SIN

Radical Evil
in Soul and Society

TED PETERS

WILLIAM B. EERDMANS PUBLISHING COMPANY
GRAND RAPIDS, MICHIGAN

Copyright © 1994 by Wm. B. Eerdmans Publishing Co.
255 Jefferson Ave. S.E., Grand Rapids, Michigan 49503

Printed in the United States of America

Library of Congress Cataloging-in-Publication Data

Peters, Ted, 1941-
Sin: radical evil in soul and society / Ted Peters.
p.   cm.
Includes bibliographical references and index.
ISBN 0-8028-3764-6. — ISBN 0-8028-0113-7 (pbk.)
1. Sin. 2. Good and evil — Psychological aspects. 3. Good and evil — Social aspects.
4. Satanism. I. Title.
BV4625.P48 1994
241'.3 — dc20   94-1519
                                                 CIP

Unless otherwise noted, the Scripture quotations in this publication are from the New Revised Standard Version Bible, copyright © 1989 by the Division of Christian Education of the National Council of Churches of Christ in the U.S.A., and used by permission.

SIN

*This book is dedicated to Martin and Derick Mzoneli
and to the future of a South Africa
where all races may live in a
just and free society.*

Contents

• CONTENTS •

viii

Acknowledgments

I wish to express gratitude to colleagues and friends for their critical review of early drafts of my work — and in some cases sharing accounts of their sinning — all of which helped to make this a better book: Carolyn Arness, Julie Bongfeldt, Ronald Klug, Ann Lammers, José Lana, Elizabeth Purdum, Roland Seboldt, Lisa Stenmark, Martha Stortz, Walter Stuhr, and Sharon Zumel. Gratitude goes as well to Jay Johnson for preparing the index.

Ted Peters

1

Introduction:
Seven Steps to Radical Evil

It was early in 1989, and I had finished preparing the manuscript for my book on the New Age, *The Cosmic Self*. It had not been published yet, but I had written a couple of articles on the subject, a brief one in *The Christian Century* and a more scholarly one in *Dialog*. Mail was coming in. So were phone calls. This is not unusual. Readers like to react to authors.

What at first I found curious and then later disturbing was a question asked of me again and again: "What can you tell me about Satanism?" Initially I turned these questions away. "I don't know anything about Satanism," I'd say. "It has nothing to do with the New Age movement." These conversations were disturbing to me because I thought the New Agers were being innocently slandered. A number of books touted in bookstores were castigating the New Age plus Satanism right along with feminism and homosexuality and everything else on a long list of things the authors didn't like. I assumed that Satanism was nothing more than a form of hype. I'm a systematic theologian. I'm not into hype.

The thought that perhaps I should take the subject seriously began when I received separate communications from two pastors in Massilon, Ohio. Neither knew the other was contacting me. Both reported a church desecration and missing children in their community. About this time I was approached by an editor at Pocket Books asking me to read a manuscript scheduled for publication the following summer, *Suffer the Child*. The author, Judith Spencer, explained that she and the publisher wanted me to offer a theologian's evaluation. The book told the story of a young girl who allegedly grew up in a Satanic cult, told from the point of view of the psychologists who recovered information about her childhood during therapy. I agreed. As I read the manuscript, I was repulsed, horrified, and terrified by the stories of ritual abuse, which included dismemberment of animals, sexual defilement of children, blood sacrifice of people, and blasphemy against God. Tears would well up causing me temporarily to stop reading, so tragic was this story of the lost innocence of childhood. If this account were accurate, I concluded, then what is going on in our society is far more serious than I had earlier surmised.

I need to know more about this, I thought. Where do I begin? As is my custom in Berkeley, where I teach at the Graduate Theological Union, I considered offering a course and then learning right along with the students. I teamed up with a professor of ethics, Ann C. Lammers. We agreed that the phenomenon of Satanism should be placed within the larger context of a theological and psychological understanding of sin and evil. Into the seminar that fall, simply called "Evil," we invited biblical scholars to help us review the Old and New Testaments. We then combed through the theological works of Augustine and Karl Barth as well as the writings of psychologists Ernest Becker and Carl Jung. The class also conducted interviews, one with a young woman named Jamie, who, while being treated for Multiple Personality Disorder, discovered that she had been kidnaped and tortured by a group practicing ritual abuse. One student, Lisa Stenmark, finished the course and then secured a financial grant to become my research assistant. Her energetic assistance during the subsequent two years has contributed much to the writing of this book.

During the period in which I have been studying the matter seriously, a number of things have become clear. First, mainline Protestant and Roman Catholic theologians of our present generation seem to have lost the ability to talk about topics such as sin. For the last quarter century or so, the theological establishment has consigned the human predicament to structures of political and economic oppression or to such systemic evils as race and gender discrimination. In the process, theologians lost interest in the internal workings of the human soul. The evils of our world have been consigned to social forces beyond the scope of our own personal responsibility. Deep down, however, it seems to me that each of us is at least dimly aware of our personal responsibility. But when our theological leaders abandon the task of helping us to understand the experiential dynamics of sin, we are left with a symbolic or conceptual void.

This has led me to a conjecture. Could we say that both New Age spirituality and the phenomenon of Satanism have rushed in to fill that void? These two are quite different things, of course — but that is the point. Each fills a different part of the void. What the New Age does is remind us that we are personally responsible for our own destiny. The responsibility — and, of course, the power — to chart our destiny lies within us, within our untapped potential, say New Agers.

This potential can take us in two directions: that of wholesome healing, as the New Age would like to see it, or that of radical evil. When New Age spiritual leaders look within, they say they do not see sin. They say they see only what is good — the beauty and bliss of the divine. But, we must ask, if the world in which we live is filled with abuse, violence, and suffering, who then is responsible? The New Age answer would logically have to be Them, not Us! Someone else must be responsible. The buck gets passed.

Enter the phenomenon of Satanism. When I speak of the *phenomenon* of Satanism, I refer as much to our belief in the existence of Satanism as I do of the actual practices of Satanists themselves. Here is what is important at this level: if we can believe that there exist organized groups of Satan worshipers who are responsible for the kidnapings, teen suicides, and serial killers that we all fear, then we can presume that the source of evil in our world is external. Evil is produced by a group that is not our group. We laughed in the 1960s when comedian Flip Wilson said, "The Devil made me do it!" As a cultural phenomenon in our own time, belief that Satanism exists is itself significant because it justifies our saying, "The Devil made *them* do it!"

The phenomenon of Satanism raises the larger question: what is the nature of sin and its evil consequences? How does Satanism fit into this larger context of human experience? The fascinating drama and brutality of Devil cults can promote outrage and fear about the threat they pose to our social fabric. We can view Satanism as one social phenomenon among many, something to be abhorred as we abhor drug crime or child abuse. We can view it as an invasion from the outside, as a *them* over against *us*. If we place this concern about Satanism within the larger context of human sin, however, the line between them and us becomes blurred. We can begin to see the connection between the inner life of our own soul and the radical evil that threatens to undo everything.

I think this latter approach is more helpful. In this book, we will look at the phenomenon of Satanism, but we will do so in the larger context of the topic of sin. Among other things, we will try to deal with a very subtle possibility: regardless of whether Satan is the source of our sin, could it be that the *blaming* of Satan or even Satanism is itself an expression of sin? The matter is tangled. We will try to do some untangling. In order to arrive at the point where we are ready to untangle the complexity, we will travel a road taking us on a tour through the various experiential dynamics of sin.

Should Sin Make Me Feel Guilty?

The topic of sin is sometimes difficult to discuss. Many of us harbor anger about the religious training we received as children. In the home, at church, or attending parochial school, many of us heard constant admonishments about God's law, our sin, and how terrible we should feel about ourselves as sinners. Strictness became identified with godliness. Sometimes strictness became a veiled form of impatience on the part of adults who had little or no sympathy for the feelings of a child, and strict discipline became a means by which impatient grown-ups could express meanness in the name of God. Because as children we tend to adopt unconsciously the values of the significant adults in our life, many of us came to see ourselves as sinners deserving only mean treatment. What we felt as guilt was in fact shame.

People who administer strict religious discipline often make the mistake of confusing sin and nature. Many of us as children were taught to fear natural tendencies within ourselves. Sexual arousal and romantic attraction, for example, are perfectly natural parts of growing up, but many misguided religious instructors have tried to instill a deep sense of guilt over what would otherwise be a quite normal field of feelings. Sexual feelings are not in themselves sinful; they are natural. Sexual inclinations need sensible control and moral direction, to be sure, but in themselves they need not make us feel guilty. By the time we grow up, most of us have learned this, but that does not necessarily free us of the residual shame induced by a neurotic form of religious upbringing. And this situation leaves some people angry about their religious upbringing — in some cases angry enough to say, "I don't want to have anything to do with discussions of sin."

Despite any misleading instruction we might have received as children, however, the subject of human sinfulness remains too important to ignore. We would do well to pay attention, to try to understand better what is going on in the world around us and in our own souls. My intent in this book is not to continue spreading unnecessary shame about natural things; rather, I want to sift through our ordinary and extraordinary experiences to discern just how it is that sin sows its poisonous seeds and reaps its polluted harvest. It is better to think about such things than to ignore them. I operate on the premise that even though better understanding may not rid our lives of sin, it will alert us to what is happening and offer insights that can become opportunities.

The Understanding of Sin in Christianity and Elsewhere

I am convinced that there is need in our time for a better understanding of the experiential dynamics of sin and their evil effects. In trying to deepen our apprehension of sin and evil in this book, I draw on numerous sources: my own experience as a child growing up, accounts of criminal activities, analyses presented by psychologists and sociologists, insights offered by philosophers and religious thinkers, images in art and poetry, and Christian theological reflection. My own perspective is influenced by my commitment to the Christian faith and my work as a professor of theology, to be sure; yet sin and evil are topics well known beyond the fences of Christian doctrine. We experience them daily regardless of our station in life, regardless of our religious commitments or cultural context. Much can be learned from listening to the wisdom of grandparents who have gained from their experiences. Much can be learned by observing children, whose behavior is a vivid reminder of the sorts of basic things that make all of us tick.

Readers from humanistic and non-Christian religious traditions should find much here in the way of shared understanding regardless of whether they are sympathetic to the Christian tradition. People of every cultural tradition and religious persuasion are able to recognize the blindness of unbridled greed and the destructive power of pride. The Christian perspective offers little that is unique here. What distinguishes the Christian apprehension of reality lies elsewhere, in its claim

5

that there does exist a gracious God who forgives sins and promises resurrection to everlasting life. But concerning sin and evil themselves, Christians and non-Christians should find much to agree about.

As you make your way through this book, you will find that I draw much from the well of insights in the scholarship of social psychologists such as the late Ernest Becker. It has been my experience that these sources have uncovered significant information in the course of their concentrated attention to, and honest analysis of, the inner workings of the human psyche both in individuals and groups. There is a drawback here, however: the vocabulary of psychologists is frequently limited by the fact that it omits reference to transcendence. We need a distinctively theological vocabulary to speak about the relationship between sin and transcendent reality.

So, we need to ask: what about specifically theological resources? As I already indicated, I don't believe we cannot rely on today's theologians.[1] This has led me to turn to the earlier generation of neo-orthodox theologians, primarily to Paul Tillich and Reinhold Niebuhr and secondarily to Karl Barth and Emil Brunner. These thinkers pounded out their understanding of the human predicament

---

1. In *Whatever Became of Sin?* (New York: Hawthorne, 1973), psychiatrist Karl Menninger complains that the theologians have abandoned the religious language of sin and turned the inner workings of the human soul over to the psychologists. Church historian E. Brooks Holifield traces the history of pastoral counseling and documents the shift that took place during the period from the seventeenth to the twentieth century, a shift away from the pastor's goal of curing a sin-sick soul's relation to God toward enhancing each person's sense of self. Admitting that he is engaging in something of an oversimplification, he traces the "movement from self-denial to self-love, from self-love to self-culture, from self-culture to self-mastery, and from self-mastery to self-realization" (*A History of Pastoral Care in America: From Salvation to Self-Realization* [Nashville: Abingdon Press, 1983], p. 351). Wayne E. Oates follows by saying that something similar has happened to the biblical concept of temptation, which is largely ignored in today's religious community. "Rage, fear, bondage, shame, guilt, worthlessness, and many others — which are abundant in the psalms and the letters of Paul especially — are labeled with psychological terms" (*Temptation* [Louisville: Westminster/John Knox Press, 1991], p. 13).

Be this as it may, I do not want to dismiss all contemporary theologians. I have found valuable contributions to our understanding of the dynamics of sin in the work of Langdon Gilkey, Wolfhart Pannenberg, and Roger Haight, who rightly recognize the decisive contributions of the previous generation of neo-orthodox thinkers as well as the insights of the ancient theological giant Augustine. Marjorie Hewitt Suchocki, Walter Wink, and Gustavo Gutiérrez are also valuable, because they help make clear the extent of systemic evil in social structures.

in the midst of the horrendous injustices and massive suffering wrought by the dominant ideologies of the twentieth century, Nazism and communism. The cauldron in which these ideological curses on human history were brewed is the human soul — our own human soul. What Becker and these theologians point out is this: *we* cannot simply blame *them* and get off easily. We must always look within when we look without. The theological thinkers of the previous generation found they could not put their faith in human decency but only in a transcendent God who is merciful, who graciously loves us.

Although the subject here is certainly familiar to all of us, some readers may be surprised by some of the things I label as sin. I include such items as tribal revenge, racism, sexism, nuclear war, unjust economic structures, and the large-scale damage being done to the environment. This may come as a challenge to those who are accustomed to restricting the concept of sin to matters such as theft or sexual indiscretion. I will suggest that the way we think about sin can in itself be sinful, because to think of sin in a strictly trivial fashion allows us to go on blindly participating in and contributing to social dynamics that wreak widespread suffering in this world.

Defining Sin and Evil

The Greek words that are translated as "sin" in the New Testament include *hamartia,* meaning "to miss the mark," as if an archer's arrow were to miss hitting the target; *adikia,* meaning "injustice" or "unrighteousness"; and *anomia* meaning "to be without the law" or "lawlessness." From the Latin word *peccatum* we get such English terms such as *impeccable,* meaning "flawless" or "incapable of sin," and *peccadillo,* a petty or trivial offense. The medievals listed seven serious or deadly vices that they said violated both natural reason and divine law: pride, envy, anger, covetousness, sadness, gluttony, and lust.[2] It is worth noting that this list of seven does not include any

---

2. Various lists of seven sins appear again and again beginning as early as the *Didache* and Tertullian. This particular septenary of vices appears in Aquinas's *Summa Theologica,* II/1, q.84, a.4, and pretty well fixes the list. We will be treating envy, covetousness, lust, and the like as forms of concupiscence. Pride is sometimes called vainglory. Sadness, or *acedia,* is sometimes referred to as sloth, idleness, or spiritual torpor (Aquinas refers to voluntary ignorance with respect to knowledge of God and the way of salvation).

actions or deeds. It is a septenary of habits or dispositions or character traits that influence our actions or deeds.

At the heart or essence of all sin is the failure to trust God. Sin is our unwillingness to acknowledge our creatureliness and dependence upon the God of grace. We pursue sin in the illusory and vain effort to establish our own lives on an independent and secure basis.[3] The effect of such sin is evil in the form of insensitivity, uncaringness, injustice, cruelty, and destruction aimed at our fellow creatures in this world. In short, sin is the failure to live up to Jesus' commandments to love God and love neighbor.

Although the words *sin* and *evil* mean nearly the same thing, I tend to use the term *evil* to refer to the effects of sin such as loss, pain, suffering, and destruction. The sinful act of gossip, for example, will result in the evil of the victim's reputation being tarnished. The sinful act of murder will result in the evil of an unjust death. The sinful act of pursuing only short-term profit may leave future generations with a planet earth that is polluted by toxic waste and robbed of its life-sustaining fertility. Sin is the cause, evil the effect.

Yet, the idea of evil covers somewhat more than just sin or the effects of sin. I am thinking here about natural evil. While I was writing this, I witnessed a minor yet tragic accident in my neighborhood. A beautiful squirrel scampered from a lawn out into the street into the path of an oncoming car. Once under the moving car, it panicked, running to and fro and finally into the path of the left rear wheel. As the car drove off, it squirmed for a moment and then gave up its life. Its mangled body lay on the asphalt with no dignity. The evil could be discerned in the terror of the little animal and in the fact that a creature of beauty was snuffed out of existence. This was an evil event, even though it was not the result of anybody's sin. It was an accident.

We should note, too, that many theologians of this period, including Aquinas, were less concerned about sin than about the seven virtues — the four cardinal virtues of temperance, justice, prudence, and fortitude and the three theological virtues of faith, hope, and love. See the *Summa Theologica*, II/1, q.61, a.1 and II/1, q.62, a.3.

3. "Sin is thus the unwillingness of man to acknowledge his creatureliness and dependence upon God and his effort to make his own life independent and secure," says Reinhold Niebuhr. "It is the vain imagination by which man hides the unconditioned, contingent and dependent character of his existence and seeks to give it the appearance of unconditioned reality" (*The Nature and Destiny of Man*, 2 vols. [New York: Scribner's, 1941-1943], 1:137-38).

Our word *evil* can refer both to sin's effects and to the suffering caused by the accidental course of nature, including disease, drought, earthquakes, tornadoes, and floods.[4]

Although natural evil cannot be disregarded, when we think of evil, we most often think of human malevolence with its accompanying deceit and destruction. For the most part, then, sin and evil overlap, and hence the terms can often be used almost interchangeably.

This leads us finally to the term *radical evil*. This is evil pursued in the name of evil. Most sinful activity is in some sense unintentional: we seek to act in the name of the good, but through blindness or self-deceit, we end up promoting evil. Radical evil, on the other hand, is deliberate evil, evil consciously embraced for its own sake. It is symbolized by Satan.

Sin as a Mystery

One item that has become clear in the course of my study is this: sin is not clear. It cannot be. No matter how much effort we invest, sin and its accompanying evil will remain unexplainable. Why? Because of the lie.[5] Because of the deceit. Inherent in sin is the denial of truth. We cover over our unwholesome motives and violent acts against others with a veneer of goodness. We sugarcoat our garbage. Everyone has a stake in hiding the truth of sin. This makes uncovering the mystery of how sin works difficult, because wherever we dig, lies rush in to fill the hole. Perhaps an objective or scholarly approach to the truth of sin is foredoomed from the start. Perhaps the only way to get at the truth of sin is through confession.

There might be another reason why sin remains unexplainable. It is inherently irrational. To tell a lie, in any event, is irrational. Lying frustrates the process of reasonable conversation and thinking. More than this, sinful activity is at bottom both self-destructive and world-

4. Some scholars assemble a more elaborate taxonomy of evil, encompassing categories of suffering produced by *moral evil* due to human sinning, *natural evil* such as the damage done by hurricanes and earthquakes, *metaphysical* or *ontological evil* such as the process of decay or entropy in the cosmos, *physical* evil such as stomachaches or AIDS, *psychological* evil such as schizophrenia or depression, and so forth.

5. "The lie is the specific evil," says Martin Buber, that the human race has "introduced into nature" (*Good and Evil* [New York: Macmillan, 1952], p. 7).

destructive. No good reason for such destructive activity can be given. Any reason we give to justify our sin is rootless. The wise theologian of antiquity Augustine suggested that sin and its accompanying evil have no being in themselves, that evil is the absence of good.[6] Evil is also the absence of being, because it seeks to dissolve or destroy what is. There is no good reason for destroying what is. Sin can give no good reason for what it is or what it does. Hence, by nature sin is not subject to a rational explanation.

Seven Steps down the Path to Radical Evil

Despite the inherently mysterious or impenetrable character of sin, we can still say something about it. After all, it is an everyday experience for each of us. So, what can we say? Here I would like to say seven things. I present them to you one chapter at a time in a sequence that I label the "Seven Steps down the Path to Radical Evil."[7] I present them as a progression. It appears to me that some forms of evil are worse than others, so I offer the seven steps as if they constitute a path to follow from innocence to maximum profanity. In our daily experience, however, we probably do not actually tread the path in step-by-step fashion. The whole of a sinful event may occur all at once, perhaps even in a flash. Nevertheless, I offer these steps as a means of parsing the phenomenon of sin, as a way to get at the component parts.

Now, some may object when I say that certain forms of sin are worse than others. It is not uncommon for a theologian to argue in the following way: all human sin is equal because all human sin is infinite. All sin is against God, and because God is infinite and eternal, our sin has infinite and eternal consequence, and hence it is wrong to limit our evaluation of a sinful act to its finite or temporal scope.[8] This

6. According to Augustine, evil is always a perversion or destruction of a previous good; it has no nature or being of its own. Even the nature of the Devil cannot in itself be evil, insofar as it is a nature. The Devil became evil through perversion of the good. See *The City of God*, 11.22; 19.13.

7. This essential structure is developed in a preliminary or skeletal form in chap. 5 of my earlier book *God — The World's Future: Systematic Theology for a Postmodern Era* (Minneapolis: Fortress Press, 1992).

8. When writing his *Cur deus homo* in the eleventh century, Anselm of Canterbury spoke of an infinite consequence to finite human sin on the grounds that each sin fails

may very well be true regarding our relationship to God, but it still seems to me that at the level of interhuman relationships we can profitably discriminate. I would much prefer my neighbor to sin by gossiping about me behind my back than to sin by murdering me on my way home from the office. At the mundane level there are degrees in the kind and amount of evil that is produced. So, if the reader will permit me the one assumption that trying to parse sin into its component parts is a potentially worthwhile exercise, let me offer for consideration the following seven steps toward radical evil.

1. *Anxiety*. Although anxiety itself is not sinful, feeling anxious readies us for sin. At the root of anxiety is the fear of loss, especially the fear of losing ourselves in death. It is the fear of dropping out of existence, the fear of extinction or loss of our own being. Anxiety is the sting of death within our lives. We are tempted to combat anxiety by erecting an illusion of immortality. We construct this illusion out of two kinds of bricks: lies to ourselves and the thefts of the strengths in others. What we experience as temptation is the desire to strike out preemptively against others, to engage in aggression, to steal their glory or money or power.

The flames of our anxiety are kindled when we confront frustration, especially in the form of humiliation. Humiliation diminishes our sense of worth, our very sense of being. It renders us helpless. Rage rises, and we are tempted to strike out with aggression.

Jenny, my wife, teaches first grade. On one occasion she had lined up her primary schoolchildren on the playground for a return to class from a period of recess. The fourth graders were passing by in the opposite direction on their way to the playground. They began to taunt the first graders, likening them to prisoners on a chain gang. In general, the much bigger fourth graders did what they could to humiliate the first graders — quite successfully. Finally one first grader on the chain gang raised his fisted arm with a defiant middle finger soaring toward

---

to give God the honor due the divine. The magnitude of our sin is measured not by the size of the sin but by the size of the offense. Thomas Aquinas later treated the matter with greater subtlety. On the one hand, we can divide sins into three domains of disordered acts, he said: (1) gluttony and lust and similar sins against oneself, (2) thievery and murder and similar forms of injustice against one's neighbor, and (3) lack of faith or hope and similar sins against God. Yet, on the other hand, because the divine order includes the orders of self and society, there is a sense in which we can say all sins are against God (*Summa Theologica*, II/1, q.72, a.4).

the sky. Jenny leaped on the scene and pressed his arm back to his waist. "Do you know what that means?" she scolded. "I dunno," he replied, "but it's sumpin' dirty." Having been humiliated so that his own being was challenged, the enraged little boy felt he had to strike out. Such is the story of the human race. When we feel that our existence as physical or psychological or social beings is threatened with nonbeing, we strike out violently with "sumpin' dirty."

2. *Unfaith.* Anxiety will take control of us and we will yield to the temptation to strike out in violence if, and only if, we lack faith. By "faith" here, I mean trust. If we trust our neighbor, we will not sin against our neighbor. The same is true with respect to God: if we have faith in the God who created us and sustains us and cares for us, we will live with courage. We will become fearless in the face of harm and resolute in the face of temptation. We will still feel anxiety, to be sure, but it will not control our lives. This is the almost magical power — more properly, the spiritual power — that faith makes available.

If we live in unfaith, however, anxiety will overwhelm us. Mistrust and fear will determine our behavior. We may begin with mild sins, complaining and gossiping. Nothing will seem right. Everyone within earshot will see our raised eyebrows and hear from us about the scandalous behavior of our mutual friends or workmates, how we have been unjustly treated, how miserable we feel. If unchecked, sin will grow in potency. We may begin to try to steal power from those superior to ourselves by spreading scandalous rumors, then progress to institutionalized means of harassment, and perhaps even go on to illegal means such as embezzlement or murder.

3. *Pride.* Pride is treating ourselves as though we were God. If we live in unfaith and trust neither God nor neighbor, then our own ego moves front and center. The ego attempts to make itself the source of life. The proud person tries to hide anxiety by smothering it under a blanket of self-control and by exerting power over others. We traditionally think of pride in terms of machismo, of bragging aloud about one's prowess. More recently, psychologists have come to associate pride with narcissism, with the quiet manipulation of others into the service of one's own psyche. The key characteristic of the proud person is a lack of empathy, the inability to experience or appreciate the feelings of others. Although it may manifest itself in women differently than in men, in both genders the key is this: pride blocks sympathetic understanding. It prevents participation in the struggles and pain of

other creatures and persons. It produces insensitivity, a capacity to ignore the suffering of others without feeling any remorse. Pride is the source of the we/they mentality, the belief that the world is made up of winners and losers and that we must always be winners.

Pride can infect both individuals and groups. Group pride leads to repression and eventually to war. Pride in one's race or in one's ethnic heritage or in one's nation leads to economic nepotism, to the practice of keeping jobs or profits within one's family, tribe, race, or nation. The flip side is prejudice and the practice of discrimination against "outsiders." When pride leads us to try to steal what belongs to the outsiders, it has produced concupiscence. If the outsiders resist, the insiders rally the troops and go to war to eliminate the resistance. Pride leads to violence.

4. *Concupiscence.* We return to Augustine for the word *concupiscence*. Sometimes translated "sensuality," it encompasses such things as desire, lust, envy, greed, and coveting. It is the desire to possess — especially the things that others currently possess. This hunger to acquire provides the motive for stealing, although it more frequently stimulates the impulse to buy. To defend itself against the attacking armies of anxiety, the concupiscent soul sets up a citadel of psychic safety constructed out of possessions: ever larger and more luxurious homes, increasingly prestigious professional positions, the most profitable stock portfolio, political influence, and so on. Concupiscence is more than merely the desire to have what it takes to survive or to be satisfied. It is an unquenchable fire of wanting and wanting and wanting. It is concupiscence that drives us to keep up with the Joneses whatever the cost. Individually, it comes to expression as beating someone else to the punch, seeking profit from someone else's loss, stealing the livelihood from someone who may wither and die because of the theft. Corporately, it comes to expression in the construction and maintenance of an international economic system that feeds the controlling classes and nations with wealth and luxury while dismissing the masses who support the system through cheap labor and the sacrifice of their natural resources. Concupiscence is akin to the passion of the ravenous wolf ripping and tearing at its prey, devouring the flesh of the slain. It is being possessed by possessions.

The model for understanding the structure of concupiscence in daily experience is sexual lust. The flame of passion ignited by the presence of someone sexually desirable seems to burn and consume the soul with bodily desire. This is love, an enthralling love that seems to overpower our mind and will. It is vivid and exciting. In less vivid and less exciting but even more destructive ways, covetousness and greed orient and organize our entire life around one thing: increasing our possessions. Like a grass fire, concupiscence burns field after field, and there is no hope that it will be extinguished until all fuel is consumed.

Long before the fuel is consumed, of course, the consumer is extinguished. The belief that possessing things can protect us from anxiety over our mortality is an illusion. This is the point Jesus makes in his parable of the rich fool. The rich farmer in this story becomes a fool because of his insatiable desire to produce greater and greater harvests, tearing down his barns to build bigger barns, and giving his life totally to the philosophy of eat, drink, and be merry. Then his divine maker suddenly confronts him saying, " 'You fool! This very night your life is being demanded of you. And the things you have prepared, whose will they be?' So it is with those who store up treasures on earth for themselves but are not rich toward God" (Luke 12:20-21).

5. *Self-Justification.* There is more to sin than overindulgence in sensual possessions. Pride and concupiscence can lead to the desire to possess what God possesses — namely, goodness. More pointedly, we may desire to take from God the goodness ascribed to the divine and apply it to ourselves. This is self-justification, the attempt to make ourselves righteous by identifying with what is good, even if it takes a lie or a scapegoat to do so. It begins with a guilty child blaming his brother for the cookies missing from the cookie jar. It is evident in the familiar rhetoric of one political party blaming another for all the nation's woes. It erupts in heinous ideologies such as Nazism, which scapegoated the Jews for having contaminated the Aryan blood. It ends finally with would-be theologians who make humanist values the standard and then blame God for crudely creating evil in an otherwise naturally good world. Its most common form is gossip, with which we verbally cut our superiors down to our own size by charging them with having committed scandalous sins. Its most dramatic form is ideology leading to genocide.

Self-justification is the denial of our own sinfulness, which is usually accompanied by an an ascription of sinfulness to a menacing scapegoat. Scapegoating combines the attribution of badness to our purported enemies with a corresponding attribution of goodness to ourselves, a phenomenon that is ultimately expressed in a holy war to eliminate the sinful menace we have identified. Once we have justified ourselves, we can justify violence against those who are not so justified. There is a lie at work here. We deceive ourselves. The curious trick of the lie is that we use the opposite of evil to justify our own perpetration of evil.

What we reject when engaging in self-justification is the possibility of goodness outside and independent of ourselves. In doing so, we cut ourselves off from the possibility of forgiveness. We implicitly reject grace from other people and from God. As the rejection of grace, self-justification is the bald expression of unfaith.

If we were to live in faith, we would be able to accept our goodness as coming from our creator God, not from ourselves. If we were to live in faith, we would be able to accept the mixture of good and bad that we find in all people, both insiders and outsiders. We would no longer feel the need to justify ourselves, and to this extent we would feel no pressure to find fault with others, to create and eliminate scapegoats.

6. *Cruelty.* Cruelty is one of the fruits of self-justification. I already suggested that one characteristic of the proud person is a lack of empathy. This lack of empathy is not simply a matter of insensitivity to the feelings of someone else. Indeed, cruel people can be keenly sensitive to the feelings of others, but they are prepared to ignore them nonetheless — perhaps even gleefully — out of a sense that they are justified in doing so. The sort of person who self-righteously takes delight in the suffering that other people experience because "they had it coming to them" is potentially cruel. Such a person crosses the line and becomes actually cruel when he or she takes the steps to cause suffering. We will define cruelty in terms of our willingness to inflict physical or emotional pain on an animal or person in order to cause anguish or fear. The pain suffered by another being is the evil effect of the sin of cruelty.

We are crossing a significant threshold at this point. I want to stress the point that we are not talking about cruelty as the unconscious or indirect by-product of unfaith, pride, concupiscence, or self-justification; we are talking about the conscious and direct infliction of suffering and pain. The cruel person may continue to engage in self-justification and its accompanying deceit, but the deliberate infliction of cruelty will be evident for what it is. The cruel person tortures other beings and considers torture to be an acceptable and desirable policy. The cruel person pursues the macabre for its own sake.

There is no way to explain adequately the joy of torturing or murdering. It is as irrational as it is sinful. Perhaps it relies on the

15

deeper lie we tell ourselves, the lie that is tied so closely to virtually every aspect of sin — namely, that we can gain our own immortality by stealing life from others. Perhaps this lie grows out of the illusion that by destroying others we can eliminate the anxiety we feel over the threat of our own extinction.

7. *Blasphemy.* The worst of the seven deadly sins on my list is blasphemy — that is, radical evil. Traditionally blasphemy has been understood as the defilement of God's name, the use of God's name in a profane way. I would like to refine this somewhat by defining it as the misuse of divine symbols so as to prevent the communication of God's grace. With this definition, we can see that blasphemy comes in two forms, covert and overt. In its covert form, blasphemy is a tool for self-justification involving the use of religious symbols to enhance our own position of power. We may appeal to the divine right of kings, for example, to justify the exploitation of peasants by royalty. Or, we may appeal to Scripture to justify slavery. In this covert form — the form of the lie — the symbols associated with God become so identified with oppression that their original intent is subverted. Instead of communicating the love of a gracious God, the symbols of salvation communicate injustice. The message of redemption is drowned out. Access to comfort is denied. Hope is destroyed. God becomes identified with evil. God becomes the scapegoat for the scapegoated.

In its covert form, blasphemy hides sin under the name of something good. In its overt form there is no more hiding. In its overt form, blasphemy is the conscious use of divine symbols in the worship of radical evil. Blasphemy is evil in the name of evil. This is where Satanism enters the picture. In Satanic religious practice, a symbolic world is constructed wherein the Devil takes the central place belonging to God. The Devil's disciples serve him through worship rituals, deliberately paying homage to the principle of evil. Explicitly excluded if not prohibited is reliance on the power or love of God. The symbols of grace are exploited in reverse: baptism is renounced in favor of loyalty to Satan; the Lord's Supper becomes a human sacrifice to Satan rather than Christ's sacrifice on our behalf; love of neighbor is transformed into love of self, and love of enemies is replaced by revenge against enemies. Selfishness, hedonism, and concupiscence in all their forms come to reign. Most importantly, death and life become so intertwined and their relationship so distorted that killing becomes confused with living. Ritual cruelty and the shedding of innocent blood are the results.

With overt blasphemy we have hit bottom. Not only do we have scapegoating and cruelty, but the victims are robbed of access to a transcendent hope that might afford them some comfort in the midst of their distress. The very symbols through which God communicates forgiveness and resurrection are stolen and pressed into the service of violence and destruction. The prostituted symbols of life become the means for inflicting spiritual death as well as physical suffering. Blasphemy renders the soul hopelessly isolated, slamming the doors shut against any word of divine grace. It is the ultimate enemy of God.

With blasphemy we have finished our step-by-step trek from anxiety and unfaith to radical evil. This is the best way I know for picturing the dynamics of sin. Yet it may be the case that the image of seven steps down the path toward radical evil is less than fully adequate. Evil is not simply progressive. I do not mean to suggest that once we step into concupiscence we have left pride behind. Although most of us who sin stop well short of blasphemy, nearly every step is present nearly all the time. What I am struggling to do here is show a logical pattern of linkage, not necessarily a chronological route. An alternative image might be that of a weed. We could identify anxiety with soil, and fear with the nutrients in the soil that are necessary to support plant growth. The weed's stem, then, would be unfaith. Protruding from unfaith would be the ugly leaves of pride, concupiscence, self-justification, scapegoating, and cruelty. "Blasphemy" would be the name of the weed in the horticulturalist's lexicon.

Satan as Symbol

We are looking at sin in its mild and radical forms, using Satan as a symbol for radical evil.[9] We need a principle for identifying evil in this radical form. The media is charged with semifanatical voices trying to frighten us by pointing to demons behind every bush. Some people

9. "The Devil is in us," writes Ruth Nanda Anshen (*Anatomy of Evil* [Mt. Kisco, N.Y.: Moyer Bell, 1972], p. 1). Using the terms *sin* and *evil* somewhat differently from the way in which we are doing so here, she speaks of sin as an occasional wrong action on the part of a person who normally wants to do what is right and who is capable of repentance. She reserves the term *evil* for what I am calling "radical evil." "The evildoer acts for the sake of the Evil, and the Evil is nothing but the satisfaction and satanic enjoyment he experiences in violation of divine and human laws and values" (p. 35).

are inclined to accuse anyone they happen to disagree with of being inspired by the Devil, and one result is that many of us are being desensitized by their cries of wolf. We hear claims of Satanic inspiration so often that we pay them little heed. So, when should we pay heed? In his book *The Prince of Darkness*, Jeffrey Burton Russell gives this clue: "Globally radical evil expresses itself in genocide, terrorism, and preparations for nuclear war. Individually it appears in actions of callousness and cruelty."[10] With this in mind, let me suggest a further criterion for discernment: *Satan is present when we hear the request to shed innocent blood.* This principle, I think, should help to identify radical evil. It should also help us to interpret the significance of the one sacrificed on the cross.

Russell's *Prince of Darkness* may be the most informative of the recent books on Satan. It vividly surveys the ways in which the Devil has been characterized throughout Judeo-Christian history, starting in the contexts of the Old and New Testaments and proceeding through Christian tradition from the patristics and classics to the Reformers and on to the modern materialists and skeptics. Russell summarizes the positions taken by theologians such as Augustine, Luther, and Schleiermacher as well as poets and novelists such as Dante, Milton, and Dostoevsky. Russell offers two reasons why he is convinced of the existence of Satan (i.e., "radical evil"). We know Satan exists intuitively, he says, because the world that comes to us in everyday experience is by no means morally neutral. The struggle between good and evil is built right into our experience. Furthermore, this evil transcends our individual human sphere. It is social. It is cosmic. The radical evil that resulted in Auschwitz and has threatened global nuclear war is a potent and whelming force that is transpersonal in power and scope.

The second reason Russell offers for acknowledging the existence of radical evil is that it accords with Scripture and tradition. Although belief in the Devil is by no means the core of religious teaching, an assumption of the existence of the Devil pervades the Bible. Russell mildly chides modern scientific materialism for trying to sidetrack the issue, and then he goes on to blast liberal Protestants who sell out to modern materialism and forsake scriptural commitments. The liberals have considered the notion of Satan to be a painful embarrassment.

10. Russell, *The Prince of Darkness: Radical Evil and the Power of Good in History* (Ithaca, N.Y.: Cornell University Press, 1988), p. 273.

They dismiss the idea of a personal Devil as outmoded, something that Jesus never really believed in (or they say that if he did believe, it was only because of the limitations of his time).[11] This attitude has left us defenseless against atheistic arguments from evil and from a realistic appraisal of the horrors of genocide in the twentieth century.

We moderns need to be careful of science, cautions Russell. Although science can examine the physical world, it really is not in a position to alter our perceptions of evil, because evil is a spiritual phenomenon. "The concept of radical evil embodied in the Devil cannot be outvoted or superseded by any developments of modern science."[12]

When it comes to salvation, Russell does not press for a Christ-centered soteriology. Rather, to the extent that he takes a position, he supports a Jesus-inspired life of love. Because radical evil is so enigmatic — a force that destroys rather than creates being or goodness — it cannot be explained. This being the case, the problem with soteriology is that it is an "ology," an attempt to explain things theoretically. The answer to evil will not be found in explaining but in living.

Like Alyosha in Dostoyevsky's *The Brothers Karamazov* listening to Ivan reciting the horrors of evil that allegedly disprove the existence of God, Russell is overwhelmed. No rational argument can counter the assault of radical evil. No theology is its match. Alyosha's final word is the final word Russell commends to the reader — namely, a life of love. Though the enemy be incomprehensible, we must fight it with weapons of love. Russell writes,

> We are called to fight evil, but we are also called to know how to fight it. Evil is not effectively resisted with hatred and with guns. Evil cannot be defeated with evil, negation with negation, terror with terror, missile with missile. The process of negation must be reversed. Only affirmation can overcome negation; evil can be integrated only by good; hatred can be laid to rest only by love. The only response to evil that has ever worked is the response of Jesus, or of Alyosha Karamazov, and that is to lead a life of love. That means what it has always meant: visiting the sick, giving to the poor, helping those who need help.[13]

11. See Russell, *The Prince of Darkness,* pp. 215, 241, 257.
12. Russell, *The Prince of Darkness,* p. 261.
13. Russell, *The Prince of Darkness,* p. 276; cf. pp. 252-53.

Russell's appeal to love here is reinforced by psychiatrist M. Scott Peck, who notes that sin and evil are tied closely to death, especially premature death in the form of killing. The word *evil* is *live* spelled backwards. Killing, whether symbolically or literally, is the means by which we seek to relieve the stress caused by our own anxiety about death, the means by which we try in vain to secure our own independent existence. The result is tension, conflict, violence, and even more stress. This leads to a question: What should we do with the killers among us? Kill them? Peck says No, because this will not provide the relief from sin and evil that we seek. "Although evil is antilife," he says, "it is itself a form of life. If we kill those who are evil, we will become evil ourselves; we will be the killers. If we attempt to deal with evil by destroying it, we will also end up destroying ourselves, spiritually if not physically. . . . Evil can be defeated by goodness. When we translate this we realize what we dimly have always known: Evil can be conquered only by love."[14] In short, we can combat sin and evil and Satan with lives of love.

While what they say is true, it is nevertheless the case that something is missing in the accounts offered by Russell and Peck. It is one thing to tell us to love. It is quite another to enable us to love. Anxiety makes loving difficult, sometimes impossible. The threat of death and the need for survival put our nervous fingers on the trigger of the weapon of sin — and it acts like an automatic weapon. Once we press the trigger, we get not a single shot but a burst of fire: self-preservation followed in a flash by self-aggrandizement and then outright selfishness. Self-justification, cruelty, and radical evil spring into the firing chamber. What does it take to remove our fingers from the trigger? Two things in particular enable us to overcome the threat of anxiety and to lead the life of love: forgiveness and the promise of life.

Forgiveness releases the grip of the lie. It permits the truth to be honestly told. It eliminates the need to draw the line between the goodness of our side and the evil of the other side. When we realize we are forgiven, we find we can borrow the goodness of the forgiver rather than working to manufacture the illusion of our own goodness. Similarly, the promise of life relieves us of the responsibility of finding immortality in our own accomplishments. We no longer need to rely

14. Peck, *People of the Lie: The Hope for Healing Human Evil* (New York: Simon & Schuster, 1983), pp. 266-67.

strictly on ourselves or try to steal life from other creatures; we can rely on the giver of life.

What these two things require, of course, is that we are loved by someone who has the power to forgive and the power to give life. This is the message that the symbols of God try to communicate. We as individuals are enabled to love if we first have been loved by others. We as a human race are enabled to love because we have first been loved by our Creator and Redeemer, God. If we in faith place our trust in this message, then blasphemy and all that leads up to it will lose its grip on our lives. We will be free to live lives of love.

Codes, Commandments, and Laws for Living

Each summer I head for the Sierra mountains on a wilderness back-packing hike. The week straddling the Independence Day holiday of 1991 found my party of eight backpackers camped on the shore of Buena Vista Lake, awestruck at the beauty of the snow-trimmed granite cliffs and gurgling waterfalls spraying into the otherwise quiet, cold lake. Hourly battles with bloodthirsty mosquitoes disabused us of any romantic notions about human harmony with nature, however.

What is important for our discussion here is the campfire conversation. Late one evening, after the mosquito army had temporally retreated from the cold and we were warming ourselves around the fire, my comrades opened up the library of their daily living to help me in my research on sin.

Our topic was pride. The medievals had labeled pride the worst of the seven deadly sins. "Not so!" said this modern group of homemakers and professionals. Pride is a good thing. It inspires. It draws us forward. It enhances self-esteem. One teacher among these campfire philosophers told the story of a grade-school student who could not talk and who felt left out. Then the lonely little boy programmed the class computer to tell jokes. The other children laughed at the right places. The mute boy beamed with a sense of accomplishment. "Now, shouldn't he be proud of his achievement? How can this be called a sin?" asked the teacher.

The campfire philosophers agreed that parents should be proud of their children, that patriots should be proud of their country, and that we all should be proud of the Oakland A's.

"So how could pride be sinful?" they asked. "When is pride constructive, and when is it destructive? Is there a line we can draw indicating where good pride ends and evil pride begins? Is there a rule that can tell us when we are okay and when we are sinning?"

This desire to have a rule or law for moral behavior goes back to the dawn of civilization. The ancient Babylonians produced the Code of Hammurabi. India sought guidance from the Laws of Manu. Israel lived by the Torah with its Ten Commandments. Such codes and commandments draw lines. If we cross the line, we sin. If we stay on the safe side of the line, we do not sin.[15] We guide our daily living with codes and commandments and the desire to be good. This is human nature, at least insofar as human nature includes human culture.

What seems to be assumed here is that *sin* refers to acts or deeds, to specific prideful activities that are evil in character or effect. Codes and commandments help to inhibit us from performing sinful acts. And, of course, this is a perfectly legitimate use of the term *sin*. Yet I believe sin is more than an act; it is also an attitude, a disposition, a habit, a vice.

The understanding of sin as act leaves much unexplained. For example, it does not explain our disposition to sin. A proud person is the kind of person who will manipulate loved ones, offend acquaintances, and pursue a selfish course in life without empathy for others. But where does the predisposition to pride come from? Is it a matter of choice on the part of the proud person? Is pride inborn? Was he or she groomed for pride by parents and teachers trying to encourage self-esteem? Is pride a defensive maneuver by the human psyche to gain protection from some threat, perhaps a perceived threat to one's dignity from the assaults of parents and teachers? And, what about group pride? Is that a matter of shared consciousness? These questions cannot be addressed if we think of sin only in terms of acts or deeds that break laws. People who *commit sins* may themselves *be sinners* as

15. Augustine defines sin accordingly as any word, deed, or desire opposed to the law of God (*Against Faustus*, 22:27). Sin is simultaneously *aversio a Deo* and *conversio ad creaturam*. Emil Brunner adds a subjective component by saying, "Only the man who knows the law can really sin — in the actual explicit sense of the word. Law and sinfulness belong together" (*The Divine Imperative* [Philadelphia: Westminster Press, 1947], p. 65).

well as part and parcel of a whole *nexus of sin*.[16] All of these together constitute the larger picture of sin.

It is this larger picture of sin that I am trying to envision in this book. The task here is not to draw up a checklist of dos and don'ts that will describe for us a sin-free safety zone for daily living. Listing dos and don'ts is an important and worthwhile task in its own right, to be sure, but it is not our task here. Rather, we should try to expand our vision to include the big picture of the dynamics of sin individually and collectively. Of course, this cannot help but suggest some guiding principles for improving our human lot, such as living lives of love.

Sin and Sins

What codes and commandments do is help us to avoid committing sins. Or, perhaps better, codes and commandments help us to identify our sins when we commit them.

But note here the assumption that we can speak of sins in the plural. The neo-orthodox theologians working between the two world wars distinguished between the state of sin in the singular and sinful acts in the plural. "One should always be conscious of the fact," writes Paul Tillich, "that 'sins' are the expressions of 'sin.'"[17] What is "the state of sin"? It is the condition in which we find ourselves estranged from God. Our relationship with God is broken, and this fundamental break causes other breaks, such as alienation from other people and even from our selves. The broken relationship with God, who is the source of all life, is what subjects us to death and to anxiety over the prospect of nonbeing. In this situation of estrangement, we act. And an act that expresses this estrangement is an act of sin.

Tillich says that it is not the disobedience to a law that makes an act sinful but the fact that it is an expression of estrangement. "Therefore," he writes, "Paul calls everything sin which does not result from faith, from the unity with God. And in another context (following

16. Karl Barth applies the idea of sin to "man himself, and himself in the totality of his existence, so that, although it does relate specifically to individual acts, it relates primarily to his life as a whole" (*Church Dogmatics*, 4 vols., ed. Thomas F. Torrance, trans. Geoffrey W. Bromiley [Edinburgh: T. & T. Clark, 1936-1962], IV/1:499).

17. Tillich, *Systematic Theology*, 3 vols. (Chicago: University of Chicago Press, 1951-1963), 2:46.

Jesus) all laws are summed up in the law of love by which estrangement is conquered. Love as the striving for the reunion of the separated is the opposite of estrangement. In faith and love, sin is conquered because estrangement is overcome by reunion."[18]

Langdon Gilkey has carried the insights of Tillich as well as Reinhold Niebuhr into his own instruction to the present generation of theologians. In addition to theory, he adds experience. Gilkey found plenty of opportunity to observe and ponder human nature under stress while a prisoner in a Japanese internment camp in China during World War II. In his account of prison life, he offers this reflection: "Sin may be defined as an ultimate religious devotion to a finite interest; it is an overriding loyalty or concern for the self, its existence and its prestige, or for the existence and prestige of a group. From this deeper sin, that is, from this inordinate love of the self and its own, stem the moral evils of indifference, injustice, prejudice, and cruelty to one's neighbor, and the other destructive patterns of action that we call 'sins.'"[19]

Original Sin?

This notion of a state of sin needs attention. As we grow and come into our own personal consciousness, we wake up to find ourselves already within the state of sin. When we commit a sin, we do not present evil for the first time to a previously innocent world. Sin was here before we arrived. We are drawn into sin by forces that surround us. In this sense we are not the sole authors of what we do.

18. Tillich, *Systematic Theology,* 2:47.
19. Langdon Gilkey, *Shantung Compound* (New York: Harper & Row, 1966), p. 233. Emil Brunner adds nuance when he argues, "Sin is an act — that is the first thing to say about sin. Only as a second point can we say: this act is always, at the same time, a state of existence, a state in which one cannot do otherwise, a state of slavery" (*The Christian Doctrine of Creation and Redemption* [Philadelphia: Westminster Press, 1952], p. 109). In explicating the concept of "being a sinner" in the whole of human existence, Brunner presses the point that a state of nature does not provide a causal explanation for why humans sin: we are not sinners in the same way that a building is a building. Rather, the human race constitutes itself as sinful through its ongoing sinful activity. Sin is an act of rebellion against God that is universal and total in scope. We enjoy solidarity in sin. See *Man in Revolt* (Philadelphia: Westminster Press, 1947), pp. 148-53.

24

There is no question that temptation to sin comes to us from beyond ourselves. It is not just an internal affair. Evil is bigger than we are. It is something in which we participate while at the same time it is something we produce through willful decision. This is another of the mysterious characteristics of evil. Philosopher Paul Ricoeur explicates the mystery as follows: if any of us initiates evil, we also discover evil; we find it already there. Evil exists within us, outside us, and before us. The story of Adam and Eve awakens us to the truth that "I do not begin evil; I continue it."[20]

Recall the story of Adam and Eve in the Garden of Eden in Genesis. In this God-given paradise, the serpent speaks to Eve, offering her an enticing argument for circumventing the will of God: God is wrong to guard privileges jealously for himself that we humans would like to — indeed, have a right to! — have as well. The point here is that a voice external to Eve addresses her and invites her to sin. Once she has heard the voice, she thinks it over, internalizes it, and then responds. Whether we think in terms of a serpent or Satan, we are acknowledging a significant component of our own experience — namely, there is a force of evil antecedent to and involved in our own human action. In the myths that developed just prior to the Christian era, the Devil was described as a fallen angel. Satan fell first, then we followed suit. The human spirit was drawn into estrangement by forces that had become alienated ahead of us.

The stories of the fall of Satan and the fall of Adam and Eve are parallel, which may mean that the former was an extrapolation based on the latter. Because Adam and Eve are the primordial parents to which we are heirs, their guilt is passed on congenitally. When the Psalmist writes, "Indeed, I was born guilty, a sinner when my mother conceived me" (Ps. 51:5), the reference is not to one of the Psalmist's mother's indiscretions. The reference is rather to the situation of sin into which we all are born, symbolized as a contagion that has been passed down not only through three or four prior generations (Exod. 20:5) but all the way back to the mother and father of our race. Sin, it seemed to Augustine, is a hereditary disease. We are in want of a cure.[21]

20. Ricoeur, *The Conflict of Interpretations* (Evanston, Ill.: Northwestern University Press, 1974), p. 284.
21. The English term "original sin" is the translation of two traditional ways of looking at it: (1) the "first sin" (*Ursünde* in German and *peccatum originale originans* in Latin) and (2) "inherited sin" (*Erbsünde* in German and *peccatum originale origi-*

Augustine used the disease metaphor to describe the fall. Good health prior to the fall consisted in our ability not to sin *(posse non peccare)* as well as the ability to sin *(posse peccare)*. In other words, we as a human race had freedom. We could choose good health, or we could choose infection. We chose the latter.

Once having made this choice, however, we lost something, something thereafter irretrievable: we lost freedom.[22] This is sometimes difficult to understand in the modern world, because we moderns so often identify freedom with the ability to make choices. Of course we have the ability to make choices between what we want and what we do not want. This is natural. But the problem of freedom arises when we believe we are able to make the ultimate choice between good and evil. The choice between good and evil is qualitatively different from ordinary daily decisions.

I may decide to drink orange juice regularly or to start exercising or to give up smoking because I believe such things will be "good" for my health. My decision in such matters will be based on what I presume to be the good. But can I in fact choose the good in the same way I choose to exercise or to stop smoking? We may think so, but this is a delusion. As moderns we seem to presume that the human

---

natum in Latin). Emil Brunner repudiates the concept of hereditary sin, saying it is not biblical (*The Christian Doctrine of Creation and Redemption,* pp. 103-4). Karl Barth objects to the conflation of original sin with hereditary sin. He rejects totally the idea of hereditary or inherited sin on the grounds that each person in each generation is personally responsible for his or her sin. We today are not guilty for what Adam did yesterday. The role that Adam plays is that of a "representative" of all humanity standing under the Word and judgment of God. "It is perhaps better to abandon altogether the idea of hereditary sin and to speak only of original sin (the strict translation of *peccatum originale*)" (*Church Dogmatics,* IV/1:501; cf. 509-10). Wolfhart Pannenberg may overstate the case, then, when he says Barth rejects the concept of original sin (*Anthropology in Theological Perspective* [Philadelphia: Westminster Press, 1985], p. 132n.143). In this discussion, I will be using the term "original sin" to refer to corporate sin as well as the propensity to commit sins that arises from the condition of human anxiety.

22. The attempt to explain this loss of freedom through the doctrine of original sin by no means leads to the idea of determinism. Emil Brunner reminds us that "the sinner is in principle capable of avoiding every particular sin. But what he cannot do is this: he cannot *not* be a sinner. . . . Sin has not destroyed all freedom, but the central freedom, the freedom to answer God as he wills it. Therefore *before God* everyone is a sinner, and all that one does, says, or thinks is sinful" (*The Christian Doctrine of Creation and Redemption,* pp. 111-12).

self enjoys some position of neutrality from which it can survey and evaluate the options before deciding. In other words, we presuppose a position of neutrality over against what is good. But can there really be any such thing as neutrality over against good? No. Anytime we presume we can stand neutral with regard to what is good, we are attempting to live outside the perimeter of what is good, outside its sphere of influence, outside its defining power. We affirm our selves in estrangement from the good.

If we think of ourselves as neutral with regard to good and evil and hence outside the defining power of what is good, then the criterion of any choice must come from within the chooser. It must be determined by the self. If we choose to get what the self wants, we are implicitly placing a higher value on what the self wants than on the good itself. We place our own selves in the position of God, who would otherwise determine and define what is good.

All of this is simply to establish the point that the doctrine of original sin in no way denies the observable fact that we daily enjoy the freedom to decide between what we want and do not want, to decide between eating a chocolate ice cream cone or a vanilla one, to decide between choosing a career in business or a career in education. But once we have left the realm of the good and established ourselves in what we at first imagined to be a neutral zone, the zone of human autonomy, then there is no way we can on our own return to the realm of the good proper. All of our decisions will inevitably reinforce our alienation from what is good. Every choice we make will only establish us more firmly in our independence and, hence, our estrangement. It is in this sense that we cannot choose the good on our own. It is in this sense that we find ourselves alienated from God and existing in a state of original sin. The freedom we have lost is the freedom to live effusively out of the divine wellspring.

Subsequent to this loss, freedom in God can no longer be understood as a birthright, as somehow given with our nature. Like someone crippled by disease, we are in need of a liberating medicine. If we are to enjoy freedom in Augustine's sense of the term, it will have to be the result of a divine act of liberation.[23]

---

23. Augustine writes, "From the bad use of free will, there originated the whole train of evil, which, with its concatenation of miseries, convoys the human race from its depraved origin, as from a corrupt root, on to the destruction of the second death,

It matters little whether the fall into sin was a historical event that actually occurred in the chronological past. What does matter is that our experience tells us that things are not the way they ought to be, that our actual selves are not who we believe we essentially are. It is this that gives rise to the sense of fall, to the belief that we have been estranged from our source of life and well-being.

Is Original Sin Fair?

There have been many objections to the idea of original sin. It seems unfair. Put most succinctly, the question we raise is this: Why should I be blamed for something Adam and Eve did? Just because Adam and Eve could not resist the temptation to eat the forbidden fruit, is it just for God to punish me and everyone else in my generation?

It was Augustine's creative metaphor of the disease that got us into trouble on this one. When he described Adam's eating of the Eden apple as the onset of the malady of sin that has been passed to all subsequent generations through genetic contagion, we began to see ourselves as suffering for what our ancestors did. Our only guilt is that we were born into Adam's family, which really involves no personal guilt at all.

The problem of fairness does not go away in the modern world. Beginning with Immanuel Kant and Friedrich Schleiermacher at the opening of the nineteenth century, modern theologians seemed to abandon the notion of an actual historical onset of the disease of sin and of an intergenerational tradition of contagion. In its place, theologians of the twentieth century put the idea of a "state of sin" as distinct from the "actual sins" that individuals commit. We are born into this state of sin, they suggested, even though we do not commit

---

which has no end, those only being excepted who are freed by the grace of God" (*The City of God,* 13.14). Alternatively, Christ "is our Liberator, inasmuch as He is our Saviour" (14.11). The Augustinian view of original sin that eventually came to dominate Western Christendom encompasses four assertions: (1) evil has existed throughout human history, (2) God is not responsible for human evil, (3) death is a consequence of human sin, and (4) God will provide salvation through the work of redemption. See Jean Delumeau, *Sin and Fear: The Emergence of a Western Guilt Culture, Thirteenth-Eighteenth Centuries,* trans. Eric Nicholson (New York: St. Martin's Press, 1990), p. 252.

actual sins until after we arrive. But these modern redefinitions do not really erase our problem. We moderns so emphasize individual autonomy and freedom that the question arises again: If I am born into a sinful state, how can I personally be responsible for that state? Why am I in need of forgiveness?

This theological doctrine seems to have tied us up in knots. The easy way out would be to cut original sin out of our religious thinking, thereby creating an apparently more just framework for evaluating each person's respective guilt or innocence. Each of us would then accept guilt for those misdeeds over which we have had complete — that is, conscious and willful — responsibility. At least this would cut our overhead down to a finite number of actions. If we could call these actions to mind, we could confess them, request appropriate absolution, and be on our way clean as a whistle. This system would have the additional advantage of providing us with the opportunity to give proper credit where credit is due. After all, there are many among us who work if not regularly then at least occasionally for the upbuilding of humanity. We should receive a pat on the back appropriate to our charitable contribution. In short, if we could eliminate the odious notion of original sin, we could produce a more logical and understandable religious system, something more along the lines of our criminal justice system. The guilty would be punished in proportion to their specific crimes, and good citizens would occasionally get cited for their positive contributions to the welfare of God's creation.

Such a system would seem eminently fair. It is a nice idea. But it is unrealistic. The world does not in fact work this way. The world into which we are born is not morally neutral. As soon as we arrive, fresh from our mother's womb, we are issued the invitation to join the party of concupiscence, aggression, injustice, and violence. The pot of the world's misery is already filled with sin and its fruit, the suffering of innocent victims. And we ourselves will add still more. This is the given.

Claremont process theologian Marjorie Hewitt Suchocki argues that we need to keep the idea of original sin if we are to account adequately for the interdependence of all things in this world. The holistic vision of reality with which she works recognizes what seems indisputable — namely, that as individuals we are who we are by virtue of our relationships to one another and to the whole. The ill-being of any of earth's inhabitants contributes to the ill-being of the whole. She identifies three relevant components for mediating both good and ill:

persons, institutions, and society. The gift of all three to us and to our progeny is to provide the parameters within which consciousness becomes self-consciousness, the structure by which our minds are ordered into a worldview. This is both bane and blessing. Insofar as it is bane, it is the perpetual origin of original sin. What Suchocki wants to emphasize is that sin is not an individual phenomenon but a social phenomenon in the sense that each individual sin is understood properly only in relation to the backdrop of sin evidenced by the human race as a whole. Solidarity, not individuality, is the fundamental basis for understanding sin. To think of sin strictly as individual acts apart from original sin is to trivialize the whole matter.[24]

Jesuit theologian Roger Haight makes a similar case. He recognizes that the structures of social institutions to which we belong may very well be destructive, may be contrary to the will of God. And we, as parts of these social structures, participate in their social sinfulness. This is not "personal sin," he insists; rather, "it is precisely social sin. As distinct from personal sin or actual sinning this social sin is an integral part of what has traditionally been called original sin."[25] This

24. Suchocki, "Original Sin Revisited," unpublished inauguration lecture, School of Theology at Claremont, 1990. See also her book *The End of Evil* (Albany: State University Press of New York, 1988). Dorothee Sölle argues that the doctrine of original sin maintains an important dialectic between fate and guilt. She reports a personal experience visiting the Netherlands following the Second World War and being rejected by the people because she was a German citizen, and they identified her with the Nazis who had killed their relatives. It became clear to her that, even though she individually had done nothing to harm the Dutch people, "by language, culture and heritage" she belonged to a human society that lived in a complex of guilt. She concludes, "I am also responsible for the house which I did not build, but in which I live" (*Thinking about God: An Introduction to Theology* [London: SCM Press, 1990], p. 55).

According to feminist theologian Mary McClintock Fulkerson, it is the grammar of discourse that mediates ill. She cites sexism as the original sin. Our Western way of speaking about God in male terms — *theo*centric rather than *thea*centric language — "has created and can continue to create forms of corporate blindness, deception, and alienation" ("Sexism as Original Sin: Developing a Theacentric Discourse," *Journal of the American Academy of Religion*, 59 [Winter 1991]: 671). Fulkerson locates original sin less in some primeval event in the past and more in the ongoing problems created by the language we speak that continues to evoke social discrimination against women. She recommends that Christian vocabulary genderize fallibility and that theologians make gender-specific sin a permanent area of investigation.

25. Haight, "Sin and Grace," in *Systematic Theology: Roman Catholic Perspectives*, vol. 2, ed. Francis Schüssler Fiorenza and John P. Galvin (Minneapolis: Fortress Press, 1991), p. 105.

is where we find ourselves everyday: trapped in structures of evil larger than we are that dispose our actions before we can take control of them. "What the doctrine [of original sin] really signifies is the profound entrapment of human freedom in a tendency to sin."[26]

In sum, the idea of original sin is an attempt to make sense out of the actual world in which we find ourselves. It is not a mere casuistic construction. The purpose of the concept of original sin is by no means to create a sense of guilt where there ought not to be any.[27] Its purpose is to interpret and explain the already existing reality of which we are a part, a reality that we may not always clearly understand.

Sin and Destiny

At the root of all this speculation about original sin is the pervasive sense that things are not the way they ought to be. The world is not the way it ought to be. My family and professional lives are not the way they ought to be. Perhaps even my own soul, my psyche, my inner life are not the way they ought to be. Reality as we confront it from day to day misses the mark. It falls short. It is not all it can be, not all it should be. We feel so estranged from the way things ought to be that we find ourselves tempted toward either despair or aggression or both. This unease or tension is so widely shared that we might think of it as universal.

To explain this split between the way things are and the way they ought to be, we project images of perfection, stories of paradise. The dominant story in Western culture is the story of the fall from paradise, the expulsion of the human race from the Garden of Eden. We feel estranged from perfection because we have fallen away from it. We once had it, but now we have lost it. It is irretrievable because we cannot go back in time to the era of paradise. We are now wandering in a wilderness of our own making. The best we can do is to be realistic

---

26. Haight, "Sin and Grace," p. 88.

27. The idea of original sin by no means suggests that we are incapable of living morally or that we cannot distinguish between good and evil people. Of course there are some people who are honest, faithful, caring, and virtuous, and there are others who are obviously dishonest, unfaithful, uncaring, and vicious. "In a word," writes Emil Brunner, "there are two kinds of sinners, virtuous and vicious, good and bad" (*The Christian Doctrine of Creation and Redemption,* p. 110).

and make our bed in the wilderness for the indefinite future. Or, by denying the reality, we can create the illusion of a present paradise either individually through unbridling our concupiscence or collectively through ideology and the march toward a righteous empire. That is to say, if we refuse to accept the reality of wilderness, we can sin more boldly and turn the wilderness into an even more vicious environment than it already is.

The story of a past fall from paradise, however, is less than fully adequate to explain the tension we sense. One problem is that with contemporary scholarly tools it is difficult to locate that alleged point in our historical past where paradise existed. Evolutionary theory seems to indicate that the struggle for survival and the competition for livelihood in the face of death stretches back with unbroken continuity to the vague origins of life itself. There is no evidence of paradise as a past reality.

Yet the sense of fallenness is pervasive. It is a reality belonging to the human psyche. Is it grounded in fact? Perhaps we should note that one of the effects this tension has on us is to drive us forward, to stimulate striving toward the good. It motivates efforts toward progress, toward individual and collective betterment, toward perfection. The key here, I think, is the orientation toward the future.[28] Dissatisfied with our state of fallenness, we look forward to rising up. We pursue the good in the hope that the future will take us beyond the sin of the past. Whether through pursuing a mystical spirituality for the salvation of the individual soul or through pursuing the transformation of nature and society in order to establish a political utopia, we are drawn to look beyond present reality toward the way things ought to be, toward visions of a future paradise. What this tells us, I believe, is that what we think of as missing the mark is less a matter of falling away from a perfect past than a matter of failing to reach the ideal of a healed future.

Is there any reason to hope that the future can overcome the past? Is there any reason to believe that, though fallen now, there may come a day when we will no longer be fallen? Or, is our dream of a future paradise a mere utopia in the literal sense — that is to say, no place? Will sin and its accompanying evil afflict the creatures on our planet forever?

---

28. Pannenberg puts it this way: "The consciousness of guilt . . . gives expression to the fact that human beings are not identical with the idea of their destiny" (*Anthropology*, p. 152).

It seems that we in our own dim and stumbling way sense that we are being called forward by our understanding of the good, by our vision of the way things ought to be. There are two prerequisites for making the transition from the present to such a future beyond evil: forgiveness of sin and life without death. We need forgiveness to cut the cause-effect tie of past aggression on present events and free the future to begin anew. And we need a life that is no longer threatened by death, or at least no longer vulnerable to the sting of death (i.e., anxiety). These are things we cannot accomplish on our own, yet they are essential. A future paradise seems impossible, and yet, for some mysterious reason, it lures us onward. Our hearts and passions ring with the sound of a new world beckoning us toward itself. The question is this: If we answer this call, will we find that the party on the other end has hung up? Or will we find that the party on the other end has initiated the call and that it is we who have been slow to answer?

2

ANXIETY
The Fear of Loss

All tremble at violence
All fear death
Comparing oneself with others
One should neither kill nor cause others to kill.

Dhammapada, V.129

Anxiety is a fear of loss. It is a sometimes overwhelming sense of insecurity. Anxiety arises when we anticipate some sort of diminishment of who we are, when we anticipate the possibility that a part of us or all of us is going to die. Anxiety is the fright we feel at the prospect of losing our existence, at dropping into the abyss of nonbeing.

Anxiety is the mark of death upon the living. Death is nothing in itself. It is the absence of life, the cessation of what once was a life. It is the nonexistence that constantly threatens our existence.[1] The

1. Whereas *fear* and *anxiety* overlap and frequently occur together, they can be distinguished. Fear has an object. We fear a particular threat, such as being hit by a car. Anxiety has no object. Anxiety is our response to the threat of nothingness, our reaction to the prospect of loss or separation from being. Much of today's understanding of anxiety extends the later work of Sigmund Freud in *Inhibitions, Symptoms and Anxiety*. Freud defined anxiety as an alarm signaling one's reaction to the threat of loss

34

haunting awareness of possible death at any moment reminds us of our limits, of our finitude.

In the event that we try to transcend those limits by wishing for infinite existence, we respond to the threat of death with fear and frustration and perhaps even rage. If we find we cannot accept our own death with grace, we may embark on a path of self-delusion, painting a picture of ourselves as immortal. In this delusionary state, beset by rising frustration and rage, we may seek to create our own immortality by stealing life from others. Whether through such trivial habits as harboring resentments and gossiping about our boss or through such dramatic action as military aggression wherein we capture the wealth and prestige of defeated nations, we try to steal the lifeblood of others in a misguided attempt to escape the anxiety caused by the prospect of our own nonbeing. Whether by ourselves as individuals or together as a communal group, we kill — figuratively or literally — in the vain hope that someone else's death will sustain our life. Anxiety, in short, is the sting of death afflicting the living.

Anxiety of Space and Anxiety of Time

Anxiety is the fear of nonbeing. It can arise in quite trivial incidents, a fact that serves to show that it is always present on the borders of our consciousness. The dimensions of space and time are important. If we sense that we are losing our space or that we have run out of time, we become destabilized, and this leaves us susceptible to despair and rage.

We need space — our own space — to exist. Each of us needs a home. If that home is a house or apartment, we all understand preconsciously that in this home we are most truly ourselves. Within this home we may even have a special room or a special chair that we mentally designate as our own domain. A home is safe. If it is not safe, it is not truly a home. Compared to any other location, home is the environment in which we exert the least amount of psychic energy

---

or separation, a reaction that is rooted in the infantile experience of separation from the mother's breast. The anxiety state in an adult reproduces this early experience, and neurotic anxiety is so painful that it inhibits creativity. Freud did not speak much about fear, preferring to speak of *real Angst* or "objective anxiety."

minute by minute to sustain our identity. If I develop a new friendship of such intimacy that I relax totally with the person, I may announce it by saying, "I feel so at home with you."

What about people who can't afford a house or apartment? Are they "home"-less? Not necessarily. Even the destitute people that one finds everywhere in India and increasingly on the streets of America's cities tend to find some spot — in an alley, in a park — that they begin to think of as their own. They will return to it periodically. If they return to find that someone else has taken it over, there may be trouble. Without our space, we don't fully exist.

As a professor, I have noticed over the years a somewhat comical pattern of anxiety of space. When a new course begins, students seem to select their seats randomly. By the second week, sometimes even by the second session, things are fixed. Students return again and again to the same seat. Nearly every student will sit in exactly the same place for the duration of the semester. Occasionally guests attend classes and innocently sit in seats that the registered students are used to occupying. Standing in front as I do, I can see the inevitable expression of shock on the students' faces when they enter the classroom and find their seats taken. It is an occasion of real disorientation, even if it only lasts a moment or two. I have sometimes announced to classes that at the final exam students will not be permitted to sit in their usual seats. This results in a sudden outburst of nervousness and then a laugh of self-revelation. The professor must be joking, of course.

We establish our space quickly and unnoticeably. Once I have found my place in line at the grocery checkout counter, I am oriented in space. If another busy shopper acts as if I'm not there and cuts in line in front of me, I get miffed. That was my space! He had no right to do that! I may even glance in consternation at my watch, as if to suggest that this interloper has also robbed me of my time. These are symptoms of anxiety. My anger is a response to the fact that the usurper is treating me as if I did not exist. If this individual had taken the time to ask if he might move in ahead of me, I might very well have waved him on ahead, even cheerfully if he had had a good enough story. His request for permission would have been a tacit acknowledgment of my existence, of my personhood. Anxiety would not have been aroused.

In addition to our sense of spatial presence, anxiety can come to expression as concern over time. Do we have enough time? When we no longer have time, we are dead.

A student who once lived in our family home would occasionally exhibit signs of nervousness. Carolyn would sit in an otherwise comfortable position biting her fingernails. When she would discover what she was doing, she would shake her hand and put it far away from her mouth. "I have agenda anxiety," she would explain. "Too many things to do and not enough time." The due dates of her class assignments and other responsibilities stayed in the front of her consciousness, so it seemed to her that she had no time to spare between the present moment and what was sure to be her doomsday. On those occasions when I felt a trifle mischievous, I would ask if she could possibly do me a favor, and then I would specify something very time consuming. I could see the anxiety rise in her like water in a bottle. The professor must be joking, of course.

One sure sign of anxiety over time is fear of the loss of our future. Without a future, we are nothing. It can strike us in two ways. First, we might fear death because death eliminates our future. This is the fear that incites us to care for ourselves, to eat right and exercise, to seek security in our daily routine, and to avoid unnecessary risks. Second, conversely, if we feel we have already lost our future, we may seek death. How frequently we have observed among couples who have been married for several decades that when one spouse dies, the other often dies not too much later. Many survivors of close marriages find it difficult to conceive of a future alone; a future alone may seem like no future at all. Routine physical ailments become life-threatening emergencies, and finally death eases the pain. Anxiety leads to confusion regarding the relation between death and life. It can also lead to confusion regarding one's own death and the killing of others. More about this later.

Understanding anxiety over space and time gives us insight into one of the most horrendous evils of the modern world, the rise of Nazism in Germany. In the wake of World War I, the victorious Allies used the Treaty of Versailles to exact heavy reparations ($33 billion in war debts) from the defeated Germans. Germany was forced to give up land. An Allied blockade caused shortages of food and raw materials. Unemployment and inflation thwarted all attempts to rejuvenate the German economy. It appeared that Germany's future had been taken away. Adolf Hitler and his National Socialist Party rose to power in part because they promised a new future, a Third Reich, a thousand years of prosperity and glory. Hitler further rallied the Germans by insisting that they needed *Lebensraum,* living space. The Nazis held out the hope of expansion in both space and time, a hope that excited a nation to the point of engaging in mass destruction, pillage, and murder.

The anxiety of space and time is at root the preconscious fear of death. Such fear can drive us to despair. Out of despair we may rise up in rage, and our rage may leave great damage in its wake.

Striking Out in Rage

When I was a seminary student pursuing the Clinical Pastoral Education requirement in 1964, I worked at the Cleveland Psychiatric Institute. On one occasion I was called to the intake office and asked to escort a new patient to his room on the ward. We exchanged greetings. As I recall, his name was Mr. Johnson. He was a large, muscular man, and I later learned that he was thirty-three years old with a wife and one child. I led him down the long hall toward the nurses' station, beyond which lay his assigned quarters. We passed an open door that led to a pool room. I caught a brief glimpse of a half dozen or so men circling the pool table with cue sticks in hand. No sooner had we stepped beyond the gaze of the pool players than Mr. Johnson whispered to me, "They're talking about me."

"Who's talking about you?" I asked.

"Those men in there. They don't like me." The words *paranoid schizophrenic* popped into my mind.

Once Mr. Johnson had been introduced to his room and to the nursing staff, he was free to wander around. He didn't. He found himself a spot on the wall not far from the pool room door. He stood nearly spread-eagle with back and arms and legs flat against the wall. His face moved from side to side so he could see foot traffic coming toward him in both directions. Shortly after he had assumed this position, one of the pool players emerged through the doorway. Mr. Johnson attacked him with a right cross to the chin. The surprised victim caught the punch and was thrown to the floor by its force. I joined a number of orderlies in overpowering Mr. Johnson and putting him into restraints.

"Why did you hit him?" I asked.

"He was going to attack me," said Mr. Johnson. He often screamed

38

during his sleep, "I don't wanna die! I don't wanna die!" On one occasion I was assigned to escort him to the bathtub.

"I won't take a bath," he told me through clenched teeth.

"Why not?" I asked.

"Because I'm afraid I'll slip under the water and drown."

We did the best we could under the circumstances. Another orderly and I put him in a tub with only two inches of water and used washcloths to get the job done. We did the washing while Mr. Johnson stood there rigid. Anxiety in the form of the fear of death had so paralyzed this man's life that he could not engage in normal human relationships or carry out normal daily functions.

Most of us are reasonably civil folk, not psychically paralyzed like Mr. Johnson. We are able to keep anxiety from overwhelming us as long as we maintain some relationships of trust, as long as we can retreat to some island of order in which our personal being is acknowledged and affirmed. We need the support of trusting and loving relationships to sustain a sense of personal worth, because the loss of that sense of worth is a form of dying. We can tolerate considerable frustration and even humiliation at work if we know we can escape to a home where things have their place and where we are loved and valued.

What happens if we return home and find it in chaos? We may then try an escape to the corner bar in hopes of finding a surrogate home there. We may try to command some respect with a bit of bravado, to get some acknowledgment of our worth from others who came for the same purpose. Like a boat looking for a secure mooring, we search for something to which we can attach our personal being. But what if the gang at the bar denies us that? And what if there is no other place to go? Then anxiety typically gives way to rage. We take it outside. Fists fly. Someone goes for a gun. Someone dies. Our morgues and jails fill up on Saturday night.

This may give us some insight into the highly publicized 1980 murder of Herman Tarnower, the *Scarsdale Diet* doctor. He was shot by Jean Harris, then headmistress of a prestigious Eastern girl's school. She had been Tarnower's lover, and she was jealous of the diet doctor's other affairs. But it was more than jealousy that led her to pull the trigger. Jean Harris had just learned that she would lose her coveted job and much of her reputation along with it. The threatened loss of her career and her social standing compounded her frustration in love, all of which seemed to constitute a loss of her being. The threat of social death sent her into a rage. She went to Dr. Tarnower's home the fateful night with no plan of escape. She seemed resigned to not having an escape. The result was somebody's death.[2]

It may also help us begin to understand the atrocity that took place at My Lai in Quang Ngai province of South Vietnam on March 16, 1968. A unit of American soldiers, elements of Task Force Baker known as "Charlie Company," massacred as many as 450 to 500 villagers, most of them women, children, and elderly grandparents. The soldiers were told to "kill every man, woman, and child in the village," to ensure that "nothing would be walking, growing, or crawling." They did. They searched through homes and huts, lined the people up, and shot them down. In some cases they opened the doors of homes and sprayed machine gun fire, killing entire families. Children were shot in open spaces while running away. In the hamlet known as My Lai Four, under the command of Lt. William L. Calley, Jr., the GIs herded villagers into groups of twenty to forty and then slaughtered them with rifle and machine gun fire plus grenades. Why? This is by no means standard military procedure.

This massacre of Vietnamese civilians can be understood in part as the attempt by some desperate soldiers to press the lid down on a pot boiling over with frustration and rage. The typical nineteen-year-old American soldier from the cotton fields of Georgia or the neighborhoods of Brooklyn was packed off to a faraway and alien place to fight in an undeclared and apparently purposeless war. The Vietnam environment was hostile at every turn, dangerous and unpredictable. There were no sure signs to warn of danger, no sure way even to identify the enemy. To the American GI, Vietnam was chaos, not order. This led to a profound inner confusion combined with feelings of helplessness and terror.

In basic training a soldier learns of the structure and ritual that characterize ordinary war. Uniforms and battle lines distinguish friend from foe. None of that applied in Vietnam. The enemy was everyone and no one, rarely visible, always moving, indistinguishable from the

2. I am relying here on the insightful interpretation of Jack Katz in *Seductions of Crime* (New York: Basic Books, 1988), p. 45. After twelve years in prison and four appeals for clemency, Harris received a pardon from New York Governor Mario Cuomo in 1992.

ordinary village peasants. Shots from nowhere, exploding mines, and children with hand grenades killed and mutilated one's buddies on a surprise basis. The GI was denied what psychiatrist Robert Jay Lifton refers to as the minimal psychological satisfactions of war. As a result, fear, rage, and frustration mounted.

Under the extraordinary stress of this unbearable situation, the Americans were tempted to view all Vietnamese as the enemy. Killing any Vietnamese became a way of retaliating at those responsible for wounding or killing their own buddies. It was a pep talk at the funeral of a slain sergeant just prior to the My Lai massacre that included the direction to "kill every man, woman, and child in the village."

One of the soldiers said that after killing a number of villagers he immediately "felt good" because "I was getting relieved from what I had seen earlier over there." This leads Lifton to enunciate an important principle relevant to our study here: killing can relieve the fear of being killed. Of course, this is an illusion, but it is a powerful illusion. By shooting villagers whom they had come to equate with the enemy — even little babies and women and older people — the soldiers thought they were finally involved in a genuine military action. They had finally managed to locate — and annihilate — their elusive adversaries. Chaos had been defeated. Order had been restored. They now could stand secure.

What is there about striking out violently and killing others that makes us think we can quell the pangs of anxiety, overcome our frustrations, relieve our rage, regain a sense of self-worth, and thereby conquer death? Killing others, conjectures Lifton, seems to relieve our own fear of being killed.[3]

---

3. Lifton, *The Future of Immortality* (New York: Basic Books, 1987), pp. 54-55. One of my students, a Vietnam veteran, pleaded for sympathetic understanding of the American soldiers at My Lai. He described the panic situation of a handful of soldiers trying to round up a large number of prisoners and hearing gunshots in the distance. If you can hear a shot, he said, it can kill you. Not knowing if the shots were friendly or enemy fire, not knowing if they were about to be ambushed by Viet Cong rising up out of village tunnels, and operating with the unwritten rule not to lose a buddy to save the enemy, the Americans at My Lai fired their weapons. He insisted that this was a rational response to an already terrifying situation. "It is no illusion that killing relieves the fear of being killed," said my student. "I have never been shot at by a dead man."

41

The Watercooler Syndrome

Murder on the scale of My Lai is an extreme experience that most of us will not confront in a lifetime, much less on a daily basis. Yet the same destructive dynamics of anxiety are constantly at work in ordinary life. Rather than literal death, they take the form of diminishment of someone's being.

One of the most common forms it takes among professional people is calumny — that is, defamation of character. I call it "the watercooler syndrome." It is the event that takes place nearly hourly in offices all across the globe, where two or three employees gather around the watercooler or coffeepot to complain about the boss. I happened to discover the watercooler syndrome quite by accident. But since I became aware of it, I have been able to recognize it in every institution I have worked for since.

My discovery began when I took a job as a security guard for Carson, Pirie, Scott, a large department store in downtown Chicago. I was interviewed by the head of security, Mr. Martinsen. I explained to him that I was a graduate student at the University of Chicago and would like a nighttime position where I could read while working.

"Would you mind if I read on the job?" I asked.

"No, not at all," he replied. "If you're reading, then I know you'll be awake."

The conversation went quite well, I thought. Mr. Martinsen was not a well-educated man, but he certainly seemed to know security work and appeared magnanimous and flexible. I looked forward to working with him.

The next night I reported to my shift, put on my guard's uniform, and dutifully made the rounds to the various security checkpoints. All six guards on that shift carried out their corresponding duties. Eventually it was break time. We gathered around the watercooler to chat. What I heard astounded me. One after another, the veteran guards berated Mr. Martinsen. They described him as autocratic, unfair, and incompetent. The Mr. Martinsen they described seemed to have no relation to the Mr. Martinsen I had interviewed with the day before. Had I missed something? Was I blind? How could I have been so mistaken? But I must have been, I thought, because these guards had worked there for months and years. In time, I conjectured, I would learn too.

Six weeks later I was called into Mr. Martinsen's office for a probationary review. After sharing my supervisor's positive evaluation of my performance, he asked kindly, "And how is your reading coming?" A pleasant conversation followed in which he sought to get to know me better and I quizzed him on the ins and outs of security work. It all ended with a handshake, and I returned to my post. Back at the watercooler the guards assembled for what I had noticed was the nightly routine of verbal snarling and sniping at Mr. Martinsen. I continued to be puzzled at the wide gulf between the person they were describing and the one I had now engaged in two conversations.

The revelation of what was taking place came many months later when the entire staff of guards was scheduled to appear before Mr. Martinsen for an annual review of operations. We all assembled quietly in our chairs. Mr. Martinsen opened with a brief speech regarding the overall security picture of the store and preparing us for special measures to be taken during the upcoming Christmas shopping season. Then he inquired of us guards, "How are things going with you?"

"Fine," each guard answered.

"No problems?" he asked, just to make sure.

"No problems," they said. Their fidgeting conveyed nervousness. Nearly all of the guards' statements were short, usually consisting of phrases such as "Yes, Mr. Martinsen" or "Of course, Mr. Martinsen." Things are going better than I had thought, I said to myself.

Yet, back on the job that night, the watercooler conversation was the same. Mr. Martinsen was berated for having his facts wrong, for passing out assignments unfairly, and for incompetence, and rumor had it that soon he would be fired by the store management. Then it began to dawn on me that the problem did not lie with Mr. Martinsen. The problem originated right here with anxiety at the watercooler. Mr. Martinsen was the boss. The very existence of the boss as a boss appeared to challenge these guards' confidence in their own existence. Mr. Martinsen was perceived to be a threat to their being, a force that somehow diminished who they were. Their obsequious yielding to his authority in the group meeting stemmed from a resignation to the perception that the boss had all the power and they had none. Mr. Martinsen was omnipotent, and he probably didn't even know it.

So, gathered around the watercooler, the guards struck out with calumny. The rage rising from their feeling of diminished being expressed itself in complaint, rumor, and gossip. This was their opportunity to engage in giant killing, in diminishing the being — or at least the image — of Mr. Martinsen just as they perceived him to be diminishing them. The employees hung the boss daily in verbal effigy.

Why didn't I react the same way? Why was I not outraged like the other guards? I think it was because I was not subject to the same anxiety. Whereas the security jobs were the careers and livelihoods of the other guards, mine was but a part-time job used to support my real vocation as a graduate student. Whereas Mr. Martinsen exercised some considerable power over their financial well-being, I tended to view him more as a peer working in a parallel profession. Had I been struck with the same diminishment of my being, might I too have struck out and tried to diminish Mr. Martinsen with complaint, rumor, and gossip?

Since this initial watercooler experience, I have remained on the lookout for the phenomenon, and I have spotted it again and again. In higher education, where I now work, I listen to students who gossip about faculty the same way the guards did about Mr. Martinsen. The faculty, in turn, hang either the dean or the institutional president or both in near daily verbal effigy. I can only surmise that similar activities are taking place everywhere. Although gossip is much to be preferred over murder, at its own level the Lifton principle appears to hold: killing others seems to relieve our own fear of being killed.[4]

The Denial of Death

Ernest Becker would agree. In fact, Becker's later work, completed just prior to his death in 1974, focused on death — especially the

---

4. Calumny — what I am here calling the watercooler syndrome — has two distinguishing features: (1) it is virtually inevitable in all situations where leadership is exerted, and (2) it represents in most cases a shallow form of anxiety-aggression. Failure to understand this can be disastrous. A dramatic case in point is the aborted Soviet coup d'état by the Committee of Eight in August 1991. The hardline communists had misunderstood the calumny of the Soviet people who, anxious for a faster pace of *perestroika,* complained about General Secretary Mikhail Gorbachev and gave him only a 17 percent approval rating. Overestimating the significance of this, the revolutionaries toppled the Gorbachev government only to find out they lacked any public support. The coup collapsed in a matter of days, and its leaders found themselves subject to prosecution. The moral is this: calumny is to be expected, but it should not taken to indicate a full commitment to change leadership.

denial of death — as the source of human evil. Becker wrote two books on the subject of evil, the second of which was the more important. He changed his mind along the way. The position of the later Becker is important for this study.

Becker grew up in a Jewish immigrant family in Springfield, Massachusetts. As a decorated American soldier in World War II, he helped liberate a Nazi concentration camp and saw firsthand the scope of human atrocity. He earned his doctorate in anthropology in 1960 from Syracuse University and went on to do interdisciplinary teaching at the University of California at Berkeley, San Francisco State University, and Simon Fraser University in Vancouver, Canada.

He wrote his first work on evil while he was in Rome in 1963; *The Structure of Evil* was published in 1968. In this early work, Becker says only a little about the topic of evil but a whole lot about social science and the need for establishing an ethic for the modern world that is scientifically grounded and socially integrated. The task that Becker set for himself was to lay the foundation for "a new, unified theory of human behavior," what he called a "science of man."[5] To this end, Becker made it clear that he divided Western history into two basic eras, the premodern and the modern. The medieval or premodern period had one advantage over the modern: it possessed a unified or holistic view of humanity. This holism stands in sharp contrast to the fragmented perspective of us moderns.

Becker's medieval holism was grounded in the Christian vision of a divine Creator who has a stake in the earth as a staging area for the work of salvation. This divine investment in our world knitted all things together in one overarching design. Human beings had a fixed and fundamental criterion for discerning the difference between right and wrong, good and evil, and they could feel that they were part of a coherent and meaningful world scheme. But this medieval view was drastically deficient, wrote Becker, because it was hierarchical. It was based on power, privilege, tyranny, coercion, and benevolent paternalism. It precluded the personal freedom that we moderns have come to deem so important. The medieval synthesis was broken by the eighteenth-century Enlightenment, and Becker was glad of it.

But the work of the Enlightenment is not yet finished, said Becker. It has left us moderns with a nagging problem — namely, the frag-

5. See Becker, *The Structure of Evil* (New York: Macmillan, 1968), p. xii.

mentation of life. Things that used to belong together have been broken apart. Fact is separated from value, science from morality, and the individual from society. The modern industrial world has "gone mad" with a preoccupation with the specific, the unconnected, the minute. What has been lost and what we need to retrieve is, in Auguste Comte's words, a *vue d'ensemble*, a view of the whole. Becker set out to construct such a view of the whole, something that would be specifically modern rather than premodern or postmodern. He wanted to bring the chaos of a disordered society under the control of identifiably Enlightenment ideals such as human freedom, dignity, and scientific reason. This is strict humanism. Becker did not follow the path taken by so many postmodern theorists who believe that the *vue d'ensemble* must retrieve some elements of the now lost religious vision in order to bring things into a comprehensive whole. Becker's only tools were science and reason. He operated with the faith that the problems modernity has created for itself can be solved by accentuating the principles of modernity itself.

How does Becker analyze the modern problem of fragmentation? He associates the split between science and morality with the problem of developing a new and secular *theodicy* (a term derived from the Greek *theos*, "god," and *dikē*, "justice"). Classical theodicy was a game played by theologians to see who could explain how there could be so much evil in the world and a God who is both all-loving and all-powerful. The problem goes something like this: because it is inconceivable that an all-loving being would permit evil to plague divine creation if it were in God's power to prevent it, we can assume either that God is all-loving but powerless to prevent evil or that God is all-powerful but not loving enough to prevent evil, but we cannot consistently say that God is both all-loving and all-powerful. Augustine's solution to the theodicy mystery, as I noted earlier, was to deny that evil is a problem by arguing that it has no genuine being, that it is the opposite of existence. Whether one follows Augustine or not, the classical task of theodicy is to justify belief in a God who both loves and has the power to effect that love in a world of sin and evil.

But with the loss of belief in divine providence during the modern period, says Becker, we must explain evil apart from God's intention or justification. Becker wanted to find an explanation that lies within the scope of our understanding of nature. But the difficulty here is that when nature is understood in terms of Newtonian science, it is value-neutral. In itself nature admits of neither goodness nor badness. What, then, is the source of evil? Becker contends that it is rooted in humanity apart from the rest of nature. He calls us in effect to replace theodicy with *anthropodicy,* to identify evil with those forces that tend to inhibit or restrict human freedom, democracy, and progress and to make human beings rather than God the authors of the criteria for discerning good and evil. He also assigns humans the responsibility of engineering some sort of victory over evil. To this extent, Becker's proposed "anthropodicy is not a theodicy: it would limit itself to the use of human powers effecting whatever they can to overcome avoidable evil."[6]

In making humans responsible for creating the criteria for discerning evil and for taking the action necessary to overcome evil, he implicitly makes us responsible for the existence of evil as well. But just how do we bring evil into existence? Individually or communally? Following Rousseau, Marx, and Dewey, Becker initially asserts that evil is a product of the community's repression of individual freedom. Making the incredibly naive assumption that human nature and goodness are synonymous, Becker says the task of the modern anthropodicy is to show scientifically that society itself with its structures of dominance has functioned to repress human liberty and alienate individual persons from their selves. Human nature would be free and good if left to itself, he says; evil arises out of social institutions that encourage class consciousness, envy, hate, competition, and coercion. In particular, the greatest single obstacle to human freedom is the existence of the free economy — the profit-oriented commercial economy — which treats human beings as means rather than ends. To combat this towering evil, says Becker, we have to take action to bring the world economy, with its accompanying political and class structure, under rational control. In short, Becker advocates pursuing an Enlightenment ideal (the freedom and dignity of the human person) via Enlightenment means (human reason and democratic control). Or, to put it another way, although we are currently experiencing alienation, we were born with an original or innate goodness, and if we can become modern enough, we can overcome this alienation and retrieve our original goodness, thereby defeating the forces of evil. It was to this end that Becker offered his "science of man."

6. Becker, *The Structure of Evil,* p. 376.

By analyzing the problem of evil in this way, he sized up the problem of modernity in terms of the relationship between the individual and society. At present there is both a theoretical and a practical split between the two, he said. As yet, the social sciences have failed to provide us with an adequate theory for explaining the relationship. Practically speaking, the alienation we moderns experience is due to the failure of society to establish a set of shared values that fosters the Enlightenment ethical ideal — namely, maximum individuality within maximum community. The alienation we experience is generated by large and impersonal social institutions that require individuals to conform, thereby repressing individual freedom and creativity. How did these institutions become impersonal and uncontrollable? We lost the sort of unifying vision that once controlled the impersonal structures of institutions.

> The twentieth century gathered all the evils that could seem possible to befall man: genocide of millions, recurrent world war, race and hate riots, famine and world-wide misery for the vast masses of men. And the outlook for the future is more of the same: atomic war, violent revolutions, mass starvation. In our time we have seen the *demonic* emerge in all its starkness and we have learned why it emerges: the demonic comes into being for man whenever he is manipulated by large impersonal forces beyond his control; forces that he is actively and uncritically contributing to. Thus, when modern man sets in motion vast social institutions but does not take critical control of them, the institutions assume their own momentum; the people who man the institutions become like ants mechanically doing their duty, and no one dares to question the routine to which the institutions conform. . . . Responsibility is nowhere; grinding power everywhere.[7]

Thus, according to Becker, evil occurs when persons are treated impersonally, and impersonal treatment arises from our failure to live out of a comprehensive vision of the whole, our failure to take a "commanding" or "unitary critical perspective." The source of evil lies not within the individual but rather at the point of contact between the individual and an impersonal economic institution. This being the case, we can overcome evil by developing an appropriate critical conscious-

7. Becker, *The Structure of Evil,* pp. 141-42; italics in original.

ness and applying that consciousness to the construction of a unitary worldview to control and guide institutions toward personal ends.

What this leads to is Becker's advocacy of an ethic of self-liberation based on what I have elsewhere referred to as the "understanding-decision-control" formula.[8] He draws a parallel and causal relationship between neurosis and social bondage. Neurosis constricts and restricts individual freedom by fostering anxiety. Such anxiety, says Becker, is due to a problem of cognition, a lack of understanding. If we are led to the understanding that we have the right and the freedom to create our own meanings, and if we "frame our problems in ever-more-explicit cognitive terms," we will unblock action, open up choices, and free ourselves. "One can convert a situation in which there is no choice to one in which there are new choices. In this way, man liberates himself by creating indeterminacy. On the individual level, the whole of ethics becomes a problem of self-liberating choice possibilities. And the strength to be ethical, we can now conclude, is really the strength to design alternatives, and to follow them out. Ah yes, to follow them out."[9]

This program of liberating the individual from neurosis by maximizing choice also serves to eliminate structures of domination in society. Why? Because people who are free to choose do not try to dominate others. *"The more choices and freedom are available to one, the less he will need to impose his narrow meanings on others."*[10] We should pause here to note how the source of evil has changed in this analysis. It no longer comes from impersonal institutions but rather from the narrowness of choice that leads to one person's domination of another. Of course, Becker might reconcile the difference here by saying that it is the impersonal institutions that narrow our range of choice. If that were the case, the means of salvation would consist in our gaining control of social institutions, personalizing them, widening our range of choice, coming to understand that more choice is available, and then actualizing our choice, thereby overcoming neurosis. Or, is it the other way around? Do we have to overcome our neurosis before we can change the institutions that generate our neurosis? Becker's analysis seems to flounder at this point.

What kind of social ethic does this imply? One that avoids reducing

8. See my book *Futures — Human and Divine* (Atlanta: John Knox Press, 1978).
9. Becker, *The Structure of Evil,* p. 259; cf. pp. 284-85.
10. Becker, *The Structure of Evil,* p. 300; italics in original.

people to their functional roles and affirms the responsibility of society to foster individual spontaneity. Becker advocated pursuing this by implementing the principles of "progressive education" as anticipated by Rousseau and developed by John Dewey. He believed that Dewey's pragmatist ethics would be vindicated and true democracy achieved if we would only treat persons as ends rather than means and open our society to the spontaneous and creative energies of our youth. In other words, the public schools should liberate youthful creativity instead of demanding conformity to what has been established.

Critical thought is paramount here. When we permit free critical thinking, there is no telling where we will come out; our future is open, indeterminate. For one thing, we open the door to progress, something in which Becker places a great deal of trust. The fostering of youthful creativity and a desire for progress constitute an ethical ideal that we must pursue if we are to maximize the individual while maximizing community. Progress requires a critical distance from what has gone before, an irreverence for tradition. "We can educate for true critical awareness, which enables the individual to draw his pride from cultural criticism, a criticism that aims for the well-being of all others *as equal ends.* . . . The program of human liberation through progressive education as social criticism is an ideal just as it was when Rousseau first proposed it over two hundred years ago. Yet we must continue to set up the ideal . . . in order to hold out for the hope for a new kind of man — in order even to support our belief in man."[11]

Progressive education should set itself to the task of cultivating the self-esteem of the individual. Self-esteem, according to Becker in *The Structure of Evil,* is the *summum bonum,* the *sine qua non* for human development, the sole means by which humans might escape the bondage of physiological determinism and become truly human. As Becker sees it, self-esteem is so fundamental a part of the nature of the living organism that it is accessible to scientific analysis and verification. "All organisms like to 'feel good' about themselves. . . . Self-feeling is at the heart of Being in nature."[12] He likens self-esteem to gravity, characterizing it as an irreducible primary property. Hence he believes that his ethic can be characterized as both naturalistic and scientifically justifiable.

11. Becker, *The Structure of Evil,* p. 301; italics in original.
12. Becker, *The Structure of Evil,* p. 328.

All of this should sound quite familiar. It's common fare in our liberal democracy. Becker put into scholarly language what we are taught in the public schools and what is assumed in the mass media. It is part of the professional ethic of the psychotherapist and undergirds garden-variety speeches at political rallies. Becker gave voice to the standard values of Western Enlightenment culture. The big question, of course, is whether he was right. Is this the way sin and evil work? And, if so, will Becker's prescription provide a cure? Or did he misunderstand something important?

Becker went on to say that self-esteem is the "surest basis for true selflessness and social harmony."[13] But on what basis did he draw this conclusion? How does accentuating the self-orientation of individuals serve to make them selfless? It seems like a *non sequitur.* Evidently he believed that self-esteem could be properly maintained only in an environment of personalized institutions and that in such an environment progressive education would foster self-esteem interpersonally. This makes a certain amount of sense, since personal development is at least partially dependent on social interaction. But this scarcely warrants the big jump from self-esteem to selflessness. If social institutions could be geared to maintain the self-esteem of individuals, on what grounds should we believe these individuals would develop into anything other than narcissists? On what grounds should we believe that competition and killing would be replaced by love and service? Becker did not really say. I don't believe he could say on the basis of his premises.

By the time Becker published his final book, *Escape from Evil,* in 1975, his analysis of the human condition had undergone a significant change. He no longer located the source of evil in social institutions that repress a primitive goodness and freedom. He now maintained that evil results from something much more basic to human nature — namely, our awareness of our own mortality and our response to it. How do we respond to death-consciousness? Becker says that we create the illusion that we can attain immortality, a thesis he had already begun to develop in his Pulitzer prize–winning book *The Denial of Death,* published two years before *Escape from Evil.* This illusion that immortality is possible, he says, leads us to perform the most heinous acts of violence against other people in a typically unconscious effort

13. Becker, *The Structure of Evil,* p. 331.

to steal their life-force in order to increase our own personal power. Our natural and inevitable urges to deny mortality and to achieve a heroic self-image are the root causes of evil because they lead us to seek power over life and death, and this leads finally to justifications for killing our enemies. Becker acknowledged that in *The Structure of Evil* he had underestimated how "truly vicious human behavior" is. In his last book, he wrote that he was finally looking "man in the face for the first time in my career."[14]

Human beings are physical creatures, animals. We are as much driven to eat, to reproduce, and to perpetuate our existence as any other animals. But we are different from the other animals to the extent that we are conscious of our mortality. We are aware that our bodies will die. In itself there is nothing wrong with this consciousness of our death. The problem is that we deny it. In fact, we go to great lengths to create systematic illusions that hide the stark realization. Becker later identifies these systematic illusions as "culture." Culture consists in a set of sacred symbols that give human life a significance transcending our death. This "symbolic denial of mortality is a figment of the imagination . . . a fantasy for which there is no scientific evidence so far," he says. Through displacement, transference, and other psychological mechanisms, we transfer our fear of death to the cultural level, and through this doorway we introduce more evil into the world than any purely naturalistic system could generate.[15]

> Each person nourishes his immortality in the ideology of self-perpetuation to which he gives his allegiance; this gives his life the only abiding significance it can have. No wonder men go into rage over fine points of belief: if your adversary wins the argument about truth, *you die.* Your immortality system has been shown to be fallible, your life becomes fallible. History, then, can be understood as the succession of ideologies that console for death. Or, more momentously, *all* cultural forms are *in essence sacred* because they seek the perpetuation and redemption of the individual life.[16]

The key link in the logic of this cultural illusion is the mistaken belief that we can transfer life from one being to another. In primitive

14. Becker, *Escape from Evil* (New York: Macmillan, 1975), pp. xvii-xviii; cf. p. 5.
15. Becker, *Escape from Evil,* p. 5; cf. pp. 89-90.
16. Becker, *Escape from Evil,* p. 64; italics in original.

religious ritual the sacrifice of the animal to assuage our guilt is prompted primarily by the desire to transfer the life-power of the animal to the worshipers. The ceremonious killing of captives affirms the power of the victorious army over death and life. The kings of the Dahomey in Africa went to war to capture slaves to sell to the Europeans. Once a year they held a festival of victory that included the ritual beheading of hundreds of these prisoners and the piling up of the severed heads. The Dahomey would sacrifice the profit they could make in selling slaves just to demonstrate their prowess, their power over the life and death of their enemies. In the arena games of ancient Rome, the audience could casually turn thumbs up for the gladiators to live or turn thumbs down to exact death. The nonchalance of the decision only served to increase the experience of effortless power. The ceremonious shedding of blood facilitates the belief that "they are weak and die: we are strong and live." The sacrifice of someone else's life for the purpose of increasing one's own power becomes the fundamental building block upon which nations and ideologies are erected and secured.

> From the beginning men have served the appetites of one another in the most varying ways, but these were always reducible to a single theme: the need for fuel for one's own aggrandizement and immunity. Men use one another to assure their personal victory over death. . . . Through the death of the other, one buys oneself free from the penalty of dying, of being killed. No wonder men are addicted to war.[17]

There is another subtle link in the logic of illusion that takes us from the fear of death to the sacrifice of others and finally to the perpetrating of evil — a belief in the heroic victory over evil. This is the paradox Becker proffers: in our very attempt to gain victory over evil, we increase evil. Becker is not speaking here of such evils as isolated incidents of street crime such as petty theft or muggings; he

17. Becker, *Escape from Evil*, p. 108. Walter Wink's analysis is similar. "We trust violence. Violence 'saves.' It is 'redemptive.' All we have to do is make survival the highest goal, and death the greatest evil, and we have handed ourselves over to the gods of the Domination System. We trust violence because we are afraid. And we will not relinquish our fears until we are able to imagine a better alternative" (*Engaging the Powers* [Minneapolis: Fortress Press, 1992], p. 231).

is concerned with evil on a massive and all-pervasive scale. Regarding evil on this level, it is his contention that good people are responsible. He repeats frequently the observation that the man who dropped the atomic bomb grew up next door, and he maintains that Adolf Eichmann bureaucratically consigned millions of people to death camps simply because he wanted to be liked by his Nazi friends. There is a dynamic of self-justification at work in the generation of such evil, a desire to identify oneself with enduring perfection. It is by offering individuals the opportunity to meld themselves into righteous and hence eternal causes that such political ideologies as Nazism and communism have produced explosions of unparalleled evil in the twentieth century. Once individuals have given themselves over to a righteous cause, they can with clear consciences give themselves over to the elimination of the enemies of that cause. In the service of a righteous cause, one can not only justify the deaths of one's enemies but also enjoy them.

By relocating the root of evil from alienating social structures to the fundamental human condition, the later Becker came as close as a nonreligious social scientist could in advocating a doctrine of original sin.[18] He was still enough of an advocate of the Enlightenment to deny that we humans are "by nature" sinful and unclean, if this means that we are incapable of overcoming our propensity for doing evil things. Becker felt he had to believe that we humans have the capacity to "escape from evil." How can we do this? Again his Enlightenment philosophy was expressed in his employment of the understanding-decision-control formula. What we need to do, he argued, is to use

---

18. This has not gone completely unnoticed in the theological community. John E. Benson, for example, argues that Becker's analysis "ends in an Augustinian theology . . . with which most of us church theologians should feel very comfortable" ("Ernest Becker: A New Enlightenment View of Evil?" *Dialog* 25 [Spring 1986]: 106). On the other hand, it has gone quite unnoticed by New Age practitioners and especially the Maharishi Mahesh Yogi, founder of Transcendental Meditation. Just prior to Christmas in 1992, he advertised in the *San Francisco Chronicle* (13 December 1992, p. A-24) that he could put an end to all big-city crime for a fee. The source of crime is stress, he said. (Is stress something like anxiety?) The cure for stress is harmony, "maintaining a balance in nature." TM experts have a method of maintaining harmony that is "based on extensive, published scientific research." These TM experts are capable of going through cities, creating harmony along with balance and positivity, and eliminating all crime within a period of only five years. The proposed fee was a mere $59.7 million per year.

the tools of psychology to analyze the human condition and come to an understanding of just how this illusion of immortality arises. Then we will be in a position to decide what to do about it. Should we decide to try to overcome evil, we might then implement scientifically conceived plans for a social design that would allow us to take control. This is what is required to make utopia a possibility.

Just what ingredients should we put into this scientifically conceived social design? Somehow we need to immunize humankind against its natural weakness, a proclivity to deny our own mortality and use scapegoating to quell our fears. We must take our base motives into account, but we cannot directly negate these motives. Becker's solution was to advocate the construction of a hate object. Hate objects already exist, of course. We hate other social classes, other nations, and the like. Becker's rather weak alternative — he spends only half a paragraph developing it — is that we should redirect our hatred toward poverty and oppression, toward the enemies of human freedom, toward those who thrive on slavery.

Becker almost recognizes how weak this suggestion is, but he does not seem to understand why. The problem is that it is self-contradictory. He has just finished analyzing how ideology, as the most virulent form of cultural symbol systems, functions to spawn evil. The essential ingredient is the righteous cause to which we as individuals give ourselves, since this provides the justification for going to war and killing off all those who do not belong to the same righteous cause. But Becker's suggestion that we make oppressors, slavers, and other enemies of freedom into objects of our hatred plays right into the hands of the ideological structure. In the end, Becker's new breed of righteous ones would simply perpetuate the apparently unending history of evil.

What leads Becker into such a self-contradiction? In trying to answer this, it is interesting to note his acknowledged dependence on philosopher William James. He quotes James frequently in *Escape from Evil*, especially his essay "The Moral Equivalent of War." What is important about this essay is that James's analysis of the human condition parallels Becker's. James admits that he is a pacifist but recognizes the great value to society provided by the soldier mentality. "Militarism is the great preserver of our ideals of hardihood," he writes; "and human life with no use for hardihood would be contemptible. Without risks or prizes for the darer, history would be insipid indeed." So the dilemma is how to eliminate war without surrendering ourselves to an insipid history. James's answer is to enlist the whole human race into a single army fighting a common enemy. What is the common enemy against which all of humanity could unite? James answers: nature. We could join together in mining and farming and fishing and building roads and boring tunnels and raising cities until a gigantic and peaceful commonwealth becomes available to all. The battle against nature is for James the "moral equivalent of war."

We might ask why Becker does not follow James in making nature the object of human hatred. The James essay appeared in 1910. Becker wrote *Escape from Evil* in the early 1970s, a time of acute ecological consciousness. We have become aware recently that in effect the human race has long been fighting for supremacy over nature but that our victories have all been Pyrrhic. The more we manage to steal life from nature, the closer we get to destroying our own life — because we humans are a part of nature too. We live in a period when we are beginning to realize that our love for nature and our love for ourselves are interrelated. Did Becker share this awareness? It is difficult to say. He did not include any analysis of the environmental crisis in his discussion of evil. Nevertheless, after having fairly carefully retraced James's argument step by step, he backed off from recounting its conclusion. He simply substituted his own conclusion — namely, we should make poverty and oppression our enemies — and never mentioned nature.[19]

The Anticipation of Nonbeing

Becker was a humanist trying to produce an anthropodicy, not a theologian trying to produce a theodicy. Yet, he had learned much

19. The relationships between our natural environment, anxiety, and sin are topics worthy of our attention. As the world population grows in size and the environment deteriorates, we can anticipate increased violence as societies compete for limited resources. A recent study arrived at the following disturbing conclusion: "Scarcities of renewable resources are already contributing to violent conflicts in many parts of the developing world. These conflicts may foreshadow a surge of similar violence in coming decades where shortages of water, forests and, especially, fertile land, coupled with rapidly expanding populations, already cause great hardship" (Thomas F. Homer-Dixon, Jeffrey H. Boutwell, and George W. Rathjens, "Environmental Change and Violent Conflict," *Scientific American* 268 [February 1993]: 38).

from theology, as his footnote citations of Paul Tillich attest. Where Becker speaks of the denial of death, Tillich speaks of pathological anxiety. Where Becker speaks of a social scientific theory of evil, Tillich speaks of the ontology of anxiety.

"Anxiety is the state in which a being is aware of its possible nonbeing," writes Tillich in his once-popular book *The Courage to Be*. He goes on to emphasize that this "existential awareness of nonbeing," this awareness of our approaching extinction, is intensely personal. Knowledge of death in general is not our concern here; an abstract or philosophical understanding of death is not relevant. What Tillich is calling our attention to is your and my own personal destiny of death and the effects the awareness of this destiny has on our personality. There is no escape. It is "the always latent awareness of our own having to die that produces anxiety. Anxiety is finitude, experienced as one's own finitude."[20]

Anxiety is painful, so we try to hide ourselves. One way to hide is in neurosis, in organizing our lives as totally as we can around fixed patterns of behavior. We imbibe deeply of tradition, especially our own little daily tradition. We eschew the challenges of new things, fearing that they will bring chaos and overwhelm the island of order and security we have created. The problem with neurosis, of course, is that it drains the vitality out of our daily life. We choose to die psycholog-

---

20. Tillich, *The Courage To Be* (New Haven: Yale University Press, 1952), p. 35. Although Tillich and Barth disagreed at many points, they shared the Augustinian view that the force of evil is felt as the threat of nonbeing, or, in Barth's term, *das Nichtige,* "nothingness" (*Church Dogmatics,* 4 vols., ed. Thomas F. Torrance, trans. Geoffrey W. Bromiley [Edinburgh: T. & T. Clark, 1936-1962], III/3:289). Pannenberg follows by referring us to "the universally present existential anxiety that precedes any actual aggression and takes the form of a vague realization of the vulnerability of one's own existence and of the threats to it" (*Anthropology in Theological Perspective* [Philadelphia: Westminster Press, 1985], p. 149). The factor of being "aware" here distinguishes Tillich from Freud, Kierkegaard, and Niebuhr, says Seward Hiltner, "for it extends anxiety beyond the function of alarm or prod to include the reception or awareness of what is being warned or prodded about. It is this extension that enables Tillich to think of even pathological anxiety as not only a warning of what is wrong but also as itself the first move toward putting it right. This position opens Tillich to the possible charge of reifying anxiety, as if it were a concrete process in itself, rather than viewing it as a factor within a larger concrete process as do Freud, Kierkegaard, and Niebuhr" ("Some Theories of Anxiety: Theological," in *Constructive Aspects of Anxiety,* ed. Seward Hiltner and Karl Menninger [Nashville: Abingdon Press, 1963], p. 64).

ically long before we will die physically. Instead of killing others, we kill ourselves, prematurely.

Another way to hide from the pain of anxiety is to join some significant group, to attach ourselves to something that appears to be immortal. This is the appeal of ideological groups. Ideologies are bodies of great and virtuous ideas combined with a zealous sense of mission. Because the ideas have the qualities of greatness and goodness, we presume that they transcend us as individuals, that they are immortal, that their truth and importance will prevail long after we are gone. We find that we can relieve ourselves of the pain of anxiety if we identify with ideological immortality to the extent that we view our own voluntary death as the means to share in that immortality. This produces a life of zeal, a life of excitement that seems to carry us beyond the rigid and ordered life of neurosis. But it only *seems* to do so. We have all witnessed friends or colleagues who have converted, who have thrown off their neurosis and accepted the invitation to invest themselves wholeheartedly in an ideological movement. While it appears on the surface that the change constitutes a swing from one extreme to the other, one thing at least remains constant: they are still engaged in a flight from anxiety, in the denial of death.

It is not difficult to understand why we have anxiety. We are all animals, finite biological creatures who face an eventual end to our metabolic processes. What is distinctive about human consciousness is that we are aware — or we can become aware if we permit ourselves — of our death in advance. We can write out our death certificate and then wait to fill in the date.

The problem created by anxiety does not arise merely from our anticipation of death, however. It arises rather from our capacity to imagine transcending death. In short, we can imagine more than reality affords us. Philosopher Eric Voegelin employs the term *metaxy* (drawn from Plato) to describe the tension we sense as finite creatures imagining an infinite existence. The metaxy is human life lived at the In-Between, the point of connection between the temporal and the eternal, between limited and immanent being.[21] But what if there is no unlimited or immanent being for us? What if the temporal is all we have? What if the eternal is forbidden to us? What if the imagined

21. See Voegelin, *The Ecumenic Age*, vol. 4 of *Order and History* (Baton Rouge: Louisiana State University Press, 1974), pp. 6, 36, 216, 330.

land of eternity is forever closed to our residence? This would produce disappointment and despair, perhaps even frustration and rage.[22]

If Søren Kierkegaard is close to being correct when he defines the human self as a relation that relates itself to its own self, then this imagined transcendence becomes part of who we are. As human beings, we find ourselves constantly transcending ourselves. We hear ourselves being called to go beyond who and what we have been. We hear the call of the eternal within the confines of our temporal existence. The decisive question, then, is whether we are merely listening to the shouts of our own deluded imaginations or whether there is in fact an eternal voice beckoning us from within and drawing us beyond. To lose faith in the latter and to yield to the former is to ready ourselves for striking out in violence — against either ourselves or others.

1 Cor. 15

Death and Guilt

Death for a human being is more than just a natural phenomenon, more than merely the process by which we drop from existence into nonexistence. It has an inherent moral component. Our ability to transcend death through our imagination leads us to render a negative moral judgment: death is wrong. Death ought not to be. But it is. Why? Perhaps we humans are responsible. Perhaps I am responsible. Perhaps we bring it on ourselves. Perhaps the wrongness of death is due to our guilt, my guilt. Perhaps death is judgment.

Modern medicine and modern psychology may be fooling us on this count. In the hospital, where so many of us spend our last hours, death appears to be a technical failure due to the inability of life support systems to carry the human body further. The death-and-dying move-

22. Edward Farley's analysis of human evil includes a similar understanding of anxiety, but he adds the notion of the tragic. Human life is tragic because sufferings of various sorts are inevitable, he says; they are the necessary conditions of creativity, affection, and the experience of beauty. "Our condition is one marked by vulnerabilities and tragic suffering that bestow a tone of discontent and anxiety on our lives" (*Good and Evil* [Minneapolis: Fortress Press, 1990], p. 130). He speaks of certain elemental passions of human agency — (1) survival, (2) interhuman confirmation and fulfillment, and (3) reality — and asserts that when these are frustrated, the result is human evil (p. 99). Farley's understanding of redemption from evil is similar to that first embraced and then abandoned by Becker — namely, liberation (p. 284).

ment in contemporary counseling operates with the naturalistic assumption that death is a part of nature, something normal and deserving of our acceptance. Yet neither the technical nor the naturalistic views permit us to give expression to the deeper wrestling that goes on inside, the inchoate sense that death is judgment. The Bible says that "the wages of sin is death" (Rom. 6:23), but we moderns have pretty much dismissed such associations as primitive and outdated. Nevertheless, the tie between death and guilt still operates in the hidden depths of our consciousness.

Tillich was aware of the connection. "We have to die, because we are dust. That is the law of nature to which we are subject with all beings — mountains, flowers, and beasts," he said in one of his sermons. Then he went on to say, "But, at the same time, we have to die because we are guilty. That is the moral law to which we, unlike other beings, are subject. Both laws are equally true; both are stated in all sections of the Bible."[23] As we move from anxiety to violence, then, we are seeking more than mere escape from finitude; we are also seeking escape from judgment.[24]

Death and the Demonic

Much of what I have just said regarding self-transcendence and sin can be restated in the language of the demonic. Tillich and most modern theologians are not likely to speak of demons as personified entities; nevertheless, they cannot avoid using the adjective *demonic* to describe the combination of external and internal compulsions toward evil that arise from anxiety.

How does the demonic work? Failing to attain immortality on our

23. Tillich, *The Shaking of the Foundations* (New York: Scribner's, 1948), p. 70. Bonnie J. Miller-McLemore offers a valuable analysis of this issue, documenting and demonstrating how the ancient biblical association of death with morality has been replaced with a strictly naturalistic perspective in modern psychology. She then shows how modern theologians such as Tillich retrieve the ancient insight while incorporating the advances made by the psychologists. See *Death, Sin and the Moral Life*, American Academy of Religion Academy Series, no. 59 (Atlanta: Scholars Press, 1988), p. 130.

24. This leads Tillich to seek a comprehensive answer to death-causing anxiety, and that answer is the message of salvation — namely, "a judgment which declares that we do not deserve to die, because we are justified" (*Shaking of the Foundations*, p. 172; see Miller-McLemore, *Death, Sin and the Moral Life*, p. 139).

own, we grab hold of some object that is mortal and then delude ourselves into believing it will make us immortal. Failing to accept our limitations, we fool ourselves into believing we are channels of unlimited power. We become demonic, Tillich says, when we treat something relative as absolute, when we treat perspectival opinion as final truth. Our faith becomes demonic when we treat something penultimate as if it were ultimate. We invoke demonic power when we treat something finite as if it were infinite.[25]

Now, saying it this way makes it appear that we are in charge, that we simply invest ordinary things with an imagined power of immortality. But this is too simple. In fact, we are confronted by temptation that comes to us from beyond ourselves. Claimants to immortal and infinite power dance before us, inviting us to eliminate our anxiety by joining in the ecstasy of their dance. They are spouting lies, of course, but the siren song of their invitation rises daily. When we accept the invitation, our interior soul becomes bound to the destiny of the exterior power, and that destiny is always death amid delusion.[26]

It would be possible for us to turn down such invitations, of course — if we had faith. Faith grants integrity and a sense of direction in our essentially finite and limited life. It grants the courage to face down the pretenders to immortality, because it trusts, despite our anxiousness, in the care of a transcendent God.

25. Tillich, *Dynamics of Faith* (New York: Harper & Row, 1957), pp. 11, 122. For Tillich, the demonic is more than human, yet it has no being of its own. It derives from negating the holy by using the power of the holy against itself. "The demonic is the Holy (or the sacred) with a minus sign before it, the sacred antidivine" (*What Is Religion?* [New York: Harper & Row, 1969], p. 85). We subject ourselves to demonic power, says Emil Brunner, when we engage in "boundless phantasy. Phantasy weaves a romantic halo of infinity around the goods of sense, and the will grasps this boundless wealth of the finite with both hands" (*The Divine Imperative* [Philadelphia: Westminster Press, 1947], p. 24); falling prey to the demonic "means being enslaved by something finite which is regarded as infinite and absolute" (p. 392).

26. Daniel Day Williams picks up where Tillich left off and offers five structural elements of the demonic: (1) *fascination* in the sense of a quickening of interest and excitement, (2) *distortion of perception*, (3) *aggrandizement* through lust for power, (4) *inertia of established systems of control* in social institutions, and (5) *ontological depth* — in the sense that the demonic erupts from beyond us and yet claims our ultimate being (*The Demonic and the Divine* [Minneapolis: Fortress Press, 1990], pp. 7-12). Williams disagrees with Tillich's characterization of the demonic as a negative principle within the category of the divine. Williams maintains that God is solely the principle of creative love.

Anxiety as the Call of God

Is anxiety all bad? There are some who argue that anxiety produces the sort of nervous energy that fuels human creativity. They cite the near pathological sense of drivenness exhibited by some of the great achievers in the fields of art, literature, science, and music. Some have gone so far as to argue that anxiety is *necessary* for creativity.[27] For the most part, however, anxiety is viewed as so painful and stifling that it inhibits creativity; it constrains and constricts. The prevailing position is that to be creative, a person must be liberated from the binding chains of anxiety. "Instead of the widely held, erroneous conviction that anxiety is a prerequisite for creativity," writes Ishak Ramzy, "it can be maintained that anxiety often blocks the creative process, or at times may instead drive it mercilessly and blindly."[28] The wisdom of the great philosophical and religious traditions of history encourages us to face our anxiety squarely and bring it under some form of control. We must confront anxiety honestly and then get a grip on ourselves. This is requisite for wholesome living in general and for creativity in particular.

How can we get control over anxiety? There are two ways: defiance and gratitude. Stoics and existentialists recommend the route of defiance, of affirming ourselves despite the threat. Christian theologians recommend relying on God's grace to affirm us in being even in the face of the threat of nonbeing, an act that should in turn stimulate within us a sense of gratitude for who we are and what we have. Seward Hiltner argues that we require something extraordinary to prevent anxiety from doing damage, "whether this be conceived by Christian theology as grace or by Stoicism and existentialism as the imaginative acknowledgment of necessity. Sartre's injunction is, finally, to a defiant and courageous kind of nobility: Are you a man or a mouse? . . .

---

27. Theologian Roger Haight, for example, sees the threat of nonbeing as double-valued: "This anxiety is ambiguous, both positive and negative at the same time. On the one hand, anxiety is the condition for the possibility of human creativity and achievement; on the other hand, it is a temptation to posit the self in being now against the threat of nonbeing or being-unto-death by proclaiming the self a fully autonomous center of being" ("Sin and Grace," in *Systematic Theology: Roman Catholic Perspectives*, vol. 2, ed. Francis Schüssler Fiorenza and John P. Galvin [Minneapolis: Fortress Press, 1991], p. 97).

28. Ramzy, "Freud's Understanding of Anxiety," in *Constructive Aspects of Anxiety*, p. 26.

Christian theology is rather less grim-lipped about what is going on. Its mood is gratitude rather than defiance."[29] Whether defiance or gratitude, in each case anxiety is something negative, something to be overcome by human assertion.

Augustine goes further, urging a positive evaluation. He suggests that anxiety may function as the call of God within the human soul. Addressing God he says, "you have made us for yourself, and our heart is restless until it rests in you."[30] The restlessness *(inquietum)* in which we find ourselves connotes something noisy, a clamor in "our heart." The reason for the clamor is loss of relationship. The restlessness is due to our existing out of communion with the source of our existence, God. But the inner inquietude is itself a divine deposit in the human soul, a reminder of the ground of our being from which we feel estranged. It is a call to faith, an invitation to trust God. Albert C. Outler offers this paraphrase of Augustine's aphorism: "You [God] provide man with the stimulus that makes him want to praise you, but you have so fixed the human condition that it is disturbed until it returns to its 'right relation' in your presence."[31]

Anxiety as the Breeding Ground for Sin

Thus we see that anxiety all by itself is not sinful. It is merely a constituent element in human awareness. It comes naturally from the metaxy experienced by an animal that can imagine being a god. It is the condition of existing as a contingent creature with a thirst for the absolute. In itself, there is nothing wrong with creaturely existence. When God first beheld the creatures of this nascent world, as the book of Genesis repeatedly reports, "God saw that it was good."

So, it is important that we distinguish between sin and finitude. Reinhold Niebuhr rightly insists that "the world of finite, dependent and contingent existence, is not evil by reason of its finiteness."[32] As

29. Hiltner, "Epilogue," in *Constructive Aspects of Anxiety,* p. 151.

30. Augustine, *Confessions,* 1.1. The original reads, "Tu excitas ut laudare te delectet, quia fecisti nos ad te, et inquietum est cor nostrum donec requiescat in te."

31. Outler, "Anxiety and Grace: An Augustinian Perspective," in *Constructive Aspects of Anxiety,* p. 93.

32. Niebuhr, *The Nature and Destiny of Man,* 2 vols. (New York: Scribner's, 1941-1943), 1:167.

finite animals, we seek to protect ourselves from the contingencies that could endanger us. This is natural. As human beings with a taste for the infinite, however, we transmute this natural desire for survival into the more grievous perils of history, replete with injustice and war. In the name of survival or security or even in a deluded attempt to define ourselves as infinite, we finite creatures may strike out aggressively. In itself anxiety is not sin, but, says Niebuhr, "anxiety is the internal precondition of sin."[33] Anxiety, we might conclude, is the breeding ground for sin. But it is also the occasion for faith.

33. Niebuhr, *The Nature and Destiny of Man*, 1:182.

3

UNFAITH
When Trusting Becomes Difficult

I have a sin of fear, that when I have spun
My last thread, I shall perish on the shore;
Swear by Thyself, that at my death Thy Son
Shall shine as He shines now, and heretofore;
And having done that, Thou hast done,
I fear no more.

John Donne, "A Hymn to God the Father"

"Anxiety is the internal state of temptation," writes Reinhold Niebuhr. Then he goes on, "It must not be identified with sin because there is always the ideal possibility that faith would purge anxiety of the tendency toward sinful self-assertion."[1] In other words, the dangers created by anxiety can be forestalled by faith. The temptation to strike out violently evaporates for a person of faith. Faith is the alternative to sin. Or, conversely, the path from anxiety to sin begins with the step of unfaith.

1. Niebuhr, *The Nature and Destiny of Man*, 2 vols. (New York: Scribner's, 1941-1943), 1:182-83. Following Luther, Niebuhr defines unbelief as "the root of sin, or as the sin which precedes pride" (1:183). See Luther, *Lectures on Genesis Chapters 1-5*, vol. 1 of *Luther's Works*, ed. Jaroslav Pelikan, trans. George V. Schick (St. Louis: Concordia, 1958), p. 147.

65

By *faith* here I mean "trust." Faith is much more than trust, to be sure, but it is worth emphasizing that the person who trusts has what it takes to render anxiety powerless. Faith as trust provides us with a sense of security even if the situation seems threatening. We take the threat of our own nonbeing up into ourselves and press forward undaunted. Faith manifests itself in us as courage. If we lack a trusting faith, then insecurity is liable to give rise to fear and then frustration, despair, rage, aggression, and violence.[2]

Faith as trust can be directed at ourselves, at other people, or at God. God is the ultimate source of such faith, as the oft-repeated twenty-third Psalm testifies.

> Even though I walk through the darkest valley,
>   I fear no evil;
> for you are with me;
>   your rod and your staff —
>   they comfort me.

The topic of faith is broad. It covers many things, not the least important of which is the nature of our bond with God. However, this is not the place for an exhaustive dissection and analysis of the whole of faith. What I wish to do is focus on those aspects of faith that have a direct bearing on our daily struggle with anxiety and the temptation to sin.

Unbelief, Pride, and Concupiscence

In his exposition of sin understood as our estrangement from God, from others, and from ourselves, Tillich begins by citing the Augsburg Confession of 1530, which says we humans are born into the world "without faith in God and with concupiscence" *(sine fide erga deum et cum concupiscentia)*. What is missing here, observes Tillich, is pride. Augustine and Luther had maintained that pride precedes the sensual

---

2. "Without faith we shrink in fear and chaos and begin generating excuses, blaming other people, bad luck, God, or the devil," writes Wayne E. Oates. "The more the excuses proliferate, the more the person, family, or group becomes dysfunctional. In the language of Alcoholics Anonymous, our lives become unmanageable" (*Temptation* [Louisville: Westminster/John Knox Press, 1991], p. 24).

sin of concupiscence. By adding pride, Tillich identifies three dimensions of sin related in this order: unbelief, pride, and concupiscence. I will follow Tillich here in part, devoting a chapter to each of these three.

What is the relationship between Tillich's word *unbelief* and the term I am using here, *unfaith*? When he uses the word *unbelief*, Tillich is speaking of more than merely a person's unwillingness to believe the doctrines of the church. Unbelief is in fact more than merely an act of the human mind. Our word *faith* is, of course, occasionally taken to mean believing a given set of teachings. Its Latin root, *credo*, from which we get our word *creed*, means "I believe." It is perfectly legitimate to associate faith with belief and hence to associate unfaith with unbelief. But Tillich is after something much deeper and more comprehensive, something more existential. He sees unbelief as an act of the total personality, including practical, theoretical, and emotional elements. As he uses it, it refers to the separation of the human will from the divine will: unbelief is the act or state in which a person in the totality of his or her being turns away from God. Tillich then offers this remark: "If there were such a word as 'un-faith,' it should be used instead of the word 'unbelief'."[3] Well, it seems to me that if the word *unfaith* says it better, then perhaps we should employ it. So we will.

What faith in contrast to unfaith does is give us courage. The person of faith recognizes realistically the threat — even the inevitability — of death. Such a person also recognizes that our life is not something we ourselves have created. It has been given us by a power over which we have no control or influence whatsoever. We are here. We have been invited here by an invisible and mysterious host. We are the guest of being. Our own being is not our own possession. If we find ourselves able to have faith, to trust in the ground and source of our life, then we will find ourselves able to accept our death. We will find ourselves able to take the threat of nonbeing up into ourselves and to press on without the debilitation of anxiety. Tillich calls this fruit of faith "the courage to be."

3. Tillich, *Systematic Theology*, 3 vols. (Chicago: University of Chicago Press, 1951-1963), 2:47.

"Do Not Be Anxious!"

The problem created by anxiety and unfaith is at the heart of the human condition described in the Bible. Shortly after the Hebrew slaves had been delivered from their Egyptian taskmasters, they found themselves wandering in the wilderness of Sin between Elim and Sinai and wondering where their next meal would come from (Exod. 16). So the people filed a complaint with Moses and Aaron, stating that they would rather have died in Egypt on a full stomach than starve to death out in the wilderness. God responded to this complaint by delivering fresh quail and then manna every morning. Moses requested that everyone take only enough to eat for a given day, trusting that a sufficient supply would appear each morning. But the people did not trust Moses. They began to take more than they could eat and to hide the extra. Whatever they hoarded, however, either spoiled immediately or made the worms fat. "Take only enough for one day!" Moses insisted. "Can you not trust the God who brought you safely out of Egypt to care for you now?" It was anxiety over the possibility of not having food in the future that led to disobedience; for those who let this anxiety gain the upper hand, the net effect was a loss of faith in God.

To people whom he describes as having "little faith," Jesus reiterates: "Do not be anxious, saying, 'What shall we eat?' or 'What shall we drink?' or 'What shall we wear?' For the Gentiles seek all these things; and your heavenly Father knows that you need them all. But seek first his kingdom and his righteousness, and all these things shall be yours as well" (Matt. 6:31-33, RSV). Both Moses and Jesus exhort us to trust God, to place our future in God's hands, and not to allow our natural anxiety over the unknown to gain control and precipitate unfaithful behavior. Trusting our future to God is the essence of faithful living.[4]

According to Martin Luther, we manifest our trust in God by accepting the divine promise, by believing God's Word. When interpreting the story of Adam and Eve, Luther notes that the serpent does not first try to tempt Eve by pointing out the loveliness of the fruit. Rather,

---

4. Jürgen Moltmann puts hope where I put faith, as trust. In his schema, the root of sin is hopelessness, which he says manifests itself in two ways: (1) as presumption, hopelessness produces a self-willed grabbing of what is hoped for by God; (2) as doubt, hopelessness leads to a resignation and a concomitant seeking after present pleasure. See Moltmann, *The Gospel of Liberation* (Waco, Tex.: Word Books, 1973), pp. 49-51.

the serpent — whom Luther identifies with Satan — contradicts God. Eve remembers God having said that she would die if she ate the forbidden fruit, but the tempter says flatly, "You will not die" (Gen. 3:4). Now, whom should Eve believe is telling the truth, God or the serpent? The temptation laid before the mother of us all is to mistrust God's word, to doubt God's promise. So Luther declares, "The root and source of sin is unbelief and turning away from God, just as, on the other hand, the source and root of righteousness is faith."[5]

A lack of trust in God leads to a lack of trust in other people, and this in turn leads to a lack of love. "Un-faith is ultimately identical with un-love," writes Tillich.[6] Even when we love others, we risk hurting them by accident; when we lack love, a life of hurting others becomes our inescapable destiny.

This concern for love raises a question: Are trusting God and trusting other people two entirely different things? In some special cases, perhaps. In some extreme moments, tortured prisoners have reported being able to trust God and only God. For the most part, however, our capacity to trust God is enhanced if not initiated by our experiences with trustworthy people. Trustworthy parents, friends, and colleagues in our daily life put our minds at ease, reduce anxiety, and enable us to operate freely in a network of trust relationships. Trust relationships make loving one another easier. What happens when such a trust network is unavailable? What happens if we grow up without ever having experienced a sustained trust relationship? If we are abandoned, is it possible to develop a sense of trust on our own? Evidence seems to suggest that the answer is No. In order to develop a sense of trust, we must first be graced by the loving presence of someone trustworthy. Without that first grace, faith *in* others and love *for* others seems foredoomed.

Psychopathic Killers as Trust Bandits

Whether or not we trust other people has an enormous effect on our interhuman relations. If we fail to trust, we kill, or at least we diminish other people's existence through manipulation, insensitivity, betrayal,

5. Luther, *Lectures on Genesis Chapters 1–5*, p. 162.
6. Tillich, *Systematic Theology*, 2:48.

and perhaps torture. Relevant to our discussion of sin is an extreme example from which we may all learn — namely, the psychopath, more technically known as the sociopath who suffers from Antisocial Personality Disorder (APD). What makes this relevant to sin understood as unfaith is the suggestion proposed by many social theorists that psychopathic criminals are the way they are because they have not developed trust relationships. The key here is relationship.[7] They cannot trust, and without such trust they become incapable of sharing mutual affection. To make matters worse, they learn the language of trust without allowing themselves the vulnerability that normally goes with it. They gain other people's confidence and then betray them. The victims, if they live through their encounters, are abandoned and humiliated. This has led Ken Magid and Carole A. McKelvey to dub psychopaths "trust bandits."[8]

One of the best-known trust bandits of recent times was serial murderer Ted Bundy. Estimates are that he raped, mutilated, and killed as many as a hundred young women from the West Coast to the East Coast, outwitting for years various police departments who sought his arrest. He was finally convicted in the state of Florida for the brutal murder of two college coeds in their sorority house bedroom and for snuffing out the life of a twelve-year-old schoolgirl, Kimberly Leach. The victims were raped and sodomized, and their bodies were mutilated. Bundy was executed, never having shown sincere remorse for the suffering he left in his wake.

One of the killer's near-victims, Carol DaRonch, lived to tell us something about Bundy's approach. On the rainy evening of November 8, 1974, as Carol was browsing in a bookstore at the Fashion Place Mall in Murray, Utah, Bundy introduced himself, giving the impression that he was a law enforcement officer. After she responded to his inquiry about the license number of her car, he told her that someone had attempted to break into her car. Would she like to accompany him to the parking lot to see if anything had been stolen? Of course. Although Carol innately trusted police officers, she did ask

7. The theory here derives from Freud, according to whom anxiety as the fear of loss in adults is rooted in the childhood experience of actual loss of relationship to the mother or other significant persons on whom the child depended.
8. See Magid and McKelvey, *High Risk: Children without a Conscience* (New York: Bantam Books, 1988), pp. 4, 7.

the otherwise pleasant man for identification. She was shown a badge and told he was an officer in the Roseland Murray Police Department. She was convinced. Once they left the mall for the rainy parking lot, Bundy coaxed her into his Volkswagen, ostensibly to escort her to the police station. Once in the car, the previously kind public servant changed into a violent demon. Realizing something was amiss, she reached for the door. He slapped a handcuff on her hand. She fought back. He swung a tire iron at her head and then drove off. Since the car was traveling at high speeds, she was afraid to jump. But when the car slowed down, she bolted out the door, screaming and waving her hands in the air to attract the attention of other motorists. She remembers Bundy waving a gun and threatening to blow her head off, but he never fired. She does not know why. Finally a couple stopped, picked the hysterical DaRonch up, and took her to police headquarters.

It is not known for certain, but it is likely that after he had lost DaRonch, Bundy went to search for another victim. Seventeen-year-old Debbie Kent disappeared that night. The key to the handcuffs that Bundy had put on DaRonch was found in the schoolyard where Debbie had gone on an errand to pick up her little brother. She has never been found.

Magid and McKelvey maintain that Bundy's psychopathic behavior was "destined from the crib."[9] Why? Because the ability to enter into trust relationships is gained only during that crucial period between birth and walking. It comes from being loved by a mother. It comes from the gift of having been cared for. It comes from having learned by experience that a bond of mutual trust is possible. Without this bonding experience, all hell breaks loose.

> What happens, right or wrong, in the critical first two years of a baby's life will imprint that child as an adult. A complex set of events must occur in infancy to assure a future of trust and love. If the proper bonding and subsequent attachment does not occur — usually between the child and the mother — the child will develop mistrust and a deep-seated rage. He becomes a child without a conscience. . . . The consequence of this failure can be individuals suffering from Antisocial Personality Disorder (APD).[10]

9. Magid and McKelvey, *High Risk*, p. 37.
10. Magid and McKelvey, *High Risk*, p. 3; see also p. 37.

Such bonding, especially during the first year, is stimulated by nature and culminated by love. The child has a need, such as the need for food. When that need goes unmet, rage wells up. The baby cries. The mother responds with milk. The need is gratified. After enough trips around the cycle, the infant comes to trust the mother. Communication and mutuality develop. When the cycle is broken, when no one responds regularly to the infant's needs in such a way as to quell the rage and establish relationship, the rage comes to dominate.

Breaks in bonding that permit the rage to dominate are plaguing our society in epidemic proportion. This is due to countless factors: professional demands on the parents' time that compete with the attention they should be giving to their children; poorly run and understaffed preschools and day care centers; bureaucratic delays in the adoption process that leave adoptive children unattached for inordinate periods of time; the cycle of child abuse, especially in families with alcoholism; teenage mothers who are unprepared to care properly for their infants; and, of course, the staggering rate at which divorces with custody battles toss children to and fro.

In Bundy's case, his infancy and youth is a log of bonding breaks. He was born in 1945 out of wedlock to Eleanor Louise Cowell, who was then twenty-two years old. His very existence apparently threatened her deeply religious family. Eleanor tried to fool the young boy into believing that she was his older sister and that his grandparents were in fact his parents. Dreading that their blue-collar neighbors might eventually call Ted a bastard, she took him across the country when he was five years old to start a new life in the state of Washington. Eleanor later married Johnnie Bundy, and the young Ted took this man's family name. When he finally learned the truth, Ted became angry at Eleanor for having wrenched him away from his grandparents and at the whole family for having sustained the lie. Magid and McKelvey surmise that bonding did not occur during Ted's first two years.

As a teenager, Bundy was successful in school. He was awarded a scholarship to the University of Puget Sound in Tacoma, where he studied psychology and then law. He was handsome and clean-cut. When he embarked on his killing spree, he was able to invent clever and elaborate ruses to lure young women to places where he could overpower them. His charm never abated. Even as a Florida prisoner awaiting execution, Bundy was able to convince a young woman that he was innocent and that she should marry him. She did.

Bundy was a trust bandit. Are there others in our society? Magid and McKelvey fear there may be as many as thirteen million psychopaths in the United States. Not all are serial killers by any means. But trust bandits can be found growing in homes and schools across the land. They can be identified by their preoccupation with fire, blood, or gore; by cruelty to others or to animals; by an inability to maintain eye contact; by an inability to give or receive affection; by an inclination to continue lying even when caught in the act; and by generally self-destructive behavior. These are children who have decided in their subconscious that they cannot trust anyone to care for them and so will not trust anyone for anything. If such children do not become the Ted Bundys of tomorrow, they will become the con artists, wife beaters, and child abusers. So Magid and McKelvey issue a clarion call:

> The killers are just the tip of a massive iceberg. The message . . . is that the chances for increasing numbers of psychopaths are escalating. We must search for answers to the pressing social problems that are helping to create unattached children. We must learn how to prevent unattached children. The solutions will not be easy or cheap, but they *must* be found.[11]

In trying to evaluate the significance of what is being said here, I note two things. Magid and McKelvey seem to operate with a deterministic premise: if bonding does not occur properly between birth and age two, then Antisocial Personality Disorder will result. But is this in fact inevitable? How can we know for certain? I suspect that Magid and McKelvey have arrived at this conclusion solely by observing APD children and adults and retrospectively concluding that bonding did not occur. But this process is problematic on a number of counts, not the least of which is that it amounts to arguing in a circle. Still, the matter is worth pursuing, because so much of what has been said about sin through the centuries and so much of what we value

---

11. Magid and McKelvey, *High Risk,* p. 43. The thesis of Magid and McKelvey might have to be qualified somewhat in light of Ted Bundy's final interview prior to execution on January 23, 1989. Bundy exonerated his family, not wanting anyone to blame his mother or father. Rather, he denounced pornography that he obtained outside the home, arguing that it fueled his desire for rape and murder. A videotape of this interview with James Dobson, entitled "Fatal Addiction: Ted Bundy's Final Interview," is available from Focus on the Family, Pomona, California 91799.

in our modern liberal society centers on the issue of human freedom. So we must press questions such as the following: If my mother failed to take up her bonding responsibility, am I forever doomed to a trustless adult existence? Does your freedom to enter into trusting relationships depend entirely on the prior gift of your mother's love? Is our capacity for trusting or not trusting determined totally by the generation that preceded us? Should we then think of sin as something passed down from generation to generation? Can later experiences of gracious love make up for what we lost during our first two years? Is transformation possible?[12]

Regardless of how these questions are answered, the central social concern raised by Magid and McKelvey is important: the safety and well-being of persons in our society *is* decisively affected by how lovingly parents care for their children. Who we are as individuals is dependent to a great measure on the relationships we have experienced. Even if it turns out that parental care — or the lack of it — is only one factor among others in determining the kind of adults we become, the responsibility on the shoulders of mothers and fathers is enormous.

Consuming Rage

Pertinent to the topic of sin is the despair-rage relationship and the aggression it produces. Psychopaths or sociopaths seem to be subject to chronic rage. We are all susceptible to experiencing acute rage, because we all experience anxiety. The fact that we have on occasion experienced acute rage should make us able to understand at least in part the most dastardly of killers.

One moment of volcanic rage in my earlier life remains etched on my mind. I spent my first eleven years growing up on North Waverly Street in Dearborn, Michigan. From the time I could walk without

12. James Q. Wilson and Richard J. Herrnstein argue that, as important as bonding may be, the bonding factor alone is insufficient to explain all of the differences among individual criminals. For example, it fails to take into account such variables as impulsiveness accompanied by an inability to foresee the consequences of one's actions and the documented correlation between limited intelligence and predatory criminality. In short, the bonding or control theory provides a partial rather than a complete explanation. See *Crime and Human Nature* (New York: Simon & Schuster, 1985), p. 65.

holding on to something, I was terrorized by the bully across the street. His name was Louie. He was a year older than I, and, though a bit smaller, he was much stronger. He relentlessly made me his target for name-calling, taunting, and what we called "a pounding." Not only were the sidewalks and neighborhood yards danger zones; he would occasionally come into my own backyard to beat me up.

My parents told me to fight back. "But if I do, he'll only beat me up all the more," I whimpered. Nevertheless, they insisted that unless I stuck up for myself Louie would continue to make my life miserable.

On one fateful winter day when I was five years old, I put on my mittens and galoshes and went out to play in the snow. I went down the street and started building snowmen with Sandy and Sheila Latham in their front yard. We were having a marvelous time. My snowman was nearly completed — I was just adding the head — when Louie showed up. He began to call me names and told Sandy and Sheila to stop playing with me. I tried ignoring him, but it didn't work. He began pounding me with his fists. I fended him off. Finally, he attacked my snowman and knocked it over. I was frustrated. I was humiliated. I flew into a blind rage from head to toe. I convulsed with uncontrollable anger. My entire body, soul, and spirit wanted nothing but evil, and evil in maximum measure. I picked up my snow shovel and swung it forcefully . . . and accurately. I caught Louie on the cheek. Blood splattered. It was a direct hit. Louie started wailing. What a joyous sound! And I had done it!

As Louie raced for home, I returned to work on my snowman. But I noticed that Sandy and Sheila had lost their enthusiasm. We all sensed that something quite wrong had occurred. I wandered home.

In the meantime, the mothers of the neighborhood were furiously exchanging telephone calls. Eventually Louie's mother phoned my mother. Then the interrogation began.

"Did you hit Louie with your snow shovel?" my mother demanded. "Yes."

"Why?"

I explained. My explanation did not elicit the sympathy I had expected.

"You should never hit anyone with a snow shovel," she stated.

"But you told me to fight back," I protested.

"Not with a weapon! A snow shovel is a weapon. You could've put Louie's eye out." She was always warning me against putting people's eyes out. I think it was her favorite warning. "This is awful," she said. When the lecture was nearing its end, she insisted that I would have to go and tell Louie that I was sorry.

"What?" I exclaimed. I tried refusing. Yet she made it clear that if I did not apologize, the punishment I would receive at home would be both painful and enduring. I consented. So my mother telephoned Louie's house and announced that I was on my way over. I put my mittens and galoshes back on and trudged through the snow. Although he lived only three doors down on the other side of the street, I found it a very long walk.

After arriving on Louie's front porch, I rang the bell. The door opened. His mother appeared holding Louie in her arms. A bandage covered part of Louie's face, as I recall. I told him that I was sorry. Louie gave me no forgiveness. Even his mother reiterated that I should not hit people with snow shovels. I had heard that before.

But the most horrendous part of the entire episode had to do with what I saw. Louie, being held at his mother's waist, had his right arm around her neck. In his left hand was a partially eaten cookie. "A cookie!" I exclaimed to myself silently. "How could she give that little monster a cookie? I got a lecture, and Louie got a cookie!" Louie's cookie has stuck in my mind ever since as a symbol of intolerable injustice and the experience of consuming rage.

One of the messages this communicates to me is that we ought not to draw the line too sharply between them and us, between the psychopathic murderers and the bulk of average people in our society. Had my snow shovel hit Louie a little differently, my name might have appeared on a list of the nation's killers.

Certainly I was not "destined from the crib" to kill. I'm assuming my mother tended to my needs lovingly when I was an infant. I know that as a child I experienced parental love and responded trustingly. Had I not been able to trust my mother, I would never have agreed even under threat of discipline to apologize, an act that ended the possibility of my expressing rage in a violent fashion. Yet, I could be dangerous, just as each of us can be dangerous under certain circumstances. The difference between Ted Bundy and most of us is that his rage was chronic, whereas ours is acute. We might say of Bundy what Isabel says to Claudio in Shakespeare's *Measure for Measure*: "Thy sin's not accidental, but a trade." But even among those of us for whom sin is "accidental," the damage can be fatal.

Take Kevin Green, for example, who at this writing sits in a California prison.[13] In June of 1985 he graduated from high school in the San Francisco Bay Area, and he was planning to enter San Jose State University that fall. He had always done well in his school's classes for gifted children, and he was anticipating equal success in college. He was proud of his accomplishments as a computer hacker. His parents and grandparents adored him and his brother Sean. His youth was a happy one.

Kevin had a potentially embarrassing secret, however. Shortly after puberty he discovered he had a sexual attraction for other boys, not girls. For some time he did not know what to do about it. Using his computer, he surveyed gay bulletin boards, and eventually he found his way to the Castro district in San Francisco and began to make contacts for sexual relations.

"I knew I could never tell my parents that I was gay," he told his court-appointed psychiatrist, Ronald Markman. "I remember what my dad once said when he was reading an article about AIDS: 'The faggots are getting what they deserve,' he said." Kevin also remembered a remark his brother made when a gay cousin was about to visit the family: "I'm gonna put a Band-Aid on my butt." Kevin presumed that the atmosphere of his family would be intolerant should his parents and brother learn his secret.

Kevin wasn't aware that Sean had tapped the family phone and recorded some of his brother's conversations with gay partners. Along with a friend, Roger Anderson, Sean hatched a plot to humiliate his brother. During a late night liaison at a beach home in Half Moon Bay, Sean and Roger broke in with a flashlight, interrupting the homosexual activity. A scuffle broke out in the midst of which Sean yelled, "I can hold this over your head now!"

Sean and Roger reported the event to Mr. and Mrs. Green. Kevin denied his homosexuality vehemently, and this seemed to convince his father.

"I'm so glad you're not gay, Kevin," said Mr. Green. "It was killing me. We agonized over this all night. I pictured you in bathhouses and bars. I thought I'd lost my son." His mother entered. Kevin again denied the truth. His mother joined the crying.

---

13. The names in this account, with the exception of that of Dr. Markman, have been changed.

Once alone with Sean, Kevin begged his brother to back up his story "in order to keep the family together." At first Sean refused, but then he agreed. He returned to his parents and recanted. But Mr. Green, a lawyer, was still not altogether certain. He telephoned Roger Anderson, who stood by the original account. Mr. Green was at least convinced that Kevin had engaged in homosexual activity, but he assumed that his son had been seduced. He summoned Kevin and demanded the names and addresses of his contacts. When Kevin refused to give him the information, he delivered an ultimatum: "If you don't do that, you can leave."

Kevin went to his room, packed, left the house, and began driving around in his 1979 Mustang, eventually pulling over and sleeping in it. When he awoke, he was confused and depressed. A sense of non-being overwhelmed him.

"I just couldn't stand to think that my Mom and Dad thought I was gay. I felt like nothing in front of them — just dirt," he told Dr. Markman. All he could think about was suicide and revenge. Despair has a way of conflating one's own death with killing others.

At the sporting goods store where he went to buy a weapon, he was told by the clerk that he could not purchase a handgun because he was underage. But an Uzi semiautomatic rifle was classified as a rifle, and he was eligible to buy that with only a two-day waiting period. Kevin paid the money, and two days later he returned to pick up his purchase. The clerk threw in a few extra clips of ammunition for good measure.

Kevin carried the Uzi in the Mustang. What would he do? He considered shooting up Sean's and Roger's cars. His intent was to humiliate Sean and Roger for "totally ruining my life." After he had destroyed their cars, he planned to commit suicide.

Kevin encountered Roger first, confronting him in a parking area near Roger's home. Kevin pleaded with Roger to take back his story so that he could have his old life back. Roger was unsympathetic. When Roger called Kevin a "faggot," Kevin pulled the trigger. The Uzi has a reputation for firing rounds at blinding speed. That day it lived up to its reputation. It took a mere instant for Kevin to fire ten shots into Roger's body.

Kevin Green is a killer but not a psychopath. Psychopaths are known to lack a conscience. Kevin has a conscience. During the manhunt that led to his arrest, he telephoned messages of love and remorse to his estranged family. Knowing he could never return, he asked that his belongings be given to his brothers. Psychiatrist Markman described the murder as having taken place in the "cold-blooded heat of passion."[14]

Kevin's rage and violence emerged from anxiety and despair. He had lost his reality, his home, and his family. He could feel the creeping power of nonbeing overtaking him. This led to the confusion between dying and killing. "I didn't want to be killed, but at the same time I did want to be killed. All I wanted to do was go home, but if I couldn't do that, I just wanted to die."

Ronald Markman has served as psychiatric consultant to numerous cases in addition to that of Kevin Green. He stresses that very ordinary persons can become murderers. "Killers come in all sizes, shapes and colors. They come from all ethnic groups, sexes, ages, religious denominations, sexual preferences, socio-economic backgrounds, and mental states," he says. "Most of the time it [homicide] is committed by people who have never committed any crimes before."[15]

Original Sin and Grace

I have been trying to emphasize the continuity between extremes, between dramatic and brutal murder on the one hand and the reactions that most ordinary people have to life's stresses and tensions on the other. The differences may be instructive as well.

There is a difference between Ted Bundy's rampage and the violence perpetrated by Kevin Green and myself. Bundy's victims were innocent. They were young women whom he simply met and picked up or who happened to be in the sorority house when he broke in. In contrast, Louie provoked me to hit him with the snow shovel. Roger provoked Kevin. Kevin and I felt unjustly treated by our victims. When I swung the snow shovel and when Kevin pulled the trigger on the Uzi, we were exacting a form of justice, retributive justice.

But I don't want to take the next step in this logic at this time. It would be easy to blame the victim, to say that Louie and Roger got what was coming to them. Yet, as I hope will become clearer as this

14. Ronald Markman and Dominick Bosco, *Alone with the Devil: Famous Cases of a Courtroom Psychiatrist* (New York: Bantam Books, 1990), p. 104.
15. Markman and Bosco, *Alone with the Devil*, p. 366.

book progresses, the temptation to blame the victim (in the name of some higher value such as justice) is part and parcel of the structure of sin itself.

In the meantime, we can make another observation. Sin is not merely an individual thing. It involves others. It emerges from a network of human relations, for good or for ill. Whether it proceeds from the failed bonding of the psychopath's parents at infancy or some later estrangement of the sort that Kevin Green experienced from his family and self, or whether it is conditioned by a web of conflicts like those I encountered with my neighborhood bully, sin is intersubjective in character. Our anxiety and rage may be our own, but whatever strengths internal and external we need to deal with them come from the significant other people in our lives.

This leads to further observations about the human situation in general. Anxiety and rage and the resulting propensity toward violence are essential aspects of the human condition as such.[16] This is the reality into which we are born. It adheres to our origin in this world. Theologians call it "original sin." Tillich refers to it as the state of "estrangement" in which we find ourselves. It never goes away. It is ever present, ever potent. At any moment one or another among us may actualize its potential, rise up in rage, and do grave violence.

What, then, prevents total anarchy? Why are our days not filled with uninterrupted brutality? Why does it seem that life is normally peaceful and that evil constitutes an interruption of that peace? The answer, I think, is grace. We have been given more than our original natures, and that "more" is what I mean by grace. Many, perhaps most of us, have been raised by mothers and fathers who loved us, who responded to our infant tears with tenderness and care, who behaved in a trustworthy way so that we could develop the habit of trusting. Our parents' gift of faithfulness to us is not something we could have asked for or demanded, yet it has made it possible for us to live our own lives with faith.

Discipline, in its own curious way, is also a gift to us from those who have gone before. The mothers of my neighborhood laid down the law: thou shalt not hit other people with snow shovels! The

---

16. "Anxiety may be taken as a universal condition for aggressive behavior," writes Wolfhart Pannenberg, "even though the passage from anxiety to aggression depends on other conditions as well" (*Anthropology in Theological Perspective* [Philadelphia: Westminster Press, 1985], p. 150).

enforcement of this and similar laws contributed greatly to the containment of barbarism and bloodshed on North Waverly Street. The enforcement of this and similar laws also helped to form the character of growing children such as myself. Once internalized, it helped me gain the self-discipline needed to channel my experiences of rage away from the shedding of blood. Such law and the order to which it aspires is also a gift of grace.

It is unfortunate that the larger American community does not have the astuteness of the mothers on North Waverly Street. If it did, we might be living with a law that says, Thou shalt not drive around with a loaded Uzi in your car. Such a law might have made the difference between life and death for Roger Anderson.

As we think about the role that parents play in bonding and that the community plays in disciplining our development — and how we are condemned to violence when such grace is absent — we need to think as well about our relationship to God. This relationship will be characterized by either faith or unfaith. If a trusting faith and a conscience can develop in children as a response to parental love, might a relationship with God develop in a similar fashion? Does God initiate a trust relationship, or is faith a matter of blind trust in the totally unknown?

The Hebrew and Christian experience of God is at least in part comparable to an infant's experience of its mother's provision of the sustenance of life. The Hebrew slaves in ancient Egypt, suffering under their vile taskmasters, cried to highest heaven for deliverance, and "God heard their groaning, and . . . took notice of them" (Exod. 2:24-25). God responded by raising up a leader, Moses, who smashed the chains of enslavement and marched the children of Israel through the Red Sea toward the Promised Land. God bonded with Israel through a covenant of trust. Though the covenant has been broken repeatedly by its human partners, God has remained faithful.

The Bible makes it clear that God does not simply leave the world to operate on its own. The divine is present not just in Israel but everywhere and for everyone. God has offered a covenant for every member of the human race, a covenant that includes the promise of resurrection from the dead. "For God so loved the world that he gave his only Son, so that everyone who believes in him may not perish but may have eternal life" (John 3:16). The promise of eternal life has the power to disarm anxiety for those who believe, for those who trust God to deliver on the promise. God's eternal being sustains our threatened being. God's faithfulness makes our faith possible, and our faith makes it possible to love others with abandon. "We love because he first loved us" (1 John 4:19).

Faith in God means first and foremost that we trust God to be faithful to the divine promise. Yet there is more to faith. God is actually present in our faith. Our mother and father, who may have loved us and evoked in us an ability to trust when we were small, are in fact absent for most of our lives. We may be grateful to our parents, but their faithful care is present primarily as a memory. Similarly, we must remember God's past faithfulness: we must remember the exodus from Egypt and the incarnation in Jesus. But we have more than mere memories. God's presence does not abate. The promise may be past tense and the fulfillment future tense, but in the present God is sustaining our existence moment by moment. Abiding in love is the key. "God is love, and those who abide in love abide in God, and God abides in them. . . . There is no fear in love, but perfect love casts out fear" (1 John 4:16, 18). Tillich reiterates this important point when he says, "Faith embraces both mystical participation and personal confidence."[17]

Accepting the Unacceptable

Death and guilt go hand in hand as signs of sin. To this point we have been concentrating on anxiety as the fear of nonbeing manifest in the confusion of one's own death with the killing of others. Closely tied to this is guilt, a topic I will address later in conjunction with justification. For the present I simply want to point out that feelings of guilt also function to diminish us, to compromise our being, to invite us to premature death. Recall that when Kevin Green was faced with losing his family, he said he felt like "nothing in front of them — just dirt." Dirt symbolizes guilt. The guilty person is someone who should either be cleaned up or discarded. As a gay son, guilty Kevin was unacceptable to his family and to himself.[18]

17. Tillich, *The Courage To Be* (New Haven: Yale University Press, 1952), p. 160.

18. Perhaps we should distinguish one's feelings of guilt from actual culpability. The issue here is not whether Kevin *should* have felt guilty regarding his homosexual proclivities; the point is *that* he felt the guilt — actually shame — and hence saw himself as unworthy, as dirt. As such, he felt he was unacceptable and subject to condemnation to nonbeing.

Would Kevin Green have been acceptable to God? Yes, he would have been acceptable to the God of grace, and this is true regardless of whether he was acceptable to his family or even to himself.

The matter of our being accepted by God even when we fail to accept ourselves occupied a great deal of Tillich's attention. Whenever addressing the topic of faith or unfaith, Tillich would remind us that our faith is a response to an act of God's prior grace. Grace is more than gifts, he says. In grace something is overcome. Grace occurs "in spite of" something that separates us and estranges us. Grace accepts that which had been rejected. Grace reunites life with life. It reconciles the self with itself. It transforms anxiety into courage and guilt into confidence.

Despair can be a reminder of grace. Despair is, to borrow Kierke-gaard's phrase, "the sickness unto death." But in its negativity, death posits life. Meaninglessness presumes the possibility of meaning. We always remain in the power of that from which we feel estranged. This leads Tillich to what he sees as the ultimate depth of sin: separated yet bound, estranged yet belonging, destroyed yet preserved. Despair means there is no escape. We cannot be released, not even through open or hidden suicide.

In what may turn out to be one of the most powerful sermons preached during the twentieth century, "You Are Accepted" (delivered August 20, 1946), Tillich sought to show how grace can present itself even in the midst of despair. "Do we know what it means to be struck by grace?" he asked. He went on to say that grace strikes us when we are in great pain or restless. It strikes us when we are walking through the dark valley of meaninglessness and empty life. It strikes us in those moments when we feel our separation more deeply than usual, perhaps because we have violated another person's life, a person whom we love or from whom we feel estranged. Grace strikes us when we are disgusted with our own being, our indifference, our weakness, our hostility, our lack of direction. It strikes us when the perfection we long for in our lives fails to appear, when we realize that old compulsions continue to reign in us just as they have for decades.

Sometimes at that moment a wave of light breaks into our darkness, and it is as though a voice were saying: "You are accepted. *You are accepted*, accepted by that which is greater than you, and the name of which you do not know. Do not ask for the name now; perhaps you will find it later. Do not try to do anything now; perhaps you will do much. Do not seek for anything; do not perform anything; do not intend anything. *Simply accept the fact that you are accepted!*[19]

In the margin of the original manuscript, scholars found a little note written in Tillich's own hand: "for myself."[20] Such an announcement of grace is for each of us, including the announcer.

That this grace applies to each of us is of inestimable importance. I was deeply moved on one occasion by a remark offered by my friend and colleague José Lana. He said that while translating Tillich's *The Courage to Be* into Spanish, he had an experience that "affected me profoundly. When I read the page where Tillich says that I am accepted even though I am unacceptable, I began spontaneously to write poetry. The verse just flowed." I pressed José to explain the connection. He responded by saying that Tillich's challenge became "a mirror to my own life. I had felt unacceptable again and again. So I constructed walls of spite and arrogance to keep others from seeing my unacceptability. But the moment I accepted my acceptance, I was overcome with . . . well, I could only say, 'hallelujah'!"[21]

Faith, then, involves our accepting our acceptance, accepting ourselves despite our apparent unacceptability. Unfaith, in contrast, involves our accepting the judgments of those who would reject us, including our own despairing selves. Unfaith involves deeming ourselves unacceptable. Continued despair is an option. Faith is also an option. Grace makes faith possible.

The traditional terms for this are *forgiveness* and *justification*. God grants us the forgiveness of our sins, and we, in faith, embrace that

19. Tillich, *The Shaking of the Foundations* (New York: Scribner's, 1948), p. 162.

20. Wilhelm and Marion Pauck, *Paul Tillich: His Life and Thought*, vol. 1, *Life* (San Francisco: Harper & Row, 1976), p. 93. Note how slippery and elusive the dynamics of faith are. Faith is not a thing one can possess. It is not reducible to a human quality, a virtue. It has rather something of an event character. Emil Brunner stress this point, noting, "Faith exists wherever God as the Holy Spirit speaks within the soul" (*The Divine Imperative* [Philadelphia: Westminster Press, 1947], p. 80). Yet faith must be more than God speaking alone. In faith one's soul must speak too, just as Tillich began to in his marginal note. The person of faith must say, "I accept my acceptance," even if doubts persist. Brunner seems to have been aware of this delicate subjective appropriation, because he added, "Faith does not consist simply in passive acceptance; it always means at the same time, an act of 'pulling oneself together'" even if "faith only exists alongside unbelief . . . for the believer is always also the unbeliever" (pp. 80-81).

21. José Lana's translation of Tillich's work is *El Coraje de Existir* (Barcelona: Editorial Estela, 1966).

forgiveness. We accept ourselves as forgiven. In trying to explain justification, Billy Graham once said that "God treats me just-as-if-I'd never sinned." Karl Barth puts it this way:

> The forgiveness of sins, or justification, is thus the total and radical acceptance of the sinner. . . . When He justifies us, God does not interpret evil as good; for He never allegorizes. Nor does He call evil good when He forgives us; for He cannot lie. But in virtue of His omnipotent compassion, and because He is Lord and Judge over good and evil alike, He makes that which is intrinsically evil good, that which is sick whole, that which is feeble glorious, that which is dead alive.[22]

A person of faith may still sin, of course — we can be justified by God and sinful on our own at the same time — but faith does make a difference. Faith relieves the external pressure to sin that may be created by the circumstances in which we find ourselves. Faith disarms anxiety. Faith helps us to realize that God is the ground of our being, not we ourselves. We need not rise up in anger when someone crowds our space: we live in God's space. We need not tie ourselves up in knots because of agenda anxiety: we live in God's time. If God should withdraw our earthly space and time, faith offers us the confidence that this is in preparation for eternal life. When we realize that eternal life is ours as a gift from God that cannot be taken away, we no longer need to deny our death. We are enabled to absorb the slings and arrows of daily misfortune without striking back in rage.

22. Barth, *Church Dogmatics,* 4 vols., ed. Thomas F. Torrance, trans. Geoffrey W. Bromiley (Edinburgh: T. & T. Clark, 1936-1962), II/2:756-57. The affirmation that God and only God has the power of life over death underpins Barth's understanding of sin as the self-deceived attempt to rob God of this power. "Sin is a robbing of God: a robbery which becomes apparent in our arrogant endeavour to cross the line of death by which we are bounded. . . . Sin is the disturbing of the relationship with God which is defined by death" (*The Epistle to the Romans,* 6th ed., trans. Edwyn C. Hoskyns [Oxford: Oxford University Press, 1977], p. 168).

4

PRIDE
Making Myself Number One

And the Devil did grin, for his darling sin
Is pride that apes humility.

Samuel Taylor Coleridge, *The Devil's Thoughts*

"Where did you get your master's degree?"

"Oh, which one?"

So goes the cocktail party conversation. "I just love to respond with 'Which one?'" the second speaker, a nurse practitioner, told me. "I'm proud of my degrees. It gives me a chance to show off a little. Is that wrong?"

She was combining irony with humor. Yet there was an issue at stake — namely, self-esteem. The conversation continued.

"Do you think some kind of pride is good, or is it all bad?" I asked. Then I tried the following: "Psychologists say that self-esteem is necessary for emotional health. If we think of self-esteem as pride, then that kind of pride would be proper, wouldn't it?"

"Oh, good." She seemed comforted that pride could be thought of as okay. Had we just arrived at the curious point where we could become proud of being proud? Does anyone these days suggest that humility might be good for our emotional health?

Pride plays a prominent role in the history of thinking about sin.

It is thought to be far more grave than the positive value of self-esteem. Pride heads the classic list of the seven deadly sins and has long been considered the seed that comes to bloom in all the others. Augustine held that "pride is the beginning of sin."[1] By pride Augustine meant the self-exaltation that results from centering our attention on ourselves when pursuing our own pleasures rather than the long-range purposes of God. Pride essentially refuses to allow God to be God. It tries to co-opt divinity for itself. This is symbolized by the manner in which the serpent tempted Eve in the Garden of Eden: if she would only eat from the tree of the knowledge of good and evil, she would become like God. Pride is the attempt at human self-divinization. Although Tillich prefers the Greek term *hubris* to the English term *pride,* he is clear in asserting that this "is sin in its total form," because it amounts to our turning away from the divine center to which we belong. He calls it "spiritual sin," saying that its main symptom is that we do not accept our own limits. It is the self-elevation of oneself into the sphere of the divine.[2]

Idolatry

The nature of pride raises the issue of idolatry, the issue of where we put our faith. Is the object of our faith worthy of it? Can we trust God, or should we put our trust somewhere else? If we decide to place our trust in ourselves, we thereby indulge in pride.

In the first commandment, the God who brought the Hebrews out of Egypt makes it clear that the people of Israel should worship only him: "You shall have no other gods before me. You shall not make for yourself an idol" (Exod. 20:3-4).[3] The Hebrew word here, *pesel,* usually rendered

1. Augustine, quoting Ecclesiasticus 10:13, *City of God,* 12.6; 14.13. Augustine places what I have called the "watercooler syndrome" on a cosmic scale. He writes, "Pride, too, is not the fault of him who delegates power, nor of power itself, but of the soul that is inordinately enamoured of its own power, and despises the more just dominion of a higher authority" (*City of God,* 12.8). The higher authority in this case is, of course, God.

2. Tillich, *Systematic Theology,* 3 vols. (Chicago: University of Chicago Press, 1951-1963), 2:50-51.

3. It is not immediately clear whether what is being forbidden here are images of other gods or images of Yahweh — i.e., images of God as revealed to Moses. Terrence E. Fretheim says both. Why would it be idolatry to make images of Yahweh? "The usual

"graven image," along with other similar Hebrew terms, is rendered *eidolon* in the Greek New Testament. Tertullian argued that it comes from the diminutive of *eidos,* meaning "form," so that *eidolon* means "formling."[4] It is from *eidolon* that we get our English word *idol.* This commandment prohibits the worship of the divine through honoring the form of a calf or a bull, for example. To put faith in something formed rather than the true God is to commit idolatry. The first commandment can be restated positively: "You shall love the LORD your God with all your heart, and with all your soul, and with all your might" (Deut. 6:5).

In the modern world we ordinarily do not think of idolatry in terms of graven images, of statues and altars. We have tended to subjectivize idolatry. Perhaps this subjectivizing began with Martin Luther and his profound analysis of the first commandment in terms of the human heart. Where we put our heart is where we orient our life, and where we orient our life tells us where we are putting our faith. The question then becomes quite practical: Are we putting our faith in the true God or in something less deserving?

> A god is that to which we look for all good and in which we find refuge in every time of need. To have a god is nothing else than to trust and believe him with our whole heart. As I have often said, the trust and faith of the heart alone make both God and an idol. If your faith and trust are right, then your God is the true God. On the other hand, if your trust is false and wrong, then you have not the true God. For these two belong together, faith and God. That to which your heart clings and entrusts itself is, I say, really your God.[5]

If we simply ask ourselves what it is that our hearts cling and entrust themselves to, we have a principle for discovering the idols in our lives. We have a tool for idol analysis.

---

answer is that this compromises Yahweh's transcendence. Yahweh is above and beyond everything in all creation. But it seems more likely that this prohibition arises more out of a concern to protect God's relatedness than transcendence. . . . Unlike plastic images, which are static and immobile, deaf and dumb, unfeeling and unthinking, and fix God at a point in time, Israel's God is one who can speak and feel and act in both nature and history" (*Exodus,* Interpretation Commentary [Louisville: John Knox Press, 1991], p. 226).

4. Tertullian, *On Idolatry,* 4.

5. Luther, "The Large Catechism," in *The Book of Concord,* ed. Theodore G. Tappert (Philadelphia: Fortress Press, 1959), p. 365.

This insight enables us to understand ourselves by asking hard questions. Do I rise out of bed each morning and find myself preoccupied all day long with financial gain, with my inadequate salary and hopes for a promotion, with the bills that are so hard to pay, with legislation that will give me favorable tax treatment? If so, then I have located my god — namely, my wallet. With eloquence, Martin Luther King, Jr., made this point for the twentieth century:

> There is so much frustration in the world because we have relied on gods rather than God. We have genuflected before the god of science only to find that it has given us the atomic bomb, producing fears and anxieties that science can never mitigate. We have worshipped the god of pleasure only to discover that thrills play out and sensations are short-lived. We have bowed before the god of money only to learn that there are such things as love and friendship that money cannot buy and that in a world of possible depressions, stock market crashes, and bad business investments, money is a rather uncertain deity. These transitory gods are not able to save or bring happiness to the human heart. Only God is able. It is faith in Him that we must rediscover.[6]

With these words we see how idol analysis can apply to civilizations as well as to individuals.[7] Langdon Gilkey applied the method to the American way of life and discovered idolatry at its heart. What is the idol we serve? Freedom, especially the freedom for each one of us to be ourselves. Freedom is sacral in character. It is ultimate. Everything else is judged according to its value relative to the one absolute value, freedom. The cultural images of freedom function as "surrogate gods in our existence, or at least as manifestations for us of the divine. For our god is whatever it is to which we give our lives, and from which we expect in turn to receive all our blessings."[8]

Tillich's approach to this is to think of faith in terms of ultimate

---

6. King, *The Words of Martin Luther King, Jr.,* ed. Coretta Scott King (New York: Newmarket Press, 1958), p. 63.

7. In the wake of the First World War, Karl Barth denounced Europe for having treated its own civilization as an idol. "It is high time for us to confess freely and gladly: this god, to whom we have built the tower of Babel, is not God. He is an idol. He is dead" (*The Word of God and the Word of Man,* trans. Douglas Horton [New York: Harper, 1957], p. 22).

8. Gilkey, *Naming the Whirlwind* (Indianapolis: Bobbs-Merrill, 1969), p. 378.

concern.[9] Whatever we are ultimately concerned about is the object of our faith. The question is whether we place our faith only in that which deserves our ultimate concern — namely, God. Anything less than God is less than ultimate; it is penultimate. Demonic and destructive powers are released when we treat as ultimate something that in fact is only penultimate. This is the heart of idolatry and the source of much of the grief in human history.

Pride enters the picture when I treat my own self as ultimate, when I trust my self more than I trust God. If it is to my own self that my "heart clings and entrusts itself," then I have entered the realm of subjective idolatry.

Tragedy

One of the problems with being proud is that, in the words of Hebrew wisdom, "pride goes before destruction, and a haughty spirit before a fall" (Prov. 16:18). This is the theme of the tragic drama of classical Greece with which the word *hubris* is often associated. It is also the theme of the myth of Prometheus. As the human race was coming into existence on earth, the Titan Prometheus snuck up to heaven, lit his torch on the sun, and returned to earth bringing the gift of fire to terrestrial beings. In the form of campfires and cooking fires, a piece of heaven had now come down to earth. Prometheus had stormed the heavenly vaults and stolen the property of the gods. For this impunity, an angered Zeus determined to take revenge. According to one myth, Zeus punished earth by sending Pandora and plaguing the planet with sin and evil. According to another myth, Prometheus himself became the victim of heavenly rage. Zeus humiliated the once-proud Titan by chaining him to a rock and permitting a furious eagle to come and lash at his flesh and eat his liver. Great is the fall for those on earth who would aspire to the powers of heaven.

Pride is also the dramatic theme of life and death in the story of Israel as reported in Genesis 1–11 and the Deuteronomic history. Not unlike Prometheus in Greece, the king in Israel becomes instructive for all of us. In the history of Israel from Saul down to the exile, the

9. See Tillich, *Dynamics of Faith* (New York: Harper & Row, 1957), pp. 1, 91, 106.

king again and again oversteps his power and falls headlong to destruction. Once this lesson is made clear, the Bible universalizes it so that the tragedy of pride applies to all human beings.

We need first to establish the connection between the king and all of humanity in the development of Hebrew symbolism. This can be done through a brief examination of the concept of dominion. According to the Priestly writer in Genesis 1:28, women and men in general are given dominion *(radah)* over the fish, the birds, and the animals that creep on the earth. But "dominion" is a royal term. It refers to the power of the ruler over subjects. In Psalm 72, which was probably sung or chanted at the enthronement ceremony, we see clearly that "dominion" means striving for justice and taking care of the poor and needy. It means ruling as God would rule.

> Give the king your justice, O God,
> and your righteousness to a king's son.
> May he judge your people with righteousness,
> and your poor with justice. . . .
> May he defend the cause of the poor of the people,
> give deliverance to the needy,
> and crush the oppressor. . . .
> For he delivers the needy when they call,
> the poor and those who have no helper.
> He has pity on the weak and the needy,
> and saves the lives of the needy.
> From oppression and violence he redeems their life;
> and precious is their blood in his sight.
>
> (Psalm 72:1, 2, 4, 12-14)

The king represents God. He is the image of God. The ancient Hebrew term for image, *zelem,* refers to a statue or idol made in the countenance of the king or emperor and placed in the town square in cities within the monarch's domain. When it is time to publish a royal proclamation, the court messenger calls the town's people together and, standing at the foot of the *zelem,* reads the king's message with derived royal authority. Analogously, the sole king of the ancient Hebrews was Yahweh; the fellow sitting on the throne was only the *zelem,* the representative.

Now what would happen should the statue forget that it is a *zelem* and seek to make itself king? This question lies behind the history of

Israelite kingship and, simultaneously, is the key to apprehending the Old Testament understanding of human nature and the Christian concept of pride.

Israel was slow in getting its first king because its faith in the immediacy of Yahweh's kingship sufficed for a relatively long time. But eventually this faith gave way to unfaith, to a lack of trust similar to that expressed when the people sought to hoard manna in the wilderness of Sin. As their trust in God diminished, they began to clamor for a king. The immediate circumstance was Philistine aggression. The tribal confederacy seemed too weak to repel enemy attacks, and the people of Israel wanted a stronger army. A king would have the authority to assemble an effective military.[10] "Give us a king," the people demanded of the prophet Samuel. "No!" replied the prophet; "only Yahweh is king." Reluctantly and against Samuel's better judgment the Hebrews got their king, but along with the king came the charismatic prophet. Whereas the judges who had ruled earlier received the charismatic spirit of God plus the power to rule, henceforth there would be a division of labor. The king would be given the power to rule, and the prophet would be given the spirit of God — a sort of theological system of checks and balances. The great fear expressed by Samuel was that the king would use his power selfishly, and so it became the prophet's commission to remind the king that he was only a *zelem* and that he should not usurp what belonged to God.

The kings failed to listen, of course. First Saul used his royal prerogatives to keep booty from battle that belonged to the offering pot. The prophet Samuel withdrew his anointing, thereby denying messiahship to Saul. Then the prophet anointed David. Saul, refusing to accept that he was no longer king, went into battle anyway, began to lose, and so ended the tragedy by impaling himself on his own sword atop Mount Ebal. The same fate awaited David, who established a magni-

10. The key passage is 1 Samuel 8:19b-20: "We are determined to have a king over us, so that we also may be like other nations, and that our king may govern us and go out before us and fight our battles." Raymund Schwager believes the key here is the desire to be "like other nations." What is at issue is mimesis or rivalry: Israel wants what the other nations want — namely, military power. This, says Schwager, is the root of sin if one interprets the Old Testament in light of René Girard's theory of scapegoating. I will return to the notion of mimetic rivalry (concupiscence) and scapegoating later. See Schwager, *Must There Be Scapegoats?* (San Francisco: Harper & Row, 1987), p. 79.

ficent kingdom but then succumbed to the trivial temptation of lust. He had Uriah surreptitiously murdered so that he could take his wife, Bathsheba, into the royal harem. Again the king had used the power of the throne presumptuously for personal gain and forsaken the dominion of justice. As a consequence, David had to endure the bloody deaths of his sons, one after the other, while he writhed helplessly in emotional pain on the royal bed. David was followed by Solomon, the most glorious and powerful king in Israel's history, whose pride led him to build a palace for himself that was bigger than Yahweh's temple, with the result that revolution tore the nation asunder permanently. The sordid drama repeated itself again and again with each petty ruler that followed until even the disunited nation disintegrated into near nonexistence during the Assyrian and Babylonian captivities. As the king goes, so goes the nation.

As the king goes, so goes humankind. What is true for the king is true for all individually and collectively according to Genesis 1–11, the final editing of which by the Priestly writer probably dates after the fall of Jerusalem and during the Babylonian exile. The point of Genesis is that as the king is the *zelem* of God in Israel, each man and woman is the *zelem* of God in the world. As the king exercised *radah* over his subjects, the human race exercises *radah* over nature. As the king's pride led him to act presumptuously and to use God's image and power for his own self-aggrandizement, so Adam and Eve in their way — and we, their children, in ours — embody the same pattern. Letty Russell describes the pattern this way: representation becomes replacement, dominion becomes domination, and self-transcendence becomes trespass.[11]

There is, curiously enough, a process of democratization going on in Scripture. The ancient or premodern mind was clearly hierarchical, giving clear precedence to the king while treating subjects, slaves, and women almost as property. But the Bible is here dignifying all of us. We are all kings, high and low, men and women. The good news is that each person has dignity, the same dignity that befits the king. The bad news is that each one of us is subject to the same pride, to the same attempt at self-divinization that precedes if not initiates the fall into destruction.

This theme runs all the way through Genesis 1–11, from individuals

11. Russell, *Becoming Human* (Philadelphia: Westminster Press, 1982), p. 78.

in Eden, to nations, and then to all of humanity, symbolized in the stories of Noah and Babel. Whereas the Adam and Eve story depicts the universality of pride and our inevitable fall as individuals, the Tower of Babel episode of Genesis 11 depicts the self-elevation and subsequent fall of groups and nations.

Motivated by the desire for civic unity and international fame, the Babel builders began construction of a tower high enough to connect heaven and earth. With a most subtle sense of humor, the Genesis author tells how God had to go down to take a look at it. Although the people were impressed with the height of their accomplishment, the God most high had to descend just to find out what was going on. How humiliating! But that is how pride works. It results in humiliation in the end.

That the word *Babel* is a sister term to *Babylon* is probably no accident. The prophet Isaiah delivered a vitriolic chastisement of the proud Babylonian empire and its haughty self-assertion, saying that it lived in an illusion of security when it was ready for a fall:

You felt secure in your wickedness,
    you said, "No one sees me."
Your wisdom and your knowledge
    led you astray,
and you said in your heart,
    "I am, and there is no one besides me."
But . . . disaster shall fall upon you . . .
and ruin shall come on you suddenly,
    of which you know nothing. (Isa. 47:10-11)

What Isaiah believed to be true about Babylon was generalized by the Genesis author to apply to all human aggregates and nations who live with the illusory presumption that they can storm the gates of heaven either by promulgating the final religion or, usually more subtly, by seeking to create heaven on earth under their own dominion.

For the proud person, the problem of pride is that it is founded on an illusion of independence. The king may think he is independent, but in fact his dominion depends on the allegiance of his subjects. We may think of ourselves as important, but our importance depends upon how others view us. Our pride has no strength of its own; we are at the mercy of others to impute worth to us. We cannot make ourselves into gods. At best, others can make us into temporary idols.

For the rest of the world, the problem with pride is that it is divisive. Proud individuals separate and isolate themselves not only from God but also from the community of creatures. In his lectures on Romans 4:7, Luther complains that proud people are individualistic *(moniacus)* and particularistic *(monicus)*.[12] Self-centered individualism and prideful particularism destroy holism. In our own century, William Temple has proposed that we think of God as the "Spirit of the Whole" and of sin as self-centeredness that seeks to deny the priority of this whole. Self-centeredness rather than God-centeredness is destructive. Sin as pride pits the individual against the totality of reality, and its claim to possession of the self cannot but deny the belongingness of the self to God and to the whole community of creation.

Narcissism and Insensitivity

One of the ways in which pride most commonly manifests itself and denies our belongingness — especially our belonging in loving relation to other persons — is as narcissism. The term comes from the myth of Narcissus, a young man so handsome that he was more taken with his own beauty than with the lovely maidens who were attracted to him. He ignored all his suitors. He so scorned the nymph Echo, who loved him passionately, that she pined away in her loneliness until nothing was left of her but her voice. The goddess Nemesis, a personification of righteous anger, decided to step in. She pronounced this curse on Narcissus: "May he who loves not others love himself." The heart of the handsome one became inflamed even more consumingly with self-love. As he bent over a quiet pool of water to get a

12. Luther, *Lectures on Romans, Glosses and Scholia,* vol. 25 of *Luther's Works,* ed. Jaroslav Pelikan (St. Louis: Concordia, 1972), p. 271. Emil Brunner describes the fundamental sin as our "rebellious breaking away" from our Creator, as a "self-chosen emancipation" in which we ascribe to ourselves a false independence. This makes each of us an "individual" in a negative sense, as a result of our having destroyed our co-existence with others. At the same time, in a distorted way, each of us has become a "non-individual" — i.e., just one more dependent member of the human species. By greedily grasping the world for our own selfish purposes, we become enslaved to the glamour of the world. Thereby we lose the freedom that only our transcendent creator can grant. See *The Divine Imperative* (Philadelphia: Westminster Press, 1947), p. 154.

drink, he saw the reflection of his lovely visage and was transfixed. "Now I know," he cried, "what others have suffered from me, for I burn with love of my own self — and yet how can I reach that loveliness I see mirrored in the water?" Leaning over the pool, hypnotized by his reflection, he fell in and drowned. Pride goes before destruction.

The reason pride is so evil is that the destruction it engenders is not limited to the proud person. Those around are made to pay the price of suffering for the narcissist's pride. The ways in which this spread of destruction take place can be subtle. It is usually painted over with the colors of loyalty or caring or noble talk. In short, it is usually covered over with lies.

In his book *The People of the Lie,* therapist M. Scott Peck uncovers some of the covert ways in which narcissism does its damage. One case is based on Peck's interview with a thirty-year-old woman named Angela who was trying to borrow a thousand dollars from her mother to buy a car. At first, Angela got no response from her mother. Then through her brother she got the message that her mother had just discovered a lump in her breast that might be cancerous. With possible medical bills in her future, it was reasonable that her mother might not be inclined to send the money. But then a promissory note arrived in the mail: her mother wrote that she would be willing to loan Angela the money if she would sign the note. The letter made Angela feel guilty. She worried that accepting the loan might compromise her mother's security by potentially leaving her unable to take care of bills for medical treatments that would be necessary to save her life. She didn't know what to do, and the dilemma was agonizing. "She always offers me something with the right hand and pulls it away with the left," Angela told Peck. Later Peck discovered that Angela's mother owned three apartment buildings and was probably a millionaire. He concluded that Angela's mother was a narcissist who used guilt to manipulate her daughter.

This led Peck to speculate on the nature of evil. He argues that it is a lack of empathy that characterizes narcissists and renders them evil. Narcissists are insensitive to the feelings of others. If I love another person, this love gives me the ability to see things from that person's viewpoint, perhaps even to feel that person's feelings. If we love others, we share and revere the feelings that are precious to them. If we love only ourselves, we cut ourselves off from anyone else's feelings. Those

96

in whom narcissism becomes total lack, "in whole or in part, this capacity for empathy."[13]

Empathy requires sensitivity and vigilance. At a recent luncheon, I heard Rembert Weakland, the Roman Catholic Archbishop of Milwaukee, offer a most instructive story.[14] He had recently made a trip to the former Soviet Union that included, among other things, performing a mass in Tomsk, Siberia. He was greeted in the city by a local news reporter who told him that she had never attended a religious ceremony of any kind and asked if she could tag along during his visit. He invited her to do so. The itinerary included an ecumenical gesture, attendance at Vespers at the local Orthodox church on the evening prior to the Roman mass. Weakland's entourage included three Roman Catholic priests who, along with the young woman reporter, entered the Orthodox church grounds, passing by two women begging near the entrance. The five walked on by. After entering the church and beginning the Vespers worship, Archbishop Weakland noticed the woman reporter leave. Worried that perhaps she felt uncomfortable in this religious setting, he followed her to the door. Looking out, he observed that she had returned to give the beggars some money. He was stunned, immediately reminded of Jesus' parable of the Good Samaritan. He had himself just passed by the two beggars without noticing them. He had taken priestly vows and given his career to a life of love and service, but now he was reminded of how easy it is for us to become inured to poverty. One sign of a living faith in God, he said, is an ability always to be moved by other people's ills.

Until recently the word we used for this was *sympathy* (from the Greek *pathos*, "pain," and *syn*, "with"). To have sympathy is to feel pain with someone else. When we love only our selves, we lack the ability to sympathize; when we love others, we express that love through a willingness to share the pain of the beloved, whether that be a spouse, a child, a friend, or perhaps even a pair of nameless starving beggars outside a church in Tomsk. It was out of a willingness to share the pain of human suffering that God submitted to the incarnation.

13. Peck, *People of the Lie: The Hope for Healing Human Evil* (New York: Simon & Schuster, 1983), p. 136.

14. The program was sponsored by the Justice and Peace Commission of the Archdiocese of San Francisco, Sheraton Palace Hotel, San Francisco, 28 June 1991.

Were God a narcissist, there would have been no incarnation. There would only have been manipulation of our souls through guilt.

Pride as Power Over

One of the sure signs of pride is what one of my colleagues, Professor Martha Stortz, identifies as the desire for *power over*.[15] She is talking about the desire to control, the ambition to dominate, the effort to enslave others and render the world subservient. She is talking about acting as though one were God.

Pride can be either quiet or loud. Angela's mother sought to dominate her daughter's psyche surreptitiously, but pride can also take an overt and public form. The proud person may seek public acclaim. In fact, such individuals might use the amount of public acclaim they receive as a barometer for measuring just how much pride they might rightfully feel. As they see it, achieving acclaim in any significant quantity requires a victory, the establishment of *power over* the competitors for that acclaim. *Power over* requires that there be winners. And hence it requires that there be losers.

The military provides the preeminent tradition of pride as *power over*. The sole reason for the existence of an army is to defeat the enemy, and frequently pride is the only reward. Winning at war is a matter of life and death. If soldiers die in battle and the nation lives on, then their lives are redeemed if the nation grants them hero status. Heroes make us proud. Had they lived, they could have been proud of themselves. New recruits become proud of their uniforms, because those uniforms identify them with a glorious history.

15. *Power over,* writes Stortz, "is gained and exercised by force, consent, law, or authority. It is the power of a South African government to enforce racial segregation upon an entire people. It is the power of husband over wife assumed in all too many marriages and buttressed by certain interpretations of Scripture and certain versions of political philosophy. It is the power of dominion over the earth that has created oil spills and a fast-disappearing cushion of ozone in the atmosphere. Insofar as this 'power over' assumes the posture of absolutist domination and totalitarian rule, it is oppressive" ("Clothed with Power from on High: Reflections on Power and Service in Ministry," *Word and World* 9 [Fall 1989]: 329; cf. Starhawk, *Truth or Dare: Encounters with Power, Authority, and Mystery* [San Francisco: Harper & Row, 1987], pp. 8-20). Power over is not always harmful, according to Stortz. Parents can provide a benefit to their children by exercising parental power properly, for example.

Sports, whether professional or amateur, have a parallel structure. Uniforms initiate a feeling of pride. The process by which competition separates winners from losers sets the stage. The fiercer the contest, the more complete the involvement of the contestants. Every aspect of the athletes' personal and group being — physical, mental, even spiritual — is devoted to one and only one task: obtaining victory. At the conclusion of the contest, the winners are permitted to hold their heads high, while losers hang their heads low. Among the ancient Mayas of the Yucatan, the winners may have been the only ones able to hold their heads up at all. Wall carvings seem to indicate that the losers at peloté may have been decapitated in the stadium at game's end.

The Badass

Militaries have organization and sports have rules. How does pride work in the absence of organization and rules? Take the case of the *badass*. The badass emerges in youthful circles, especially gang life on the streets of America's large cities. The badass can be a lone individual of either gender, though most often it is a male individual in a group of badasses. The term *bad* indicates deviance from wider social values, and *ass* connotes a combination of toughness and meanness. The point of being a badass is to intimate aggression, to hint at conflict and presume to be the winner in advance.

Pride is shown in the walk, which is meant to intimidate. Today in East Los Angeles, the walk of pride is called the "barrio stroll." It is a slow, rhythmic walk with flamboyant arm movement, chesty posture, and head up toward the heavens. The badass can identify himself as such by employing the barrio stroll at the right time.

Jack Katz claims to have formulated a systematic understanding of the badass in terms of his special way of walking and numerous other symbolic gestures of deviance. He identifies three levels or degrees of intimating aggression. The first is toughness. Someone who is "real bad" is tough, impervious, heedless of the opinions others hold about him. The walk posture and similar gestures are meant to say, "You see me, but I'm not here for you; I see you, but you're here for me only if I say so." The second level is disaffection from social convention, perhaps even to the point of barbarism. The badass engages in activity

99

meant to convince others that he is not subject to their influence. As an alien to prevailing conventions, he can say, "Not only am I not here for you, but I come from a place that's flat beyond the control of your world." Third, the badass must on occasion demonstrate the reality of his toughness through explosions of rage. In order to remain credible, when he says "I mean it," the badass has to back it up with aggressive action consistently. When he offers these demonstrations of gratuitous meanness, he is in effect announcing, "Not only do you not know where I'm at or where I'm coming from, but I can mess you and your world up good whenever I want to."[16]

In the larger dominant society with its competitive economy that marginalizes large segments of humanity — a society and economy that seem to grind out new losers on a daily basis — the marginalized losers need to find a way to win or at least to develop a sense of self-worth. Perhaps adopting the badass persona is a way of transforming oneself from a loser into a winner, a way of turning humiliation into pride. Regardless of the motivation, however, the result is narcissism in an aggressive and destructive form.

Is such narcissism total? Is the badass totally evil? Peck's criterion, recall, is empathy, and according to Katz's analysis, the badass communicates zero empathy. But if we can find some empathy (or sympathy) in the badass, then what?

I encountered a version of the barrio stroll while serving as an inner-city pastor on the south side of Chicago. There it was called "styling." My congregation conducted a program aimed at delinquent youth on parole. Two parole officers and I would meet with a group each Tuesday evening to address problems of social adjustment in the period just after release from jail. One Tuesday evening, four of the young men, all African Americans, entered in an animated state.

"The cop kicked us out of the library," William complained, "and for no reason at all!" We asked for more details.

"Them cops got it in for us," Steve said. "We just walked into the library, got no further than the main desk, an' the cop told us to hit the road."

16. See Katz, *Seductions of Crime* (New York: Basic Books, 1988), pp. 80-81. This attitude is by no means merely countercultural. The badass is culturally celebrated by the film industry with such actor heroes as Clint Eastwood, Charles Bronson, and Sylvester Stallone in his role as Rambo.

"Certainly you must've done something to provoke him," pressed Mr. Vogner, one of the probation officers.

"We done nothin' wrong," they all insisted.

Mr. Chadwick, the other probation officer, suggested we do some role playing as we had in the past. "William," he said, "you stand here and play the cop. You other three guys go outside and walk back into the room exactly as you walked into the library."

We all took our places. The three walked in with their tam hats, part of the uniform of the Black P. Stone Nation, cocked down to their eyebrows. The walk was a familiar one. They were styling. Styling gives the message: the badass has arrived.

"Okay, Mr. Policeman," Mr. Chadwick said to William, "would you throw these three guys out?"

"I sure would!" responded William. "Man, this is a library. These dudes come in here lookin' like they own the whole joint, lookin' around for their friends so's they can talk an' carry on. They sure ain't here to read!"

We then asked each in turn to play the role of the cop. Finally, they all agreed that their walk had been provocative. They found they were able to see themselves through the policeman's eyes. Two Tuesdays later, the group of four proudly announced that they had gone back to the library and apologized to the cop.

Tribalism and Group Evil

Writing during the Great Depression of the 1930s, Reinhold Niebuhr made a startling distinction between the moral capacity of individuals and that of groups. He argued that a high-minded individual is able to love self-sacrificially and pursue justice disinterestedly but that a group is intrinsically incapable of self-sacrificial love. No group can set aside its own vested interest in an effort to seek social justice. "As racial, economic and national groups they take for themselves, whatever their power can command."[17] The only way groups can relate to one another

17. Niebuhr, *Moral Man and Immoral Society* (1932; reprint, New York: Scribner's, 1960), p. 9. Elsewhere he writes, "The chief source of man's inhumanity to man seems to be the tribal limits of his sense of obligation to other men" (*Man's Nature and His Communities* [New York: Scribner's, 1965], p. 84). Ernest Becker also fears the group,

is as power versus power. It has been my experience that Niebuhr's insight is accurate. Relevant to the issue at hand is the observation that we are brought to the brink of aggression and violence when individuals take pride in the groups to which they belong.

The oldest form of the group relevant to the discussion of sin is the tribe. Theoretically, tribalism goes back to at least the second chapter in the story of human history. If the human race in fact stems from a single Eve, whether we establish this biblically or genetically, at its nascence the race must have been one. Soon after, however, it fragmented into families, then clans, and finally tribes. Most contemporary religious and cultural leaders praise the family as the bulwark of society's noble values. Yet this is naive. A closer look will reveal that when the family takes on the form of tribal identity it contributes to some of the most heinous evil besetting the human race.

The first thing to note is that the tribe considers outsiders to be less than human. Perhaps we need to be somewhat self-conscious as we discuss this matter. The notion of the human being as a universal category was discovered in classical times by Plato and Jesus in complementary ways, and it was retrieved and promulgated by the Enlightenment in the eighteenth century. It is only from this Enlightenment perspective that we can look back and see that tribes uniformly dehumanize outsiders. Outsiders are simply that: outsiders.[18] Tribal eyes are blind to any other relationship.

Cannibalism, which is difficult for Enlightenment people to comprehend, is rendered comprehensible when we recognize that the people eaten are outsiders. Their status may be above the animals but certainly below that of what is considered truly human — namely, the in-group or tribe.

Language reveals what is going on here. The biblical Hebrews thought of themselves as the "chosen people" of God, and this sep-

---

especially a group that has formed with a tribe or clan mentality, because "of the great stake that the organism has in blowing itself up in size, importance, and durability. . . . [It] carries the conviction of ultimacy" (*Escape from Evil* [New York: Macmillan, 1975], pp. 12-13).

18. The moral impact of the category *humanity* is frequently underestimated. The very existence of the idea of a single human race functions to combat tribalism by identifying all outsiders as insiders. All of us, regardless of family or tribe, belong to a single human race. Only after such a category is invoked can we begin to use such corollary categories as human rights, individual freedom, and democracy.

arated them from all the Gentiles, the *goyim*. The Navahos called themselves *Dine*, meaning "the people." No non-Navaho was viewed as an equal. Turning to the other side of the fence, the European settlers in North America began to speak of Navahos and other native Americans as "savages," a rank decidedly below that of the so-called civilized Europeans. This language reveals that tribalism is by no means limited to those sharing a common genetic ancestry. It is more of a social-psychological mechanism that functions to divide insiders from outsiders. Even though the ancient Greek philosophers could conceive of a universal human race, it was the Greek language that gave us the word *barbarian* to demote everyone who is not like us. The German Nazis tried to assert that they belonged to a superrace by describing everyone else as *Untermenschen*, as less than and subordinate to what is fully human. The tribal mind-set works to define others right out of the human race.

The tribal mechanism functions to soothe an otherwise sensitive conscience into killing. It was difficult for young American men living in a liberal society in the 1960s to be sent to Vietnam to pull triggers. The soldiers picked up the habit of calling the Vietnamese "gooks." It is much easier to shoot a gook than it is to kill Mr. or Mrs. Diem.

Pertinent to our discussion of sin is the *lex talionis*, the law of blood revenge. Blood revenge is the way of obtaining justice in a tribal setting. Sometimes it applies intertribally, but its primary function is to guide the behavior of competing families or clans within a tribe. As a method for attaining retributive justice, the law works like this: if you shed my blood, then I shed yours. An eye for an eye, a tooth for a tooth. If you slay my brother, then I slay you. Your brother in turn will slay me. My sister in turn will slay your sister. And so it goes. Each warring clan is justified in perpetuating the shedding of blood. Clan warfare tacitly creates a new definition of what is human: my family is human, yours is not. What constitutes the tribe — who's in and who's out — is constantly undergoing revision depending on the course of blood revenge.

One of the primary objectives of civil government — by *civil* I mean modern and urban-centered, not gracious or genteel — is to blunt the damage caused in blood revenge by turning the task of justice over to a neutral authority, to a police force and judicial system.[19] Our

19. The notion of the city — or the kingdom, understood in the ancient world as an empire of city states — as our only hope for overcoming tribal revenge is reflected

modern civilization has sought to eliminate the deleterious effects of tribalism through the establishment of democratic institutions. It has been only partially successful, however. This is because tribalism is a mental mechanism. It constantly takes new forms. On the streets of our large cities it takes the form of gang identification, a tribe of badasses. On a larger scale it expresses itself in racism and nationalism.

The way pride functions here is to elevate the self through identification with a group that is assumed to be omnipotent or immortal or both. We deliberately cultivate a family feeling among the members to gain bonding power. Simultaneously we raise a wall between the in-group and the outsiders, dehumanizing the latter. Soon a mind-set of war takes over. We look for justification and opportunities to render the outsiders powerless and subject to mortality. We try to steal their lifeblood.

What about empathy or sympathy? Essential to the tribal mind-set is the dulling of our sympathetic sensibilities. Take for example the teachings of Heinrich Himmler, who headed the SS during the Nazi period in Germany. The Germans were his tribe, united by common blood, and he permitted no sympathy for non-Germans.

One principle must be absolute for the SS man: we must be honest, decent, loyal, and comradely to those of our own blood and to no one else. What happens to the Russians, what happens to the Czechs, is a matter of utter indifference to me. . . . Whether the other nationalities live in comfort or perish of hunger interests me only insofar as we need them as slaves for our society; apart from that, it does not interest me. Whether or not 10,000 Russian women collapse from exhaustion while digging a tank ditch interests me

---

in political symbols of salvation such as the kingdom of God, the New Jerusalem, and Augustine's "City of God." The point is made in a hymn by Frank M. North, "Where Cross the Crowded Ways of Life":

Where cross the crowded ways of life,
Where sound the cries of race and clan,
Above the noise of selfish strife,
We hear your voice, O Son of Man.

Till all the world shall learn your love,
And follow where your feet have trod;
Till glorious from your heav'n above,
Shall come the city of our God.

only insofar as it affects the completion of the tank ditch for Germany.[20]

In the movie *Apocalypse Now,* which tries to interpret the U.S. military action in Vietnam in terms of Joseph Conrad's novel *The Heart of Darkness,* lack of empathy is key. When the Americans lose the ability to connect with the feelings of the Vietnamese people, it marks a stage on the road to the heart of dark evil. In an early scene the Americans invade a village. The roar of the helicopters and weapons and Wagner's music blasting out of loudspeakers frightens the villagers into running. Helicopter gunners shoot down the fleeing children in a schoolyard. Homes, buildings, livelihoods, and lives are destroyed wantonly. The military commander whoops and hollers and waves his cowboy hat to cheer his troops on. In the middle of the shooting he sits down for breakfast and says wistfully, "I love the smell of napalm in the morning. It smells like victory."

Patriarchy and Homophobia

Patriarchy and homophobia are commonly experienced forms of pride that do not fit neatly in the categories of either individual narcissism or group self-interest. They belong somewhere in between, perhaps as the expression of some physiological or genetic predisposition. The generally larger physical stature of men in most parts of the world may tend to make it easy for them to lord it over women. And just as some recent research seems to suggest that a certain percentage of the population has a genetic predisposition to homosexual attraction, we may eventually discover that the revulsion much of the heterosexual population feels toward homosexuals is similarly innate. Regardless of such speculations, we should note that patriarchy and homophobia combine internal and external components. There is a compelling force that works within the psyche, and this is reinforced by certain values available in the surrounding culture. Perhaps we should think of these two as psychocultural forms of pride that produce an underclass of women and homosexual persons who find themselves suffering in silence.

•

20. Himmler, quoted by Joaquim Fest in *The Face of the Third Reich,* trans. Michael Bullock (New York: Pantheon Books, 1970), p. 115.

105

Our word *patriarchy* combines two terms, *patri,* meaning "father," and *archē,* the important Greek word that means "beginning" or "that which governs." In short, *patriarchy* means men govern. The social science textbooks I read in school as a child said that there are two kinds of societies, patriarchal and matriarchal. We happen to live in a patriarchal society. The terms were presented as value neutral. Since the rise of the women's liberation movement in the 1960s, however, *patriarchy* has developed clearly pejorative connotations. The assertion is that men have traditionally governed badly or illegitimately. Patriarchy is now identified with the oppression of women.

There are considerable psychocultural grounds for this complaint. Something happens to young boys as they pass through puberty. They discover their bodies are gaining newfound strengths. I can remember my brother Rob at age fourteen picking up my mother and carrying her around the house. She would holler half jokingly "Put me down!" but this would only increase the size of the mischievous smile on his face. Carrying mom around was a declaration of independence, an assertion of Oedipal power, an establishment of his incipient manhood.

What I have identified as *power over* becomes a consuming enterprise. Whether through engaging in athletic competition, achieving academic recognition, bullying in groups, fighting in the schoolyard, or the like, the boy seeks to become a man by establishing his self-worth through victory, through aggressive action that establishes himself a winner and someone else a loser. But his victory cannot be solely his own. He needs the admiration of a group. He grasps self-worth only insofar as someone else is willing to grant it to him. Teams and cliques and even gender identification become factors. For some, the belief that boys are better than girls serves as one more easy step up on the ladder to self-worth.

But what develops is by no means just another version of group pride or tribalism as we have defined it. This is because the opposite sex lives within the boy's soul. Deep down he knows he cannot live apart from his mother or from the powerful attraction he feels toward the girls at school or in the neighborhood or the media. He feels the power from within — sometimes uncomfortably, sometimes painfully. Should he seek to gain victory over this too? Should he pretend that he is unaffected by the girls around him? Should he demonstrate his dominance over his emotions through meanness toward the opposite sex? Unless a man gains genuine self-understanding and self-control as he matures — unless he gains the capacity for empathy — the confusion over establishing self-worth may take the form of harassment at the office and wife-beating at home.

Perhaps our cultural norms can be thought of as lacking maturity, as coddling the underdeveloped egos of the male gender. Perhaps patriarchy can be understood as a form of pride that ensures all men a false sense of self-worth. When braves of the Huron and Mohawk tribes were frustrated or angry with their failure in hunting or war, they would accuse one another of behaving like women or frightened dogs — that is, like weaklings. In locker-room chatter, boys will often use such sexual shorthand as "cunt" or "pussy" in referring to women, thereby reflecting a doublemindedness: on the one hand, such references acknowledge the extreme attractiveness of the woman, but on the other hand, they serve to render the woman into an object that can be used and disposed of at will.

Add to this psychological mechanism a structure of male dominance in social institutions, and the sad result is that the girls and women in our culture do not get a fair shake. Traditionally the activities of the males have served to establish the criteria for achievement and excellence; the activities of females have been considered trivial and mundane by comparison. Men have been assumed to be stronger and more responsible, women weaker and less productive. Thus the entire structure of our culture stands as an impediment to opportunities for women to strike forward and make recognizable contributions to the social whole. A woman with grand ideas, energy, ambition, and self-confidence must daily confront what appears to be a silent conspiracy to prevent her from accomplishing anything. She becomes frustrated at traveling a road blocked by a long line of what she perceives as unfair barriers propped up by male pride. Her perceptions are accurate.

Homophobia has some parallels to patriarchy. The term has come into usage recently to refer to prejudice against gay men and lesbian women in much of Western society. *Homo* refers to homosexuality, and *phobia* to an inordinate or unfounded fear. Fear, whether legitimate or irrational, can lead to violent defensive reactions. Pride in general is a defensive reaction to anxiety. Homophobia can be understood, I think, as one way that pride expresses itself.

One of the psychiatric social workers with whom I worked at the Cleveland Psychiatric Institute described the local bar conversation in the neighborhood as having the function of establishing masculinity through communicating bigness: "Big truck! Big drinker! Big penis! Big! Big! Big!" Such bars are exceedingly dangerous places for gay men. The presence of a homosexual man triggers something within the others, some sort of defense. Perhaps there is a lingering fear within the heterosexual man that he is less heterosexual or less masculine than the image he has projected to his buddies would indicate, and this fear motivates attempts to reestablish or reassert his masculinity through ridicule or even physical assaults. The Castro and Polk Street areas in San Francisco are not infrequently visited by carloads of thugs, usually young men in their late teens and early twenties who have driven in from the suburbs, who hunt down gays walking the streets. They stop the car, jump out, and proceed to beat the homosexuals into unconsciousness. Then they jump back into their cars and drive home, probably high on the "smell of victory."

Some maintain that gay bashing is justifiable because homosexuality is sinful. They reason that gay bashing (like AIDS) is a form of divine retribution. By beating gays they are indirectly serving a righteous God. But, as I will argue later, the very attempt to justify violence by placing oneself on the side of the righteous against alleged sinners is itself part of the structure of sin.

Gay bashing, like patriarchy, is morally inexcusable. It is loveless. It lacks empathy. It exudes pride through victory, through making oneself a winner and someone else a loser.

Can Women Be Proud?

Does our discussion of pride thus far apply only to men, or can women be proud too? Is pride a gender-specific issue? Some contemporary feminist theologians complain that proscriptions of pride are repressive to women just when they need to develop a greater sense of self-worth. Such feminist discussions of sin have been a leaven, giving rise to new and intriguing insights.

The discussion began with a perceptive and pioneering article by Valerie Saiving (Goldstein) published in 1960. Saiving explores the possibility that some experiences of women are qualitatively different from those of men, and this difference should be taken into account when trying to understand the nature of sin.

Saiving asserts that men are universally aggressive. Because of this, a theology of sin aimed at men should be aimed at containing aggression. Men would do well to hear the Christian teaching that love — especially self-giving or *agape* love — is the highest virtue. Instead of dominating, men should give of themselves. Instead of seeking *power over*, men should seek to empower others. If men could be convinced to love one another, the deleterious consequences of their aggressive behavior would effectively be contained.

This sounds quite reasonable to me. Saiving is careful to separate the disease from the cure. The disease or sin is aggressive behavior; the commandment to love one another is the way we cure it. There is no suggestion here that Christian theology has been endorsing male aggression; to the contrary, it has sought to contain it. Saiving is not blaming the tradition here. While there is much more to morality than just this, I think Saiving is off to a good start.

Once she has made this initial point, Saiving proceeds to ask whether there might be something gender-specific about women's sin. After all, she says, men tend to give their lives over to "becoming," whereas women are more occupied with "being." Men tend to cut themselves off from nature through creative work, whereas women are more closely bound to nature. With these observations in mind, Saiving suggests that the fundamental temptation confronting women is not pride but the denial of a sense of self. "The temptations of women as women are not the same as the temptations of man as man," says Saiving. "They are better suggested by such items as triviality, distractability, and diffuseness; lack of an organizing center or focus; dependence on others for one's own self-definition; tolerance at the expense of standards of excellence, inability to respect the boundaries of privacy, sentimentality, gossipy sociability, and mistrust of reason — in short, underdevelopment or negation of the self."[21]

21. Saiving, "The Human Situation: A Feminine View," in *Womanspirit Rising*, ed. Carol P. Christ and Judith Plaskow (San Francisco: Harper & Row, 1979), p. 37. Among those who have responded to Saiving's thesis is Susan Thistlethwaite, who applies the sin of the diffused self to herself but adds some specificity. Diffusion of self is specifically the sin of American white middle-class women, she says, including herself among them. It is not the sin of African-American women, who, though treated as "other" by a racist society, prevail against the odds. To make matters worse, says Thistlethwaite, as a white liberal she is tempted to compound her sin by bonding "with black women under an *undifferentiated* label of 'sisterhood'" (*Sex, Race, and God: Christian Feminism in Black and White* [New York: Crossroad, 1991], pp. 85-86). Ruth Nanda Anshen recognizes this phenomenon, which she calls "empty altruism,"

I think Saiving is both correct and mistaken. She certainly has done us a formal service by perceiving and disclosing the relationship between peculiarly male proclivities and theological explication of symbols for sin. Materially speaking, however, the actual list of women's temptations reveals that Saiving herself may still be working too much out of a bias toward the male situation. As a case in point, let's examine briefly the temptation to triviality. Let me simply ask what is wrong with triviality. Is there a commandment against it? No, the commandments forbid us to live a life without love; they do not forbid triviality. Did Jesus chastise the Pharisees for following trivial pursuits? No, not exactly. He chastised them for hypocrisy. Why then does Saiving consider triviality sinful? Let me offer a hypothesis: the pursuit of trivia looks sinful because men feel driven to do important things and feel guilty if they are failures in life, and Saiving unconsciously applies this standard — a standard she herself has identified with the male gender — to women.

Let's look at it another way. Is there anything good about triviality? One quality that often accompanies triviality is attention to details. The mother and homemaker who occupies her mind with the proper amount of water softener to add when washing the diapers, who analyzes the nutritional content and taste of the various brands of baby food, and who rushes her child off to the hospital emergency room whenever she hears a strange cough is likely to be quite a bore to the men she speaks with at academic seminars or cocktail parties for friends in the professional world. She may not have spent much time thinking about how to solve the nation's unemployment problem, she may seldom express much outrage at recent failures to bring representatives of the nuclear powers to the negotiating table, and she may not grasp

---

but she applies it not to women in general but rather to those people, regardless of gender, who pursue "altruistic professions." She describes it as "the fanatic occupation with and devotion to others, their needs and desires. It is an altruism morally and spiritually without merit because it does not emanate from a well-formed, self-confident ego. Whether innate or acquired as the result of destructive experience, this empty altruism replaces and compensates for the ego's loss by living the lives of those to whom its feeling, thoughts, and actions are dedicated. This type of disintegrated self, not easily recognizable but frequent in all so-called altruistic professions, is of no interest to the Devil, for there is no point of attack. It is genuine altruism that interests him — altruism sustained by a well-developed self — for that is a unique phenomenon which carries with it the potentiality of saintliness" (*Anatomy of Evil* [Mt. Kisco, N.Y.: Moyer Bell, 1972], p. 65).

the intricacies of recent proposals for health care reform. The fact that she does not dwell on these issues may be conspicuous in contexts where professional men and women do dwell on them. If the antidote to sin is thought to be shouldering concern for the big and important things in our world, then the woman who stays at home and, as Saiving says, remains close to nature may easily become ashamed of her ostensible triviality.

But what appears to be boring at a cocktail party is absolutely essential to our survival as a human race. What an idealist characterizes as trivia may actually be the very act of love that makes human life possible. The attention to the minute and practical details that sustain health and nurture growth is a priceless treasure that is often overlooked by those whose eyes are fixed on the elusive end of the idealist's rainbow. Now my point here is by no means to baptize trivia wholesale. I simply wish to point out that, despite her insightful suggestions, Saiving may still be looking at sin through androcentric glasses, and this perspective might have caused her to jump to the premature conclusion that triviality is inherently sinful, blinding her to its possible tie with incarnate love.[22]

Despite this mild criticism, I believe we should thank Saiving for being careful not to build an insurmountable wall between men and women. She perceptively recognizes that the concept of sin applies to a single human condition. The problems created by our desire to achieve great things and the destructive aggression this releases pose a temptation for both men and women. Saiving's point is that within this broader human problem there are some specific qualities of female experience that have been overlooked and that need to be brought into theological explication.

Saiving's pioneering thought was pre-ideological. A decade and a half later, ideological feminists picked up her work and incorporated it into their program, declaring women's independence from all an-

---

22. In trying to present a gender contrast to male striving for dominance, Nel Noddings offers these appreciative lines for the woman involved in daily caring: "A woman knows that she can never win the battle against dust, that she will have to feed family members again and again (and that no meals are likely to go down in history), that she must tend the garden every year, and that she cannot overcome most of its enemies but must treat them with the sort of moderation that encourages harmony" (*Women and Evil* [Berkeley and Los Angeles: University of California Press, 1989], p. 182).

drocentric points of view. Later feminists argued, among other things, that the traditional male proscription of pride ought not apply to women. Carol P. Christ wrote that "the traditional doctrines of sin and grace encourage women to remain in their form of sin, which is self-negation or insufficient assertion of will."[23] What women need, she argued, is self-affirmation and a greater assertion of the female will. In short, women need power.

Where will women get this power? Answer: from worshiping the goddess. The rise of neopagan goddess worship is first of all a rejection of the Hebrew and Christian religious traditions on the grounds that the male symbolism for God is repressive to women. The clearly voiced assumption is that religious symbols are both models *of* divine existence and models *for* human behavior. If we think of God in terms of male symbols such as Father or Son, then we will be inclined to think of men as socially superior to women.[24] Feminist critics argue that the Christian understanding of God gives the impression that female power can never be fully legitimate or wholly beneficent. In contrast, goddess worship provides a means of liberation and empowerment for women.

The goddess spoken of here is not *out there*. She is not a transcendent being. She is found within women. She is a divine personification of feminine principles. Three characteristics identify the new understanding of the goddess: (1) she is a divine female who can be invoked in prayer and ritual; (2) she symbolizes natural processes close to women's experience, such as life, death, and birth; (3) she symbolizes the women's liberation movement and its declaration of the legitimacy and beauty of women's power. Worshipers of the goddess meet in small groups on full moons, solstices, and equinoxes to celebrate symbolically the waxing and waning energies in the universe and in themselves.

It appears that what we have here is a return to old-fashioned idolatry. It is the deliberate positing of a divine reality other than that revealed through Moses to Israel. There may or may not be any graven images involved, but conceptual images play a vital role. The entire theology depends on the assumption that we copy our mental image of the divine in society. Even if the goddess has no independent or transcendent existence of her own, the mental construct of the goddess

23. Christ, "Why Women Need the Goddess," in *Womanspirit Rising,* pp. 283-84.
24. See the Introduction to *Womanspirit Rising,* pp. 2-3.

grants us — at least the women among us — the power of the goddess. The point of goddess worship is to enhance self-esteem.

Tertullian in the third century stumbled on an insight that might apply today — namely, whenever we make and worship an idol, we are in fact worshiping something human.[25] The something human in this case is the affirmation of a woman's self-worth and her power in society. Goddess worship is admittedly a projection onto heaven of the vision of the empowered woman on earth. Goddess worship is at root the worship of the human woman herself. Perhaps we have here a case of pride as subjective idolatry — that is, the elevation of the self into the sphere of the divine.

In some ways the advocate of neopagan goddess worship is reminiscent of the badass. Like the badass who expresses dissatisfaction with his plight as a member of a marginalized minority, the neopagan feminist expresses dissatisfaction with the subordinate status of women. As the badass seeks to affirm his self-worth through the barrio stroll and his declaration of independence from the dominant middle class, the radical feminist declares her independence from patriarchy by rejecting classical religious tradition.

Now, we might raise again the concern for empathy. Is feminism in general or neopagan feminism in particular aimed at eliminating empathy? No, not necessarily. While repudiating the classical understanding of sin, Carol Christ says two things about the will that are helpful here. First, the woman's will needs to be empowered. "A woman is encouraged to know her will, to believe that her will is valid,

---

25. Tertullian, *On Idolatry*, 15. Virginia Ramey Mollenkott provides a clear example of the logic: "Because God is womanlike — women are Godlike" (*The Divine Feminine* [New York: Crossroad, 1987], p. 78). Although Mollenkott is seeking a biblical rather than a pagan feminism, what is important is the way in which she says a woman is Godlike. A woman is not Godlike because she achieves virtue, because she loves as God loves or because she has achieved a holy life. Rather, she is Godlike by birth, by nature. The argument is that women are by nature the channel of divine power to the world. But this assertion implicitly denies the existence of the God proclaimed by Israel and Christianity in favor of a feminist form of naturalism. Nel Noddings, for example, speaks of God as a "psychic reality" produced by whimsy or personal longing: "To me, when that longing for holy communion arises, God is clearly female. As I hold a new infant, or dive through a marvelous ocean wave, or spot one of my grown children at the airport, or feel the warmth of the sun on my back as I garden, or listen to a gentle snore from my sleeping husband, I speak thanks to someone like Ceres — a deity who loved her child as I would like to be loved" (*Women and Evil*, pp. 243-44).

and to believe that her will can be achieved in the world." Such a remark leads us to ask: Is this will-to-power merely a copy of male aggression in women's dress? No, not necessarily. This leads to the second point: Christ says that her goal is a "positive affirmation of personal will in the context of the energies of other wills or beings."[26] The emphasis here is on cooperation, community. Feminists want power, but not necessarily *power over.* They reject love understood as self-sacrifice, to be sure, but they endorse love understood as sharing.

It may be worth noting a subtle point in this feminist argument: it is legitimate to use the goddess to enhance women's power in society because the Christian doctrine of God has allegedly been used to enhance the power of men. Carol Christ is quite candid about this point: "Goddess symbolism undergirds and legitimates the concerns of the women's movement, much as God symbolism in Christianity undergirded the interests of men in patriarchy."[27] What she is saying here is that men were wrong to use traditional religion to undergird patriarchy in the past, but since they did so, women are now justified in responding in kind, in adopting the same flawed strategy. In short, two wrongs make a right.

But is Carol Christ making correct use of the facts? The difference between her argument and that of Valerie Saiving is instructive. Saiving maintains that the classical Christian position identifies pride as a sin and in doing so seeks to contain male aggression, not enhance it. Thus she holds that it is not the intent of Christian doctrine to promote pride. Carol Christ, on the other hand, contends that it is the intent — or at least the function — of Christian teaching to endorse the domineering interests of men. The situation is complicated somewhat by the fact that Saiving focuses on the Christian understanding of sin, whereas Christ focuses on divine symbolism. Nevertheless, Christ insists that Christianity defends what Saiving says it repudiates. In my judgment, the Saiving analysis is the more theologically accurate, even though Christ's concern about the historical church's endorsement of patriarchy definitely needs to be addressed.

It appears to me that some of what has been passing as feminist analysis has in fact amounted to ideological attempts to exonerate women and scapegoat men, and I have made an effort to look into

26. Christ, "Why Women Need the Goddess," p. 284.
27. Christ, "Why Women Need the Goddess," p. 276.

the matter further when I could. In the context of studying the nature of sin and evil, I took opportunities to quiz many of my women students. For one thing, I asked them how sin evidences itself in their lives personally. No one who responded blamed all the evil in the world on the male gender. All admitted their own sinfulness. Women are just as susceptible to pride as men, they told me, but their pride does manifest itself somewhat differently. They viewed women as less given to boasting and bravado but more given to narcissism and manipulation. In the final analysis, therefore, pride seems to constitute a common human predicament.

Perhaps I should pose one more question before departing from this subject: Where should we draw the line between a healthy sense of self-worth and the destructive force of pride? Where does healthy self-esteem end and destructive pride begin? Perhaps we could use the presence of empathy as a litmus test and say that pride begins when our sensitivity to the feelings of others begins to diminish. A healthy sense of self-worth may even strengthen our ability to feel the feelings of others. The ability to sympathize does not depend on a poor sense of self. Pride, understood as a loss of sympathy, seems to belong in a different category.

Sympathy (or empathy) is a decisive criterion, and yet it can be risky to invoke it. For one thing, we risk self-justification in doing so. I might reassure myself that as long as I feel empathy, it follows that I have a healthy sense of self-worth, in contrast to other people whose actions suggest that they do not feel empathy — Nazis, say, or patriarchal men or homophobes — and who must therefore be prideful and hence sinful. In other words, using this criterion might put me in the position of being proud about my empathy.

So I think it may be better to leave the question unanswered. One of the complicated aspects of human sin is that it leads us to draw lines, especially lines between what is right and what is wrong. Like the nurse practitioner who wondered if it was wrong to be proud of her academic degrees, we would like to be able to draw a line and put ourselves on the right side of it. But the problem is that this sort of thing only produces more pride. Once again sin seems to be inescapable. That is what theologians have meant by the controversial term *original sin*. Original sin is an inevitable component of human living. It is ever present and ever subtle. Even the attempt to understand sin is perilous, since we are easily tempted to define sin in such a way that it applies to other people's thoughts and actions and not our own. We laugh at the buffoon who boasts of his humility along with his other fine virtues, but it's no joke. Sin is often that viciously circular.

Pride and Mutually Assured Destruction

The proverb "Pride goes before destruction" (Prov. 16:18) takes on a certain haunting quality in the context of planetary politics. If we think on a global scale, we find ourselves in the midst of an expanded form of the ancient feud between clans but now with the threat that blood revenge might do away with the human community entirely. It is frustrating that in an age in which travel and telecommunications have made it possible for more people than at any other time in history to envision the reality of a single worldwide human community, we continue to splinter into an increasing number of factional nation-states. There is no global justice system analogous to domestic civil justice systems that might serve to break the cycles of international and interracial violence. The sheer impenetrability and intransigence of the problem defy solution by the most brilliant minds and most loving souls living in our world today and seem to provide convincing evidence even to those outside the church that we are in the grip of something equivalent to what Christians call original sin. If only some sort of sacrifice could be offered to stem what threatens to be the final deluge of human violence, even modern people might opt for it. But, alas, no way of escape has as yet captured our imaginations. We are left with the sheer terror of the times.

The stockpiling of nearly fifty thousand nuclear weapons during the cold war brought our world to a state of critical mass, where the detonation of one bomb might precipitate a chain reaction of destruction that could spell the end of the human race and much of the natural world as well. For nearly half a century following World War II we stood nervously on the brink of the nuclear pit excavated by the policy of deterrence formulated by the NATO leaders and the Soviets: if you believe we are willing to use our nuclear weapons to destroy you utterly, then you are unlikely to use your nuclear weapons against us. Journalist Jonathan Schell dubbed it a policy of mutual assured destruction — *MAD* for short.

Through this balance of terror we found ourselves in the position

116

of holding a knife at the throat of those on the other side of the brink, while ironically imposing the same threat of death on ourselves and all whom we love. We do not need to go to the theologians to find a characterization of our situation since 1945 as sin. The scientists do it for us. According to the director of the Manhattan Project, J. Robert Oppenheimer, the bombings of Hiroshima and Nagasaki marked the fall from innocence of the modern age. Oppenheimer's words will long be remembered: "Physicists have known sin." Princeton physicist Freeman Dyson describes the possession of our nuclear arsenal as "a manifestly evil institution deeply embedded in the structure of our society." We have become servants to this evil. We have sold ourselves into atomic slavery.

Is emancipation possible? The thaw in the cold war initiated by the personal warmth of Mikhail Gorbachev and extended by the fall of the Soviet empire has given us a brief respite, a moment to sigh in relief. Yet the danger is by no means over. The nuclear weapons still exist, and nations with appetites more aggressive than those of the Soviets are struggling to obtain them. New alliances and new configurations of friends and enemies simply change the direction in which the missiles are aimed.

In a somewhat utopian fashion, Jonathan Schell argues that it is as much within our power to rid ourselves of the horror of nuclear weapons as it was within the power of our ancestors to rid themselves of the horror of slavery. Our generation needs to make a conscious choice, he says, to lift the nuclear peril by resolving to escape "this pervasive corruption of our lives." Such an escape would require of the nations involved a "pre-emptive repentance" for the "original sin" committed at Alamogordo and Hiroshima.[28]

Here, completely outside conventional theological circles, our experience with the human predicament is rising to articulation, and those who wish to give it voice find they must use the symbols of sin in order to express the depth of the despair we are experiencing. The self-assertion, the hubris of autonomous nations threatens the health if not the very existence of the global community as a whole. Yet now that the original sin has been committed, what can a single nation do? If it

28. Freeman Dyson, *Weapons and Hope* (San Francisco: Harper & Row, 1984); cf. Jonathan Schell, *The Fate of the Earth* (New York: Knopf, 1982) and *The Abolition* (New York: Alfred A. Knopf, 1984).

continues the path of deterrence, the finger it keeps perpetually poised over the trigger of the nuclear arsenal may grow progressively more shaky or numb and increase the likelihood of accident, miscalculation, or carelessness. If it engages in repentance and unilateral disarmament, it risks inviting a preemptive strike from the other side. If the human race were capable of acting as a whole in its own best interests, we could make decisions of global consequence to reduce and eventually eliminate the peril. But in our world where individual nations are sovereign and have the initiative — where the ancient precivil system of clan revenge is now writ large — there is no way that one can act directly in behalf of the good of the whole. Augustine was right: in our present situation we cannot not sin — *non posse non peccare*. Or, to quote journalist Strobe Talbott, commenting on the work of Dyson and Schell, "An escape from mankind's suicide threat remains elusive, a goal we might, in our wisdom, approach, but never, in our state of sin, achieve."[29]

Pride and Holism

I suggested earlier that one of the problems associated with pride is that it breaks our sense of belongingness, our sense of bond with God or with other people. It separates and isolates us. It fragments. And when it leads to manipulation or aggression, it initiates dissonance if not violence. The peace and serenity of the whole community is broken. One way to conceive of the significance of pride in terms of the overall understanding of reality is to employ the whole-part dialectic. The problem is then cast in this way: the pride of the part threatens the health and harmony of the whole.

I find the work of William Temple to be helpful in creating a holistic vision that puts pride in its place. Temple, an English theologian who served as the Archbishop of Canterbury during the second third of the twentieth century, maintains that there is a close relationship between God and the whole of reality, a relationship so close that they are functionally equivalent regarding the issue at hand. God is "the Spirit of the whole."[30] Self-centeredness in any part of the whole

29. Talbott, *Time*, 11 June 1984.
30. Temple, *Nature, Man and God* (1934; reprint, London: Macmillan, 1960), pp. 376, 390.

constitutes sin. Temple is clear here that self-centeredness is the problem and not selfhood per se. God has carefully brought individual selves into existence — the existence of human selves is part of the divine plan — but the meaning and value of each self is found in its relation to that grand plan. Each one of us finds our respective goodness in our relationship to the whole of the ongoing creative process. Temple underscores the point that this process of divine creation is characterized by complementarity and synthesis. The true aim of the human soul is to glorify God, and to do this I must center myself in the life of the whole rather than in my self as an independent self.

Temple notes that the natural self is capable on occasion of engaging in acts of disinterested love, what I have here been referring to as empathy and even self-sacrifice. As an example, Temple reminds us of how a person's love for a disabled spouse or another member of the family may lead to years of dedicated service and care. One's patriotic devotion to the homeland, to cite a second example, may lead to a soldier's ultimate sacrifice for others in battle. Though we are individual selves, we are by no means enslaved to brute self-centeredness. There are spiritual forces that can call us beyond ourselves and lead us to greatness.

After acknowledging these noble expressions of the human spirit, Temple goes on to reflect on the realities implied by the doctrine of original sin. The vitiation of self-centeredness is never complete. Two facts need to be noted. First, self-giving is usually based on some sense of affinity for the person to whom the giving is directed. The beloved invalid belongs to the lover via the family, and the lover to the beloved. The patriot belongs to the country and the country to the patriot via the equivalent of tribal identity. In these two examples we find devotion to the other as an extension of devotion to oneself. Second, the community to whom this disinterested love is directed is always a limited community, not the whole of reality. Beyond one's family are other families and clans and tribes that are not natural recipients of the spouse's attentive care. Beyond the soldiers' nation are other nations for which they will not be motivated to lay down their lives. Temple reminds us of the grim fact that disinterested love and self-sacrifice — these highest of human virtues — are perfectly compatible with clan rivalry, including blood revenge and international war. He argues that anything less than centering oneself on the all-inclusive whole contributes to evil and hence to disintegration.

We humans cannot be saved, nor can either individuals or society attain perfection, except through the total elimination of all competitive self-centeredness. The severity of the problem is enhanced by the fact that the self cannot free itself from its self-centeredness. This is the paradox. As long as the self retains the initiative, it can only fix upon itself and further establish itself as the illegitimate center. Yet, somehow it must be uprooted from this center and be drawn to find its center in that which is beyond itself, in what Temple calls the "Spirit of the whole." In this case, one could not even say that the true aim of the human self would be to attain its own salvation, because even the pursuit of individual salvation would only further establish the self as the center and ensure its perdition. Thus, says Temple, salvation can be experienced only by those who have ceased to be interested in whether or not they are personally saved, only by those who have given themselves over completely to the Spirit of the whole.

If Temple is correct, we would seem to be in an impossible situation. How did we become trapped in this blind alley with no exit? Temple is careful to endorse some of the points we established earlier regarding finitude and sin: he affirms that finite selfhood is in itself something good. But as he ponders the issue, he comes closer and closer to making finitude responsible for our sin. The step from selfhood to self-centeredness becomes so short that Temple wonders if God had not meant from the beginning for us to fall into sin. "It is not wicked to be finite," he writes, "but it is so improbable as to be beyond all reasonable estimate of practical possibility that finite selves, if left to themselves, should not be wicked."[31] We can see Temple's struggle here. The very problem of sin, when cast in terms of the whole-part dialectic, becomes a problem of finitude. How can the part center itself on the whole when its very nature is to center itself on itself? Could it really be that God intended us to sin? Are we back in Eden again, blaming the serpent?

Temple does not go as far as Hegel, who suggested that the fall may have been a fall upward, an ascent to higher consciousness (in the sense that a knowledge of the difference between good and evil is preferable to ignorant innocence). Even though Temple does not follow Hegel here, he does affirm that the fall indirectly contributed to a good. This is because the dynamic movement of the whole has

31. Temple, *Nature, Man and God*, p. 369.

the ability to transform the evil of the part and compel it to participate in the good, in the greater good. In this sense evil is subordinate to, yet lifted up into and synthesized with, what is good. For example, says Temple, error can provoke questioning that leads to further truth. The climax of art occurs when the artist takes the otherwise repellent and hostile elements of experience and welds them into the completeness of aesthetic harmony. As the crowning instance he cites the crucifixion of Jesus, which is extremely bad if taken as an isolated event but, when viewed as the pivotal point in history, is supremely good. Hence, argues Temple, the incorporating power of the Spirit of the whole is also a transforming power that indirectly draws up and synthesizes even our sinfulness into God's overall plan for the creation.

In sum, Temple defines God in terms of the "Spirit of the whole" and sin as self-centeredness that seeks to deny the priority of this whole. Salvation consists in shifting the center of the soul's life from itself to God. But, we must observe, this change is impossible for the self to accomplish on its own, because the very attempt only reinforces its self-centeredness and precludes a genuinely disinterested effort. What is called for, we must conclude, is some form of divine grace. Temple envisions this grace in terms of the transformative power of the whole.

I believe Temple is on the right track. Perhaps he does not emphasize as much as I would like the role of temporality and the yet outstanding future. I want to argue that at present there is no genuine whole in anything but a formal sense. For a true wholeness of the whole, wherein the actual centeredness and communion of all things express only the Spirit of the whole, we must await the finishing of the old creation and the advent of the new. In short, the whole about which Temple speaks is the whole promised by God in the resurrection of Jesus and communicated to us in the symbol of the new creation.

What this means for our understanding of sin is that the prideful assertion of the part not only disrupts the harmony of the whole but also tends to fixate us on the present moment rather than the coming future. It declares the present to be absolute. It closes us off to future transformation. It repudiates trust in the God of the future by elevating not only the self but also present reality to the sphere of the divine. It is this mistake that warrants the inexorable truth of Proverbs 16:18,

"Pride goes before destruction." Time marches on. Any decision to fix oneself in present reality is ultimately suicide, because present reality always gives way to the future. What is present will soon become the dead past. The harmonious whole that harbors life is the future whole to be wrought by God. Only faith in the God of the future has what it takes to recenter the self in that which is truly divine.

5

CONCUPISCENCE
Lusting after What They Have

Life is uncertain. Let's eat dessert first!

Anonymous remark at dinner

Concupiscence may be a strange-sounding word to our modern ears. Yet what it refers to is all too familiar: it means "desire," what is sometimes called "sensuality." It is the particular form of sensual desire associated with envy, greed, avarice, and coveting. The New Testament word is *epithumia* (Col. 3:5; 1 Thess. 4:5).[1]

A member of my family goes shopping when she gets depressed. The worse she feels, the more dresses she buys. These shopping binges are evidence of concupiscence at work. At its deepest level, concupis-

---

1. The problem is not desire per se, but rather evil desire, *epithumian kakēn* (Col. 3:5). Desire in the form of *erōs* is essential to love, even to the love of beauty or truth or theology, according to Tillich. Tillich distinguishes *erōs*, desire emerging from a personal center, from *epithumia*, desire without a personal center, what Freud referred to as libido. The latter refers to our normal drive toward self-fulfillment, toward the establishment of a personal center in relationship to what we love. Such fulfillment results in pleasure; frustration of this drive results in pain. This is normal, says Tillich, and so we should remove all theological prejudice against it. The real problem lies with perverted *epithumia* that lives solely from the pleasure-pain principle apart from the pursuit of self-fulfillment. See *Love, Power, and Justice* (New York: Oxford University Press, 1960), pp. 28-31.

cence creates the illusion that having constitutes being, that consuming can combat anxiety. It fosters the illusion that getting and owning will actually make us immortal.

Concupiscence includes envy or mimetic desire — that is, the desire to have what others have. We have a concupiscent cat. His name is Socrates. Rescued as a kitten after our dog, Buck, had killed his mother, tiny Socrates grew up on my desk, so to speak, keeping me company while I pursued my research and prepared for classes. Until he was four months old, he was strictly an indoor cat. We kept him isolated from the outdoor cats. We also kept him on a strict diet of cheap dry cat food. My cousin Jim, a vet, had told us that if a pet never tastes anything different, it will be happy with dry pet food. So we undertook this family experiment in nutrition and budget. Socrates seemed contented in his ignorance about culinary alternatives. Well, perhaps it was inevitable, but one day an older and wiser cat made it into the house and sat in front of our refrigerator. When one of us entered the kitchen, this cat would waltz around, meow loudly, and rub affectionately against our legs. When the refrigerator door opened, it grew more excited. Socrates witnessed what was going on and began to mimic the excitement, not knowing at all the reason for it. I took out a scrap of turkey meat, at which point the outside cat went into a frenzy of jumping and hollering. Socrates went into a similar frenzy. As soon as I had given the turkey to the outside cat, Socrates tried to steal it. Unsuccessful, he turned to me and demanded a like share. Without even having tasted meat, Socrates knew he desired it because the other cat had desired it. From that moment on, Socrates was a carnivore.

Concupiscence is the passionate desire to get something, to have it. Traditionally concupiscence has been identified with sexual lust. The word derives from the root *cupere*, "to desire," as does *Cupid*, the Latin counterpart of the Greek god Eros. Cupid is the impish baby of Venus, the goddess of love (as Eros is the child of Aphrodite for the Greeks). The arrow from Cupid's bow depicted on our Valentine's cards each February sticks in our hearts and refuses to let go. Erotic or sexual attraction can be gloriously delightful while it enslaves us. Lust, in short, is a powerful drive that can overwhelm us with the promise of ecstasy.

Lust and life seem to go together. The promise of sexual pleasure makes us feel really alive, at least for the moment. One of the campfire philosophers I mentioned in an earlier chapter said, "Oh, don't take lust away from me. Lusting is fun. I'd never do anything, but it makes me feel so alive!" We feel concupiscent when we are driven by lust. What I want to point out here is that this sense of being driven by the sort of desire exemplified in sexual lust is what gives concupiscence its power.

More generally, concupiscence is the desire to acquire, to own, to indulge, to take pleasure, to consume. It causes us to covet and disposes us to greed and avarice. Critics of the established social order during the Renaissance announced that greed and avarice were tearing soul and society apart. In a print dedicated to *Elck* (Everyone) now found in the Mayer Van den Bergh Museum in Antwerp, Flemish artist Brueghel the Elder announces that we are all united in the anonymity of sin but no one is aware of his or her responsibility. The alchemist tries to fabricate gold. The merchant is lost amid bundles of merchandise. The soldier conquers. Brueghel's caption reads:

Everyone only seeks his own interest.
Everyone in all enterprises only seeks himself.
Everyone on every occasion aspires to wealth.
Everyone tugs for the longest end.
All people have only one desire: to own.[2]

The insatiable human appetite for possessions, sex, and the like has often been identified as the root of all evil and suffering in the world. Stoics, Hindus, and especially Buddhists locate the source of sin in human desire or craving and identify the path of salvation with overcoming desire or craving. An ancient Buddhist-Hindu myth of the human fall into sin from the primordial golden age begins by describing an aboriginal state of disembodied mind. Without a body, the mind dines only on joy, free of sexual distinctions, free of lust and greed. The earth is fragrant and sweet as honey. Then one individual tastes the earth's sweetness, and desire begins to overtake him. Others follow the example. This causes their bodies to become solid. As their bodies take on flesh, they differentiate into two sexes. Passion arises. Couples build huts to conceal their sexual intercourse. Greed rises up.

2. Breughel, quoted by Jean Delumeau in *Sin and Fear: The Emergence of a Western Guilt Culture, Thirteenth-Eighteenth Centuries*, trans. Eric Nicholson (New York: St. Martin's Press, 1990), pp. 132-33.

One man steals another's field near the hut. From such beginnings, so the myth goes, theft, censure, false speech, and punishment become the human lot in life.[3]

In our own time, concupiscence as the desire to own is expressed most saliently in the consumer mentality. It is the assumption that we should be engaged constantly in buying and having. It fuels our efforts to escape the tension of anxiety by overindulging in the details of ordinary daily life and its activities. The result is what Reinhold Niebuhr calls "unlimited devotion to limited values," what Thomas Aquinas refers to as turning inordinately to mutable good.[4]

Concupiscence is a perversion of love. "I just love to go shopping!" says the bumper sticker. At the store we fondle newly manufactured products and imagine how they'd look in our homes. It gives us a feeling of power to have sales clerks attending to our wishes. Our love for shopping becomes a perversion, however, when it marginalizes higher forms of love, when it replaces our love for truth, our love for other people, or our love for God. Augustine presupposes that there is an order to nature and that concupiscence consists of preferring the things that are lower in that order over the things that are higher, of desiring what is inferior. Concupiscence inverts means and ends. Augustine was willing to grant transitory enjoyments such as shopping

3. See Wendy Doniger O'Flaherty, *The Origins of Evil in Hindu Mythology* (Berkeley and Los Angeles: University of California Press, 1976), p. 33. Within Christian theological discussion, concupiscence in the form of covetous greed is frequently identified as the root source of other sins. See Aquinas, *Summa Theologica*, II/1, q.84, aa.1, 2. Richard K. Fenn takes a similar position and adds a modern psychological explanation: the experience of breaking the bond with our mother in infancy leaves us filled with dread, and dread manifests itself as the desire to consume. "Each individual is born with a passion for consumption," he says, "an insatiable hunger to fill the self with the contents of the world. That desire, uninformed by the awareness of a sharp distinction between the self and the world, is often experienced as a desire for fusion with the source of life. . . . The residues of infancy remain in every adult in the form of a greed that cannot be entirely satisfied" (*The Secularization of Sin* [Louisville: Westminster/John Knox, 1991], p. 98). The fatal fault — namely, the breaking of our bond with the source of our life, our mothers — takes the form of what I call the anxiety over space, and this in turn leads to aggression. Fenn goes on to say, "The desire for return to the land, to one's source in the original matrix, is a particularly consuming and potentially destructive passion. That is why I am treating it here as the basis of sin: the fatal fault underlying both anger and envy" (p. 20).

4. See Niebuhr, *The Nature and Destiny of Man*, 2 vols. (New York: Scribner's, 1941-1943), 1:185; and Aquinas, *Summa Theologica*, II/1, q.77, a.4. See also Luke 12:20; Romans 8:6; Galatians 5:16; and Plato's *Timaeus*, 90.

to their proper place amid a complex of loves that are ultimately ordered toward love of the everlasting God; but when such mundane desires begin to consume all our energies and crowd out love for God, he condemns them as fruits of concupiscence, as evidences of a life given over to envy, lust, and consumption.[5]

The amount of wealth one possesses is irrelevant with respect to one's capacity for concupiscence. It infects the poor and the rich alike. In impoverished societies it may come to expression in envy of the rich and in the use of theft or pillage or legislation or revolution or whatever may be necessary to secure one's own livelihood even if it involves denying the livelihood of others who are equally desperate. In the bourgeois and wealthy classes of our society, we deny spirit and sink into sensuality by engaging in unbridled consumption: traveling, redecorating, night-clubbing, drinking, partying, and generally living a conspicuous high life. Since 1950, per capita energy use in the United States has increased 60 percent, auto travel has more than doubled, air travel has jumped 2,500 percent, and the use of plastics has multiplied 2,000 percent. Consumption in Japan has increased even more rapidly.

Some identify the desire to consume with the love of money. The New Testament tells us that "the love of money is a root of all kinds of evil" (1 Tim. 6:10). Socrates — the philosopher, not the cat — said that the love of money is the cause of wars.[6] If this were a simple matter, we might suppose that we would only have to provide enough money to those who love it in order to prevent a lot of damage. Unfortunately, this is not how things work. It would not be possible to provide *enough* money to those who love it. No matter how much we get, we want

---

5. Two points regarding Augustine need to be noted here. First, he contends that concupiscence is rooted in pride. This may not be obvious, but he argues that the drive to accumulate things is one way in which the self seeks to glorify itself. Pride expressing itself through envy leads to aggression and perhaps violence. Second, Augustine's analysis fails to account for something very important — namely, the self-destructive nature of sin. He does not speak of the sort of aggression that is directed inward toward the self. One of the important discoveries of Kierkegaard in the nineteenth century and the discipline of psychology in the twentieth century is that the self can treat itself as violently as it treats others. "Augustine had not yet fully thought out the consequences of sin for the relation of human beings to themselves," says Pannenberg. "Only in the modern age has sin been described in a consistent way as a distortion of human subjectivity" (*Anthropology in Theological Perspective* [Philadelphia: Westminster Press, 1985], p. 146).

6. Plato, *Phaedo*, S.66.

more. An ancient Hindu maxim packages the wisdom: trying to eliminate a person's lust for wealth by giving him or her money is like trying to put out a fire by putting butterfat on it. Concupiscent love cannot be satisfied.[7] At best it can only be controlled.

Concupiscence is not limited to individuals. It can imbue a social structure. The economic structure of the modern industrial world is fundamentally concupiscent. Capitalism depends on the production of what Karl Marx called "surplus value," the excess value or profit that results from the mass production of goods. Surplus value is tied to freedom — or so we have convinced ourselves. The greater our ability to control and reinvest surplus value, the more freedom we have. Marx identified the desire to gain control of the surplus of others as the primary drive between classes and between nations. Since the Industrial Revolution, the nations of Europe and North America and more recently Japan have gained control of much of the world's surplus value. They have situated themselves at the center of the global economic system. By establishing a periphery of underdeveloped economic colonies around the world, they have managed to keep raw materials flowing cheaply to the center and manufactured goods flowing back to the peripheral markets. The surplus value accumulates in the center. One of the most significant justice issues associated with this process is the fact that in parts of the Third World, efforts to produce cash crops for export are choking out local food production.[8]

---

7. Aristotle distinguishes two kinds of desire for wealth, one that meets basic needs and one understood as limitless concupiscence. Regarding the second, he says that "as their desires are unlimited, they also desire that the means of gratifying them should be without limit" (*Politics*, 1.9 [1258a, 1]). Thomas Aquinas dubs the first "natural concupiscence" and the second "non-natural concupiscence," the desire to be rich beyond fixed limit (*Summa Theologica*, II/1, q.30, a.4). Perhaps this distinction is what leads Roger Haight to give concupiscence a most charitable interpretation: "because of the resistance to freedom that stems from the spontaneous and determining desires or impulses of nature, it is impossible to commit the self completely and fully [to God]. . . . Concupiscence in this sense is not an evil; it is simply the finite condition and actual situation of human existence" ("Sin and Grace," p. 97).

8. The Sahel region in Africa is a good case in point. In a region where there has been starvation on a massive scale for a decade, cotton is being exported at record rates. Five Sahelian nations — Burkina Faso, Chad, Mali, Niger, and Senegal — produced a record 154 million tons of cotton fiber in 1983-84, helping to drive prices down on the world market and hence making cotton goods a little cheaper in the First World. But while increasing amounts of arable Sahelian land were being diverted from food crops to cotton, millions were approaching or succumbing to starvation. The

In such cases, the system is doing more than just draining the surplus. The very livelihood of millions of people is being appropriated to line the already well-lined pockets of the First World. More than mere money is at stake. The human cost in poverty and susceptibility to starvation, disease, and death is staggering.

"Poverty means death," says Gustavo Gutiérrez, making his own assessment of the human cost.[9] In his groundbreaking book of 1971, *A Theology of Liberation,* this Peruvian parish priest argued that development in the northern hemisphere is systematically dependent on underdevelopment in the southern hemisphere. The impoverished peasants of Latin America are chained to the wheels of an international economic mill that grinds them into the soil from which the cash crops grow. The concupiscence at the economic center that neglects the welfare of the periphery consigns the periphery to death. The health and wealth of the core drain the life force from the outer skin, which, having served its purpose, is then peeled away and discarded. "It means death due to hunger and sickness, or to the repressive methods used by those who see their privileged position being endangered by any effort to liberate the oppressed."[10]

Stealing Life from Our Children

The theft of livelihood takes place not just between hemispheres but between generations as well. Current consumption is increasing at such a rate that our planet will be unable to sustain its support of the human race indefinitely. Mother earth's ability to nourish the life she has spawned is diminishing. We are draining earth's milk faster than it can be renewed. The livelihood of future generations is in serious jeopardy.

In 1990, I was asked by St. Mark's Church in San Francisco to preach a sermon commemorating the twentieth anniversary of Earth

---

present economic order rewards Third World landowners for growing cash crops rather than feeding their own people. See *Our Common Future,* produced by the U.N. World Commission on Environment and Development (Oxford: Oxford University Press, 1987), p. 68.

9. Gutiérrez, *We Drink from Our Own Wells* (London: SCM Press, 1984), p. 9; see also pp. xv, 28.

10. Gutiérrez, *We Drink from Our Own Wells,* pp. 9-10.

Day. In preparation, I did some research to find out what had happened during the two decades since the inauguration of the event. I was astounded at the degree of deterioration of our planet's ability to sustain life. Deforestation and desertification have been devastating. During this twenty-year period, the world lost 200 million hectares of tree cover. This is an area roughly the size of the United States east of the Mississippi River. In most cases, the lost forests were replaced with deserts, which grew by 120 million hectares, claiming more land than is currently under cultivation in China. We lost 480 billion tons of topsoil to erosion — the equivalent of almost all of the acreage under cultivation in India. The loss of forest contributed to a further reduction of our planet's ability to process carbon dioxide, a greenhouse gas contributing to the threat of global warming. And the shrinking supply of cropland made it that much more difficult to provide food for the 1.6 billion additional people added to the world's population during the past twenty years. Following worship on that Sunday in 1990, the congregation walked out to a spot near the parking lot, ceremoniously planted a tree, and dedicated itself to caring for the earth that sustains the lives of us and our progeny.

This symbolic gesture was admirable, but it will take much more than the mere planting of a few trees to turn back the tide of environmental destruction. The degree to which the human race has fouled its own nest is overwhelming. As we continue to deplete nonrenewable natural resources such as petroleum, we enhance the wealth of a few in the short term while diminishing the prospects of the whole of humanity in the long term. We have but a half century left of oil reserves, 65 percent of which are in the Persian Gulf. Despite the shock of skyrocketing prices in the 1970s, the industrialized world has increased its consumption steadily. We are approaching a showdown of supply and demand. Some observers have remarked that "the world's addiction to cheap oil is as destructive and hard to break as an alcoholic's need for a drink."[11]

11. Christopher Flavin and Nicholas Leussen, "Designing a Sustainable Energy System," in *State of the World 1991,* ed. Lester R. Brown (New York: W. W. Norton, 1991), p. 23. Flavin and Leussen recommend a total conversion of our economy to renewable energy sources, principally solar energy. The sun, they say, could provide a cheap and sustainable source of energy and an energy industry that is decentralized, permitting lesser developed countries to leapfrog the First World into the new state of technology.

Our addiction to oil, coal, and natural gas will eventually reach a limit due to dwindling availability, but the pollution of our biosphere may constrain us before we can exhaust the supplies. The burning of fossil fuels is now spewing six billion tons of carbon dioxide and other toxins into the air annually — greenhouse gases that are accumulating in the atmosphere, trapping solar radiation, and gradually heating the planet. Rising temperatures are almost certain to increase already alarming rates of desertification, to raise sea levels through melting the polar ice caps, and to cause unpredictable turbulent weather. The decade of the 1980s included six of the hottest years in the past century, perhaps indicating that global warming is beginning to take hold.[12] Other gases are producing acid rains that are killing plant and animal life in our forests and lakes. The *Waldsterben* (death of forests) in Germany has awakened Europe to the threat caused by acid rain, and the death of nearly ten percent of the 240 lakes in the Adirondack region of New York state has awakened some North Americans. Still other gases are damaging upper-atmospheric ozone, exposing the planet's surface to greater amounts of ultraviolet radiation, which is known to damage plant and animal life in a number of ways, including increasing the likelihood of cataracts and skin cancer in human beings. Measurements indicate that from 1969 to 1986, the ozone decreased by 1.7 percent overall, with 3 percent decreases in portions of the northern hemisphere over North America, Europe, and Asia.[13] Even if we could somehow halt the production of all of these damaging gases today, the effects of those we have already released would persist for decades to come.

Befoulment of our life support system by industrial waste is increasing, and virtually no one wants to claim responsibility. From 1980 to 1985 the U.S. Environmental Protection Agency recorded 6,928 ac-

12. The hottest years in a century of record-keeping were 1980, 1981, 1983, 1987, 1988, 1990, and 1991. A slight drop in temperature occurred in 1992. Source: J. Hansen and S. Lebedeff, cited by Lester R. Brown, Hal Kane, and Ed Ayres in *Vital Signs 1993* (New York: W. W. Norton, 1993), p. 69.

13. See Cynthia Pollock Shea, "Protecting the Ozone Layer," in *State of the World 1989* (New York: W. W. Norton, 1989), pp. 77-96. U.N. leadership in June 1990 led to an agreement by ninety-three nations to halt by the end of the century the production of the chloro-fluorocarbon gases believed to be principally responsible for the depletion of the ozone layer. Research is still underway to find safe and effective substitutes for these gases.

cidents — an average of five per day — in which toxic chemicals and radioactive materials endangered personnel and the environment. A congressional research team in 1985 concluded that nearly half of the 1,246 hazardous waste dumps surveyed showed signs of polluting nearby groundwater. The Office of Technology Assessment estimates that at least 10,000 hazardous waste sites in the U.S. now pose a serious threat to public health and are in dire need of being cleaned up. The Superfund set up by the U.S. Congress to underwrite cleanup in 1980 has been a miserable failure, getting bogged down in litigation and expending more money on attorneys' fees than on the tasks at hand. In the process we have discovered that the problem may be many times worse than estimated when the program began.

Under the leadership of Lester R. Brown, the Worldwatch Institute offers the following assessment of our situation:

> Every major indicator shows a deterioration in natural systems: forests are shrinking, deserts are expanding, croplands are losing topsoil, the stratospheric ozone layer continues to thin, greenhouse gases are accumulating, the number of plant and animal species is diminishing, air pollution has reached health-threatening levels in hundreds of cities, and damage from acid rain can be seen on every continent.[14]

The World Commission on Environment and Development sponsored by the United Nations examined such trends and sought to draw out their implications for economic justice. The members observed that poverty pollutes. If the present generation is to reverse its present slide toward ecological suicide, it will have to eliminate poverty around the globe. We need to think holistically.

> The Earth is one but the world is not. We all depend on one biosphere for sustaining our lives. Yet each community, each country, strives for survival and prosperity with little regard for its impact on others. Some consume Earth's resources at a rate that would leave little for future generations. Others, many more in number, consume far too little and live with the prospect of hunger, squalor, disease, and early death.[15]

14. Brown, "The New World Order," in *State of the World 1991*, p. 5.
15. *Our Common Future*, p. 27.

Such observations have led to a recent parting of the ways between two academic disciplines, economics and ecology. Economists analyze trends in terms of savings, investment, and growth. The economist's point of view prevails in the offices of industry, finance, government, and international development agencies. But two very important costs are typically omitted from the economist's calculations: the human costs and the environmental costs. Ecologists follow a different track, attending to the relationships of living things with each other and with their environments. Ecologists note that corporate profit and loss statements neglect to include mention of the long-term effects on civilization and on the biosphere of the depletion of nonrenewable resources and the abandonment to the future of expenses for cleaning up toxic and nuclear waste. Ecologists worry about what it will cost our progeny a century from now to protect themselves from the dangers we have bequeathed them, while economists seem to ignore the issue.

Could it be that the scientific discipline of economics is itself evil? Is it part of the lie? By hiding the true cost of our consumption, the science of economics salves our consciences so as to permit ever-increasing vampirism, a vampirism that might well — however inadvertently — eventually mean the death of us all.

Some voices are calling for a revision or rehabilitation of economics, a reordered discipline that will incorporate ecological concerns. Whereas traditional economics takes as its principal assumption individual self-interest, revisionists Herman E. Daly and John B. Cobb, Jr., among others, make the person-in-community the central category. "We believe human beings are fundamentally social and that economics should be refounded on the recognition of this reality. We call for rethinking economics on the basis of a new concept of *Homo economicus* as person-in-community."[16] The Daly and Cobb approach is holistic, looking at the whole of the human race geographically and temporally united. Sin, in such a scheme, would logically consist of asserting the part to the exclusion and even damage of other parts or

16. Daly and Cobb, *For the Common Good: Redirecting the Economy toward Community, the Environment, and a Sustainable Future* (Boston: Beacon Press, 1989), p. 164. In a similar plea to stop the ravaging of earth, philosopher Holmes Rolston III proposes an ecological ethic based on the presumption that "self-interest and benevolence are not necessarily incompatible" (*Philosophy Gone Wild: Environmental Ethics* [Buffalo: Prometheus Books, 1989], p. 24).

the whole. "To commit oneself finally to anything less than the whole is, in this perspective, idolatry."[17]

To commit oneself to the whole over time is to commit oneself to the concept of sustainability. "The basic value of a sustainable society, the ecological equivalent of the Golden Rule is simple," writes Worldwatch Institute researcher Alan Durning: "Each generation should meet its needs without jeopardizing the prospects of future generations."[18] We are in imminent danger because the present generation has shown itself to be willing to consume and consume with little or no regard to this equivalent of the Golden Rule.

In light of this, I am using the classical term *concupiscence* to describe the rapacious and insatiable appetite that dominates the present generation and its willingness to ignore the possibly irreparable damage it is causing. Through chosen blindness and desire unencumbered with moral considerations, the present generation has numbed its conscience so as to permit one final orgy of production and consumption that will eventually leave a Mother Earth denuded of her life-giving resources and her future children wallowing in our waste. A line on the jacket of one of Lester Brown's books makes the point: "We have not inherited the earth from our fathers, we are borrowing it from our children."[19]

The Lust for Power

At the heart of concupiscence is the denial of our own limits expressed through the consumption of someone else's life-giving power.[20] Those of us who profit from today's First World economies are like vampires, thriving on the blood of unseen victims. Our vampirism is virtually invisible, of course. We see no sign of it in our daily routine as we cash our paychecks and head for the shopping centers. Yet our whole

17. Daly and Cobb, *For the Common Good*, p. 383.
18. Durning, "Limiting Consumption," *The Futurist* 25 (July-August 1991): 13.
19. Brown, *Building a Sustainable Society* (New York: W. W. Norton, 1981).
20. In this connection, Reinhold Niebuhr uses the term *greed* to refer to "man's inordinate ambition to hide his insecurity in nature. . . . Greed as a form of the will-to-power has been a particularly flagrant sin in the modern era because modern technology has tempted contemporary man to overestimate the possibility and the value of eliminating his insecurity in nature. Greed has thus become the besetting sin of a bourgeois culture" (*The Nature and Destiny of Man*, 1:191).

economy is based on this concupiscent structure: the desire to consume someone else's life-giving power.

The theft of someone else's life-giving power probably began in our prehistory with the ceremonious eating of the heart of the strong animal that the hunters had slain. It was believed that the strength of the animal was somehow transmuted into increased strength for the hunters. It continues with the systematic slaying of those captured in war. In an earlier chapter I noted Ernest Becker's analysis of the kings of the African Dahomey who captured members of inland tribes to sell to slave traders. Not all the captured were sold. Once a year, hundreds would be lined up and the Dahomey would cut off their heads. They were willing to give up financial profit for the exhilaration of demonstrating their power over weaker peoples. Becker says the public display, humiliation, and execution of prisoners is psychologically very important, because it affirms that "they are weak and die; we are strong and live." The killing of others affirms our own illusory power over life.

The greatest excitement conceivable for a human being is confronting the risk of death and winning a skillful victory over it. We have an insatiable hunger for this excitement. Hence the establishment of the arena games in ancient Rome, in which the staging of perpetual life-and-death struggles became the pastime. Thumbs up meant life to the gladiators; thumbs down meant death. To control life with such a casual gesture is to consume the power of life taken from those we control. By sacrificing others, we fuel the fire of our own self-aggrandizement and pursue the impossible task of obtaining immunity against our own death.

Concupiscence as the consumption of the life of others still undergirds our social order, if a little less obviously. But the calm day-to-day routine of civil society is only a thin veneer covering a substrate of rapacious violence. The relentless drive to obtain and maintain military superiority — even if we never actually fight the war — seems to rely on the same illusion that it is possible to take power from the projected victim. Today our gladiators fight in the war rooms of the Pentagon and on our television screens, shedding imaginary blood and producing cardboard heroes. Although we might breathe a mild sigh of relief over the fact that the violence of the war room and the TV networks is a fiction, the relief may not last long. This fiction still emerges from the basic human desire to consume life by taking power from others, and we have learned from the history of our own century that at any moment this potential violence can break out into the actual destruction of our world.

To this point I have been describing concupiscence as the desire to consume material things, as seeking to avoid anxiety by losing ourselves in the senses, in the things of the earth from which we sprang. But there is more to it than this. This drive to escape the bounds of our finitude may express itself in nonmaterial ways as well. We humans are inclined to combine soil with spirit. Concupiscence can also come to expression as a lust for consuming spiritual realities.[21]

One form of spiritual concupiscence involves entering a castle of ideas and refusing to dirty oneself any longer with thinking about actual experience. Some seek to protect themselves within a fortress of doctrines and view everyone outside the fortress as an enemy. In times past the attempt to become solely spirit took the form of ruthless religious intolerance — for example, the repression of the lower castes in India, the confessional wars among Christians in Europe, and the Muslim *jihad* against the infidels. In our time, soilless spirit takes the form of political ideology. Forms of nationalism such as Nazism and forms of internationalism such as communism give us the illusion of immortality by making us part of a great group spirit, by offering us opportunities to become part of a great enduring purpose worthy of the sacrifice of our individual lives. Soilless spirit in our emerging postmodern setting is associated with each transformationist ideology that promises a qualitatively new reality externally through political revolution or internally through spiritual discipline or in some cases both. Such political ideology accompanied by religious zeal is a disguised form of military vampirism, an attempt to suck the life-force from the enemy in order to prop up one's own vision of self-attained immortality. The root problem here is that finitude gets forgotten as infinite desire seeks infinite fulfillment.

It is this that makes concupiscence both a material and a spiritual matter. Power is the key. The concupiscence of both our personal and our corporate being is fueled by an insatiable lust for power. For those who have lost rational and moral self-control, power becomes a sacred

---

21. Thomas Aquinas spoke to this issue. He concluded that although concupiscence pertains properly to our sensual or material appetites, it can appear to apply to our desire for higher matters of the spirit such as wisdom (*Summa Theologica*, II/1, q.30, a.1).

goal, a wholly consuming interest. In this regard, fanatics illustrate in the extreme what is going on inside all of us more modestly. A case in point is Herman Goering. Goering wanted to consume power, and yet power cannot be consumed; it can only be identified with, participated in. Goering got as close to power as he could by becoming a Nazi. Hitler was the personification of the power with which he identified. He treated the Führer as the sacred, the absolute. Just as the "Catholic Christian is convinced that the Pope is infallible in all religious and ethical matters," Goering said, "so we National Socialists declare with the same ardent conviction that for us, too, the Führer is absolutely infallible in all political and other matters having to do with the national and social interests of the people." In bestowing the symbol of infallibility on Hitler, Goering elevated him to the level of ultimacy and, through identification, he elevated the Nazis and himself to that level as well. Goering's adoration of Hitler's power carried him into religious ecstasy.

> We each possess just so much power as the Führer wishes to give. And only with the Führer and standing behind him is one really powerful, only then does one hold the strong powers of the state in one's hands; but against his will, or even just without his wish, one would instantly become totally powerless. A word from the Führer and anyone whom he wishes to be rid of falls. His prestige, his authority are boundless. . . . It is not I who live, but the Führer who lives in me.[22]

Goering's paraphrase of Paul's statement in Galatians 2:20 ("It is no longer I who live, but it is Christ who lives in me") underscores the mystical overtones of his concupiscence. He believed he was consuming the greatest spiritual and material commodity of all, ultimate power.

What about Sex?

The word *concupiscence* is seldom used in conversation these days, and if it is, we are not likely to think first of wanton shopping, economic oppression, environmental degradation, or totalitarian power. What is most likely to come first to mind is sexual lust. This is no accident.

---

22. Goering, quoted by Joaquim Fest in *The Face of the Third Reich*, trans. Michael Bullock (New York: Pantheon Books, 1970), p. 75.

The traditional association owes much to Augustine, who tied the two tightly together. Augustine came to the Christian faith in his adult years and subsequently confessed his misspent youth. While sowing his wild oats, he fathered a child out of wedlock. In his spiritual pilgrimage, Augustine reflected on his own experience of sexual desire, trying to understand it as a form of love that had somehow become misdirected. He explained that he had become an erotomaniac, a sex addict. When lust takes hold, it is all consuming. It blocks our openness to God. "Clouds arose from the slimy desires of the flesh and from youth's seething spring," wrote Augustine. "They clouded over and darkened my soul, so that I could not distinguish the calm light of chaste love from the fog of lust. Both kinds of affection burned confusedly within me and swept my feeble youth over the crags of desire and plunged me into a whirlpool of shameful deeds."[23] It is important to note that what Augustine is identifying as sinful here is not the body of his lover or even sexual relations per se but rather his experience of being consumed by the desire to consume. He grieves over his loss of control over his own soul, the ceding of his spiritual love for God to the carnal love of what is less than God.

As I read it, Augustine is using this experience of lust as a model for sin in general, a means by which to make the sinful structure of our daily experience more evident. Because sexual desire is virtually universal among mature individuals, it provides a good example of the ways in which concupiscence works in many aspects of our lives. Only a few paragraphs after speaking of how his spiritual vision had been diminished by the fog of lust, Augustine relates a famous story about the time he stole pears off a neighbor's tree. He was motivated not by a desire for the pears as such, but rather by sheer perversity.

I willed to commit theft, and I did so, not because I was driven to it by any need, unless it were by poverty of justice, and dislike of it,

23. Augustine, *Confessions,* 2.2. Having defined *concupiscence* as "the unlimited desire to draw the whole of reality into one's self," Tillich refers to "physical hunger as well as to sex, to knowledge as well as power, to material wealth as well as to spiritual values" and chastises Augustine (and Luther as well) for reducing concupiscence to the striving for sexual pleasure (*Systematic Theology,* 3 vols. [Chicago: University of Chicago Press, 1951-1963], 2:52; cf. Alexander C. Irwin, *Eros toward the World: Paul Tillich and the Theology of the Erotic* [Minneapolis: Fortress Press, 1992], p. 28). It is my judgment that Augustine understood that concupiscence incorporates much more than just sexual desire.

138

and by a glut of evildoing. For I stole a thing of which I had plenty of my own and of much better quality. Nor did I wish to enjoy that thing which I desired to gain by theft, but rather to enjoy the actual theft and the sin of theft.[24]

The point is that there is no point to this sin. Augustine's theft cannot be reduced to some need or principle. It cannot be explained by anything other than a willful decision to take someone else's livelihood. The placement of these two texts in sequence leads me to think that the passage on sexual lust is intended to ready us for the pear theft, so that we will begin to see the breadth and depth of concupiscence. We are born with it. It belongs in the category of original sin. We inherit it from the generation that has preceded us. Our wills are bound to it. We need God's grace to liberate us from our bondage to limitless desire and to draw us toward a love for what is good. Concupiscence enslaves us. God frees us.

There is much going on here. It would be a serious mistake to walk away from Augustine's analysis with the conclusion that concupiscence has to do solely with sexual lust or, worse, that there is something intrinsically sinful about sexual love.[25] To do so would be to trivialize the idea of sin; at the very least such a strategy would sidestep a confrontation of the complexities and horror of the evils we have been discussing thus far.

Many among Augustine's friends and foes seem inclined to make this mistake. Much of the Christian tradition down to the present day has

24. Augustine, *Confessions,* 2.4. Margaret R. Miles has offered a similar comparison of these two passages from the *Confessions,* thus offering some corroboration for my thesis that it is not sex per se but rather compulsive lust in general that characterizes Augustine's notion of concupiscence. "Having identified the structure of all concupiscence as pleasureless enjoyment of compulsively acquired objects," writes Miles, "Augustine uses the incident of the pear theft to illustrate rather than a more titillating story of sexual misbehavior" (*Desire and Delight: A New Reading of Augustine's "Confessions"* [New York: Crossroad, 1992], p. 26).

25. I believe Wayne Oates would agree. He fears that our concern for sexual morality may be masking the real problem — namely, our pride. "Before we equate temptation with sexual desire, we must let God teach us what other desires are hiding beneath this cover. . . . The desire to be in God's place with no limits, to have all knowledge, and to be an exception to all other mortals, for example, rarely receives our attention. Pride separates us from the reality of our humanness, our ignorance, and our companionship in frailty with our fellow creatures" (*Temptation* [Louisville: Westminster/John Knox Press, 1991], p. 19).

clung tenaciously to a rather rigid set of sexual mores, citing Augustine along with Tertullian and others to buttress its moral dominance.[26] Foes of this traditional morality in our own generation have indulged in a good deal of Augustine bashing as they have pressed their point of view.

But more blame is laid at Augustine's doorstep than he deserves. The energy driving society and religion toward tight control of sexual activity (the cardinal principle of which is that sexual intercourse should take place only within marriage) comes from a variety of sources that far outweigh Augustine's lone contribution to Western culture. The Old Testament includes the commandment against adultery, and the New Testament includes frequent proscriptions against fornication. But even appeals to the authority of the Bible are driven by a more universal human motivation: the need to control, the desire to maintain order in the face of possible chaos. Sexual energy is powerful. Uncontrolled, it can wreak untold sorrow in the form of shame, jealousy, rivalry, and violence. Fear of this sorrow leads us to seek to impose both inner and outer control — personal control over our own

26. Why did Christianity become so rigidly anti-sex? Ernst Troeltsch says the origins of Christian emphasis on virgin purity are obscure, especially in light of the fact that the Bible more generally demonstrates an appreciation for the ordinary pleasures of life. Troeltsch speculates that the ancient Roman empire may have exerted an influence on the development of Christian values: "The civilized world of that day was suffering from a nervous disease which sought purification and support in religious ideas" (*The Social Teachings of the Christian Churches,* 2 vols. [New York: Harper, 1960], 1:106). This cultural desire for purity may have fostered growth of the ascetic ideal within the Christian priesthood. By the time of the medieval and Renaissance periods, the Christian conscience was plagued with guilt over sin in general and lust in particular. The world-denying spirituality of the monastics had spread in significant ways to the laity. According to the *Doctrinal de sapience* (1604), "A lewd glance, an impure thought with the least complaisance, these are deadly sins that condemn you to the everlasting flames." Quite predictably, extramarital relations remained forbidden, but beyond this, all sexual pleasure *within* marriage was also forbidden. In 1444 Franciscan Nicolo de Osimo said that marital sex could be considered sinless only if there were no "delectation of pleasure." Confessional manuals were built on Augustine's notion of the three goods of marriage: (1) *proles,* or procreation; (2) *fides,* or faithfulness, referring to performing one's sexual duty; and (3) *sacramentum,* or the indissolubility of the marital bond. Although a minority approved of making love for the sake of pleasure, the dominant view in the church was that pleasure as a sexual end even within marriage was sinful. Jean Delumeau comments that preachers who instilled fear regarding the dangers of marital sex "were trying to justify to themselves their own celibate life-style" (*Sin and Fear: The Emergence of a Western Guilt Culture, Thirteenth-Eighteenth Centuries,* trans. Eric Nicholson [New York: St. Martin's Press, 1990], p. 435; cf. pp. 214-20).

internal desires and social control over relationships. Like the other objects of concupiscence, sexual energy is something that we like to imagine we can tame and harness for our own purposes, but it is a wild horse and it is not easily broken.

Sex as Dirt

We need to digress here a bit and take a closer look at the matter of sex and why it has traditionally been associated with sin. I believe the roots of the association stem from deep-seated psychological factors — a fear of impurity on the one hand and a desire to gain control over potentially chaotic forces on the other.

When writing his important book *The Symbolism of Evil,* Paul Ricoeur placed sexual impurity in the category of defilement — that is, at a level of symbolic experience prior to that of sin. Sin involves the ideas of freedom, moral choice, and personal responsibility, but defilement involves a sense of contamination that precedes questions of innocence or guilt. For example, both the individual who commits incestual rape and the individual who is a victim of incest experience a loss of purity. What was clean has become unclean.

How can we explain this? We cannot. One of the points made by Ricoeur's phenomenological method is that we can only observe the phenomenon, recognizing that all explanations are dependent on what we observe. The Christian doctrine of sin is itself an attempt to explain rationally our more primitive experience, which is pre-rational in character. Defilement, like other manifestations of evil, resists comprehensive explanation by anybody.[27] Thus, when Christian theologians such as Augustine began to develop a doctrine of original sin and attempted to explain sexual impurity in terms of a free decision, complications and even contradictions were bound to appear.

In his fascinating book *Dirt, Greed, and Sex,* L. William Countryman endorses Ricoeur's assertion that sexual morality is rooted in the question of defilement. Countryman, a New Testament professor at the Church Divinity School of the Pacific and the Graduate Theological Union in Berkeley, examines the Bible and concludes that its pronouncements concerning sexual practices center on issues of purity

27. See Ricoeur, *The Symbolism of Evil* (Boston: Beacon Press, 1967), pp. 4, 236-39.

and impurity. A violation of the Holiness Code in Leviticus rendered a person unclean (hence Countryman's use of the word *dirt* in his book's title). Purity entails the avoidance of dirt.[28] More specifically, maintaining purity involved keeping dirt from entering the body, as outlined in rules governing what sorts of foods one might eat and outlawing certain sexual activities such as bestiality, homosexuality, incest, and adultery. Bodily cleanliness was meant to be symbolic of Israel's ethnic purity, reflecting the sharp distinction between the clean people of God and the unclean Gentiles.

The ministry of Jesus and his followers was aimed in part at breaking down the divisive barriers of ethnicity. The difference between the clean and the unclean remains, but it takes a turn inward. Rather than physical cleanliness, Jesus and Paul press for "purity of heart." Dirt is now associated with the intention to do harm. It comes from the inside out, not the outside in. The New Testament cuts the ties between physical cleanness and divine favor. Purity of heart is to be found in gentleness, unity, love, and justice. "If the gospel is indeed 'God's power for salvation to everyone who believes' (Rom. 1:16), then it must welcome the leper, the menstruant, the uncircumcised Gentile, indeed all the unclean without exception."[29] The change to inner purity shifted the foundation for ethics.

What about sex? To get at what he views as the central issue, Countryman introduces a second category: property.[30] The cardinal sin of the Bible's property ethic, he says, is greed. He argues that the notion of impurity has been replaced by that of greed in defining sexual sin. Greed *(pleonexia)* is akin to lust and refers to our inner desire to possess another person's property — his or her spouse, for instance — through adultery.[31] In this sense, greed becomes a social

28. See Countryman, *Dirt, Greed, and Sex* (Philadelphia: Fortress Press, 1988), p. 11.
29. Countryman, *Dirt, Greed, and Sex*, p. 142.
30. The etymology of *property* in English pertains to what "is proper to" each person. Property, writes Countryman, "is the wherewithal of being human in this age — which can also become, by grace, the wherewithal of becoming a fit citizen of the age to come" (*Dirt, Greed, and Sex*, p. 248).
31. See Countryman, *Dirt, Greed, and Sex*, pp. 109, 148. When interpreting Jesus' statement in the Sermon on the Mount that "everyone who looks at a woman with lust has already committed adultery with her in his heart" (Matt. 5:28), Countryman says, "Jesus was asserting that adultery does not consist primarily in the sexual union of two people at least one of whom is 'one flesh' with another person; it consists rather in the intention, acomplished or not, to take what belongs to another" (p. 178).

offense, disrupting the unity of the community. The ultimate affirmation of a property ethic is the assertion that we belong to Christ and Christ to God (1 Cor. 3:23).[32] Sexual desire is a natural appetite, and Christians need to guide their appetites in ways that are consistent with the fact that they are the property of Christ. This requires mutual support and communal harmony.

This rereading of the Bible does not lead to an endorsement of unbridled sexual license, however. Countryman acknowledges that Jesus and Paul condemn divorce, adultery, incest, prostitution, and homosexual promiscuity. However, he adds a subtlety:

> A Christian sexual ethic that remains true to its New Testament roots will have to discard its insistence on physical purity. . . . To be specific, the gospel allows no rule against the following, in and of themselves: masturbation, nonvaginal heterosexual intercourse, bestiality, polygamy, homosexual acts, or erotic art and literature. The Christian is free to be repelled by any or all of these and may continue to practice her or his own purity code in relation to them. What we are not free to do is impose our codes on others. Like all sexual acts, these may be genuinely wrong where they also involve an offense against the property of another, denial of the equality of women and men, or an idolatrous substitution of sex for the reign of God as the goal of human existence.[33]

Countryman concludes his book by affirming sex as a positive gift from God that "is to be received with delight and thankfulness."[34]

32. It is important to note that in Countryman's interpretation, the notion of property rights in Old Testament times was tied to a patriarchal hierarchy that subordinated women, slaves, and children. By making all believers the property of God, the New Testament transforms the notion of property. One of the results is equality between the sexes. See *Dirt, Greed, and Sex*, pp. 188, 241-42.

33. Countryman, *Dirt, Greed, and Sex*, pp. 244-45. Although he constantly casts his argument in terms of property ethics, Countryman probably relies more on an assumed notion of natural appetite than he himself acknowledges. For example, he maintains that for homosexuals the attraction to the same sex is natural, and on this basis he says that "to deny an entire class of human beings the right peaceably and without harming others to pursue the kind of sexuality that corresponds to their nature is a perversion of the gospel. Like the insistence of some on the circumcising of Gentile converts, it makes the keeping of purity rules a condition of grace" (*Dirt, Greed, and Sex*, p. 244). In short, he is arguing that the gospel frees our natures as long as communal harmony is not broken.

34. Countryman, *Dirt, Greed, and Sex*, p. 266.

But perhaps he says this too easily. If it is such a good gift, why do we frequently feel guilty about sexual desire? Why do we experience lust as a power that seems to control us? Why has sexual temptation so often been associated with the demonic? Why are Christians — including Countryman himself — willing to characterize celibacy as a gift?[35] If sex is a gift to be greeted with delight, then what warrants the celebration of celibacy? Is this not contradictory?

My point is that there seem to be certain enigmas built into our experience with sexuality, enigmas that become complexities if not outright contradictions at the level of theology. Although Countryman has made an argument that the New Testament repudiates the purity-dirt basis for constructing sexual ethics and substitutes the property-greed formula, he does not account for the amazing persistence through the centuries of defilement thinking. Nor does he wrestle with the intellectual problem — Ricoeur's problem — of trying to track the path from the experience of defilement up into a theoretical (i.e., theological) understanding of free will and sin.

Though the ideas of dirt and greed do bring to expression some aspects of our experience with sexuality, I wonder if another metaphor might not be more appropriate. Perhaps sexual desire is akin to nuclear power, which can be devastatingly destructive in a wartime context and crucially beneficial in a medical context. Sex is explosive. When we drop our guard, it contaminates. In the context of love, it produces the greatest experience of tenderness. Apart from love, it can be abusive and dehumanizing. In short, sex is a supra-individual power of considerable force, an ambiguous force that sometimes lends us energy and at other times seeks to control us from within. The task of ethics with regard to our sexuality, it would seem, is to provide guidance and control that will ensure that it is wholesomely productive and not wantonly destructive.

A Sexual Explosion

That sexuality will continue to be a powerful force in the foreseeable future can be illustrated by the explosion among the Presbyterians in 1991. The pressure had been on for three decades to liberalize sexual

35. Countryman, *Dirt, Greed, and Sex,* pp. 245, 264.

codes. The so-called sexual revolution of the 1960s, including as it did the widespread use of birth control devices and the rise of the women's liberation movement, helped to make the sex-within-marriage restriction appear anachronistic. Growing numbers of people showed a willingness to grant the legitimacy of gay rights, some even endorsing the notion of homosexual marriages. The rise in the number of divorced clergy and the demand in many quarters to ordain openly gay men and lesbian women engulfed one mainline denomination after another. Feminists were injecting words such as *justice* and *abuse* into the sexual vocabulary. In an attempt to respond discerningly to the many challenges these social changes were posing to the traditional moral vision, the Presbyterian Church U.S.A. commissioned a three-year study. The first result was a bombshell in the form of a carefully drafted study document entitled "Keeping Body and Soul Together: Sexuality, Spirituality, and Social Justice." The second result was an explosion of controversy that rocked the denomination from sea to shining sea.

The report contained more than forty recommendations, but interest focused almost exclusively on the handful that were controversial. Under the banner term "justice-love," the document recommended that Presbyterians not seek to begin their interpretation of Scripture with an objective reading of text and tradition but that they let their contemporary experience as sexual beings inform how they read the Bible. What this led to in the report was a legitimation of homosexual relationships, approval of sexual activity for adults who are not married, and endorsement of sexual education curricula and experimentation with masturbation for teenagers. John Carey, a pastorally sensitive scholar who chaired the Special Committee to Study Human Sexuality, wrote, "Human sexuality is intrinsically good. . . . The church needs to recover an understanding of personhood that has a legitimate place for the erotic and the affirmation of our bodies."[36] The authors of the report insisted that they did not condone sexual immorality. To the contrary, they said, by asserting the essential goodness of sexuality, the

---

36. Carey, "The Work and Vision of the General Assembly's Special Committee to Study Human Sexuality," *Presbyterian Outlook,* 11 March 1991, p. 6. At this writing, the Evangelical Lutheran Church in America has set out to walk the same path taken by the Presbyterians. It has produced a parallel document with a parallel set of recommendations entitled "The Church and Human Sexuality: A Lutheran Perspective."

value of sexual and spiritual wholeness, and their commitment to eros and passion, they were advocating mutuality, consent, integrity, responsibility, and fidelity. Within this framework they sought to grant dignity to all persons as sexual persons, whether heterosexual or homosexual, single or partnered.

The members of the Special Committee voted ten to six to accept the final draft. The minority of six wrote their own report. The minority subscribed to a more traditional hermeneutic. They asserted that in matters of faith, life, and salvation, the Bible has precedence over all other authorities, including any knowledge or experience we currently possess regarding sexuality. On this basis, the minority report upheld the view that marriage is the proper place for sexual relations and that the virtue of faithfulness — a faithfulness that mirrors God's faithfulness — ought to be characteristic of marriage. On the basis of its reading of the Bible, the minority report condemned homosexual practices to be unacceptable deviations from God's will for humankind. It added that homosexual persons must nonetheless be treated with great respect, love, and empathy.

At the Baltimore Convention Center in June 1991, the outraged General Assembly of the Presbyterian Church U.S.A. voted resoundingly 534 to 31 to reject the Special Committee report. The assembly also issued a disavowal of homosexual practices and reaffirmed its commitment to "the sanctity of the marital covenant between one man and one woman."

The liberal Presbyterians took a beating not only from their traditionalist confreres but also from secular critics. Writing in *The New Republic,* Camille Paglia lashed out at the Special Committee's assumptions about human sexuality and what she characterized as its capitulation to current feminist ideology. Despite its ostensible attempt to be compassionate, she said, the report is "a repressive, reactionary document. Its language is banal, its ideas simplistic, its view of human nature naive and sentimental." She further charged that its assumption of "the basic goodness of sexuality" projects "a happy, bouncy vision of human life" that ignores the seamy side, focusing on tender, safe, clean, hand-holding gays and lesbians rather than pederasts, prostitutes, strippers, pornographers, and sadomasochists. Paglia also objected to what she saw as the report's suffocating feminist frame of reference that puts the blame for all human sexual problems (e.g., rape within marriage) "on an unjust social system, a patriarchy of gigantic and demonized dimensions blanketing history like a river of molasses." Finally, Paglia denounced as arrogance the report's presumption of having the answer to what is in fact an insoluble problem. "The report is rooted in the arrogant, condescending, welfare-agency model of life: there all those poor, troubled souls out there whom we privileged, superior, all-knowing people must 'help.' But no one — least of all, liberal Presbyterians — can ever solve the problem of love."[37]

Christian Century editor James M. Wall, a conscientious spokesperson for what he calls the "liberal religious community," was saddened by the whole episode. He believes the Presbyterian study "correctly linked sexuality with commitment and responsibility." The problem facing liberal Christians, he wrote, is that they try to walk delicately "between the inflexible moralists on the one side and the freedom-worshipping secularists on the other." This requires sensitivity and subtlety. It is difficult to do, perhaps even impossible. "As a result the document was pilloried by religious moralists and by secularists, both of whom assume that religion is supposed to condemn and control, not guide and sustain. Confronted with this dual attack, a confused and embarrassed Presbyterian General Assembly retreated from its honest attempt to search for the meaning of a religiously based sexual commitment."[38]

Noting this, I forecast that future attempts at moral revision will be met with a similar fate, and it will seem to be due to deeply held commitments regarding God's will. The assumption that God's will revealed by religion is supposed to condemn and control human sexual behavior runs wide and deep. This is not due simply to ostensible narrow-mindedness on the part of Augustine.

37. Paglia, "The Joy of Presbyterian Sex," *New Republic,* 2 December 1991, pp. 24-27.

38. Wall, "Moral Wisdom and Sexual Conduct," *Christian Century,* 4 December 1991, p. 1124. *Time* magazine illustrated Wall's concern when it assured unbelievers that they have an interest in this religious faction fight because Christian convictions have an impact on social policy. Essayist Richard Brookhiser would not sell the defenders of tradition short by accusing them of blindly upholding the status quo. He wrote that sexual conservatives see themselves as defending divinely given guides to human behavior. No compromises. No live and let live. On issues of sexual morality, opponents face each other across a fissure in philosophical bedrock. See "Of Church Pews and Bedrooms," *Time,* 26 August 1991, p. 70.

Augustine Bashing

As I suggested above, Augustine bashing has become a new intellectual sport.[39] Many like to engage in this sport because it mixes together sex, religion, and righteous indignation. A case in point can be found in the work by Elaine Pagels, a religion professor at Princeton and author of the award-winning *Gnostic Gospels* (1981). The views she expresses in a later book, *Adam, Eve, and the Serpent* (1988), concern us here. Her stated objective in this work is to offer the reader a historical review of the patristic origins and development of the kind of Christian sexual morality that has led to the present controversies. This may appear to be a boring agenda, but Pagel's unabashed antipathy toward Augustine's doctrine of original sin generates some real excitement.

The question that provides the volume's focus is this: Since representatives of early Christian orthodoxy had lifted up the idea of moral freedom as central to the gospel, why is it that the majority of Christians for the last 1600 years have capitulated to Augustine's idea of moral bondage?[40] Citing ancient fathers such as Irenaeus, Tertullian, Clement, and even Pelagius, Pagels emphasizes that they considered *autoexousia* — the moral freedom to rule oneself — to be virtually synonymous with the gospel.[41] Her most vivid examples are celibate women martyrs such as Thecla, Perpetua, and Felicitas. By choosing celibacy, these heroic women freed themselves from family responsi-

---

39. Augustine provides a ripe target for those engaged in giant killing, for few even approach his stature in Western culture. Historian Delumeau observes that "the work of the Bishop of Hippo was immense. It covered all the great dogmatic, moral, ascetic, and mystical problems of Christianity, and moved our civilization toward the awareness and thorough study of the human individual's inner workings." Augustine is cited authoritatively on both sides of most every important controversy. In addition to providing the standard for orthodoxy in medieval scholasticism, Augustine was the herald of humanism through Erasmus as well as the patron theologian of the Reformation through Luther. Calvin described Augustine as superior to all dogmas, and the Jansenists praised him as doctor of doctors, discerning, solid, irrefutable, angelic, seraphic, most excellent, and ineffably admirable. "The great Augustinian themes — cognition, love and wisdom, memory and presence — have fed European thought for many centuries. Throughout the years, every Christian renaissance has drawn from Saint Augustine as from an ever-flowing spring" (*Sin and Fear*, p. 261).

40. See Pagels, *Adam, Eve, and the Serpent* (New York: Random House, 1988), p. 152.

41. Pagels, *Adam, Eve, and the Serpent*, p. 99.

bilities to devote themselves solely to matters of the spirit. By choosing rebellion against Roman emperor worship — rebellion that put them on the path to martyrdom — they gave expression to a strength of human will that no political power could destroy. With regard to their own sexual inclinations, Pagels cites Mother Teresa's characterization of the women as "athletes" for God who triumphed over their natural proclivities.[42]

These women went to their deaths while the Christian church was an oppressed minority, alienated from the Roman establishment. But the situation changed when Constantine became emperor and the Christian church became officially established. Political support for the Christian church provided the new context within which Augustine — according to Pagels's interpretation — repudiated human freedom. Although Pagels says she does not want to reduce theological advances to political agendas, she hints that Augustine's picture of human beings enslaved to sin was politically convenient. If we as individuals cannot control ourselves, then we need a big government such as Rome to do so.[43]

The Augustine that Pagels describes seems self-contradictory. On the one hand, he maintains that prior to the fall, Adam and Eve possessed so much freedom that their choice to sin produced all the suffering and death that has occurred ever after. Human freedom has — or at least once had — the power to alter nature. On the other hand, those of us who live after the fall are now helpless victims of our lusts and passions. We cannot rise above our desires. Our wills are bound. We are powerless to do anything but suffer the indignity of living a fated existence, victims of our ancestors' destiny. Using the works of Julian, Pagels criticizes Augustine for confusing sin and nature. In what she presents as a refutation of Augustine's position, she argues that sexual desire and mortality are not the result of a sinful decision but that they are natural aspects of our finite constitution as

42. Pagels, *Adam, Eve, and the Serpent*, p. 83.

43. Pagels, *Adam, Eve, and the Serpent*, pp. xxvii, 120, 145. Not all contemporary women interpreters are Augustine bashers. Margaret R. Miles reads Augustine's *Confessions* quite sympathetically and yet asks Pagels's honest question regarding the neglect of women's perspective on desire. "It is ultimately the passivity — the intellectual and practical laziness — of generations of Christians who adopted Augustine's formulations without discernment of their concrete effects within their societies that is to be blamed for the destructive effects of Augustine's ideas" (*Desire and Delight*, p. 99).

human beings. No human decision, she says — not even the decision of Adam and Eve — could alter the course of nature.

I offer three thoughts. First, I think that Pagels's interpretation of Augustine might be a bit one-sided or incomplete. Although she cites the *Confessions* and *The City of God,* she overlooks Augustine's essays "On Free Will" and "The Spirit and the Letter" and those parts of *The City of God* that describe the infusion of God's Spirit that gives us freedom.[44] Augustine does indeed affirm human freedom — but as a gift of God's grace! It is simplistic to describe Augustine as a theologian who repudiates the gospel of freedom.

Second, it is equally simplistic to contrast pre-Augustinian *auto-exousia* with what Pagels characterizes as Augustinian bondage of the will. She fails to take account in the sources she cites of the suprahuman factor in evil — namely, the Evil One. Of course the early Church Fathers affirmed human free will, but they did so against a backdrop of suprahuman demonic powers. The Devil and his angels seek to enter the human mind and persuade us to participate in apostasy.[45] What this reflects — and sexual temptation may be a prime example — is our experience of powerful external forces seeking to influence us to do their bidding. It is within the whelming flow of such forces that we assert the freedom to choose between what is better and what is worse. We are engaged in an unending struggle to determine just where the external forces leave off and the internal freedom takes over, because at root these two apparently contradictory things belong to the selfsame experience of evil.

Third, even granting the weaknesses in Pagels's presentation, I think she does make a positive contribution to the current discussion by lifting up what seems to me to be an obvious fact — namely, that sexual proclivity and human mortality are essential aspects of our human nature. We were created sexual beings before the fall. We need not categorically identify spontaneous sexual desire with a sign of our fallenness. There is a widespread neurosis afoot in Christendom, and despite Augustine's penchant for nuance and thoroughness, what has been communicated through the centuries is the misleading message

44. Augustine, *The City of God,* 22.30.
45. See, for example, Justin Martyr, *Second Apology,* 7; Irenaeus, *Against Heresies,* 4.24; Athenagoras, *A Plea for the Christians,* 27; Origen, *On First Principles,* 3.3.5; and Methodius, *From the Discourse on the Resurrection,* 3.2.

that we should feel guilty over natural things. I do not believe we should feel guilty over natural things. The world is waiting for the sage who can distinguish for us genuine guilt from artificial or neurotic guilt.

Eve and Evil

One thing Augustine bashing rightly does is put us on the trail of a possible distortion in our understanding of sin, especially concupiscence, stemming from the unbalanced influence of too many male theologians. In particular, I believe we can identify a distorting mechanism at work within the male psyche that has been either overlooked or inadequately understood by many who deal in such matters. It takes the form of displacement, a phenomenon Jesus alerted us to when he told us to remove the log from our own eye before trying to remove a speck from someone else's eye.

To describe how this displacement works, let us begin with a look at the fall. In the Art Institute of Chicago hangs a 1544 painting by Augustus Cordus, "The Fall of Man with Scenes of Creation," which will serve as an example. Adam and Eve sit nude in the Garden of Eden sharing a single apple. Over Eve's left shoulder the serpent is craftily whispering into her ear. What is noteworthy about this painting is the serpent. It has the body of a lizard but the head of a miniature human woman. The face of the serpent resembles the face of Eve herself. Cordus is implicitly placing the burden of responsibility for the fall on the woman. Sirach 25:24 similarly indicates that sin has its beginning in a woman. But the original story in Genesis says no such thing. When Adam tries to pass the buck by blaming "the woman you [God] gave me," God is not fooled. God does not declare Adam to be an innocent victim of someone else's deceit. Man and woman are equally guilty, and both receive the same forcible expulsion from the garden. If this is the original symbol, what accounts for the tendency to associate Eve alone with the source of evil? Is Genesis including in its very portrayal of sin the tendency of men to blame women for their own fallenness, which in effect is sin compounded?[46]

---

46. A contrast between the biblical account and a Greek parallel is noteworthy. According to Hesiod, Zeus, in his anger over Prometheus's theft of the sun's fire, sent the beautiful woman Pandora to earth. She was the means by which Zeus punished

I would like to test the hypothesis that the phenomenon of temptation for males has had an identifiable and perhaps deleterious influence on Christian spirituality and theology. Here is how it works. We begin with the demonstrable fact that most men beyond the age of puberty experience a physiological reaction when their eyes fix on a sexually attractive woman. Sexual desire is unquestionably biological in origin; it is universal and cannot be dismissed as just one more cultural form. Yet sexual lust has an enormous impact on culture. It is reflected in the ancient literature of Asia and Europe, being the driving theme of Jupiter's exploits in Ovid's *Metamorphoses* and the reason Rama's lovely wife, Sita, was kidnapped in the Indian epic the *Ramayana*.[47] Certainly the contemporary entertainment industry exploits this male proclivity to an absurd degree with increasingly perverse portrayals of male fantasies. Even Jesus acknowledged what is going on here when during the Sermon on the Mount he described a man as committing "lust in his heart" when sizing up an attractive woman. Because of the universality of the phenomenon and the near impossibility of a man ever ridding himself of this fact of nature, it is likely that Jesus made this point with a tinge of humor. How is it possible to stop it? By cutting out one's eye and throwing it away? This is absurd! Jesus' main point was that commitment to God's law can be interpreted so stringently as to call us to go beyond our natural inclinations. It is clear that we have the capacity to resist the temptation to commit adultery even though we cannot rid ourselves of the inclination to do so. Among other things, Jesus is giving us the practical advice of catching temptation at its initial stage.

Is it possible to say that, unfortunately, later generations lost their sense of humor? Did they take Jesus literally and mistakenly confuse

---

the human race. Hidden behind her seductive beauty was divine revenge. When Pandora opened the forbidden box, out flew the evils that have plagued us ever since. Unlike Eve in the Garden of Eden, who was originally good, the woman in the Greek myth was originally evil and bore the divine intention to bring harm to earth. From the Hebrew and Christian point of view, the female gender is not inherently evil.

47. Hinduism provides a particularly convoluted form of theologically based misogyny. The Hindu view of evil is tied to karma and the cycle of rebirth. Each rebirth starts the soul once again on the path of a life of suffering. The fact that women give birth makes the female sex particularly responsible. The ascetic mind-set of Hinduism pictures women as drawing men down into the realm of the physical with its accompanying decay and death. Sex and death come together. Wendy O'Flaherty adds that "abstract goddesses were cited with increasing frequency as the cause of evil on earth" (*The Origins of Evil in Hindu Mythology*, p. 27).

temptation with sin? If so, this might account for the perverted spiritual asceticism that seeks to rid the male mind of what Jesus called "adultery of the heart." Men in monastic orders were asked to take a vow to the Almighty to do the unnatural and the impossible — to eliminate lust. Perhaps a few spiritual virtuosos were able to accomplish it, but by far the vast majority of monks were simply left with the struggle, a struggle they could not win but would feel too guilty to give up on. Even though they never committed acts of adultery, they felt as guilty as they would have had they done so. Their souls could never be purified from the basic biological drive or even from the inclination to appreciate the warmth of feminine tenderness. This led to inevitable frustration and a concomitant sense of unworthiness. Even for those in the church who never took vows or entered religious orders, the very fact that the monk or nun was hailed as a moral ideal heaped piles of guilt upon the internal stirrings of the human sexual drive.[48]

At this point, displacement — passing the buck — steps in with its distortion. The woman comes to be viewed as the temptress. The inability of the virtue-seeking man to overcome his lust is sublimated into an anger at the woman, whom he blames for his own lack of self-control. Society now introduces dress codes that de-sexify the woman. Strict rules of segregation go into effect. These measures are aimed at helping men to control the uncontrollable. A woman who reveals too much of her body or who walks where she should not is interpreted as "asking for it." Because the male psyche is all tied up in knots, the resulting frustration and anger are displaced and transferred to the woman. Thus arise secondary symbolism and verbal allusions that closely associate the female gender with the weakness of the human race as a whole.[49]

---

48. This component in the history of misogyny arises from the false belief that physical sex is inherently evil, a belief that comes not from the Bible but from "Platonic Hellenistic mysticism," says Emil Brunner. "This idea, actualized in the Catholic ideal of virginity, was not wholly overcome by the Reformation; above all it became powerful in Puritanism and Pietism, and more or less unconsciously and secretly it has determined the thought of Christendom down to the present day. It is a sign of the terrible anti-Christian inheritance, and it has wrought infinite harm and disaster" (*The Divine Imperative* [Philadelphia: Westminster Press, 1947], p. 364).

49. In a diatribe against wearing jewelry and dying hair, Tertullian in the third century demanded that Christian women dress humbly. In an argument that associates the weakness of the human race as a whole with women in particular, he says the following to the woman reader: "You are the devil's gateway: you are the unsealer of

Objectively speaking, of course, this is not fair. Women are not to blame for male biology or the misunderstanding of what should constitute Christian spirituality. But the difficulties of displacement here should not be underestimated in either their subtlety or their power. They may be reflected realistically already in the Garden of Eden story itself, where Adam tries to blame Eve. Eve then tries to blame the serpent and, by implication, God, who allegedly got them all into this mess by creating them in the first place. Passing the buck is part of the dynamic of sin. So complex is this process of displacement that we ultimately end up blaming God for our predicament.

I do not want to suggest by this that women do not similarly wrestle with the problem of temptation and displacement. If the manner in which women wrestle with sexual desire is not identical to that of men, it is at least parallel. Christian nuns who take the vow of chastity confront similar challenges to their commitments. And there is nothing peculiarly Christian about this type of spirituality. Sexual abstinence for a few days was part of the prehunt ritual in archaic hunter societies, and celibacy is considered a sign of spiritual merit in the most sublime mystical traditions. Mother Krishnavai of Ananda Ashram in India, a Hindu saint who commands great respect and admiration, claims that she realized she was on the brink of cosmic consciousness when she found she was completely devoid of sexual desire. She says it took forty years of self-denial and meditative discipline to reach this point.

Western society is by no means the only one with a tradition of dress codes and public behavior formulated to reduce the unleashing of male sexual aggression. The full covering of women in Islamic culture and

---

that (forbidden) tree: you are the first deserter of the divine law: you are she who persuaded him whom the devil was not valiant enough to attack. You destroyed so easily God's image, man. On account of your desert — that is, death — even the Son of God had to die" (*On the Apparel of Women*, 1.1, in *The Ante-Nicene Fathers*, 10 vols., ed. Alexander Roberts and James Donaldson [Grand Rapids: William B. Eerdmans, 1885-1897], 4:14). If Tertullian were writing today, we would surely judge him to be chauvinist and manipulative. He scapegoats women and then blames the victimized woman even for the death of the Savior.

Delumeau points out the misogynist elements in the theology of sin from the thirteenth to the eighteenth centuries in the "iconographic evocations of *Frau Welt* (Dame World), who is exquisitely beautiful in front and repulsively ugly behind. For the monastic world, woman could easily represent the ultimate in decay insofar as she incarnated a self-evident image of sin and death. As a matter of fact, antifeminism and the macabre were intimately linked" (*Sin and Fear*, p. 47).

rules for riding on separate sides of the bus in India serve to limit the mobility and opportunity of women. Such mores may at bottom be an expression of a love-hate relationship that society as a whole has with its women, a love-hate relationship produced by the frustration of the male psyche. Social structures serve to control women because the men are worried that they may not be able to control themselves. Symbolically the woman comes to look like a temptress, and theologically an inordinate amount of emphasis is placed on sin as concupiscence. Judged by modern standards of gender equality, such theology functions to restrict the freedom of women and as such is clearly unjust. But if we have in fact uncovered the underlying psycho-social structure of the injustice, then we must grant that the ascetic ideal in Christian spirituality is not the sole source of this social misogyny but rather one aspect of a larger and perhaps even universal human predicament.

What theologians need to do first is formulate an *inclusive concept of sin* and then take note of its gender-specific expressions. I have already spoken of sin as the human attempt to fixate the present and resist God's future — that is, to absolutize our own part and sacrifice God's whole. As Letty Russell puts it, sin is breaking away from community; it is the "refusal to be radically helped."[50]

50. Russell, *Becoming Human* (Philadelphia: Westminster Press, 1982), p. 80. Russell is a feminist theologian who seeks an inclusive understanding of sin, in contrast to some feminist theologians who speak of sharp divisions between the genders and attribute to men most of what has been traditionally considered sin. Nel Noddings, who is clearly a non- or even an anti-theological feminist, recognizes as I do here that the image of the woman as temptress derives in large part from male projection. But she proceeds from this to the customary Augustine bashing, arguing that the feminist's perspective on evil is essentially different from the male perspective. Women have a privileged position, she says repeatedly, by which she means that because women have been victimized they have a better understanding of evil. She contends that the good and evil dimensions of reality are more naturally integrated in the woman's consciousness, enabling her to play a virtual messianic role as a transformer of society by fostering relationships. Women transform by reconciling disputing parties, she says, whereas men break relationships by clinging to an understanding of virtue as principle. But in effect Noddings is comparing male sins with female virtues here. No wonder they look so different. See *Women and Evil* (Berkeley and Los Angeles: University of California Press, 1989), pp. 19, 34, 35, 81, 240.

Before concluding this discussion, I'd like to make one more interesting observation about Noddings's position: she breaks the association between evil and sin. Sin is traditionally defined as evil committed against God, but God plays no essential role in Noddings's view of evil. Instead, she associates evil with the pain of broken human relationships. The net result is evil without sin. I take very seriously the feminist critique

Although we must begin by assuming that men and women are equal partners in the one world of sin, perhaps in light of the discussion in the chapter on pride we can say that the distinctively male form of sin is self-assertion, whereby the community of the whole is broken by the male desire to dominate. Perhaps the distinctively female form of sin derives from excessive dependence — that is, the failure to develop an independent self and thereby make a creative contribution to the community as a whole.

Granting this, we should note in addition that many in the Christian tradition have committed sin in the very act of formulating a doctrine of sin. Careless teachings about sin have led to misogyny, which is itself a sin. In our own time this process is being reversed by some feminists who are rewriting history so that men are to blame for the world's troubles and women are exonerated. This only adds to the problem, however. Once we put a wall between the genders, mud seems to fly in both directions. I would suggest that two things are required at this juncture: an affirmation that sin is universal plus a confession that mud belongs on *our* side of the fence, whichever side that may be. We must be both evangelical and critical to admit that even theologians tend to break community by blaming only one gender for a problem belonging to us all.

Specifically, the subtle sin to which I am referring, common to both genders, is *self-justification* through *scapegoating*. It begins with the desire to know the difference between good and evil in the Garden of Eden. Once we know the difference and can draw the line between good and evil, we are tempted to put ourselves on the good side of the line. This then justifies us in condemning those whom we identify as standing on the bad side of the line. Once it is clear to us that we are good and the others are bad, then in the name of justice we may condemn the others to suffer punishment. In order to pull this off with a clear conscience, we call on the help of an ideology that justifies our doing violence to others. Our ideologies reinforce our certainty that we are in the right by hiding our own guilt from us. We can hide if we can pin our guilt on someone else. This brings us to the concept of

of the long-standing misogyny associated with the Christian tradition, but I believe that this misogyny can be judged sinful on the basis of the criteria bequeathed us by this same tradition. I see no advantage in an ideology that controverts the tradition or seeks to divide the genders on the essential structure of sin.

scapegoating and the twisted tendency to seek self-justification through the sacrifice of someone else who is innocent. This subtle but damaging dimension of sin will occupy our attention in the next chapter.

Addiction and Grace

Supposing my interpretation of Augustine to be correct — namely, that he cited sexual lust as a template on experience to render the structure of sin more visible — it is nonetheless the case that in the midst of the confusions wrought by recent controversies regarding liberalization of sexual mores and feminist discontent with tradition, this template probably cannot serve us as well as it served him. Could we find another template that would be more illuminating in our context? One candidate might be the concept of addiction. Contemporary investigators seem to say much about addiction today that Augustine said about concupiscence in his time.

Addiction and its twin, codependence, are processes over which we are powerless, says Anne Wilson Schaef. Addiction takes control of us and leads us to become progressively more compulsive and obsessive. We are probably all familiar with substance addictions such as dependence on alcohol or narcotics. We can also develop substance addictions to nicotine, caffeine, and even food. With this pattern in mind, we can also identify *process addictions,* one example of which is an addiction to money. Addiction to money is progressive: it takes more and more to achieve a fix, and eventually no amount is enough. People addicted to money or similar processes (e.g., gambling, sex, work, religion, worry) deny certain inner feelings and look for relief from anxiety from the outside. Addicts are typically caught up in addictive social systems, which include codependents — people who are addicted to the addicts. Both addicts and people in addictive relationships are characteristically obsessed with controlling what is out of control, especially their inner feelings.[51] How extensive are addictive relation-

51. See Schaef, *When Society Becomes an Addict* (San Francisco: Harper & Row, 1987), pp. 22ff., 41ff. Schaef places fear in the role that has been assigned to anxiety in our discussion. "Fear permeates the Addictive System," she writes. Female codependents "are always fearful because they believe that they cannot exist without male validation and approval" (p. 93).

ships? When Schaef adds up the number of alcoholics and codependents in the United States, she gets a number larger than the total U.S. population.[52] She settles for describing our entire society as addicted.[53] Although Schaef decries the theological idea of original sin, she makes one of the best contemporary cases for the existence of original sin.[54] She helps us to understand the human predicament, but, having dismissed any consideration of divine grace, the only means of salvation she proposes is perpetual psychotherapy.

Gerald G. May takes up the same concern, analyzes addiction, and concludes that the only remedy is grace. Although he is a medical doctor, not a trained theologian or scriptural scholar, May believes he knows what sin is: It is that which turns us away from love. Two forms of sin turn us away from love, he says: repression and addiction. Of the two, addiction is worse because it enslaves us. "While repression stifles desire, addiction *attaches* desire, bonds and enslaves the energy of desire to certain specific behaviors, things, or people. These objects of attachment then become preoccupations and obsessions; they come to rule our lives."[55] He concludes that only grace — defined as the active expression of God's love — can liberate us. According to May, grace is the most powerful force in the universe. It can transcend repression, addiction, and every other internal or external power that seeks to oppress the freedom of the human heart. Grace is where our hope lies.[56]

52. Schaef, *When Society Becomes an Addict,* p. 15.

53. Schaef's book is misnamed. The title is *When Society Becomes an Addict,* but it contains no analysis of society as a whole; Schaef discusses only individuals in society.

54. Schaef is mercilessly critical of Christianity, attacking the idea of the martyr on the grounds that martyrdom is simply a form of the disease of codependence (p. 33). She charges the church with teaching niceness (p. 58). She contends that by teaching eternal life, the church retards change in people's earthly life (p. 101). She does not bother to back these charges up with documentation or even argumentation. After distinguishing between religion and spirituality, Schaef attacks theology on the grounds that it employs reason. "Spirituality cannot be approached only through the left brain. Left-brain theologies teach us to rationalize, objectify, and be logical about our spiritual selves. The trouble is that spirituality has nothing to do with rational, objective, logical thinking. It has to do with the *experience* of the spiritual self, which tends to be irrational, nonobjective and illogical" (p. 92). What this anti-church and anti-theology prejudice leads to is a description of addictive behavior without reference to God. It is illuminating but less than complete.

55. Gerald G. May, *Addiction and Grace* (San Francisco: Harper & Row, 1988), p. 3.

56. See May, *Addiction and Grace,* pp. 4-5.

Included in May's list of addictions we find a good deal more than just drugs and alcohol: nicotine, caffeine, sugar, chocolate, work, performance, responsibility, intimacy, being liked, helping others, and so on. In themselves such things are not evil, but when they become obsessions they rob us of our willpower. One part of the will wants to be free while the other part wants to remain addicted. Resolutions fail. The slavery resides within. If we are to break free, we need nothing short of a transformation of desire. May has no need to bash Augustine here, because Augustine himself understood clearly what we are rediscovering today — namely, that we need grace to free us from ourselves to become our true selves.[57]

How do we overcome our addictions? *We* don't. God does. How? May believes with Augustine that each of us has an inborn yearning for God.[58] God calls us from within. We need only heed that call. Spiritual discipline can help. This doctor's prescription for overcoming addiction is prayer, meditation, and action. These add up to listening to the divine call, to allowing ourselves to develop trust in God. Our measure of faith is the degree to which we trust the truth of grace.[59] Trust permits the human spirit to flow with the divine spirit, personal power with divine power. It is grace working through our faith that returns to us our freedom.

Through grace, with our assent, our desire begins to be transformed. Energies that once were dedicated simply to relieving ourselves from pain now become dedicated to a larger goodness, more aligned with the true treasure of our hearts. Where we were once interested only in conquering a specific addiction, we are now claiming a deeper

57. In his *Confessions* (8.5), Augustine speaks of something very similar to our current concept of addiction — namely, sin understood as the force of habit that binds the will and keeps it asleep. The need for grace is reiterated by twentieth-century Augustinians in terms of the "impossible possibility." Barth and Niebuhr reached at least a partial agreement at this point. They parted ways over a distinction between what is real and what is unreal. Niebuhr argued that love is unreal in the sense that it is the unattainable ideal. Barth maintained that it is sin that is unreal. "Barth and Niebuhr both used the term 'impossible possibility,'" notes George Hunsinger, "but in diametrically opposite ways. What for Barth was the touchstone of reality (love) was for Niebuhr the 'impossible possibility,' whereas what for Barth was the 'impossible impossibility' (sin) was for Niebuhr the touchstone of reality" (*How to Read Karl Barth: The Shape of His Theology* [New York: Oxford University Press, 1991], p. 39).

58. May, *Addiction and Grace,* pp. 1, 92.

59. May, *Addiction and Grace,* p. 130.

longing, and we are concerned with becoming more free from attachments in general, for the sake of love.[60]

When May speaks of cases in which this formula has been invoked, he uses words such as *deliverance* and *miraculous*.[61]

The model of addiction and codependence can help to illuminate the state of concupiscence in which we find ourselves. We are born into it. We initially inherit at least our disposition if not our actual patterns of behaving from the families into which we are born. And we pass it on to our children. It confronts us as a conflict that rages within us while taking the form of an obsession with something outside us. We are addicts because the outside has become the inside. We do not want to be addicts, but our wills are bound. We cannot by our own reason or strength transform ourselves. We need grace. We need a loving and transforming power that comes to us from beyond, a power that makes us into who we truly are.

60. May, *Addiction and Grace,* p. 150.

61. May, *Addiction and Grace,* p. 151. May proposes a version of cooperative grace here. He emphasizes the role of human will in deliverance so that we do not too easily say it is entirely God's business. Right along with the rest of the history of theologians from Augustine onward, May frets because he cannot "explain the coinherence of grace and will" (p. 156). Join the crowd, Dr. May.

6

SELF-JUSTIFICATION
Looking Good While
Scapegoating Others

*People, real people, rarely choose evil. . . . We do evil in the
name of some overriding good — usually, paradoxically, the
conquest of evil.*

Nel Noddings, *Women and Evil*

"He is a sinner," you are pleased to say.
Then love him for the sake of Christ, I pray.
If on His gracious words you place your trust —
   "I came to call sinners, not the just" —
Second His call; which if you will not do,
You'll be the greater sinner of the two.

John Byrom, "Self-Righteousness"

Down deep each of us knows four things: (1) we know that we are
going to die; (2) we know that concupiscence will fail to give us
immortality; (3) we know the difference between good and evil; and,
although we may not know it for certain, (4) we suspect that good
may be eternal. In order to maintain the illusion that concupiscence
will in fact succeed, we invent lies — lies that identify us with what is
good. Sometimes these lies identify some others as evil, justifying the

161

conclusion that they should die and we should live. Identifying ourselves with the good is called *self-justification*. Identifying others with evil is called *scapegoating*. The two fit together like a nut and a bolt.

In this chapter we turn to perhaps the most subtle and dangerous dimension of sin. It involves much more than the mere perpetration of evil. It involves the twisting and contamination of the good. It is important to note that in the Garden of Eden story, the tempting serpent is not described as the most evil of God's creatures but as the most subtle, the most crafty (Gen. 3:1). It is also important to note the content of the temptation — namely, to gain the knowledge of good and evil. Why would we want the knowledge of good and evil? So that we can become like God. What is God like? God is good.

Now, the logic here is counterintuitive. It flies in the face of the way we think things should work. We are prone to ask: Isn't it good for us to seek the good? And, if we are to know the good, do we not have to know evil by way of contrast? Is it not the case that the good people among us are those with a conscience, those who try hard to distinguish good from evil? And, once we distinguish between good and evil, is it not our duty to identify ourselves with what is good? If we are to be moral people, we should try to make ourselves good and to stamp out evil, right? It seems right. But the Adam and Eve story says just the opposite. Why? Because of the subtle nature of the mechanism of self-justification. It blinds us. It distorts the truth.

In the Garden of Eden story, note that once the sin of eating the forbidden fruit is discovered, a chain of self-justifications ensues. Adam blames Eve, thereby implying that he is innocent. Eve blames the serpent, thereby implying that she is innocent. And who made the serpent? God, the creator of all things, of course. God is indirectly blamed for creating the serpent and putting the temptation in the garden in the first place. Adam and Eve have learned to draw the line between good and evil, and they immediately try to place themselves on the good side of the line, even if this means placing God on the evil side.[1]

This pattern of self-justification runs deep in the human character and leads to the scapegoating of nature, of other people, and even of

---

1. This is Luther's analysis, to which he added, "This is the last step of sin, to insult God and to charge Him with being the originator of sin" (*Lectures on Genesis Chapters 1–5*, vol. 1 of *Luther's Works*, ed. Jaroslav Pelikan, trans. George V. Schick [St. Louis: Concordia, 1958], p. 179).

God. The problem this creates for God is that it makes it almost impossible for him to make his divine goodness known, because we are constantly trying to steal that goodness for ourselves. Divine self-revelation becomes exceedingly difficult. God — at least the gracious dimension of God — will be evident only to those who aren't trying to justify themselves.

I Didn't Do It!

When I was six years old and attending the Charles A. Lindbergh Elementary School in Dearborn, Michigan, the boys in the neighborhood formed a most interesting ring of bicycle reflector thieves. One day I saw Bobby from across the street open a bag and reveal a dozen or so bright red reflectors. They gleamed from within the bag like jewels in a cache of buried treasure. His brother Billy and also the notorious Louie about whom I wrote earlier had similar bags.

"Where'd you get those?" I asked, filled with mimetic desire.

"I'll show you," Bobby answered. Then he took me to Roony's drugstore, where two Schwinn bikes were parked out front. "I saw them go in for a Coke," he said. "We've got plenty of time." We each took a bicycle. I laid myself down behind the rear wheel and reached up to unscrew the nut behind the fender. The reflector and nut came loose easily. We both ran home with our prizes, and I began my collection. I had learned the method, so it was not long before I, too, had a bag full of stolen reflectors, many of which I could never have afforded to buy with my allowance money.

But how could I enjoy them? I could not display them to anyone other than my partners in crime. I could not take the best ones and put them on my bike without one of my parents asking me where I had gotten it. All I could do was wait until the family had gone to bed at night and then sneak into my desk drawer to admire my spoils.

Eventually word traveled around the neighborhood that children going to and from school were losing their reflectors in unusually high numbers. Suspicions arose. My mother put me on the spot: "Have you been stealing reflectors?" Nope. After repeated interrogations, I could feel the pressure building. I thought I might be able to relieve the pressure with a little squeal.

"I think I saw Bobby with a bag full of reflectors," I said. My mother was by no means stupid, so my tactic was doomed to failure. Eventually the truth came out, I had to give up all the reflectors, and I received an appropriate punishment, even though I cannot at the moment recall what it was. Giving up the reflectors was bad enough.

Looking back on the reflector incident, I can see at work in me the same concupiscence that Augustine experienced when stealing the pears. And even though I knew I was guilty, I wanted others such as my family to keep thinking of me as an honest child. Hiding the loot constituted a physical lie, a pattern of dishonest behavior. When confronted with interrogation, I justified myself first with an outright lie and later with a misleading truth. The function of the misleading truth was to divert accusations from me to Bobby. My self-justification led me to scapegoat Bobby. I wonder what Bobby was telling his parents.

As I mentioned earlier, my wife, Jenny, teaches first grade. Each morning the arriving children place the items they have brought for "share time" (Jenny's version of Show-and-Tell) on the shelf behind her classroom desk. One morning there appeared a crystal rock of striking beauty. Some child was planning on sharing this favorite rock at the appointed time in the afternoon. Over lunch period the crystal rock disappeared. The theft called for disciplinary action. Jenny addressed the class sternly: "Unless the crystal rock is put back on the shelf by two o'clock, we will not have any more share times." At two o'clock, little Leslie opened her desk and there beheld the missing crystal.[2] She brought it to the teacher's desk whimpering that she had not been the one to steal it. Because of other observations Jenny had made that day, she was convinced that Leslie was innocent. The guilty party or parties had slipped the rock into her desk to make Leslie the scapegoat for the class. Here we have an innocent scapegoat.

Scapegoats may be either innocent or guilty. We may even engage in mutual scapegoating while engaging in mutual self-justification. One day Adrian came to Jenny on the playground during recess complaining that Andrew had hit him. "I wasn't doing anything, and he slugged me." Jenny went after Andrew and benched him. Ten minutes sitting on the bench watching while the other children enjoy the recess is a formidable punishment. Jenny sat down next to Andrew and asked what had happened. "Adrian came up behind me and tried to strangle me. So I punched him." Assuming that Andrew was telling the truth, we can see

2. The names of the children have been changed in these accounts.

that Adrian had tried to pretend that he was the victim, the innocent one. So he sought out the judge, the teacher, to inflict recompense on Andrew, his intended scapegoat. For his part, Andrew admitted just enough guilt to accept the punishment, but even in his admission he sought to justify himself as the innocent victim of Adrian's sneak attack. Who knows what went on prior to the attempted strangulation?

The motive for self-justification and scapegoating in the first grade is obviously hedonistic — that is, the motive is to avoid the pain of punishment and perhaps enjoy the pleasure of seeing someone else punished. As we grow up, various people in authority, such as parents and teachers and eventually bosses, mete out the punishment and pleasure, and we develop behaviors that we hope will *look good* to them, behaviors that are pleasing, that will pass judgment and set the stage for rewards rather than punishment. We quickly internalize these behavior patterns, and once that happens, we may well unthinkingly ascribe to God in heaven the role of punisher and pleasure giver. In our minds we construct the image of a God of justice who functions like an overgrown parent or teacher, and then we try to justify ourselves before this imagined deity. We try to make ourselves look good for God. This is not the real God, of course. This is the God we have projected in our imaginations for the purpose of validating our lies.

In September of 1990 the Canadian town of Provost was greeted with the "Alberta Aryan Fest." White supremacists held a weekend rally in celebration of their own special amalgamation of hatred, bigotry, and self-aggrandizement. The scapegoats such groups typically blame for the world's problems are Jews and blacks. The Aryans ascribed to themselves the monstrous title "The Church of Jesus Christ–Christian Aryan Nations."[3] Like the first graders using their teacher to do their

3. The event upset most of the residents of Provost, but it also led to some significant reflection. "The obvious misuse of the cross of Christ," wrote Pastor Ted Arndt, "spurred our people to focus more clearly on the real meaning and purpose of the cross, prompting us to uphold a higher way of life found in Jesus Christ" ("The Aryan Weekend in Provost," *The Canadian Lutheran*, January 1991, p. 21A). This reminds me of Reinhold Niebuhr's description of self-justification as the "sin of self-righteousness" in terms of a progression from moral pride to spiritual pride. Religion is no rescue here; indeed, it is part of the problem. "Religion is not simply as is generally supposed an inherently virtuous human quest for God. It is merely a final battleground between God and man's self-esteem. . . . The worst form of intolerance is religious intolerance, in which the particular interests of the contestants hide behind religious absolutes" (*The Nature and Destiny of Man*, 2 vols. [New York: Scribner's, 1941-1943], 1:201).

dirty work, the white supremacists used religious symbols to appeal to transcendent values in support of their dirty work. Later in this book I will argue that this sort of self-justification constitutes the sin of covert blasphemy.

Righteous Slaughter

This God whom we choose to serve — or, more accurately, the God whom we want to make serve us — may not appear in highly refined theological form. We are usually more comfortable with a vague notion of some sort of transcendent value, an inchoate belief in an eternal good.

In this respect, I am fascinated by sociologist Jack Katz's analysis of crimes of passion. Katz asked shoplifters, burglars, vandals, and murderers why they did it, and he got a lot of "self-justifying rhetoric." After extensive interviewing and analysis, he concludes that criminals in general and killers in particular seek to embody, "through the practice of 'righteous slaughter,' some eternal, universal form of the Good."[4] The form it typically takes is that of righteous rage to which someone else has to be sacrificed.

Katz cites a case of spouse murder as an example. Two weeks prior to the homicide, John's wife told him that she didn't want him anymore and that she planned to leave home and move in with her lover. John begged her to stay in the marriage for the sake of the children. She refused to discuss the matter. Upset, John went out and bought a rifle, thinking he might use it to kill himself. His wife left as she had said she would, but then returned on Mother's Day to ask for the children. John again begged her not to take them, but she ignored his pleas. During the argument the children became upset and started crying. John told her to look at the children and see the damage she was doing. The wife replied that she "didn't give a damn about the children." John grabbed a knife and stabbed her to death. Later he tried to justify his action on the grounds that he was defending the

---

4. Katz, *Seductions of Crime* (New York: Basic Books, 1988), p. 9. Katz argues that theories of crime that depend on materialist motives are inadequate because they do not account for the appeal to a transcendent good experienced by the person committing the crime.

children's moral sensibilities. In his mind, caring for the welfare of his children transcended all other considerations in his conflict with his wife. He viewed caring for children as a universal good. In the end, he placed so high a value on defending children against a wayward parent that, in a fit of humiliation and rage, he was willing to sacrifice his wife's life to secure this good.

Katz also presents the case of Francine Hughes, who had suffered frequent beatings throughout her fifteen-year marriage. Tired of living as a welfare mother, she enrolled in a business college in hopes of improving her situation. When her husband, James, tried to prevent her study, they argued, and he started beating her. Their daughter, then twelve years old, telephoned the police. The officers showed up, but they left without making an arrest. When James went into the bedroom to take a nap, Francine took advantage of his defenseless state, poured gasoline all around the bed, and lit it. James died in the flames. In her hysterical confession and court defense, Francine claimed that the murder was justified because she had been victimized. This was not a mere matter of physical self-defense, however; it was a spiritual matter. Francine was defending the good. Specifically, she was defending a version of the American dream — namely, her right to better herself through education and escape the welfare rolls by getting a job. She felt that James had to be sacrificed on behalf of her understanding of the American dream. The jury was sympathetic. Francine was acquitted — not on the grounds that the murder was justified but on grounds of temporary insanity. Even if Francine had been temporarily insane, however, she was certainly rational in claiming that her momentary irrationality would be understood by others as righteously inspired.[5]

5. The social atmosphere in North America is currently colored by the widespread use of the term *abuse* applied to the treatment of women by men, and this may influence the way we interpret such cases. In her attempt to establish that women have a privileged position regarding the understanding of evil, Nel Noddings concedes that Ernest "Becker and others are not necessarily wrong when they say that men hurt one another out of fear and the desire to overcome evil." Still, Noddings wants to apply the theory that the fear of death resulting in violence applies to men but not to women. "Women too are afraid," she says, "yet we rarely explode into physical violence" (*Women and Evil* [Berkeley and Los Angeles: University of California Press, 1989], p. 122). Unfortunately, the facts do not support Noddings's view. Although it is the case that most murders of strangers during a crime are committed by men, violence against loved ones is by no means gender specific. Women murder their spouses and children at almost the same rate as men. Cf. Katz, *Seductions of Crime,* p. 47.

According to Katz, people experiencing humiliation and rage feel that they are transcending boundaries of time. The combination of rage and righteousness focuses an individual's consciousness completely on the here-and-now, as if the present moment were all that existed, as if it were eternal. People feeling righteous rage cannot focus on the future consequences of their actions. Unable to see any end to the humiliation they are experiencing, unable to discern any reasonable path from the unbearable present to an tolerable future, would-be killers leap to a righteous plateau and identify themselves with an eternal good. Their aggression is linked to an identity with some socially approved value — their status as father, mother, property owner, defender of the American way, or the like. In the moment of rage, they search frantically for "something that will end what cannot be taken anymore — and an eternal moral peace. The blindness to the practical future implications of the moment gives rage, with all its fury, a soothing, negative promise that humiliation painfully lacks. This is its great comfort. . . . It blows up the present moment so the situation becomes portentous, potentially an endless present, possibly the occasion for a destruction that will become an eternally significant creativity. This is the spiritual beauty of rage."[6]

Such impassioned attacks are quite frequently preceded by aggression through cursing. It seems natural to move toward an assault with shouts of retaliatory humiliation such as "bastard," "whore," "bitch," "nickel-and-dime drunk," and the countless other appellations that are meant to identify the victim as falling outside the camp of what is lovable, dignified, or righteous. Cursing is meant to degrade people, to classify them as pollution in an otherwise good world. Or, as Katz puts it, it is meant to shift people symbolically "into an ontologically lower status."[7] Self-righteousness would seem to require this. The line is being drawn between a higher good and a lower evil, and the killer wants to be on the upper side of the line.

Group Pride and Prejudice

Cursing as an outburst of expletives is familiar to us all. Yet cursing can become a habit, a structure of social consciousness that renders

6. Katz, *Seductions of Crime*, p. 31.
7. Katz, *Seductions of Crime*, p. 36.

the cursed ones less than human and, therefore, fit to kill. One group can curse another group, as we noted in our discussion of tribalism. Here I want to take another look at the phenomenon in the context of prejudice. Prejudice is a social curse that has the function of making people feel justified in their efforts to dehumanize others.

In partnership with prejudice is pride, group pride. The origin of group pride, says Scott Peck, is narcissism. Group narcissism occurs naturally in children as they form clubs and cliques that declare all those outside the group to be inferior or evil or both. In the military this natural childhood propensity is cultivated and revered for the friendships and loyalty it creates. The military tries to foster esprit de corps by distributing group insignias, unit standard flags, shoulder patches, trophies for winning at group competition, and the like. The flip side of esprit de corps is what Peck labels "enemy creation," or hatred of the "out-group."[8] The entire effort has but one aim: to kill whoever happens to be the enemy when war breaks out. If war has already broken out, the task is easier. In the case of Vietnam, American soldiers diminished the enemy by referring to them as "Gooks" and associating them with the worldwide communist conspiracy. In Operation Desert Storm in 1991, the evil of the Iraqi enemy was established through repeated comparisons of Saddam Hussein to Adolf Hitler.

The prejudice pattern is fairly obvious when we look at children's cliques and the ways in which it is deliberately fostered in military campaigns. Yet prejudice can also be invisible. In its more subtle and more pervasive form as a cultural value, it is more difficult to discern. Racial prejudice is an important example of how a curse can be so built into a cultural milieu that its purveyors are nearly blind to their own patterns of self-justification and scapegoating. Racial prejudice also provides an instructive example of how original sin works: it is a form of self-justification and scapegoating that is passed down from one generation to the next, a tradition of sin we may unknowingly inherit and perpetuate.

Perhaps I should qualify what I said about the invisibility of prejudice. Although those who are prejudiced are nearly blind to the fact, the victims of the prejudice have no difficulty in perceiving it. The

---

8. Peck, *People of the Lie: The Hope for Healing Human Evil* (New York: Simon & Schuster, 1983), p. 225.

Jew in Auschwitz and the black in a South African detention center are acutely aware that a social curse can kill.

Prejudice is so automatic that it becomes second nature. We might say that prejudice sleeps for the person of pride. In its sleeping state it is dangerous for those being scapegoated. Once awakened, however, it becomes visible. Then the prideful face a choice either to continue the prejudice for another generation or to combat it.

I can remember with some vividness an experience of awakening. I was eighteen years old. It was my first day on the campus of Michigan State University, where I was entering as a freshman. We were unpacking and moving into the dormitory, Bryan Hall. Perhaps eight or so of us had gathered in one room to get to know one another. We each reported our hometown. When my turn came I announced with obvious pride, "I come from Dearborn, the best city in the state of Michigan. It is the home of the Ford Motor Company and Mayor Orville L. Hubbard. There are no niggers living within the city limits, and none ever will as long as Orvie is mayor."

One soft and unidentified voice could be heard to say, "Well, I don't think that's anything to be proud of."

I was shocked. "An all-white city is not something to be proud of?" I could not believe my ears. As I look back on it, that was the first time I had ever heard anything less than praise for my racist upbringing. At that moment I could not comprehend what was being said to me. It was a challenge, and it took me a considerable amount of time to integrate the challenge into my thinking. It is easy to underestimate how thoroughly one's worldview can be determined by family and communal consciousness, rendering one opaque even to something as obvious as this.

At home in Dearborn I had been confident that I possessed the truth. My milieu provided the criteria for truth. I bought into the myth that Dearborn had shown leadership in its public school system, had the cleanest streets of any major city in Michigan, and provided the home for the largest single manufacturing company in the world. How proud we were of the Ford Motor Company, which brought raw iron ore down the Detroit River to the Rouge Plant and then rolled brand new automobiles off the other end of the assembly line at a rate of one per minute. We even had our own city camp, Camp Dearborn. How frequently as a child I could remember driving via Michigan Avenue toward Wayne and passing through Inkster. "That's

170

where all the niggers live," my dad would say. "Aren't we glad we don't have to live in Inkster." Of course I was glad I didn't have to live in Inkster. And we were all grateful to Dearborn's mayor, Uncle Orvie, for keeping the walls high against the chaos of Detroit on one side and Inkster on the other so that Dearborn would remain lily white! This was my truth — actually my myth — up to the age of eighteen, a truth that became subject to considerable alteration during my year as a college freshman.

The months of dorm life that followed were as educational as my formal studies.[9] Willie Boyken lived in the room next to mine. Willie was an African American. He played lineman on the MSU varsity football team, no mean accomplishment in those days, when the Spartans found themselves frequently in what was then the most prestigious of championship showdowns, the Rose Bowl. Willie was six-foot-seven and weighed 285 pounds. It was all muscle. He could run the hundred-yard dash wearing all of his equipment in 9.7 seconds. Physically he was the embodiment of all that a mortal man could become, and more. I sat in awe listening to the pontifications and vituperations of this Greek god. Willie was the first black person I had ever known by name.

Down the hall lived Larry Venyah, a black foreign student from Africa. Larry and I went places together, and he stimulated my interest in learning more about his continent. We became friends. Just prior to the Christmas break, I asked Larry if he would like to come home with me to spend the holidays with my family.

"You live in Dearborn, right?" he asked.

"Yes."

"You know I wouldn't be very welcome in Dearborn. The people there do not like the color of my skin. I wouldn't feel very comfortable.

---

9. My education regarding race and prejudice necessarily included repentance and conversion on my part. Patrick R. Keifert has written perceptively about this dynamic: "The drive of the self in the face-to-face encounter is to reduce the other to analogies of the self and to justify this reduction of the other through violence against the other, through either overt physical, emotional, and spiritual violence or the more covert violence of projecting intimacy upon the other. The various systems of self-justification show themselves on the social and psychological levels as sexism, racism, and classism. A profound change and reversal must therefore take place in this self-justifying, ego-centric self. It must die and be reborn a self-for-the-other" (*Welcoming the Stranger* [Minneapolis: Fortress Press, 1992], p. 86).

Thank you for the invitation, but I believe I will be making a trip to Canada over Christmas."

Again, I was shocked, surprised, and disturbed that my hometown had such a reputation. I had assumed that Dearborn was the home of the superior and the good, but the very fact that it represented itself as such was alienating people like Larry. I was beginning to understand, but each such interchange only suggested that matters were much more serious than I had reckoned. My slowness to understand was due to the fact that I was so deeply invested in the Dearborn mind-set. I thought and felt the way Dearborn felt and thought. Dearborn was the filter through which I interpreted reality. One reason these interchanges shocked me so much was that my mind-set — the filter that structured my picture of reality — was coming apart, and no new mind-set had yet taken its place. When I went home for the holidays I began to look at Dearborn with somewhat different eyes, almost as if I were a stranger. I had been partially awakened, and it was beginning to occur to me that the sweet dreams of my youth were someone else's nightmare.

This created anxiety. The challenges I was encountering at MSU were threatening my being, at least the mind-set dimension of my being. I could have responded by following one of two paths. In order to relieve myself of the pain that such anxiety brings with it, I could have tried to defend Dearborn's way of life in an effort to keep my original mind-set intact — I could have rolled over and returned to the sleep of my youth. Or I could have sought out further challenges and additional friendships with people of other races in the hope that a new and more wholesome mind-set might some day emerge. I probably would not be writing these words had I chosen the first path. Still, I can sympathize with those who choose that path, because the temptation is powerful. This experience has taught me how invisible and insidious race prejudice can be. We are born into it. We drink it right along with our mother's milk. It is a form of original sin, a form of sin that originated before we came along, a sin that we inherit, a sin that we commit, a sin that we pass along to our children and grandchildren. And to those against whom such racial prejudice is directed — to the victims of hatred today who might become the victims of righteous slaughter tomorrow — this intergenerational sin looms as an insurmountable curse threatening others with nonbeing.

Ideology

We have looked at self-justification as it occurs in children either to cover guilt or to scapegoat, and we have looked at self-justification in rage during righteous slaughter along with group pride and racial prejudice. Virtually all of these dynamics and more come together in ideology. By *ideology* I mean an articulated belief system that aspires to offer a unified explanatory vision in answer to personal, social, political, and perhaps religious problems. An ideology typically begins by describing a crisis in a given context. Then it rewrites history to blame one or another group for precipitating the crisis. Finally, it suggests a solution that protects the interests of a favored group. Ideologies can be local, as in the case of a stockholders' coalition trying to restructure corporate management, but more frequently they are comprehensive in scale. One kind of radical feminism, for example, promotes a grand vision stretching back to the dawn of human history, back to a primordial matriarchal harmony that was lost in a fall into patriarchal alienation, and now calls for social transformation and retrieval of the lost harmony.

Certainly the most potent ideologies of the twentieth century, ideologies that have wrought massive human misery and destruction on a global scale, are easily identifiable: Nazism and communism. Once in power, they sponsored totalitarian rule, forced labor camps, mass murder, and international war. The structure of self-justification and scapegoating became the order of the day for all over whom they ruled. While recognizing this, we must also be alert to the fact that numerous ideologies are running around among us today. They come and go. They vary in scale. Yet, they differ from Nazism and communism only in the extent to which they command less political power. Preventing their rise to power should be the first priority of every free society. We cease our vigilance regarding the dangers of ideology only at great peril.

One victim of the Stalinist version of communism who had a lot of time to think about it is Aleksandr Solzhenitsyn. A prisoner for nearly two decades in the series of Siberian labor camps he calls the Gulag Archipelago, he learned firsthand how it felt to be arrested secretly, tried unjustly, and led off to an unknown destiny. The camps were the totalitarian government's secret way to eliminate political opposition and church leadership. Millions of Russians and other ethnic groups were arrested in waves from the 1920s to the 1970s. They suffered degradation, overwork, and malnutrition, and many died.

Those immediately involved in the handling of the prisoners were by no means the authors of the regnant ideology. They were the low-level officials, specialists in inflicting injustice, experts in torture, and yet mere cogs in the great machine. In all respects, the icy-faced jailers were like any other human beings.

Solzhenitsyn tells a story set in the Big House in Leningrad during a German attack in the 1940s. A woman prisoner was being taken to interrogation by an impassive, silent woman guard with unseeing eyes. Suddenly, bombs began to explode around them. Terrified, the guard threw her arms around the prisoner. The embrace indicated how desperate she was for human companionship and sympathy. When the bombing stopped, she withdrew her arms. Her eyes became unseeing again. "Hands behind your back! Move along!" she said sternly to the prisoner. "There is no merit in that — to become a human being in the moment of death," says Solzhenitsyn.[10] Still, the story allows him to make an important point — namely, that the inflicters of injustice are not a special breed of evil people. There is every possibility that we would act the same way if we were in their shoes. We cannot divide the human race into two groups, the evil ones and us. "If only it were all so simple! If only there were evil people somewhere insidiously committing evil deeds, and it were necessary only to separate them from the rest of us and destroy them. But the line dividing good and evil cuts through the heart of every human being. And who is willing to destroy a piece of his own heart?"[11]

This acceptance of the universality of the human predicament that includes both jailer and prisoner readies us to attend to what Solzhenitsyn has to say about ideology. "To do evil a human being must first of all believe that what he's doing is good," he tells us. "It is in the nature of the human being to seek a *justification* for his actions."[12] One of the most heinous forms of such justification is ideology.

Ideology — that is what gives evildoing its long-sought justification and gives the evildoer the necessary steadfastness and determination.

10. Solzhenitsyn, *The Gulag Archipelago* (New York: Harper & Row, 1974), p. 172.
11. Solzhenitsyn, *The Gulag Archipelago*, p. 168.
12. Solzhenitsyn, *The Gulag Archipelago*, p. 173, italics in original.

That is the social theory which helps to make his acts seem good instead of bad in his own and other's eyes, so that he won't hear reproaches and curses but will receive praise and honors. That was how the agents of the Inquisition fortified their wills: by invoking Christianity; the conquerors of foreign lands, by extolling the grandeur of their Motherland; the colonizers, by civilization; the Nazis, by race; and the Jacobins (early and late) by equality, brotherhood, and the happiness of future generations.

Thanks to *ideology*, the twentieth century was fated to experience evildoing on a scale calculated in the millions.[13]

Communism like many other ideologies has been international in scope. Nazism, in contrast, is a form of fascism and is limited to one nation. Even the allies during World War II were not able to escape ideology completely. For them it took the form of nationalism or patriotism. Philosopher John Herman Randall, Jr., found this distressing. "Whatever its origin and its ultimate value," he wrote, "patriotism is beyond doubt the most widespread social ideal of the day; it is the modern religion, far stronger than Christianity in any of its forms, and to its tribal gods men give supreme allegiance. Nationalism is almost the one idea for which masses of men will still die. . . . Patriotism is, in practice, invidious: it lives by hatred of the foreigner."[14] Ideology and patriotism are two forms that tribalism takes in the civilized world.

Culture Wars: Our Virtues Are as Sinful as Our Vices

Now let me interject that it is not my intention to engage in reductionism here. I am not reducing human sin to the social phenomenon of forming social identity. Quite the contrary. I am suggesting that the process of forming social identity through tribalism, patriotism, or ideology is fraught with temptations to commit violence against outsiders and that this is the expression of the sinful condition in which the human race finds itself. The fires of prejudice are fueled by the deep desire to be morally correct — that is, to know the difference between good and evil and to stand on the side of the good.

13. Solzhenitsyn, *The Gulag Archipelago,* p. 174; italics in original.
14. Randall, *The Making of the Modern Mind* (1940; reprint, New York: Columbia University Press, 1976), pp. 668-69.

What have come to be known as the "culture wars" in contemporary America may provide an illustrative example. In the past it was easy to identify mutual prejudice between religious groups. The confessional wars between Roman Catholics and Protestants devastated Europe for a century from 1559 to 1689. The Enlightenment *philosophes* who influenced the founding of the American republic in the eighteenth century viewed religion as the root cause of much social unrest. They predicted that as our society advanced, we would outgrow our need for religious "superstitions," and in outgrowing these superstitions we would outgrow the social divisiveness that results from religious conviction. The architects of American government gave us the First Amendment to the U.S. Constitution to prevent any one sectarian group from getting the upper hand. Despite their efforts to this end, the nineteenth century witnessed the growth of a generic Protestant prejudice against Roman Catholics. In the 1830s a genre of literature appeared that depicted Catholic priests and nuns as sexually immoral, and mob actions led to numerous attacks on convents, churches, and seminaries. Toward the end of the century, a parallel genre of literature depicted Jews as unscrupulous in business and a threat to the social fabric. In the century since, however, relations between Protestants and Catholics and Jews have improved greatly. Protestant leaders have repented of their past prejudices. And especially since the election of Catholic John F. Kennedy as president and the convening of the Second Vatican Council, Americans have come to trust one another more across religious lines.

But this has by no means put an end to the religious battles. America is beset with its own version of a *Kulturkampf*, a culture war. Who is not astounded at the intensity and tenacity of the Right to Life and Pro-Choice movements in the struggle over abortion on demand? How can we explain the verbal venom in the debates over gay and lesbian civil rights and sexual practices? What accounts for the feminist reinterpretation of the history of human relations and the fearsome anxiety it arouses in defenders of "family values"? These new battle lines do not conform to the old religious lines, but they are definitely religious — or, better, definitely *moral*. A liberal Roman Catholic can voice the same degree of antipathy toward a right-wing Roman Catholic as a liberal Episcopalian can toward a right-wing fundamentalist. Orthodox Jewish rabbis lie down on the sidewalk side by side with evangelical Protestant clergy and Roman Catholic priests in efforts to shut down abortion clinics. What is going on here?

One way to describe it is cultural conflict. James Davison Hunter defines cultural conflict as "political and social hostility rooted in different systems of moral understanding." Now, at first this looks like garden-variety tribalism — that is, adherence to an ideology that places us in the in-group and our enemies in the out-group. But there is more going on here. Note that Hunter roots the cultural conflict in *moral understanding.* "Let it be clear," he continues, "the principles and ideals that mark these competing systems of moral understanding are by no means trifling but always have a character of ultimacy to them."

The quality of *ultimacy* makes these moral understandings "religious" in a general sense. It is the combination of morality and ultimacy that marks the danger. What accounts for the tenacity and ferocity on both sides of each of these cultural battles is the identification of those involved with an ultimate moral order, identification with what adherents to each ideology presume to be ultimate justice or goodness or righteousness. The temptation is to create a *moral ethnocentrism* that is justified through identification with the ultimate moral order. As with other tribalisms, our loyalty can be measured by the amount of courage we exhibit in taking a stand against those who adhere to a competing moral — what we might call a competing "immoral" — order. "The nub of political disagreement today on the range of issues debated — whether abortion, child care, funding for the arts, affirmative action and quotas, gay rights, values in public education, or multiculturalism — can be traced ultimately and finally to the matter of moral authority," says Hunter. "By moral authority I mean the basis by which people determine whether something is good or bad, right or wrong, acceptable or unacceptable."[15] When Hunter cites "moral authority" as the ultimate authority, he seems to be sending us back to the Garden of Eden, to the tree of the knowledge of good and evil and the human propensity to see oneself as justified by identification with the good.

My point here is not to pick sides in the culture wars. Nor do I wish to propound a limp ideology of inclusivity that takes the passion out of moral activism. Rather, I simply want to suggest that in order

15. Hunter, *Culture Wars* (New York: Basic Books, 1991), p. 42.

to understand sin, we must be able to see it right in the very heart of our most moral endeavors.[16]

This is why religion — all religion, the Christian religion included — poses a threat to genuine faith in God.[17] The religious vision of a moral universe that justifies its adherents by virtue of their membership in the "in" moral or cultural group closes our eyes to the need to find justification in God and not ourselves.[18] Only when we wake up to realize how we participate in the structure of moral self-justification and its concomitant scapegoating will we be able to recognize that our virtues are as sinful as our vices. This is the damnable structure of human sin from which there is no escape except through divine grace. The message of the gospel is that our justification comes from God, not from ourselves. Without faith in the God who justifies, our only recourse is to turn to hypocrisy.

Hypocrisy

Jesus seems to have had a low tolerance for tribalism and for self-justification in every form. When confronted with Jewish ethnocentrism, Jesus would grant that he had come first to the Jews but then to the world. His parable of the Good Samaritan depicts an outsider, not a Jew, performing obedience to the law of love. Jesus kept alive the ancient Hebrew code: be kind to the foreigner, be hospitable to the sojourner. The God of Israel is the God of all nations, he insisted, and faith can be found even among the Gentiles. More relevant to our discussion here than Jesus' opposition to exclusivism, however, is his repeated condemnation of hypocrisy.

16. Karl Barth wrote, "Is it not remarkable that the greatest atrocities of life — I think of the capitalistic order and of the war — can justify themselves on purely moral principles? The devil may also make use of morality. He laughs at the tower of Babel which we erect to him" (*The Word of God and the Word of Man*, trans. Douglas Horton [1928; reprint, Gloucester, Mass.: Peter Smith, 1978], p. 18).

17. Karl Barth asked, "Is not our religious righteousness a product of our pride and our despair, a tower of Babel, at which the devil laughs more loudly than all the others?" (*The Word of God and the Word of Man*, p. 20).

18. "The totality of our depravity," says Gerhard Forde, "consists in the blindness: We do not even see that *our virtues are as sinful as our vices*" ("Christian Life," in *Christian Dogmatics*, ed. Carl E. Braaten and Robert W. Jenson, 2 vols. [Philadelphia: Fortress Press, 1984], 2:453; italics in original).

I have found the teachings of Jesus somewhat enigmatic on this subject. It is obvious that Jesus is opposed to sin. But what kind of sin? One might presume he would take strong stands against such things as organized crime, swindling, murder for hire, and the like. Or one might expect that he would speak out against social injustice, the exploitation of the poor by the rich, the misuse of power by the Roman rulers, and the like. Or one might wish he would condemn child abuse, wife beating, rivalry for inheritance, and the like. But this is not what we find. Instead, Jesus expels his venom against those whom he calls hypocrites. Who are the hypocrites? Usually the most respected and revered citizens and religious leaders of the community.

At first glance, it appears that Jesus' objection to the hypocrites is that they are outer-directed: they don't rely on genuine inner strengths. This is the definition of *hypocrite* we find in our dictionaries: a person who seeks to gain public approval by pretending to have moral or religious commitments that he or she in fact does not possess. In his Sermon on the Mount, Jesus says,

> And whenever you pray, do not be like the hypocrites; for they love to stand and pray in the synagogues and at the street corners, so that they may be seen by others. Truly I tell you, they have received their reward. But whenever you pray, go into your room and shut the door and pray to your Father who is in secret; and your Father who sees in secret will reward you. (Matt. 6:5-6)

The problem here seems to be that hypocrites do not have a deep personal commitment, but they want others to believe they do.

Yet hypocrites are motivated by more than a mere desire for public approval. They draw a line between good and evil and place themselves on the good side of the line. The line serves as the criterion for judging others to be morally inferior. It sets up a we/they dualism. It justifies exclusion tactics. It permits prejudice. With humor and sarcasm, Jesus goes after the hypocrite again in his Sermon on the Mount:

> Do not judge. . . . Why do you see the speck in your neighbor's eye, but do not notice the log in your own eye? Or how can you say to your neighbor, "Let me take the speck out of your eye," while the log is in your own eye? You hypocrite, first take the log out of your own eye, and then you will see clearly to take the speck out of your neighbor's eye. (Matt. 7:1a, 3-5)

Behind this desire to see specks in the eyes of others — that is, to see evil in others so that we can judge ourselves to be morally superior — is the deep-seated psychic conspiracy to justify ourselves. I refer to this as a psychic conspiracy because in our minds we try to co-opt God into our plan for self-justification. But of course God will not be co-opted, so the hypocrite cannot help but be blinded to the truth of the situation. One of Jesus' most difficult tasks was to find a way to penetrate the wall that keeps the hypocrite's soul shut up in darkness. Jesus' parable of the Pharisee and the Publican makes the point:

> Two men went up to the temple to pray, one a Pharisee and the other a tax collector. The Pharisee, standing by himself, was praying thus, "God, I thank you that I am not like other people: thieves, rogues, adulterers, or even like this tax collector. I fast twice a week; I give a tenth of all my income." But the tax collector, standing far off, would not even look up to heaven, but was beating his breast and saying, "God, be merciful to me, a sinner!" I tell you, this man went down to his home justified rather than the other; for all who exalt themselves will be humbled, but all who humble themselves will be exalted. (Luke 18:10-14)

In this parable the tax collector has two advantages over the Pharisee. First, when the tax collector draws the line between good and evil, he is willing to place himself on the evil side. This enables him to see himself realistically, to avoid the smugness of the Pharisee. Second, he recognizes the important truth that God is gracious, that God grants forgiveness to even the worst of sinners, and that by granting this forgiveness, it is God who justifies us. We do not justify ourselves. These are insights beyond the purview of the hypocrite.

Hypocrisy, with its self-justification and exclusion of outsiders, spells death. Jesus minces no words when making this point:

> Woe to you, scribes and Pharisees, hypocrites! For you are like whitewashed tombs, which on the outside look beautiful, but inside they are full of the bones of the dead and all kinds of filth. So you also on the outside look righteous to others, but inside you are full of hypocrisy and lawlessness. (Matt. 23:27-28)

Hidden behind the facade of publicly professed godliness is the secret home of a dead soul.

One of the problems with death in the human soul is that it does not just lie there inert. Even though death is a form of nonbeing, for some difficult-to-comprehend reason we experience death as a power, a power of destruction. Especially when we challenge the dead with a call to resurrection, as Jesus did, the dead rise up only to reap more death. The darkness rises up to blot out the light. Self-justification kills the soul within and the scapegoat without.

The Scapegoat

The concept of the scapegoat is complex. The term *scapegoat* was given to us by William Tyndale. It is connected with the ancient Hebrew tradition of Yom Kippur, the day of atonement. According to Leviticus 16:8-22, two goats were chosen. The first goat was sacrificed. Its blood was sprinkled ritually on the mercy seat. The second goat, the living goat, was held still while the high priest laid his hands on its head, confessing all the sins of the people of Israel, and ritually heaping them onto the goat. Then the goat was driven out into the wilderness, symbolically bearing the sins of Israel away.

In contemporary common parlance, we have come to use the word *scapegoat* to refer to any person or group made to bear the blame for others or to suffer in their place. This common usage is probably more helpful in trying to discern how sin works.

What I have found significant in recent treatments of the subject of human evil is that the scapegoat plays a prominent, even decisive role. The first characteristic that Scott Peck assigns to the personality disorder he names "evil" is "consistent destructive, scapegoating behavior, which may often be quite subtle."[19] He defines evil in psychological terms as "the use of power to destroy the spiritual growth of others for the purpose of defending and preserving the integrity of our own sick selves. In short, it is scapegoating."[20] Peck draws ex-

---

19. Peck, *People of the Lie*, p. 129. A notable exception to my observation here is theologian Edward Farley, who in his book *Good and Evil* (Minneapolis: Fortress Press, 1990) seems to overlook the scapegoat mechanism. Farley sees the root of human evil in the discontent caused by elemental human passions when confronting the vulnerability and tragic structure of life, but he does not seem to recognize how we use self-justification and scapegoating to delude ourselves that we can overcome vulnerability and tragedy.

20. Peck, *People of the Lie*, p. 119.

amples from family situations in which parents who are frustrated with themselves but wish to maintain the facade of success scapegoat their children. Child abuse is the result. Peck could have used the term *hypocrite* to good effect here. What distinguishes the scapegoater, as we noted earlier, is a lack of empathy for the victim.

In an investigation of the logic of scapegoating, Ernest Becker cites the following insights of Otto Rank: "The death of the ego is lessened by the killing, the sacrifice, of the other; through the death of the other, one buys oneself free from the penalty of dying, of being killed."[21] This is why we are addicted to prejudice and war. Hypocrisy also enters the picture, making it difficult for us to discern what is really happening. We create an illusion of self-righteousness — that is, we pretend that we are the champions of liberty fighting for human rights when in fact we secretly wish for the other's death and our own immortality. In the grip of this illusion, we cannot gain control over social evils such as prejudice or war. Becker writes,

> The logic of scapegoating, then, is based on animal narcissism and hidden fear. If luck, as Aristotle said, is when the arrow hits the fellow next to you, then scapegoating is pushing the fellow into its path — with special alacrity if he is a stranger to you. . . . The logic of killing others in order to affirm our own life unlocks much that puzzles us in history.[22]

Violence and the Social Order

While the insights of Peck and Becker concerning the mechanism of scapegoating are definitely on target, the phenomenon is still more complex. What remains to be explained is why, if we are always consumed with prejudice, we are not constantly at war. Why is it that when our prejudice is called to our attention we decry it? Why is it that the regnant values of our society — almost every society — are concerned with preserving the peace? The answer is that social justice and international peace are good, and as something good they too communicate life and convey a sense of the eternal that helps to relieve

21. Rank, *Will Therapy and Truth and Reality* (1936; reprint, New York: Knopf, 1945), p. 130.
22. Becker, *Escape from Evil* (New York: Macmillan, 1975), pp. 109-10.

anxiety. We humans have a genuine desire for order, for social stability if not harmony. At the same time we harbor the secret desire to steal the livelihood of others. How do these two fit together?

On this question I have found the work of René Girard, a French literary critic and professor of anthropology at Stanford, very instructive. Because of our propensity for rage and violence, all societies live under the constant threat of uncontrollable violence. Recognizing this, Girard offers the thesis that each society engages in some form of scapegoating — sacrifice — aimed at stemming the tide of violence and establishing social order. Whether consciously or unconsciously, we believe that the flood of uncontrolled violence can be dammed up and its destructive force averted through a controlled act of ritual violence — through the killing of a scapegoat.

Girard uses the word *sacrifice* here because the party against whom the ritual violence is directed is a substitute for the guilty one. We have all encountered something like the following sequence: a man gets chewed out by his boss at work, goes home and yells at his wife, and she scolds her child, and the child kicks the dog. The problem is that once anger is provoked and the urge to commit violence is aroused, there is no stopping it until it has taken a victim. As we have already noted, in tribal societies that have no criminal justice system, the law of clan revenge prevails. Clan vendettas and blood feuds can gradually decimate two populations. Every act of violence is considered a reprisal. No crime is considered to be an unprecedented offense; it is always revenge for a prior crime. There is no way to retrieve the original crime, to right it and put an end to the deadly spiral. In order to break the cycle, one side must offer up an innocent victim. It cannot be the person who committed the last act of revenge in the chain; it has to be someone else if the cycle is to be broken.

This leads Girard to conclude that the fundamental truth about violence is that, "if left unappeased, violence will accumulate until it overflows its confines and floods the surrounding area. The role of sacrifice is to stem this rising tide of indiscriminate substitutions and redirect violence into proper channels."[23] The purpose of sacrifice, then, is to restore harmony to the community, to reinforce the social fabric. Everything else, says Girard, stems from this.

23. Girard, *Violence and the Sacred* (Baltimore: The Johns Hopkins University Press, 1977), p. 10.

Who should be sacrificed? It makes little difference whether it is a human being or an animal. What is important is that the sacrificial victim resemble the members of the community but not be identical. Consequently, a given community can sacrifice social undesirables, slaves, small children, or even the king. Sacrificing the king has the added advantage of satisfying the rage expressed in the watercooler syndrome. It is not necessary, obviously, for the sacrificial victim to volunteer for the honor.

This mechanism is difficult to see in modern Western society — for good reason. Since the Enlightenment, we have sought to eliminate clan revenge and sacrifice. In part, this is what democracy is all about. The way it applies is that we seek to establish an impartial justice system backed up by a strong police force. We cede authority to the courts on the supposition that they will punish only the guilty. We hope that this punishment of the guilty will put an end to any further retaliation or violence. The success of the justice system depends on its ability to suppress revenge. We say of a convicted criminal that he or she owes a debt to society. This is not literally true, of course. The debt is owed to the victim of the crime. But in a civil judicial system, we transfer the debt to the state in order to eliminate the need for revenge by the victim or the victim's relatives. Today's judicial system replaces yesterday's sacrificial system. Both have been devised to end the spiral of violence.

To the extent that the justice system is successful and clan revenge is reduced to a minimum, we no longer sense the public need for sacrifice. But when the criminal justice system is circumvented or fails, this more fundamental psychosocial structure surfaces. Competition among Mafia families and street gangs provides a good example: the cycle of reciprocal violence proceeds apace until someone quite innocent, someone random or even quite treasured, becomes the victim. Then remorse breaks the cycle and a new order is established.

Girard wants to better understand the madness of collective violence in our era, and he believes the key lies in a study of the archetype of the scapegoat.[24] The scapegoat mechanism is likely to click in when (1) we are confronted by a cultural crisis, such as a plague or a war, that obliterates stable social differences; (2) we make a symbolic accusation — that is, we identify the cause of the crisis with some rep-

24. See Girard, *The Scapegoat* (Baltimore: The Johns Hopkins University Press, 1986).

184

resentative of moral breakdown; and (3) we select certain *victims* who ostensibly embody this moral breakdown, usually people belonging to a minority and having distinctive marks such as color, sickness, madness, religious affiliation, or class status. The line between good and evil is drawn. The just turn to mob action against the unjust in an effort to purge themselves of the evil that precipitated the crisis.

How does the scapegoat archetype help us to understand the nature of the human condition? Girard cites Jesus Christ as the pivotal example. The martyrdom of the innocent carpenter from Nazareth reveals the oppressiveness of the scapegoat system and the fruitlessness of seeking self-justification through the persecution of others. Christ, the lamb of God, exposes the hypocrisy of the scapegoat mechanism. The cross event destroys the mob's self-justifying belief in the guilt of the victim. Scapegoats can no longer save, because witchhunts and pogroms and persecutions have been demystified. Christ crucified is the final scapegoat, the one who puts an end to the possibility of self-justification through scapegoating.

Girard argues that this approach leads to the most coherent reading of the New Testament texts as well as the most coherent understanding of where the Christian religion went wrong. It is the best way to understand Jesus' sharp criticisms of the Scribes and Pharisees for persecuting and killing the prophets, for shedding the blood of the innocent going all the way back to Abel.

> Therefore I send you prophets, sages, and scribes, some of whom you will kill and crucify, and some you will flog in your synagogues and pursue from town to town, so that upon you may come all the righteous blood shed on earth, from the blood of righteous Abel to the blood of Zechariah the son of Barachiah, whom you murdered between the sanctuary and the altar. Truly, I tell you, all this will come upon this generation. (Matt. 23:34-36)

The blood of righteous Abel? Abel was slain by his brother Cain, and this began the history of clan revenge — the history of justifiable murder — that has lasted down to the present day. It is not merely the Scribes and Pharisees to whom Jesus is speaking. It is to the whole history of the human race.[25] By speaking in this way, Jesus is revealing the hidden

25. See Girard, *Things Hidden since the Foundation of the World* (Stanford: Stanford University Press, 1987), pp. 159-64.

truth: our social structures are built to cover our violence. The Word of God that Jesus pronounces is this: stop the cycle of violence! Love your enemies! Turn the other cheek! Do not repay evil for evil!

It is significant that the fact that our social structures are founded on violence should be hidden. Jesus uses the metaphor of the tomb to describe those who mask violence — glistening white on the outside but filled with rotting flesh and death on the inside. Jesus challenges us to take this hidden death out into the open and acknowledge it. We need to tear the cover off deceit and hypocrisy. We need to recognize the lie as a lie. The lie, says Jesus, comes from the father of lies, Satan, who was "a murderer from the beginning, and has nothing to do with truth" (John 8:44, RSV).

Those to whom Jesus spoke so pointedly did not like to hear what he was saying. They could see that Jesus threatened the social order they were maintaining. To protect that order, they had to make Jesus into a scapegoat. To prevent Jesus' revelation from exposing the truth, the dark powers of death rose up to put him to death.[26] Jesus was crucified in an act of legal ritual and mob violence that were both aimed at restoring peace to the community. The New Testament texts reveal clearly the scapegoat structure at work.

> So the chief priests and the Pharisees called a meeting of the council, and said, "What are we to do? This man is performing many signs. If we let him go on like this, everyone will believe in him, and the Romans will come and destroy both our holy place and our nation." But one of them, Caiaphas, who was high priest that year, said to them, "You know nothing at all! You do not understand that it is better for you that one man die for the people than to have the whole nation destroyed." He did not say this on his own, but being high priest that year he prophesied that Jesus was about to die for the nation, and not for the nation only, but to gather into one the dispersed children of God. So from that day on they planned to put him to death. (John 11:47-53)

26. Girard's theory suggests that the scapegoat is normally random. Does that apply here? Not according to Raymund Schwager, who has attempted to apply the Girard theory to the biblical understanding of atonement. Schwager sees Jesus as the "necessary" scapegoat on the grounds that Jesus' preaching created the conflict. See *Must There Be Scapegoats?* (San Francisco: Harper & Row, 1987), p. 191. Girard's argument does seem to lead to Schwager's conclusion.

What we see here is the deliberate attempt to maintain social order through sacrifice. Jesus threatened the status quo and ran the risk of invoking reprisals by the Roman army. He had to be put to death to ensure that the whole nation would not be destroyed. After sending Jesus back and forth between the Roman and Jewish tribunals, "Herod and Pilate became friends with each other that very day" (Luke 23:12, RSV). The political friendship was founded on ritual death.

Of decisive importance for us today is that the New Testament writings that tell us of Jesus' execution do not participate in the cover-up. Rather, they expose it. The legacy of this execution of the innocent is that the retelling of the story of the cross reveals the founding mechanism of violence. The New Testament account is there for everyone to read, and it calls us to dismantle the power of social scapegoating in our own time, to turn our attention in love to the victims.[27]

Girard seems to think it essential to contend that the value for us of what happened to Jesus is not connected with the idea of sacrifice. "There is nothing in the Gospels to suggest that the death of Jesus is a sacrifice," he says, "whatever definition (expiation, substitution, etc.) we may give for that sacrifice. At no point in the Gospels is the death of Jesus defined as a sacrifice."[28] Why is Girard opposed to using the concept of sacrifice? It seems to fit his theory so well. He says it is because the death of Jesus is supposed to put an end to all further sacrificing, all further scapegoating. Jesus is a *scapegoat*, not a sacrifice.

Evidently, Girard believes that the concept of sacrifice is necessarily related to a belief that the gods are violent. If we believe that the divine powers are violent, then scapegoating is justified. But the God of Jesus Christ is not violent. Any attempt even within biblical theology to make God appear violent only constitutes one more act of hiding

---

27. See Girard, *Things Hidden since the Foundation of the World*, p. 192. Perhaps this can help us to understand Barth's assertion that only when we know Jesus Christ do we really know that we are sinful human beings, and what sin is, and what it means for us (*Church Dogmatics*, 4 vols., ed. Thomas F. Torrance, trans. Geoffrey W. Bromiley [Edinburgh: T. & T. Clark, 1936-1962], IV/1:389). One of Girard's friendly critics is Walter Wink, who says that the revealed scapegoat mechanism explains some but not all violence. Wink's own theory of the "myth of redemptive violence" is more generic and common, making scapegoating a subset (*Engaging the Powers* [Minneapolis: Fortress Press, 1992], p. 153).

28. Girard, *Things Hidden since the Foundation of the World*, p. 180.

our murderous propensity.[29] "To say that Jesus dies, not as a sacrifice, but in order that there may be no more sacrifices," writes Girard, "is to recognize in him the Word of God: 'I wish for mercy and not sacrifices'. . . . The Word of God says no to violence."[30]

Girard is confident the New Testament Gospels back up his reading. When it comes to the letter to the Hebrews, however, Girard has a problem. Hebrews 9:26 reads, "He has appeared once for all at the end of the age to remove sin by the sacrifice of himself." Jesus is literally described as the "single sacrifice for sins" for all time (Heb. 10:12). Girard argues that the author of Hebrews fails to examine carefully the structure of sacrifice that presupposes a violent deity. Even so, Girard does take comfort in noting that the letter to the Hebrews acknowledges that Jesus Christ is the final sacrifice and hence forbids any future sacrifices. Such sacrifices continue in our own time in highly disguised form, of course, but the message is nevertheless clear: the sacrifice of a scapegoat — any scapegoat — is contrary to God's will.

Girard says that the great sin of the Christian religion is that it has failed to examine carefully enough the point of God's revelation in Jesus Christ — namely, that our God is not a God of sacrifice and violence. If we persist in picturing God in terms of the mechanism of sacrifice, we will find ourselves justifying prejudice against the enemies of the church who threaten what we hold as truth. The history of the Christian faith is soaked with violence and persecution.[31] At the same time, due to the revelatory event of the cross, our Western culture is undergoing a demythologizing of the mechanism of sacrifice, and this is making it increasingly difficult to get away with attempts at scapegoating.[32]

29. On this basis, Girard is unsympathetic to apocalyptic literature such as the book of Revelation. The apocalyptic vision presents God as the vindicator of his chosen clan, as judging between the righteous and the unrighteous and then clobbering the unrighteous. In contrast, the kingdom of God announced by Jesus is a voluntary community of nonviolence. See *Things Hidden since the Foundation of the World*, pp. 186, 196, 203.

30. Girard, *Things Hidden since the Foundation of the World*, p. 210. Nonviolence is Walter Wink's central point. "Our lives are *founded* on violence. Oppressors and oppressed alike live in a violent system. Some wish to maintain their grasp on the good life, others to seize it for themselves. Nonviolence threatens the powerful because it would require relinquishing unjust advantage. But the powerless may fear it just as much, for it appears to nullify their hopes of assuming power by the very means used to keep them subjugated: violence" (*Engaging the Powers,* p. 239; italics in original).

31. See Girard, *Things Hidden since the Foundation of the World*, pp. 224-25.

32. See Girard, *Things Hidden since the Foundation of the World*, p. 174.

In my judgment, the characterization of Jesus Christ as the final sacrifice in the book of Hebrews and the characterization of Jesus as the final scapegoat in Girard's work are functionally the same. It is not the case that God approves of scapegoating and disapproves of sacrificing. The Christ event signals that God wants to put an end to both.

Justification by Faith

What is revealed here is that God — the true God, not the one our imaginations have manufactured — refuses to be co-opted into our schemes of self-justification and scapegoating. The entire mechanism is shattered when it becomes clear that God has identified with the scapegoat rather than the righteous ones who slaughter with the best interests of the existing social order at heart. When we engage in self-justification, we take a stand against God, even if we are convinced that we are identifying with God.

Among other things, this means that we should rely on God to justify us, not upon ourselves.[33] Forgiveness is the sign. While hanging from the cross just prior to his death, Jesus prayed for those who were crucifying him, "Father, forgive them; for they do not know what they are doing" (Luke 23:34). There is no clan revenge on God's part. Through Christ, God redeems — not by retributive justice but by forgiveness. The divine enemy is not destroyed but reconciled. Using forgiveness as a means of reconciliation is the divine agenda. God has offered to justify us as a gift of grace. With this gift in hand, we don't have to rely on the justice we find — or fail to find — in ourselves.

One way to look at this is to suggest that when God draws the line between good and evil, God places the incarnate divine self on the evil side. This is not to say that Jesus indulged in sin but that God identifies with the sinner rather than the righteous. In our human haste to engage in self-justification, we are constantly dividing the world into good and evil and putting ourselves on the good side — a strategy that in itself accounts for a large part of the sin that divides

33. Although most of us might assume that morality is good, Emil Brunner says that "it is precisely morality which is evil." The problem is that people striving to be moral want to make themselves good, and "this state of mind constitutes the source of all falsity, for it is the denial of the fact that the Good is always a gift of God" (*The Divine Imperative* [Philadelphia: Westminster Press, 1947], p. 71).

the world. God, on the other hand, seeks to overcome the division and thereby dismantle the mechanism of scapegoat violence. God submits to scapegoating rather than condoning or engaging in it.

God may consent to be the victim of scapegoating, but God also triumphs over it. The sign of victory is Jesus' resurrection on Easter. With this act, God broke the power of death in two ways. First, the power of death as nonbeing was overcome: nonbeing no longer has the final word. God creates new life out of death just as he first brought the creation into existence out of nothing. To have faith in the God of resurrection is to bind oneself to a power greater than death. Second, the sting of death was overcome. By the "sting of death" I mean anxiety, fear, and the resulting structure of sin that steals life through emotional or physical aggression. Near the end of his great chapter on resurrection, Paul writes,

Death has been swallowed up in victory.
Where, O death, is your victory?
Where, O death, is your sting? (1 Cor. 15:54b-55)

Faith binds the faithful person to the death and resurrection of Jesus Christ. Or, to put it another way, the Holy Spirit makes this event of death and resurrection present to the person of faith, and this presence delivers power for life in the here and now. Instead of stealing power from other scapegoats, the person of faith draws the power of life — everlasting life — from the scapegoat intended by God to end all scapegoating. In his eloquent testimony to baptism, Paul says, "We have been buried with him by baptism into death, so that, just as Christ was raised from the dead by the glory of the Father, so we too might walk in newness of life" (Rom. 6:4).

The person of faith steals life from God, so to speak, so that there is no need or desire to steal it from other creatures. And stealing life from God is no theft, because God offers it freely. This is divine grace.

Fruits of Faith

Like a seed coming to flower, faith blossoms fruitfully in a number of ways. First, it undercuts the need for self-justification. The person of faith becomes aware that God is gracious and that in grace it is God who justifies. Or, to reverse it, once people of faith are relieved of the burden of self-justification, they can perceive the gracious dimension of God's love. This has considerable import concerning our image of God. Those who believe in a God of justice may well believe that self-justification is necessary for salvation. Those who believe in no God at all may feel that self-justification is necessary to get ahead in this life. But those who believe in a God of grace recognize that self-justification is an insult to heaven. Faith in a God who graciously justifies eliminates the temptation to insult heaven.

A second blossom of faith is a new understanding and commitment regarding scapegoats. The person of faith who identifies with Jesus will be inclined to identify with scapegoats everywhere. Faith will make it difficult to side with parents abusing their children, with white supremacists engaging in bigotry, with an unchecked capitalist economy exploiting the oppressed masses in underdeveloped countries, with unbridled industrial consumption raping the earth, with theological schemes trying to blame God rather than ourselves for the human predicament. Faith leads us to want to side with the victims. Faith inspires us to share the power of divine life with those from whom livelihood is being stolen.

A third blossom is realism, the end of naiveté regarding the particularity of sin. Sin is universal, and we can admit it. Solzhenitsyn was right: good and evil cut through the center of *every* human heart — scapegoats included. One of the ironies of sinfulness is that those who try to work aggressively in behalf of the rights of the poor and oppressed often fall prey to the temptation of ideology. Ideologists tend to overstate if not even glorify the dignity of those being scapegoated. They paint pictures of the victims as innocent, perhaps even as saints. The truth is, they may not be saints. Nor do they have to be. Reinhold Niebuhr frequently noted that the righteousness of a cause does not accrue to the righteousness of the individuals who champion that cause. The victims of injustice may not themselves be just. Faith in the God who justifies permits us to be realistic rather than romantic about such victims.

Fourth, this realism permits us to acknowledge that even the person of faith is a sinner. By soothing our anxiety with the promise of resurrection, faith undercuts the root motive for sinning, but by no means does it transform us into something totally supernatural. We remain the animals that we are, still subject to limits of finitude and their accompanying fears. We remain participants in cultural and social

191

systems that encompass us and stain us with inescapable structures of prejudice, exploitation, and violence. There is no place we can go to avoid systemic evil. We cannot take a psychic shower and cleanse ourselves of the sins of our society. There is no action we can take regardless of our noble motives that might not have some negative consequence. We belong inescapably to a nexus that is shot through and through with sin. We can do no better than to live as forgiven sinners rendering our best judgments and taking what we deem to be the most wholesome actions. People of faith are, to use Martin Luther's vocabulary, *simul justus et peccator,* simultaneously saint and sinner. Such realism does not justify quietism, however. To Philipp Melanchthon, Luther once wrote in a letter, "Be a sinner and sin boldly, but believe more boldly and rejoice in Christ who is victor over sin, death, and the world."[34] Faith yields the confidence to press on in a sinful world with freedom and vigor.

34. Luther, in a letter to Melanchthon, in *Letters I*, vol. 48 of *Luther's Works*, ed. Gottfried G. Krodel and Helmut Lehmann (Philadelphia: Fortress Press, 1963), p. 282.

7

CRUELTY
Enjoying My Neighbor's Suffering

"Life is a mess . . . in the end it will cease to move. The big eat the little that they may continue to move, the strong eat the weak that they may continue their strength. . . . What do you make of these things?"

— Jack London, *The Sea Wolf*

A few years back Judith Shklar wrote a book, *Ordinary Vices,* the first chapter of which is entitled "Putting Cruelty First" — first, that is, on the list of the seven deadly sins. Shklar argued that cruelty is worse than pride. Cruelty is the *summum malum,* the supreme evil. While I have some problems with Shklar's overall argument, I think her thoughts about cruelty are well worth considering — particularly her definition of cruelty as the "willful inflicting of physical pain on a weaker being in order to cause anguish or fear."[1] I would only add that cruelty can involve psychic and spiritual as well as physical pain.

---

1. Shklar, *Ordinary Vices* (Cambridge: Harvard University Press, 1984), p. 8. Beyond her discussion of cruelty, I believe Shklar stumbles in trying to draw out the significance of what she is saying. God does not play a role in her analysis, and since pride is essentially a sin against God, she is quick to dismiss its significance. She accords cruelty decisive importance on the grounds that it hurts people. She then states that her opposition to cruelty places her "outside the sphere of religion" (p. 9)

193

Cruelty marks a transition in our treatment of sin and evil. There is some continuity with the categories of sin we have already investigated — cruelty describes what the proud and concupiscent person engaged in self-justification does to the scapegoat — but there is also a break. To this point, our description of sin has included an element of blindness. We pretend not to see the consequences of our actions. We choose ignorance. In this ignorant state, we can inflict great pain and yet keep our capacity for sympathy intact. If we are inadvertently confronted with the dark side of our reality, we rationalize. We may even feel sympathy for the victim, and yet the blindness continues. It is a function of our belief that the victim deserves the pain, and that we the perpetrators are but agents of some higher force of righteousness. We impose suffering as a means to achieve a higher end, an end that we embrace even if the victim does not. As sinners, we may engage in cruelty, but we pretend either that we do not see it or, if we do see it, that we regret its necessity.

But there is also a sense in which cruelty takes on a kind of life of its own. Torture quickly becomes an end in itself. The cruel person begins to enjoy watching the suffering of the victim and deliberately devises new methods of inflicting pain. The suffering of others works like a drug; the cruel person needs increasingly larger doses to attain the same high. The ultimate fix is the death of the other. What accounts for this perverse pleasure? Perhaps the Lifton principle applies here: killing others relieves our own fear of being killed.

Once a person begins to enjoy cruelty, the door is open for blasphemy. I am here defining *blasphemy* as the stealing of the symbols of salvation. In Chapter 8 I will argue that blasphemy has multiple levels; the level I am concerned with here combines overt acts of cruelty

---

— but this only indicates that she has a superficial understanding of both pride and religion.

Jean Delumeau offers an interesting theory to explain why cruelty did not appear on the medieval list of the seven deadly sins despite the fact that it should have. Western civilization began to discover its own cruelty through its depiction in art during the fourteenth to sixteenth centuries, a period of religious wars and advancing secularization. But the list of the seven deadly sins was prepared by cloistered monks who were battling inner spiritual sins such as envy and lust. The monks were not tempted to cruelty. Its omission, says Delumeau, is "all to their honorable credit" (*Sin and Fear: The Emergence of a Western Guilt Culture, Thirteenth-Eighteenth Centuries,* trans. Eric Nicholson [New York: St. Martin's Press, 1990], p. 243).

with an accompanying symbol system that justifies them. The worst example of cruelty is Satanism, the practitioners of which deliberately inflict pain and engage in sacrifice as an intentional expression of evil.[2] The essence of blasphemy in Devil worship lies not merely in the fact that cruelty is given transcendent justification but in the fact that the transcendent ground is itself depicted as evil. Lower evils are justified because they serve a higher evil, not the good. Short of Satanism, however, cruelty as the willful infliction of pain on weaker beings is still all too familiar.

Toads and Firecrackers

Is there built into the human psyche a force that propels us toward wanton destruction? Is there a deep-seated desire to contaminate the clean, pollute the pure, spoil the fresh, dissolve the solid, kill the living? If so, what is its source?

Behind my family house in the North Waverly Street neighborhood was a small swamp. By the end of the summer it would pretty much dry up, but each spring it was teeming with critters and crawlers. One of my deepest joys as a little boy was to spend hours tiptoeing through the reeds, watching the birds and butterflies, overturning rocks to see what would squirm out, pouring water from one can to another to see what I had caught. One of the biggest thrills was to catch a crayfish — not an easy task, because they are able to jet backward quickly when they sense danger. After a good deal of frustration and practice, though, I got so I could sweep down with an empty soup can and catch a crayfish shooting straight into my path.

There were no frogs in this swamp. Maybe you need year-round water for frogs. In any case, this was a big disappointment. But we did have toads — hundreds of little ones in the spring and larger ones during the summer. I had a good time finding, handling, loving, and

2. This seems to be the case phenomenologically, as I hope to show here, and also mythologically, as Ruth Nanda Anshen reports: "The Devil requires from his followers neither fear nor love. Loyalty is all he demands. . . . For the Devil is distinguished by absolute emotional frigidity. Just as he does not ask for love or fear, he is himself free from these emotions. Indeed, he is free from all emotions except hate and its sadistic derivatives, such as cruelty and insidiousness" (*Anatomy of Evil* [Mt. Kisco, N.Y.: Moyer Bell, 1972], p. 121)

letting them go. I felt that I and the animal world belonged to one another.

I shared a great deal of the curiosity and adventure of the swamp with the other boys and girls in the neighborhood. Sometimes we would go crayfish catching together and compare collections. We would trade toads and butterflies and flying grasshoppers. The swamp was central to the knee-high and belt-high community of North Waverly.

Yet there was to my observation a sinister presence: cruelty. When Bobby and Billy caught crayfish, they'd pull their legs off one at a time. "Look how it makes 'em squirm," they'd say, laughing. They'd stick a firecracker into the mouth of a toad, light it, and laugh when bits of toad exploded in all directions. To this day I do not understand that laugh.

I also felt the sinister presence on the baseball diamond, in connection with a certain ritual. In those days we used Louisville Slugger bats made of wood. When you stood up to the plate to hit, it was important to face the trademark on the bat barrel. If the trademark faces the batter, the ball will connect with the cross grain of the wood, and the bat will stay intact. If you turn the bat ninety degrees, the ball connects with the flat of the grain, and the bat is more likely to break. It seldom actually breaks into pieces, but if it cracks, it's just as useless as if it had.

I discovered a trick that could keep a cracked bat in operation and reduce the drain on my allowance. If I fastened a cracked bat tightly in a vice and drilled a small hole straight through from the flat side, I could insert a tiny screw that would hold it together. The operation would render the bat almost as good as new. I began attending night-league baseball games in the area and begged the teams for their broken bats. This kept me in good supply.

My old nemesis Louie didn't see it this way. If we heard the sound of a bat cracking during a baseball game — it makes a distinctive sound — Louie would run over and pick up the bat. No matter who owned the bat, Louie would pick it up. He would then grab the heavy end and bang the handle on the ground. With each bang the crack would grow in size. After a half dozen or so bangs, it would splinter in two. I would beg him not to do this and volunteer to take it home and fix it for whoever owned it. "No," Louie would insist. "It's broken. Let's break it!" Just why Louie would take pleasure in ensuring the destruction of the bat was confusing to me then. It is still confusing now.

Lycanthropy

Wolf symbolism has long been used to point to the powers of wanton destruction that well up in human life. As the saying goes, *Homo homini lupus* — "humankind is a wolf to humankind."[3] "Beware of false prophets," warned Jesus, "who come to you in sheep's clothing but inwardly are ravenous wolves" (Matt. 7:15). Chaucer alludes to this passage in "The Parson's Tale," speaking of "the Devil's wolves that strangle the sheep of Jesus Christ." The assumption here is that wolves — and certain humans among us — devour the innocent to satisfy their own rapacious appetites. Medieval legends spoke of *L'homme savage,* the savage man or wild man, who combined human and wolf traits. This led in the fifteenth century to stories of the werewolf who raided the human community to commit acts of depravity and sexual indulgence. Tales such as Little Red Riding Hood and the Three Little Pigs perpetuated the fear among children with descriptions of the Big Bad Wolf who could speak, deceive, and devour. The German submarines of World War II were described by news correspondents as wolf packs prowling the North Atlantic, thereby implicitly characterizing the Third Reich as a beast of abominable cruelty and greed preying on Europe.

At the turn of the twentieth century, as the theory of evolution came to be more broadly disseminated, people began to ask how closely our human nature is tied to our animal nature. Have we in the civilized world advanced to the point of having left our animal nature behind? Or does the beast lie just below a thin veneer of culture, waiting to leap out and destroy? No one asked these questions more poignantly than novelist Jack London, whose *Call of the Wild* was standard college freshman reading for decades. It is the story of a San Francisco dog, named Buck, who is taken to Alaska, where the latent viciousness of the wolf emerges from deep within him. This parallels London's own experience during the Alaskan gold rush of the 1890s, when civilized men went off to the wilderness and there devolved into snarling wolves, inflicting unspeakable cruelty on one another. Deep

---

3. Delumeau reminds us that the original phrase was longer and carried a double message: *Nosce teipsum: homo homini Deus. Homo homini lupus* — "We humans find ourselves between beast and God" (*Sin and Fear,* p. 144). This double message is what I have referred to as the *metaxy,* the tension of existing at the in-between. Without God, we sink into the vicious abyss of the beast.

within our evolutionary past our ancestors killed for the sheer joy of killing, says London, and their legacy lives just below the surface of our civilized consciousness. He describes both Buck and his human owners in these terms.

> All that stirring of old instincts which at stated periods drives men out from the sounding cities to forest and plain to kill things by chemically propelled leaden pellets, the blood lust, the joy to kill — all this was Buck's, only it was infinitely more intimate. He was ranging at the head of the pack, running the wild thing down, the living meat, to kill with his own teeth and wash his muzzle to the eyes in warm blood.[4]

Much of London's literary work can be understood in terms of lycanthropy, as a quest to understand the wolf nature that lies dangerously latent in the human soul.

In our own time, some animal rights advocates are saying that the wolf has gotten a bad rap. In an attempt to prevent the species from becoming extinct, they are trying to undo centuries of folkloric association of the wolf with evil by describing the animal as the harmless and innocent victim of human projection. I consider protecting wolves from human destruction to be a worthwhile enterprise. But I still think it worthwhile to look at the traditional wolf symbolism for the light it sheds on us, if not the wolf itself. This symbolism helps us ask questions about human nature, even if these questions become unanswerable. And there remains much we do not know about the wolf in any case, as Barry Holstun Lopez points out:

> In the past twenty years biologists have given us a new wolf, one separated from folklore. But they have not found the whole truth.

---

4. London, *The Call of the Wild* (New York: Airmont, 1964), p. 50. Going back to the dawn of Western literary history, to Homer's *Iliad* (Book 16), we find the following reference to Achilles's Achaean soldiers: "They fell in like flesh-eating wolves in all their natural savagery, wolves that have killed a great antlered stag in the mountains and rend him till their jowls are red with blood, then go off in a pack to lap the dark water from the surface of a deep spring with their slender tongues, belching gore, and still indomitably fierce though their bellies are distended." The analogy continues by introducing the wolf-sheep relationship: "They [the Achaean warriors] harried the Trojans like predatory wolves harrying lambs or kids and snatching them from under their dams when they are lost on the mountains through the shepherd's carelessness and the wolves seize their chance to pick off the timid creatures."

For example, wolves do not kill just the old, the weak, and the injured. They also kill animals in the prime of health. And they don't always kill just what they need; they sometimes kill in excess. And wolves kill each other. The reasons for these acts are not clear. No one — not biologists, not Eskimos, not backwoods hunters, not naturalist writers — knows why wolves do what they do.[5]

Nor do we know for certain why humans do what they do.

Torture

One way we humans wash our "muzzle to the eyes in warm blood" is through torture. Torture is the deliberate inflicting of pain as a means to a political end or as an expression of cruelty. It comes in psychological and physical forms, both of which capitalize on anxiety. Let me discuss two examples.

The first is that of Heidi Michelsen. Heidi came to Berkeley to study for the Lutheran ministry in the fall of 1987. She took a part-time job working for me doing secretarial and organizational work. She was popular on campus and known for her thoroughness in attending to community responsibilities, and students and staff and even faculty got in the habit of saying "call Heidi" when something needed to be done right. She was an excellent student, energetic, compassionate, with a strong faith and a deep commitment to justice in an unjust world. This led her eventually to concern for the suffering of the poor amid the civil war in El Salvador. She took Spanish language lessons and then in the fall of 1989 headed for a small Salvadoran village near San Miguel to serve her internship. She lived with a village family, slept on a straw cot, heartily embraced local life, and quickly came to love the people.

On Reformation Day of that year, October 31, Heidi was arrested by the Salvadoran army and taken to Third Brigade headquarters in San Miguel. She was then transferred to the jail operated by the Treasury Police. The abduction would have been secret, but witnesses on the street reported it to her supervising pastor, Rev. Walter Bairez, who telephoned us in Berkeley, where Pacific Lutheran Seminary president Jerry Schmalenberger put diplomatic wheels into motion to

5. Lopez, *Of Wolves and Men* (New York: Scribner's, 1978), p. 4.

secure her release. It was a difficult process. At first, U.S. State Department officials refused to help on the grounds that "she shouldn't have been down there."

The arresting soldiers, bearing M-16 rifles, paused briefly at the entrance to the Treasury Police headquarters, just long enough for Heidi to witness a bruised and beaten man being carried out. He had been badly tortured, was unable to walk by himself, and his eyes were watering profusely. The message was subtle yet emphatic: this might be in store for Heidi. Then they began the long and arduous process of interrogation. It was clear from their questioning that they had come to view church workers as enemies of the state. They asked Heidi about her knowledge of Marxism and demanded to know the names of villagers with whom she was associated, obviously seeking to uncover or to manufacture the plausible threat of a communist conspiracy to overthrow the Salvadoran government. At about 9:00 P.M. they introduced a new interrogator, whom Heidi described as bearing a "slimy leering look of evil." He began skillfully: "I really admire you Americans."

"Why?" Heidi asked. Having elicited a response from her, he craftily guided the conversation to the point of a sexual advance and then turned mean.

"When we men in El Salvador first have sex with our women, they get hurt." He had successfully conveyed the message that Heidi risked being sexually abused if she did not cooperate. "They were playing with my mind to fill me with fear," Heidi later told me. The threat of physical pain became psychological torture. The psychological fear was an extension of the threat of physical pain.

Unsatisfied with the answers their prisoner was giving, the Salvadorans took fifteen-minute shifts all night long in order to deny Heidi sleep and wear her down. Sneering cynically only inches from her face, they would shout taunts: "Does the fan bother you? Would you like a glass of water?"

The commander in charge, General Vargas, was caught off guard when telephone calls from the United States revealed that the outside world knew of Heidi's incarceration. Arrangements were made to transfer her to the Treasury Police station in San Salvador, the capital city, so that she could meet U.S. Embassy personnel. It was agreed that Rev. Bairez should escort the entourage to the capital, because the death squad history includes accounts of prisoners being kidnaped and murdered while being transferred from one prison to another.

The scheduled departure time was 6:00 A.M. At 5:30 A.M. the guards announced that it was time to leave. Heidi noted that the car was not a military vehicle and that she was being turned over to men wearing civilian clothes. It is common knowledge that this is how the death squads operate. Fearing what might be in store, Heidi asked for rest room privileges, which were granted. She went into the ladies room, locked and barred the door, and refused to come out until Rev. Bairez had arrived at 6:00. It worked, and the transfer went smoothly.

On arrival in San Salvador, she saw another prisoner who had been beaten, this one even more badly than the first. In the Treasury Police waiting room, Rev. Bairez waited with a church lawyer. The U.S. Embassy official showed up, a man whom Heidi describes as inept, "poor at speaking Spanish, and scared shitless." Before the officials would turn Heidi over to American authorities, they demanded that she sign a document stating that she had not been beaten, kicked, drowned in water, shocked by electricity, or suffocated. "Does psychological torture count?" Heidi asked. She was told that it did not. She signed. At this moment the U.S. Embassy official left the room to make a phone call. Before he could return, soldiers blindfolded Heidi, whisked her down a long hallway and into another building, and deposited her in another interrogation room. Now that she had signed a document exonerating the Salvadoran authorities, she feared they could do anything. They left her alone. What was she to do? She was helpless. So she dug into her memory. She recited the Twenty-third Psalm, the Lord's Prayer, and the Apostles' Creed. Then she began to sing and sing loudly Luther's Reformation hymn "A Mighty Fortress Is Our God." She told me she found great comfort in lines such as "though the hordes of devils fill the land . . . the kingdom's ours forever!" Her singing bolstered her courage.

The guards returned with a blank document and asked for her signature. Knowing their custom of filling in treasonous charges above such signatures, Heidi refused to sign. The guards were astounded at her resolute will. "They thought I was just some bimbo they could bluff, that I would get scared and flee home," she told me. "They didn't expect me to stand up to them." The guards blindfolded her again, forced her into a car, and drove off, again capitalizing on her fear of torture. The car simply went around the compound and dropped her back off at the waiting room. The paperwork done, Heidi was taken directly to the airport and flown back to Berkeley.

Heidi's safe return made us feel like the Hebrews had been delivered from slavery in Egypt. Among a hundred other questions I asked her was why she thought these people had treated her this way.

"I'm not sure," she said. "The slimy guy who made the sexual threat clearly enjoyed the suffering. The principal interrogator, though, seemed to be following orders. I think he was masking any care for me he might have been feeling. He had to work to put a sinister look on his face. General Vargas was just cynical, saying that he would not want to be responsible should I turn up dead. What was behind it all was the government's fear of what I represented — namely, international solidarity with the poor and our stand for human rights. They viewed it as an us/them situation, and I was part of the enemy."

Heidi learned that some soldiers in El Salvador were actually trained in torture. They would begin by brutalizing animals. Neophytes cut the throats of puppies, and then work their way up to humans. Torturers needed to be trained to overcome their initial revulsion at shedding blood.

What Heidi did not know at the time was that her arrest was the first chapter in a larger story. We now know that the Salvadoran government had concluded that church leaders and intellectual leaders with international connections were enemies of the state. In the days following Heidi's arrest, thirteen other Lutheran international church workers were abducted. After a worldwide public outcry, they turned up in detention centers and were deported. An Anglican pastor, Luis Serrano, was secretly arrested and not released for months, until a worldwide delegation of Anglican prelates showed up in El Salvador demanding an accounting of their colleague. On November 16, 1989, soldiers invaded the Central America University in San Salvador and brutally murdered six Jesuit professors along with their housekeeper and her daughter. One cannot help but recall the words of the Salvadoran Archbishop Oscar Romero, whose dedicated ministry on behalf of the poor of his country a decade earlier led to his martyrdom in the cathedral at the hands of a death squad: "Sin caused the death of the Son of God; sin continues to cause the death of the children of God."[6] Anxious on its seat of power, the insecure government struck out in violence — violence that included

6. Romero, quoted by Gustavo Gutiérrez in *We Drink from Our Own Wells* (London: SCM Press, 1984), p. 99.

the psychological torture of Heidi and the washing of the military muzzle in human blood.

Let us turn to a second example. In January 1987 I received a letter from my bishop expressing alarm that one of our Lutheran pastors was being illegally detained in a South African prison for anti-apartheid activities and might be subjected to torture. The bishop said the South African government could be influenced by public opinion, and he requested that we write letters to the U.S. State Department and to President P. W. Botha asking that Rev. Tshenuwani Simon Farisani be released. I wrote to both. So did a number of other people. Eventually twenty-six thousand such letters arrived at the U.S. State Department, and I presume an equal number were dumped on President Botha's desk. With this pressure and the help of Amnesty International, Farisani was released, put under the ban, brought to the United States, and eventually arrived in Berkeley, where, by coincidence, at this writing he is a visiting scholar and working with me toward a doctorate in theology.

This had been Farisani's fourth time in prison. A member of the Venda tribe whose mother had converted to Christianity, he came under the influence of a German missionary, Hannah Lechler, when he was a child. He began his anti-apartheid protesting already in his student days, joining Steve Biko and the Black Consciousness Movement in Natal in the early 1970s. As a pastor and eventually dean (deputy to the bishop) of his conference, Farisani preached a God of love, justice, and equality. Such preaching did not produce the sort of compliant blacks the government wanted. Authorities responded to Farisani's ministry with a series of arrests beginning in 1977.

Torture was part of the prison fare. The motive was to persuade leaders such as Dean Farisani to sign documents falsely confessing that they and their compatriots were guilty of communism, treason, and terrorism. His interrogators frequently acknowledged that they knew he was innocent, but they also told him, "No one gets out of this room alive unless he says and does what we want." During his third detainment, the arrested pastor was told to stand on his head against the wall with legs spread apart. In this position he was kicked from all angles. The police captain kicked his genitals. As the humiliated Farisani rolled in pain, the captain said, "I am determined to destroy your manhood, those dirty testicles that make you feel like a small bull." Then they threw the helpless prisoner in the air several times and let him fall onto the concrete floor. They lifted him by the hair and yanked out his beard. Then came the worst: electric shock. The guards connected wires to various parts of his body, doused him with water, and turned on the current. "My whole body shook, my insides danced," Farisani has written. "It was the most excruciating pain of my life. I wondered if it could be worse in hell."[7]

Why such cruelty? Does the political motive explain it? "Human beings can be very cruel to one another," says Farisani. "They can become beasts." He reports how one of the women guards would engage in what I have identified as cursing. "You will excrete, you excrement!" she would yell. Even when off duty, she would come to the cell area and taunt the male prisoners verbally.[8] Inflicting pain was more than just a job for her. It was recreation.

In his poems and in personal conversation, Farisani speaks of those who engage in cruel practices as having double personalities. They are hybrids of human and beast, combinations of the image of God and a perversion of that image. At home they are loving and responsible parents. On the job something of a beastly nature comes out of them that permits them to torture, maim, and kill.[9] To what extent these people have been trained for the job of torture and to what extent their previous disposition for cruelty recommended them for this position remain a mystery to at least this reflective victim.

In a certain ironic way, Rev. Farisani's torture was itself an answer to prayer. During his first detainment, he was placed in solitary confinement. From his lonely cell he could hear prisoners in other cells undergoing interrogation and torture. The screams penetrated the walls and pierced his own soul. Their pain became his pain.

I had to listen to screams like these for almost three months. . . .
The human screams would filter through all the disguises and reach

7. Farisani, *Diary from a South African Prison* (Minneapolis: Fortress Press, 1987), p. 71.

8. Farisani, *Diary from a South African Prison,* p. 67. Rev. Farisani told me that subsequent to his release from prison, he met this jailer coming out of an office building in Pretoria. He greeted her in a friendly fashion, asking her how things were going. She exhibited obvious embarrassment but managed to explain in a courteous and genteel manner that her family life was going fine and that she had quit her job with the prison system. Later Farisani learned that she had lied. She continues to hold the same job.

9. See his poems "The Beast Man" and "Man Beast," in *Justice in My Tears* (Trenton, N.J.: Africa World Press, 1988).

my human ear, breaking my human heart. Then I would fall on my knees and cry softly, at times silently, to the Lord despite my previous disappointments with him: "Oh God, you source of justice and love, opponent of oppression and exploitation, enemy of apartheid and torture, where are you? The murderers are let loose. The wolves are plundering. Can't you hear the desperate screams, the begging for mercy, the forced confessions? Can't you hear the boasting of the godless? Where is your love? Where is your care and concern? Where is your being? Please God, let them come to torture me rather than have me listen to the screams of my brothers and sisters. Amen."[10]

The wolves are plundering. Where is God's love? It is difficult to see, but it is partly revealed in the heart of a lamb who would take the place of the other sheep.

Doubling

How is it that Farisani's jailers (and perhaps Heidi Michelsen's jailers) could inflict such torture on the job and yet to all appearances live morally upstanding lives at home and in the community? Robert Jay Lifton suggests an answer with the concept of *doubling* — that is, a division of the self into two functioning wholes, each of which acts as an entire self. Although there are some similarities between doubling and multiple personality disorder (e.g., both conditions can be precipitated by extreme stress), doubling is a milder psychological condition that permits an otherwise well-integrated person with a conscience to engage in heinous criminal activity. It permits an individual to engage in evil without violating his or her conscience.

Lifton developed the concept of doubling in connection with a study of the doctors who worked for Himmler's SS during the Second World War. These physicians engaged in medical experiments sponsored by the Nazis for ideological and military purposes. Among their other responsibilities, these doctors also had to make determinations about which of the Jewish prisoners arriving at the death camps would be assigned to work programs and which would be consigned to the gas chambers. The doctors supervised the mass executions, and in

10. Farisani, *Diary from a South African Prison*, p. 36.

some cases personally executed individuals with lethal injections. What began as a racial eugenics program involving sterilization procedures in 1933 progressed to a program of euthanasia in 1939 and eventually became the "Final Solution" for racial and political undesirables. The border between healing and killing was erased in these doctors. Lifton calls it the "healing-killing paradox."

One important strategy that these medical people employed to carry on with their tortures was "technicizing" — that is, translating all their activities into technical tasks that could be measured by ordinary standards of efficiency. One SS doctor told Lifton, "Ethics was not a word used in Auschwitz. Doctors and others spoke only about how to do things most efficiently, about what worked best."[11] They managed to adopt this strategy not by eliminating their consciences as such but rather by transferring them to the state. They subjected their consciences to Auschwitz criteria for what is good: duty to the fatherland, loyalty to their professional colleagues, improvement of living conditions at the death camps, and efficiency of operations. They subordinated the deaths of millions of innocent people to these ends, thereby freeing the consciences of their original selves.

Elsewhere in their lives, these medical people were loving family members, responsible in their community, supportive of culture, appreciative of music and the opera. They were the pillars of society, the ostensible shepherds of our civilization.

What does this mean? Are we all potential wolves in shepherd's clothing? Is there lurking just below the surface of our civilized values and habits some sort of primitive beast just waiting for the license to emerge? Is that what ideologies such as Nazism do — provide the license? Does protecting the security of the government in power give us the right to engage in cruelty? Lifton notes how the doctors tried to believe in the doctrines of Nazism that appealed to the mystical bond of the present generation with the historic *Volk*, with the Teutonic gods of nature. To realize *homo homini lupus*, need we only release the bonds of order in selected departments of life and free the rage from within? Lifton concludes that each of us harbors an evil potential that can be invoked by doubling. "That evil is neither inherent in the self nor foreign to it. To live out the doubling and call forth the evil is a moral choice for which one is responsible, whatever

11. Lifton, *The Future of Immortality* (New York: Basic Books, 1987), p. 91.

the level of consciousness involved. By means of doubling, Nazi doctors made a Faustian choice for evil: in the process of doubling, in fact, lies an overall key to human evil."[12]

Lifton's analysis is valuable as a description of a phenomenon, but it is not in itself an explanation. He says that doubling is the key to human evil. But before we presume we have opened the lock on the mystery, let us return again for a moment to sociopathic criminality.

Cruelty without Conscience

The concept of doubling helps us to understand how people can engage in cruel behavior and still retain their consciences. But what about cases in which there seems to be no conscience? In the San Miguel prison, Heidi Michelsen confronted one interrogator with a conscience and one without. Cruelty can come from either.

Social scientists seem to agree that a defining characteristic of Antisocial Personality Disorder is a lack of conscience. Psychiatrist Ronald Markman refines this a bit, suggesting that the psychopathic criminal knows the difference between good and evil, between right and wrong. What such a person lacks is any inclination to apply it, to be good in any authentic way. In fact, the knowledge of right and wrong simply helps psychopaths to lie more effectively, to engage in self-justification aimed at convincing others to think highly of them. There is no blindness or self-deception here, nor any doubling: people who have no internal need to feel righteous have no need for doubling. The self-justification of psychopathic criminals is all for show. And it opens the door to cruelty as an end in itself.

Lawrence Bittaker and Roy Norris were in and out of prison from age eighteen on. Their rap sheets listed convictions for burglaries, robberies, assaults, and other felonies. They met each other at the San Luis Obispo California Men's Colony in 1978. It is often said that prisons are colleges for crime. If you put habitual criminals together for long periods of time, it is only reasonable to suppose that the plans they formulate in concert will be more sinister than any they might have assembled alone. Bittaker and Norris found that they shared a desire to dominate, rape, and brutalize women. They shared fantasies,

12. Lifton, *The Future of Immortality,* p. 201.

hatched plans, and eventually graduated from criminal college with honors and a hunger to ply their trade.

Bittaker and Norris teamed up in Los Angeles. They needed the right place to carry out their plans and settled on a remote area in the San Gabriel mountains. They also needed the right kind of vehicle. They purchased a 1977 GMC cargo van with a sliding door and no side windows. The sliding door would make it easy to kidnap people: they could simply pull up next to the victim, open the door, grab, and run. The two hunters started cruising the beaches looking for game: Pacific Palisades, Redondo Beach, Hermose Beach, Manhattan Beach, Venice, Santa Monica. They lived on beer and marijuana.

On June 24, 1979, they kidnaped sixteen-year-old Cindy Schaeffer. When Cindy screamed, they cranked the van radio up full blast to cover her shrieks. Once at their lair in the San Gabriel mountains, Norris announced that it was time to party. He forced Cindy to perform oral sex on him. Then Bittaker raped her. Then the two argued over who would get to kill her. Cindy lost the argument. They strangled her with a coat hanger and threw her body over a cliff. This established the procedure they would follow repeatedly.

Next to be kidnaped was eighteen-year-old Andrea Joy Hill on July 8, 1979. Again at the San Gabriel spot, they tortured her by driving an ice pick through her ears into her brain and took photographs as she died.

On Labor Day, September 3, 1979, they picked up two hitchhiking teens, Jackie Gilliam and Leah Lamp, and held them prisoner for two days at the mountain retreat. They used a tape recorder to capture the girls' screams while they tortured them, and then murdered Jackie with an ice pick to the brain and smashed Leah's head in with a sledgehammer.

On Halloween of that year, Norris and Bittaker kidnaped sixteen-year-old Shirley Ledford and raped her in the van. They recorded her screams while they sodomized her and pinched her with pliers. To make her scream louder, they smashed her elbows with a hammer. Finally they strangled her with wire. Curious about what the press would do if they discovered the body, they dumped Shirley in an ivy patch at the front of a Sunland neighborhood house.

At first no one connected the five rape-murders. Roy Norris's pride over his exploits led him to brag about his accomplishments to a former prison buddy, Joe Jackson — a mistake that eventually led to his arrest and conviction. Norris admitted to the killings and offered to give information to convict Bittaker as part of a plea bargain. He claimed that everything had been Bittaker's idea and that he, Norris, had only gone along for the ride. Bittaker, in turn, wrote a book, *The Last Ride,* describing the rape-murders, and in each instance he blamed Norris for inspiring the crimes. He said it was Norris who led him deeper and deeper into a life of crime. Bittaker went so far as to claim that he had tried to save the girls' lives but that he had been overpowered by Norris. This game of lies is characteristic of sociopathology. There is no trust, no true loyalty. The sociopath's self-justification is a sham, a device to ward off punishment. The jury was not taken in by this miserable attempt at mutual scapegoating. Bittaker was sentenced to death. Norris was sentenced to forty-five years to life, and will be eligible for parole in 2010.

Ronald Markman assures us that Bittaker and Norris are not insane, not mentally ill. They are psychopaths, he says, or more accurately sociopaths. They may be clever enough to fake psychotic behavior while in custody (Bittaker bragged about doing just that), but they do not actually suffer from psychosis. Rather, sociopaths are "incapable of learning to play by the rules."[13] We can count ourselves fortunate if such people engage in no more than petty crime and bounce in and out of jails. But some percentage will develop into individuals like Bittaker and Norris, who, without any internal controls over their impulses, proceeded to rape and torture and kill without hesitation or remorse.

Sadism

Having identified a conscience that does not require an internal identification with the good, might we take one step further and identify an outright philosophy of cruelty? Something like this turned up during the Enlightenment in the form of Sadism. The Enlightenment sought to free the Western conscience from alleged crudities of religious loyalty by appealing to innate principles of nature. Some individuals sought to take giant steps beyond all religious constraints on human morality and decency. Sometimes in secret societies, sometimes

13. Ronald Markman and Dominick Bosco, *Alone with the Devil: Famous Cases of a Courtroom Psychiatrist* (New York: Bantam Books, 1990), p. 257.

publicly, philosophies appeared that gave ideational expression to the way of the wolf.

Our word *sadism* comes from the surname of Donatien-Alphonse-François, Marquis de Sade (1740-1814). The Marquis de Sade was a common criminal who spent nearly half of his life in prison for debauchery and petty crime. While in prison, he wrote profusely. He was a relativist and an atheist. One implication of atheistic relativism is that there cannot be any absolute good. He denied any transcendent ground for the distinction between right and wrong. He denied that there is any universal purpose to life or to the human struggle beyond what nature has bequeathed us. Appeals to God or to the Devil meant nothing to de Sade's view of reality.

De Sade's observations of nature led him to conclude that fortune and success smile on the wicked as often as on the just.[14] He saw no good reason to live justly. In fact, he felt it more reasonable to live unjustly. He maintained that the wicked are more clever, smart enough to seize each opportunity to increase their own wealth and prosperity, and hence more likely to attain fortune and success.

This opens the door to hedonism. If our world is intrinsically valueless, argued de Sade, then seeking personal pleasure is the most sensible thing to do. It follows that if torturing someone gives you pleasure, you should pursue torture.[15] If other members of society do not enjoy torture, they need not engage in it themselves, but they have no right to appeal to a transcendent good in order to forbid you to go on torturing. Morality and virtue are fantasies. Mercy, love, and kindness are perversions.

The argument goes on. Sexual pleasures are more intense than most,

14. According to the Marquis de Sade, crime is natural, and it gives more pleasure than the conventional virtues. Crime, he wrote, always has "a character of grandeur and sublimity which prevails over and will always prevail over the monotonous and effeminate attractions of virtue" (*Les 120 Journées de Sodome* [1785], in *The Thought and Themes of the Marquis de Sade,* ed. Lorna Berman [Kitchener, Ont.: Ainsworth Press, 1971], pp. 124-25).

15. "Cruelty, far from being a vice, is the first sentiment inculcated in us by nature. . . . It is then a virtue and not a vice" (*La Philosophie dans le Boudoir,* in *The Thoughts and Themes of the Marquis de Sade,* p. 142). De Sade distinguishes two types of cruelty: "One, born of stupidity, not reasoned or analyzed, makes the individual like a ferocious beast and gives no pleasure; the other, the fruit of the extreme sensitivity of the organs, gives pleasure." He asserted that this second kind of cruelty appeals especially to delicate women (p. 143).

so they should be pursued without restraint. Under certain circumstances, crime can be even more thrilling than sex. If we combine them, we get sex crime, more intense than either by itself. The greatest delight for de Sade came from performing acts of cruelty on children, especially if the cruelty included degrading and humiliating the child. The most pleasurable act he could imagine involved the humiliation of a child, physical torture, and sexual abuse culminating in murder.[16]

In his criticism of de Sade, Jeffrey Burton Russell complains that the "very core of his doctrine is that he pays no attention to others' choices at all, including that of his victim."[17] That is to say, de Sade's hedonistic values cohere only for the individual who engages in cruelty for pleasure, not for the victim of that cruelty. Values that support acts of evil cannot be universal; they can only support one party over against another.

In order to make values apply to all equally, one has to appeal to some principle that unites all persons, to some transcendent ground. One might appeal, for example, as Confucius and Jesus do, to the golden rule: do unto others as you would have them do unto you.[18] Such an appeal to the golden rule presupposes a universal grounding for the good. Confucius appealed to the will of heaven, Jesus to the will of God. This is something a relativist gives up. Once a sense of the universal good has been lost, there is no moral ground for constraining cruelty.

Stealing the Symbols

Cruelty in mild or extreme forms is the inevitable product of our sinful behavior, of the progression of pride, concupiscence, and self-justification. At the early stages of our movement into sinfulness, we

16. De Sade's naturalism justifies murder. "The man who destroys his fellow man is to nature what the plague or famine is; he produces the destruction which nature needs for creations" (*The Thoughts and Themes of the Marquis de Sade*, p. 130). When it comes to cannibalism, de Sade says the "best type of human flesh is that of little boys" (*Ailine et Valcour*, in *The Thoughts and Themes of the Marquis de Sade*, p. 100).

17. Russell, *The Prince of Darkness: Radical Evil and the Power of Good in History* (Ithaca, N.Y.: Cornell University Press, 1988), p. 212.

18. Augustine took up the problem of the relativity of values from culture to culture. Of course customs differ, and what is considered right in one society is considered wrong in another. Does this then deny the existence of an absolute sense of what is right? By no means, says Augustine. The golden rule, for instance, "cannot be altered by any diversity of national customs" (*On Christian Doctrine*, 3.14).

do not intend to be cruel. We act in the name of some good. We think of ourselves as just or righteous. We may be fooling ourselves, but at least the symbol of the good remains our life's guide. The reasoning of the Marquis de Sade, however, is one example of the ways in which we begin to make a transition away from the symbol of the good, at least the transcendent good. The symbols upon which we have relied to create moral order amid chaos fall away. By positing a valueless universe, we unlock the cage that previously restrained the inner wolf and wash our muzzles to the eyes in warm blood.

The next step in the progression involves a transition from cruelty to blasphemy. We are moving in the direction of deliberately manipulating symbols for the purpose of heightening the degree of suffering caused by cruelty. In addition to the physical pain, cruelty in the form of blasphemy adds intolerable psychic or spiritual pain. Before taking this step, we should note something about the victims of torture.

Despite the excruciating circumstances in which they found themselves, Heidi Michelsen and Rev. Farisani were able to maintain a level of sanity because they could appeal to their own inner strengths, strengths established by the symbols of their faith. When Heidi was being interrogated and threatened, she began to sing "A Mighty Fortress Is Our God," a hymn that reminded her that God is her protector. No matter how much physical pain her captors threatened to inflict, her faith promised to sustain her inner integrity. Built into Heidi's psyche is a reservoir of spiritual strength on which she can draw simply by calling to mind the symbols of her faith.

Farisani told me that during the long lonely periods in prison and in the midst of unbearable torture, the theodicy problem arose repeatedly. When suffering, he would plead with heaven, demanding answers: "Do you exist, God? If you exist, do you bless only white people and curse black people? Here I am trying to be loyal to my faith, but you, O God, only crush me with unfeeling absence. Why?" He expressed his agony in the language of faith, even if he gave vent to his doubt in doing so. During the arrest process, the police would take away his Bible and other religious literature. The one Bible they could not take away, he says, was the one in his memory. He would mull passages over in his mind. The symbols of his faith were alive and gave him the internal strength he needed in at least three ways. First, he prayed. Like Augustine and Paul before him, he lifted his

212

anguish and doubts up to God in prayer. Second, he offered comfort to other prisoners undergoing similar hardships. He never ceased serving as a pastor, even inside prison walls. Third, and most remarkably, when he was in deepest despair, he encountered God in prescient visions. Farisani knew that, regardless of the unjustness of his suffering, he was not alone. God was present.

Both Heidi and Tshenuwani possessed internalized symbol systems that provided transcendent meaning and enormous strength in the face of threats to their safety and well-being. They had faith that even if the physical world were destroyed, the spiritual world would bear them on beyond. When attacked from the outside, they could retreat to safe harbor on the inside.

Now suppose, in the conscious service of evil, we were to try to destroy those internal strengths. In addition to physical pain and psychological fear, suppose we would try to inflict spiritual cruelty. How might we go about it? We would try to manipulate the symbol system so that the victim's internal consciousness could find no access to transcendent strength, no safe harbor for the psyche. With this kind of planning, we are on the way toward blasphemy.

Perhaps it would be helpful to consider an example of how the prostitution of symbols works. When preparing for the seminar on evil I mentioned in Chapter 1, my colleague Professor Lammers and I interviewed a woman named Kathy.[19] We also had Kathy come to class to tell her story. It goes like this:

When she was twelve years old, growing up in the Los Angeles area, one morning Kathy was kidnaped while walking to school. Three men whisked her off the street, forced her into a car, and threw a burlap bag over her head so that she could not see what direction they were traveling. When the bag was removed, she found herself in a house under construction in an unfamiliar neighborhood. Before her stood the three abductors, whom Kathy described as Nazi-like skinheads in their twenties who carried themselves in disciplined militaristic style. Beside her stood two other little girls her own age, neither of whom she recognized.

"Do you know why you are here?" asked the man whom Kathy eventually came to view as the leader. Of course the petrified girls could not answer. The question was repeated again and again, inter-

19. The name is changed here to protect her anonymity.

spersed with remarks such as, "We are here to feed off love. Do you know what it means to feed off love?"

Then began a long and complicated form of brainwashing in which the captors posed questions and then employed punishments and rewards to induce the girls to give the proper answers. Each of the girls was taken to a separate room. Kathy was stripped and placed on the floor in a sitting position with her legs spread. Her interrogator began silently. He took a large dagger and ran the point very slowly across the surface of the skin on her legs toward her vaginal area and then away. After a while, he had established the movement of the knife as the constant. When he would stop the movement, Kathy's level of fear would rise, because she didn't know what would happen next. Then the knife would move again. The captor could not maintain his stone-faced demeanor completely. The procedure caused him to become sexually aroused. He forced the knife handle into Kathy's vagina and ejaculated over the blade. Once relieved, he returned to the conditioning process. His objective was to get Kathy's reflexes under his control so that she would be more likely to respond with the proper answers to his litany of questions.

Kathy didn't know what was happening to the other two girls. She heard occasional screams of terror, more from one than the other. Now and then, the girls would be brought together for enigmatic lectures on the nature of love. Then they would be separated again. The process of conditioning leading toward the symbol of "feeding off love" continued throughout the day.

In our interview with Kathy, she seemed to feel that it was important to describe herself as having grown up in a dysfunctional family with an uncaring mother and abusive father. This told us that over the years she had developed ways of dealing with the stress of potentially violent circumstances. She described herself as having been able to learn quickly even under the duress of her captivity and torture. If she could only ascertain what the men actually wanted, she thought, she would agree to do their bidding.

The haunting phrase "feed off love" was the key, she concluded. Late in the day, almost at nightfall, the three nude girls were brought into the living room of the unfinished house. A large table was situated in the center. The three men took the little girl who had screamed most frequently and forced her to lie on the table. "Now has come the moment to feed off love," the leader announced. Kathy said that

214

by this time she knew what she was supposed to do. She took the dagger and plunged it into the girl's heart. Blood spewed forth while the victim squirmed and died. Kathy watched as the three removed the sacrificed girl's heart, cut it up, and ate it. As Kathy and the other nameless girl were being ushered out of the living room, she could see two of the men dismembering the body and placing the parts in garbage bags.

Kathy was returned to her interrogation room, tied to a wall stud, and left alone. She concluded that it would only be a matter of time before she and the other remaining girl would be killed. She had to do something radical. At that moment, she said, a great sense of calm and intense concentration came upon her. She described it as "a presence." "Do you mean an angel?" I asked. "Maybe," she said. "I'm not sure what it was. I just call it a presence." What the presence did was grant Kathy assurance that she would survive.

Some of her captor's paraphernalia remained in the room, including a knife. She was able to wriggle sufficiently to draw the knife toward her, sever the ropes, and escape out a window to safety. The fate of the girl left behind is unknown. No arrests were ever made. We have no knowledge of the group other than that given in Kathy's testimony.

At the time of her kidnaping, Kathy was part of a Jewish family. She later converted to Christianity and now belongs to an Episcopal church. Along with three other victims of ritual abuse, Kathy has relied heavily on the priest at her home congregation to help her work through the trauma buried in her memory. Each celebration of the Eucharist provides a jolting reminder of the horrors they experienced. When the priest raises the elements above the altar and announces that the congregation will be drinking the blood and eating the body of Christ, all the terror and pain of the/literal cannibalism they were forced to witness comes roaring back to their consciousness.

In the case of Kathy in particular, the symbol of love was contaminated for years.[20] What is the true meaning of love? The overwhelming power of the conditioning and ritual to which she was exposed has

20. "To sin is to deny love," writes Gutiérrez (*We Drink from Our Own Wells*, p. 97). The double cruelty that leads to blasphemy in Kathy's case is that love is denied in the name of love.

burned a connection in her mind between love and a cruel death. In addition, the question-and-answer procedure led to an internalization of the cult's values that eventuated in Kathy's actually embracing her captor's designs and purposes. She granted internal consent. She found herself wanting to kill. She was a voluntary accomplice. The men had managed not only to capture her body but, for at least that one moment, also her soul.

8

BLASPHEMY
Satanic Rituals and the Destruction of the Inner Soul

So farewell hope, and, with hope, farewell fear,
Farewell remorse! All good to me is lost;
Evil, be thou my Good.

John Milton, *Paradise Lost*, bk. 3, ll. 108-11

There are two kinds of blasphemy. Both seek to sever the tie between the name of God and the grace of God. The first form, covert blasphemy, is the more subtle of the two. It involves using the name of God directly or indirectly in order to hide evil behind a veil of righteousness. It is hypocrisy. It presumes the goodness of God and then tries to co-opt that goodness to cover over insidious injustice. The danger of this form of blasphemy is that those who see through the hypocrisy may get the impression that language about God is intrinsically deceitful. Blasphemers tarnish the name of God to the point that people no longer think to call on it to ask for divine grace. One of the heinous examples of this form of blasphemy in the late twentieth century is the Afrikaners' use of belief in God to justify the apartheid system in South Africa. To a black South African who has felt the iron heel of racial injustice, the name of a gracious God may provide the only grounds of hope for deliverance. When the perpetrators of oppression claim this God as their own possession, they leave

217

the oppressed with no symbol of hope, nothing to hang onto. They steal the symbol of divine grace away from those who most need it. Tshenuwani Simon Farisani recalls Jesus' beatitudes when he writes,

> Whoever robs one of these blacks of the least of his human rights,
> And teaches that apartheid is from God,
> he shall be called heretic in the kingdom of God.[1]

This form of blasphemy consists in invoking the name of God in order to justify oneself and contaminating the name of God in the process.

Here, we will be taking a closer look at a second kind of blasphemy, overt blasphemy. This less subtle form of blasphemy (Greek *blasphēmia*) is classically defined as the dishonoring or reviling of the name, being, or work of God through slander, cursing, or showing contempt. It is a denial of God's holiness. It is a repudiation of God's saving work. It is a rejection of God's grace. It is a defamation of God's character. It takes the form of employing divine symbols for the purpose of disavowing all loyalty to the God of love and salvation. Worse, it employs these symbols to prevent others from gaining access to the God of love and salvation.

It is this second kind of blasphemy that I call "radical evil."[2] By deliberately advancing the symbols of evil, it repudiates the sham

---

1. Farisani, *In Transit* (Grand Rapids: William B. Eerdmans, 1990), p. 121. Nearly four decades ago, when writing his book on ethics, theologian George Forell used South African apartheid as a prime example of taking the Lord's name in vain. The proper use of God's name is to fight injustice, not baptize it: "The second commandment calls us to speak up against unrighteousness wherever we find it, to speak for the downtrodden, the exploited, the hungry and the naked everywhere" (*Ethics of Decision* [Philadelphia: Fortress Press, 1955], p. 114).

2. The term *radical evil* may call to mind its use by Immanuel Kant in book 1 of *Religion within the Limits of Reason Alone*. According to Kant, evil arises not out of the arena of physical sensation but out of a decision of the human will. Furthermore, willful evil decisions emerge out of a prior tendency to evil. The human "evil heart" is radically evil in that it destroys all moral maxims. This would certainly seem to suggest that radical evil is something from which we as humans cannot extricate ourselves. Emil Brunner compliments Kant for providing the best possible philosophical argument apart from Christian revelation that only an act of divine grace can redeem humanity from this state of radical evil; see his *Man in Revolt* (Philadelphia: Westminster Press, 1947), pp. 125-29; and *The Christian Doctrine of Creation and Redemption* (Philadelphia: Westminster Press, 1952), p. 95. This is an important debate, but my use of the term *radical evil* has nothing to do with it. I employ the phrase to refer to the worst case of blasphemy — namely, the pursuit of evil in the name of evil.

218

allegiance to goodness found in hypocrisy.[3] I call it *radical* evil because it cuts the soul off from consolation; it vitiates goodness at the roots *(vitiatum in radice)*.

The Kingdom of Hell

I would like to begin this consideration of blasphemy by returning to the terrifying story I mentioned in Chapter 1 of the young girl who claimed to have grown up in a Satanic cult. The case study, presented by Judith Spencer in her book *Suffer the Child*, is told from the point of view of the two psychotherapists who have been treating the girl for Multiple Personality Disorder (MPD) since 1983. The subject, referred to in the study as Jenny, is said to have created over four hundred personalities as a method of psychic survival in the face of abuse received at the hands of the cult. The therapists have been seeking to reunite the fractured array of personalities and recover a single whole identity. Among other things, this book portrays the nightmare that a victim of ritual abuse experiences.

Born to a mother who was a member of a Satanic cult, little Jenny was herself initiated into the cult while she was still a preschooler. She heard pseudo-scriptures being read that blasphemed God and praised Satan. She watched people engage in sexual intercourse on the Devil's altar. She witnessed the torture and sacrifice of dogs, cats, chickens, squirrels, and goats. She saw limbs being amputated and blood flowing into waiting drinking cups. She and other children were occasionally placed on the altar beneath a priest with dagger in hand. Blood was drawn from her vagina and bits of her skin were scraped off for use in a eucharistic ritual in which the worshipers, whipped into a frenzy by drugs and alcohol, would actually drink human blood and eat human flesh. Spencer's book receives its title from a statement that Jenny repeatedly heard the priest make: "Suffer the little children to come unto him, for of such is the kingdom of hell." This, in my

---

3. I am suggesting that we can distinguish ordinary hypocritical sin, in the pursuit of which we can still retain some reverence for the goodness of God, from radical evil, in the pursuit of which we intentionally enter into opposition to God. Radical evil is Satanic. Ruth Nanda Anshen writes, "What the Devil exacts is ever one and the same: the hatred of God. In this respect, he is inexorable" (*Anatomy of Evil* [Mt. Kisco, N.Y.: Moyer Bell, 1972], p. 120).

judgment, is the blasphemy: by stealing words of Scripture that bear the power of salvation and twisting them into the service of Satan, the priest was robbing his victims of psychic access to symbols that could bring comfort.

When she was five years old, Jenny took part in a Satanic wedding ceremony in which she became the Devil's bride. As part of the ceremony, she was suspended above a naked woman who had been drugged into unconsciousness and stretched across the altar. She was handed a dagger and told to kill the woman beneath her. She did as she was told. Presumably the sacrificed woman provided the flesh and blood for that night's ritual.

Jenny was taught the meaning of the symbols. The dagger stands for manhood, the chalice for womanhood. Church came to mean distress. She was taught that she must not look upon the Christian cross or listen to words blaspheming her master, the Devil. To participate in baptism or communion in a Christian church would mean certain death. The aim of such blasphemy is to close the door all the more tightly against the salvific power of symbols of grace.

Jenny was also taught theology. Evil persons cannot go to heaven. They go to hell, a place of burning ruled by Satan. Those who serve Satan also go to hell, but they will not burn. The highest rank in hell would be reserved for them.[4] Why would this theology attract anybody? The fact that both Jenny and her mother were born out of wedlock might be relevant. They referred to themselves as "bastards." Perhaps people who present themselves that way, who start out thinking of themselves as no good and contaminated with evil, will be more inclined to think that an invitation to become a disciple of Satan and receive the reward of an upper berth in hell sounds good.

The Four Faces of Satanism

Before we proceed much further in our analysis of the dynamics of sin, perhaps we should try to establish just what we are talking about when speaking of Satanism, or what I call *radical evil*. We first need to divide the topic between the theological understanding of Satan on

4. This Satanic theology is reminiscent of that in Milton's *Paradise Lost* — "Better to reign in Hell, than serve in heaven" (bk. 1, l. 263).

the one hand and Satanism as a contemporary social phenomenon on the other. We will tackle the social phenomenon first. I would not want to suggest that getting straight on the facts regarding contemporary Satanic practices is easy, however. We must be vigilant in pursuing the facts lest we lead ourselves astray.

Satanism as a social phenomenon is protean, frequently changing its visage in recent history. Since 1980 it has had at least four faces. The first is *classic Satan worship,* which can be traced back at least as far as eighteenth-century France. This form of Satanism mimics and repudiates everything Christian: the Devil replaces Jesus Christ as Lord, the black mass replaces the Eucharist, and so on. Classic Satan worship appears to exist in our era in small, highly secretive groups who engage in ritual torture and murder. In almost all contemporary cases, Satan worship is associated with illegal drugs. The purpose of ritual murder and the subsequent eating of human flesh is twofold: to gain power from the victim and to desensitize cult members, readying them for criminal assignments. Many skeptics maintain that classic Satanism does not exist in our time. I believe there is sufficient evidence to prove that such groups do in fact exist, but I suspect they are self-styled independent groups and not organized in any comprehensive conspiracy.

The second face is that of *public Satanism*. The present tradition began with the teachings of Aleister Crowley (1875-1947), a hedonist who claimed for himself the mark of the beast (the number 666) mentioned in the book of Revelation and prophesied that Satan's second coming was imminent. The Crowley tradition lives on in the Church of Satan founded by Anton Szandor LaVey, who declared in 1966 that the Satanic Age had begun. LaVey served as a consultant during the filming of Roman Polanski's 1968 movie *Rosemary's Baby,* in which the birth of a Satanic messiah is presented as a parody of the birth of Christ. One of LaVey's early disciples, Michael Aquino, broke away to form the Temple of Set, hoping to distance himself from the repudiation of Christ associated with traditional Satanism and to establish ties instead with the Egyptian god Set. Contemporary Crowleyism teaches that Christian morality is oppressive because it blocks expression of our more genuinely human propensities to take unbridled pleasure in sex and power. These public organizations demand protection from prosecution under the First Amendment and claim that they themselves do not engage in criminal activity.

221

The third face is that of the *lone teenage dabbler* who fantasizes through role-playing games and identifies with heavy metal music. These interests may be combined with indulgence in drugs and sexual orgies, though not necessarily. Mental health workers tell me that such teens have a distinct profile: they are loners who begin to explore esoterica by themselves. This may lead to mail-order purchases of Satanic paraphernalia and the reading of Anton LaVey's *Satanic Bible*, which they tend to take much more seriously than its author did. Such teens are very susceptible to suicide. They may also team up with a small number of close friends to experiment with the occult and sometimes engage in antisocial activity such as the desecration of churches.

In rare cases, dabblers may become serial killers such as Richard Ramirez, the Night Stalker, famed for holding up his hand during his trial to display the number 666 inscribed on his palm. At this writing, Ramirez has been convicted of thirteen murders and is facing trial for another. In a gesture of obvious self-justification, he told a television audience that "serial killers only do what governments do, but on a smaller scale." He added, "I gave up on love and happiness a long time ago."[5] Ramirez is an example of the fourth category, *self-styled Satanists*, consisting of criminals who borrow Satanic themes as a rationale for their antisocial behavior.

The category of the self-styled Satanist may overlap with those of the teenage dabbler and public Satanism. In San Francisco during the late 1960s, there was some overlap in membership between the Church of Satan and the Church of the Process of the Final Judgment, a group founded as a breakoff sect of Scientology in 1964. Process Church theology tied together Christ and Satan and reversed the fifth commandment to read, "Thou *shalt* kill." One person influenced by the Process Church was Charles Manson, who in 1969 asked his "family" to ritually murder Sharon Tate, the wife of the director of *Rosemary's Baby*, Roman Polanski. A decade later, the Process Church was implicated in the Son of Sam serial killings in New York City.

Closely tied to these four faces of contemporary Satanism is the inadequately understood problem of cult survivors such as Jenny in *Suffer the Child*. To date our only access to such survivors, three quarters of whom suffer from Multiple Personality Disorder, is through psychotherapy. To complicate matters, books about the phenomenon

5. *A Current Affair*, 14 October 1991.

have themselves become factors in the phenomenon. The 1980 publication and 1985 paperback republication of *Michelle Remembers,* by
Michelle Smith and Lawrence Pazder, virtually inaugurated the present
chapter in the history of Satanism's significance. The book reports
what Michelle told her psychiatrist, coauthor Dr. Pazder, regarding
her experience growing up in a Satanic cult during the 1950s on
Vancouver Island. Unable to remember consciously the horrors she
had undergone, Smith depended on therapeutic techniques to recover
them. Pazder helped Michelle recall her past and then, through the
book, to divulge it to others. It may turn out that many of the images
that have come to be identified with contemporary Satanism have been
stimulated by this and similar books.

Satanism as a Phenomenon

Whenever we speak of a *phenomenon,* we are speaking about how
something *appears* to someone. The term *phenomenon* derives from
the Greek word, *phaino,* meaning "to appear." In our usage, the idea
of a phenomenon encompasses both the thing that is perceived and
the person who is doing the perceiving — both the object and the
subject. In the case of contemporary Satanism, the nature of the object
is determined in part by who is doing the perceiving. It is in this light
that we can identify three basic levels of the phenomenon: (1) the
Satanism movement, (2) the anti-Satanism movement, and (3) the
anti-anti-Satanism movement. Because our access to information about
Satanism is in many ways constrained by these three competing takes
on the phenomenon, a simply factual analysis of the situation is virtually impossible at the present time.

We have already reviewed what seem to be widely accepted as the
four faces of Satanism in North America. But one step back from this,
a dispute continues to rage over whether Satanists do in fact exist at
all. And among those who agree that they do exist, there is disagreement over whether they constitute a broad conspiracy that can be
blamed for a long list of crimes. What the anti-Satanists perceive leads
them to say Yes in both cases.[6]

6. Sociologist David G. Bromley assigns the name Anti-Satanism Movement (ASM)
— the capital letters and acronym certainly seem to assure a genuine if not official

Who are the anti-Satanists? They include sensationalizing journalists such as television personalities Geraldo Rivera and Oprah Winfrey, who, in the name of serving the public interest, present lurid details of unspeakable horror.[7] They include scholars such as Carl Raschke, who, in his controversial book *Painted Black,* tries to connect a wide variety of criminal activity with Satan's underground. They include hundreds of therapists who are working with MPD clients. They include numerous parent groups seeking to supervise day-care centers. They include law enforcement agencies large and small across the country, many of which have developed specialists in cult crime. And they include evangelical and fundamentalist preachers who decry the widespread deterioration of family life and corruption of youth through drugs and heavy metal music.

How do anti-Satanists describe the present situation? Larry Kahaner, a police investigator, gives us the big picture:

> I found a hidden society, much larger and more disquieting than the world of [public] Satanism alone, a place few people know exists. . . . It is the underworld of "occult crime." . . . The crimes are frightening: a homicide where the decapitated victim is sur-rounded by colored beads, seven coins and chicken feathers; ritual sacrifices at wooded sites where black-robed cultists mutilate animals on altars; other homicides where the corpses are found drained of blood with symbols such as a pentagram or inverted cross carved into their chests; drug and pornography rings with nationwide con-nections to occult groups; carefully executed grave robbing; Satanic rituals and human sacrifices involving children — fantastic stories

status — to those holding what he calls a "countersubversion ideology." The "subver-sion" that the ASM counters is, of course, Satanism. Bromley introduced the term in a paper entitled "Satanism: The New Cult Scare," which he presented at the Fifth Annual International Conference on New Religions, sponsored by the Institute for the Study of American Religion in Santa Barbara, California, 16-17 May 1991. A version of this paper appears in *The Satanism Scare,* ed. James T. Richardson, Joel Best, and David G. Bromley (New York: Aldine de Gruyter, 1991), pp. 49-72. I have introduced the terms "Satanist movement" and "anti-anti-Satanist movement" as extensions of Bromley's terminology, even though the term *movement* may imply more unity among Satanists than there actually is.

7. Geraldo's show included specials on Satanism in broadcasts on 19 November 1987; 6, 24, and 25 October 1988; 29 November 1988; and 1 March 1989. Oprah's show featured similar segments on 30 September 1986; 17 February 1988; and 31 January 1989.

told by hundreds of children in scores of preschools throughout the United States, all of them relating similar horrors.[8]

The anti-Satanists are convinced of the existence of a massive underground network of organized Satanic groups who practice ritual worship of the Devil, sponsor molestations of children in preschools, kidnap or breed their own children for ritual purposes and the production of child pornography, torture animals and sacrifice human beings in versions of the black mass, practice cannibalism, and continue to recruit our nation's young people through heavy metal music and games such as *Dungeons and Dragons*.

A colleague recently brought me a flier he had received from the Schiller Institute in Livermore, California, entitled "Save Your Child's Life!" It is addressed to "Parents" and opens with the line "Strike back against the child kidnappers and child murderers!" It recommends that action be taken to halt the sale of heavy metal recordings, to shut down occult bookstores, to keep children from playing Dungeons and Dragons, to restrict the activities of such organizations as Wicca and the Ordo Templi Orientis, and to garner political support for the Satanic Rituals Prohibition Act. "Most suspect what is going on," the flier states. "They're just waiting for a call to arms."

This is the perception of the anti-Satanists. Now, who are the anti-anti-Satanists? They are a curious amalgam of social scientists, skeptics belonging to the Committee for the Scientific Investigation of Claims of the Paranormal, law enforcement personnel who are disenchanted with their anti-Satanist colleagues, and Satanists themselves. Many anti-anti-Satanists doubt that Satanism exists at all in the form of a widespread conspiracy; they dismiss the incidents that excite the anti-Satanists as sporadic copycat manifestations that mimic the image presented by the anti-Satanists. In other words, the anti-anti-Satanists accuse the anti-Satanism movement of being the author of the Satanism movement. They either find the anti-Satanists to be a curious phenomenon to study or, more seriously, charge them with being the truly dangerous element in our society.[9] Some oppose

8. Kahaner, *Cults That Kill: Probing the Underworld of Occult Crime* (New York: Warner Books, 1988), p. vii.

9. Sociologist Marcello Truzzi is one of the relatively few anti-anti-Satanists who flatly deny the existence of any Satanists. Most anti-anti-Satanists acknowledge the existence of public Satanism, for instance, such as Anton LaVey's Church of Satan —

anti-Satanism on the basis of narrow identification of the movement with evangelical and fundamentalist Christian forces; they contend that the beliefs of these Christians are incompatible with the worldview of an ostensibly secular society, and they dismiss these Christians as ideologists who are scapegoating the Satanists. In other words, the real enemy to our society is not Satanism but rather anti-Satanism.

What are the points at issue between the anti-Satanists and the anti-anti-Satanists? First, the scope of the so-called Satanist movement. Anti-Satanists frequently say that there are 50,000 to 60,000 ritual sacrifice victims each year. One parent of a child in the McMartin Preschool case told a Geraldo audience that 1,200 children had been molested in the city of Manhattan Beach alone — a city with a total population of only around 32,000. The Schiller Institute flier claims that 1.8 million children have disappeared in the United States. Are such statistics credible? No, say the anti-anti-Satanists. David Bromley dismisses as implausible the claim that Satanists obtain their victims by abducting children. The best estimates of law enforcement agencies place the total number of children abducted by strangers annually in the United States between 200 and 300. Even if all of these stranger abductions were by Satanists, they would not come close to meeting the alleged demand for victims. Furthermore, even if there were only as many as 10,000 human sacrifices conducted by Satanists per year (rather than the figure of 50,000 more commonly cited by the anti-Satanists), and if Satanism dates back to the 1950s as ritual abuse survivors commonly report, this would have produced 400,000 victims — a total rivaling the 517,347 war-related American deaths from World War II, Korea, and Vietnam combined. Yet, according to Kenneth Lanning of the FBI, on whom Bromley depends here, not a single casualty of the Satanic movement has been discovered.[10]

> A satanic murder can be defined as one committed by two or more individuals who rationally plan the crime and whose primary motivation is to fulfill a prescribed satanic ritual calling for the murder. By this definition, the author has been unable to identify even one

---

the sort of thing that has a listing in the phone book. Satanism in this form is clearly hard to deny. But the anti-anti-Satanists are united in denying the existence of a widespread Satanic conspiracy. See *The Satansism Scare,* p. 8.

10. Bromley, "Satanism: The New Cult Scare." Bromley is most helpful in delineating the points at issue.

documented murder in the United States. . . . It is highly unlikely that they could kill several people, every year, year after year, and not be discovered.[11]

A second point at issue has to do with the degree of organization in the Satanist movement. The anti-Satanists describe complex rituals sponsored by a huge and complex underground network. Anti-anti-Satanists say there is no evidence of a common belief system, set of rituals, or organizational apparatus. Despite anti-Satanist descriptions of elaborate rituals, anti-anti-Satanists have found no written sources that trace their historical development or spell out the philosophy of the secret ceremonies. Despite the contention that a conspiracy exists, no one has been able to produce correspondence, membership lists, telephone logs, travel records, bank accounts, meeting places, crematoriums, or equipment used in the production of pornographic films or videos.

A third point of contention has to do with what counts as evidence. What about the desecration of churches and the vandalism of cemeteries? What about reports of mutilated animal corpses? Anti-Satanists interpret these as evidence of cult crime. In a state park near Allenstown, New Hampshire, in May 1989, for example, it was reported that six cats were found hanging in a tree near a decapitated dog. A woman out for a walk with her dog said she found a makeshift altar with the carcass of a mutilated beaver on it and another beaver skin nearby. The police sergeant in charge of the investigation looked for a link between the sacrifice of the animals and drugs or heavy metal music. As a result, the mayor of Manchester, New Hampshire, tried to ban the appearance of a heavy metal band in town for fear that it might precipitate more animal mutilations. Anti-anti-Satanist author Robert D. Hicks investigated and determined that in fact no dead cats had been found hanging from trees and that the beavers had been legally trapped. Other dead animals occasionally reported in the park turned out to be road kill that had been stacked by the park service for later pick-up.[12] With regard to the overall picture, Bromley says that church and grave desecrations and animal mutilations have a long

11. Lanning, "Satanic, Occult, Ritualistic Crime: A Law Enforcement Perspective," *Police Chief* 56 (1989): 62-83.

12. Hicks, *In Pursuit of Satan: The Police and the Occult* (Buffalo: Prometheus Books, 1991), p. 330.

history in America. Only recently have they been identified with Satanic cult activity. In any event, there is no evidence of a recent increase in the number of these incidents.

A fourth point at issue is the question of how Satanists could have avoided detection if the frequency and enormity of their offenses is as great as that claimed by the anti-Satanists. Is this an airtight conspiracy? Why haven't the children spoken out? The anti-Satanists contend that the children have been so terrorized and intimidated that they have been unable to reveal their victimization to anyone. When they do speak, what they say is so bizarre that it is dismissed as fantasy. In addition, say the anti-Satanists, certain high-ranking police officials are themselves Satanists and manage to deflect investigations. Judith Spencer told our GTU seminar that many respected community leaders are secret practitioners, including undertakers who get rid of all evidence in their crematoriums. It is claimed that therapists who happen to gain access to the unspeakable memories of their patients are intimidated by warnings of harm should they go public. The relatively small number of survivors is simply interpreted as testimony to the ruthlessness and effectiveness of the Satanism movement.

Bromley believes the anti-Satanists contradict themselves. On the one hand, they describe the Satanists as a tightly organized, powerful, infallible network that leaves no evidence of its large-scale programs of abduction, human breeding, and sacrificial activities. On the other hand, they maintain that Satanic groups leave behind an easily discovered trail of clues such as animal carcasses and open graves that demand official investigation. Bromley goes on to argue that not a single defector has managed to leave with any type of organizational records. Historically, such radical groups have been shown to be particularly prone to schism, defection, and internecine conflicts. This absence of defectors from the Satanic movement is striking.

A fifth point at issue is the credibility of the accounts that people suffering from Multiple Personality Disorder have given to their therapists. I have already mentioned three cases of cult survivors with MPD: Kathy, Jenny (*Suffer the Child*), and Michelle Smith (*Michelle Remembers*). There are currently hundreds of therapists in the United States treating clients for MPD resulting from a history of ritual abuse. Despite the fact that the clients do not know one another and come from a variety of geographical locations, they tell strikingly similar stories of Satanic abuse.

The regnant theory among professionals and anti-Satanists is that MPD is a subclass of dissociative disorders. In this case, the child in the abusive situation is so overwhelmed with terror and pain that the personality cracks or splits into multiple personalities. The continuity of identity, memory, and consciousness is disrupted. One discrete personality is consigned to the trauma of stress and pain. The other personalities, known as *alters,* escape by forgetting. The memory of the abuse is pressed down and covered over as a means of psychic protection. What happens in therapy, so the theory goes, is that these previously forgotten experiences are brought to the surface as the therapist tries to talk with each of the personalities. Because it is theorized that the fragmenting is itself a form of self-hypnosis, therapy frequently includes the technique of hypnotic regression. The therapeutic goal is not always the same. In some cases the goal is to bring all personalities to the surface and then integrate them. In other cases the goal is to choose one personality and make it dominant. MPD is quite gender-specific; nine out of ten people diagnosed with it are women.

The accounts of an extensive Satanic underground gained from MPD survivor testimony sound convincing to therapists for a number of reasons: the clients tell their stories with evident emotional pain, they reveal the same stories under hypnosis, the stories are internally consistent, and patients from various parts of the country give very similar accounts.

While anti-anti-Satanists do not dismiss MPD accounts casually, in the end they consider them unconvincing as evidence of widespread Satanism.[13] For one thing, says Robert Hicks, survivor testimonies stand alone without any corroborating evidence. No police investigations have ever supported survivor allegations. In addition, Hicks contends that MPD sufferers are not particularly credible on the grounds that they cannot discriminate between fantasy and fact. He contradicts the opinion of therapists when he asserts that even with hypnosis, it is difficult to gain a coherent account from a MPD sufferer.

---

13. One runs a variety of risks in challenging the accounts of the survivors of ritual abuse. "When a growing number of individuals believe that they experienced satanic rituals as children, their beliefs become, in effect, 'eye-witness testimony.' Refuting such testimony becomes a formidable task for those questioning the satanic conspiracy's existence. Indeed, those who question such claims run the risk of being accused of revictimizing the person making the statements" (*The Satanism Scare,* p. 11).

Hicks does not doubt that MPD victims have suffered some form of abuse, but he argues that this does not mean that we should take literally what they say regarding cult activity.[14]

In some cases, survivor accounts can be discredited outright. In her book *Satan's Underground: The Extraordinary Story of One Woman's Escape,* author Lauren Stratford not only claimed that she been a victim of ritual abuse (and that she had the physical scars to prove it) but also introduced the startling concept of the breeder. She said she had been forced to give birth to three infants who were subsequently killed, two in snuff-porn movies and one in a Satanic ritual. But even after checking closely, researchers writing for *Cornerstone* magazine found they could not verify the times and dates Stratford had given in her book. The physical scars she attributed to the Satanic cult appeared in fact to have been self-inflicted. Most decisively, this alleged breeder of three babies showed no medical evidence of ever having been pregnant.[15] The publisher of *Satan's Underground* ceased distributing the book in 1990, apparently in response to the revelations.

Discounting those cases that can be discredited directly, we still

---

14. See Hicks, "Police Pursuit of Satanic Crime, Part II," *Skeptical Inquirer* 14 (Summer 1990): 382. Some critics even question the link between early trauma and the development of MPD. "It has not been proven that childhood trauma causes MPD," writes Frank W. Putnam. "An independent verification of alleged abuse, which often occurred 10 or more years prior to being reported in therapy, is almost impossible for the average therapist to obtain" (*Diagnosis and Treatment of Multiple Personality Disorder* [New York: Guilford Press, 1989], p. 47).

15. See Gretchen and Bob Passantino with Jon Trott, "Satan's Sideshow," *Cornerstone* 18 (1990): 23-28; and Philip Jenkins and Daniel Maier-Katkin, "Occult Survivors: The Making of a Myth," in *The Satanism Scare,* pp. 132-33. Jenkins and Maier-Katkin write, "We can already discern the early stages of a troubling process that permits the almost unlimited manufacture of survivors and their grisly tales. Ideological and theoretical changes within the therapeutic community have contributed to a dramatic increase in the numbers of self-described occult survivors. . . . As survivor tales proliferate, the sheer volume of apparent evidence may convince some of the truth of the charges. We would suggest, however, that many of these stories should be seen as little more than derivative of the first few accounts, and that those first few accounts are themselves highly questionable" (pp. 141-44). Such questionableness has led to controversy. "If we want to stop ritual abuse, the first step is to believe these brutal crimes occur," writes Elizabeth S. Rose in "Surviving the Unbelievable," *Ms Magazine,* January/February 1993, p. 45. The question of whether memories of childhood ritual abuse can be trusted is addressed in a two-part series of articles by Lawrence Wright entitled "Remembering Satan" in *The New Yorker,* 17 May 1993, pp. 60-81, and 24 May 1993, pp. 54-76.

have to ask how we can explain the remaining similarity of accounts provided by patients in diverse locations who do not appear to know one another. Anthropologist Sherill Mulhern has a theory: the therapists constitute a professional subculture that has been building the idea of a cult conspiracy into its diagnosis of MPDs since 1984, when the First International Conference on Multiple Personality/Dissociative States was organized in Chicago. The communication among professionals has produced an aura of plausibility around the conspiratorial blood cult image. "The alleged victims of satanic cults are not so much saying the same things as they are being heard the same way," says Mulhern.[16]

Anti-anti-Satanist Robert Hicks offers a broader thesis: Satanism is an urban legend that is being spread by a coalition of anti-Satanists including therapists, clergy, and "cult cops." The legend began, Hicks contends, with the publication of *Michelle Remembers* in 1980. Prior to that there were no such cult survivor accounts.

Relying on the work of Sherill Mulhern, skeptic Jeffrey Victor agrees with the urban legend explanation.[17] The constant in the MPD stories, he says, is not the traumas of the patients but rather the ideology of the therapists. Psychiatrists, psychologists, and social workers have been duped by their own groupthink. They have come to accept the existence of Satanic cults through seminars and conferences that enforce group conformity. The main agency is the International Society for the Study of Multiple Personality and Dissociation. Program participants return to their practice and then introduce the ritual abuse formula to their patients during therapy. Victor contends that MPD patients have a chameleonlike, manipulative personality, and they feed therapists the kind of stories they feel the therapists want to hear. Therapists want to hear stories of cult abuse, so they get them.

Suspicion that the source of the problem lies with the therapists rather than the clients led to the March 1992 formation of the False Memory Syndrome Foundation of Philadelphia. The Foundation has collected three thousand accounts of families accused by an adult child — mostly women in their twenties, thirties, and forties — of incest and

---

16. Mulhern, "Satanism and Psychotherapy: A Rumor in Search of an Inquisition," in *The Satanism Scare,* p. 158.
17. See Victor, "Satanic Cult Survivor Stories," *Skeptical Inquirer* 15 (Spring 1991): 274-80.

Satanic ritual abuse. Four hundred fifty of these families have had to defend themselves against such charges in court. The charges arise when therapists use hypnosis to uncover the alleged memories of abuse. The FMS Foundation views hypnosis as a suggestive tool that intrinsically has the potential to create false images. Without denying the existence and tragedy of actual cases of incest and child abuse, the Foundation contends that not every accusation can be true. In questionable cases it calls for caution and critical assessment until the truth be found.

A sixth point at issue is the credibility of law enforcement people who specialize in cult crime. If we in fact are dealing with an urban legend, then perhaps its origin can be traced back to a specific incident that was marked by a combination of sincerity and hasty judgment. Here is the story as I understand it:

In the early 1980s, Sandi Gallant of the San Francisco Police Department was investigating ritual sexual abuse, noting how Satanic symbolism was frequently found at the crime source. After doing some background research, Gallant typed up a brief police manual on Satanic crime, complete with a half dozen pages showing Satanic symbols. She was telling investigators that if they were to find any of these symbols associated with a crime, they should suspect Satanic involvement. Her informal photocopied and stapled manual was sent first to the Los Angeles Police Department, which consulted it in connection with graffiti produced by a local gang called the Stoners. The report was then reproduced by the Baldwin Park Police, and from there it traveled via Xerox machine from one police department to another until it was eventually distributed to law enforcement people around the entire nation.

Gallant's report at first failed to discriminate outright Devil worship from neopaganism, which is a more generic nature religion. Representatives of Wicca — neopagan goddess worshipers and practitioners of witchcraft — approached Gallant to explain that they do not advocate criminal activity. Gallant learned from the conversation and began to draw the distinction. In the years since, she has matured in many of her assessments. But it is too late to retrieve the now almost ubiquitous police manual. So police are now on the alert almost everywhere, and they believe they are pursuing an epidemic of cult crime. When we mix in media attention and the vituperations of apparently outraged evangelical preachers, we have the formula for widespread confusion and misunderstanding.

Anti-anti-Satanists such as Robert Hicks, who is both a law enforcement officer and a skeptic, are critical of so-called specialists in cult crime for their lack of professionalism. He argues that cult cops gain all their knowledge from seminars and workshops rather than from any actual encounters with Satanic groups. He asks his readers for restraint and critical analysis: "Some cult survivors *may* be telling accurate accounts of human sacrifice; satanic cults *may* be running day care centers; and playing Dungeons & Dragons *may* lead some children to acquire the Black Arts. If such phenomena exist, then they must be proved."[18]

We ought finally to note that the anti-anti-Satanists have an unarticulated but nevertheless obvious additional agenda — namely, to combat the influence of conservative Christianity in America. Through guilt by association and innuendo, they repeatedly reduce the anti-Satanist movement to an expression of fundamentalism. They operate with a psychological conspiracy theory of their own that attributes to the anti-Satanists the following hidden logic: if Christians can get the public to believe in Satan, then they can convince the public to believe in God. Jeffrey Victor reports having found a therapist attending a conference on cults who told him that the existence of Satanism confirms her belief in God.[19]

Hicks contends that "fundamentalist Christianity drives the occult-crime model. Cult-crime officers invariably communicate fundamentalist Christian concepts at seminars . . . and they sometimes team up with clergy to give seminars on satanism."[20] Hicks hints that because Sandi Gallant has identified herself as a "born-again Christian," and despite her conscientious attempt to learn from new evidence, he concludes that she "still has not distanced herself from conspiracy claims."[21] In a telephone interview with me, Detective Gallant described

18. Hicks, *In Pursuit of Satan*, p. 12; italics in original.

19. Victor, "Satanic Cult Survivor Stories," p. 279.

20. Hicks, "Police Pursuit of Satanic Crime, Part I," *Skeptical Inquirer* 14 (Spring 1990): 279. The *Skeptical Inquirer* is published by the Committee for the Scientific Investigation of Claims of the Paranormal. In the spirit of science and skepticism, this group is dedicated to stamping out superstition. CSICP's chairman and one of its key spokespersons, philosopher Paul Kurtz, describes his task of making an apologetic for scientific or secular humanism in *The Transcendental Temptation* (Buffalo: Prometheus Press, 1986).

21. Hicks, *In Pursuit of Satan*, p. 85.

Hicks's assertions as "totally stupid." She reported that Hicks had never spoken with her and said she has no idea where he got his information. "Although I was in a sort of panic at first, trying to understand what was going on," she said, "I always strove to be objective regarding the evidence." Furthermore, Gallant described her perspective as "balanced" in that she believe the problem is relatively isolated and opposes the idea of a large-scale Satanist conspiracy. Despite Gallant's "balanced" view, Hicks insists that there is an anti-Satanist conspiracy. "The satanic cults *are* scapegoats for a variety of social ills, and I view such scapegoating as a product of xenophobia stoked by a millenarian fear. The cult-cop world-view entertains, although unwittingly, a racism that is supported by a fundamentalist Christian vision that seems apocalyptic in respect to a coming millennium."[22]

I would like to offer a few observations about Hicks's theory. He claims that the anti-Satanists are engaged in scapegoating. But how can you have an effective scapegoat if there is doubt that the scapegoat even exists? Scapegoats normally receive displaced punishment, but Hicks contends that there is no one there to receive it. Does the accusation of scapegoating really fit here? And what about millenarian fears? He injects this from out of the blue. Most absurd of all is the accusation of racism. On what grounds does Hicks charge cult-crime specialists or any other proponents of anti-Satanism with racism? If anything, anti-Satanists argue that the leaders, not the marginalized, of our communities are providing the leadership of the cults. There is no suggestion whatsoever that racial minorities are being picked on here. Why is Hicks so vehement? Perhaps it is a matter of prejudice against fundamentalist Christians.

Radical Evil at Matamoros

One might think that the case of the Matamoros cult killings, which provided ample physical evidence and prisoner testimony and generated extensive photographic press coverage, would settle the dispute between the anti-Satanists and the anti-anti-Satanists. But it has not.

What we know now is that Adolfo de Jesus Constanzo was born

22. Hicks, *In Pursuit of Satan*, p. 23.

in 1962 and raised in Miami by his mother, who introduced him to the mysterious practices of Santeria, a cult religion from her native Cuba that combines elements of primal religion and Roman Catholicism. After moving to Mexico, Constanzo became a sort of ecumenist of the black arts. He evidently apprenticed himself to sorcerers in various Afro-Cuban and Haitian voodoo cults, including Palo Mayombe and Abakua. He was known as a *mayombera* or *bruja* or *Tata Nkisi*. Constanzo admitted to practicing a combination of Santeria and Palo Mayombe, but since it is the custom among Mexican members of these sorts of religions to associate themselves in public conversations only with religions that are closer to legitimacy (e.g., a practitioner of Santeria will publicly admit only to practicing "Christian Santeria" or "white Santeria"), we can assume that he was in fact most probably a practitioner of Abakua. The Abakua engage in torture, human sacrifice, and mystical cannibalism. In Mexico, the ripping out of a beating human heart calls to mind ancient Aztec rites of sacrifice, and this practice was revived by the Constanzo cult. Constanzo's ritual chants were in the Bantu language, so his practice was also known as Regla de Congo or simply Congo.[23]

By the mid-1980s Constanzo was living in Mexico City and had gathered a small group of followers who believed that he could predict the future with tarot cards. He earned money by performing religious rites of cleansing known as *limpias*. His clients consisted of narcotics traffickers, government officials, and the elite of Mexico's entertainment business. Each limpia included a ritual of human sacrifice. A homosexual or prostitute from the Zona Rosa district would be invited to attend or perhaps kidnaped. The victim would be stripped naked and placed willingly or unwillingly on the ritual altar. At Constanzo's priestly instruction, assistants would slit open the individual's chest and remove the heart, and then all present would drink blood directly from the heart. The victim's brain and other body parts would then be removed and placed in a cauldron along with other symbolic items connoting death, and the resulting mixture would be consumed by all present. Inflicting terror and pain just prior to death was deemed important, because it was assumed that fear placed the victim's soul totally in the killer's hands. The priest typically tortured the victim

23. Jim Schutze, *Cauldron of Blood: The Matamoros Cult Killings* (New York: Avon, 1989), pp. 116-17.

prior to execution as a means of capturing the dead soul's power so that it could be redirected for the use of the living. Constanzo explained that this procedure guaranteed his paying customers mystical power for professional success. He performed two to three limpias per week, and his wealthy customers paid $30,000 to $40,000 for the sorcerer's service.

One woman seeking revenge against another party reports that she went to Constanzo to negotiate a cleansing and a hex. Her host greeted her by saying, "This is the house of the devil." After explaining what she wanted, Constanzo stated, "If you want to be cleansed, when you leave here, you will no longer have God, but you will have other forces to call upon for inner strength. . . . Here — the one they call the devil. I offer him to you, as I offer you to him." It appears that this was too high a price for the woman, a Roman Catholic, to pay. "The truth is, I only love God," she said. "I didn't want to have anything to do with them."[24]

Enough people did want to have something to do with Constanzo and comrades, though. The money rolled in. Constanzo developed an aristocratic lifestyle, purchasing several homes and cars with cash. Then he decided to boost his income to even higher levels. After initiating Sara Aldrete, a young coed from Texas Southmost University in Brownsville, Constanzo used her as sex bait to snare a wealthy drug dealer, Elio Hernandez. Once he had the drug trafficker's attention, he offered a deal. In exchange for half the profits of Hernandez's marijuana and cocaine sales to U.S. customers, Constanzo would initiate him into the cult and provide him with magical powers to increase his U.S. market. Hernandez agreed and was fully initiated at the Santa Elena Ranch on the outskirts of Matamoros just across the border from Brownsville, Texas. It took two sacrificial murders for Elio Hernandez to get the technique correct; one of the victims was his cousin, whom he killed by mistake.

Sara Aldrete was impressed by the Hollywood movie *The Believers,* because it seemed to dovetail with the practices Constanzo had developed. She persuaded Hernandez and previous disciples to watch this film repeatedly, on the grounds that incorporation of some of the movie's ideas would help weld the newly expanded cult together into one big happy family.

24. Schutze, *Cauldron of Blood,* p. 225.

Constanzo told Hernandez that the ritual sacrifice of an American citizen, a gringo, was key to their gaining magical power over U.S. border authorities and an expansion of their drug market. This led to the March 14, 1989, kidnaping of Mark Kilroy, a premed student at the University of Texas who had come to Matamoros for spring break. At the worship center in the Santa Elena Ranch barn — which included an altar adorned with various religious symbols such as a Buddhalike figurine, Santeria candles, Roman Catholic candles, and objects associated with Haitian voodoo, Palo Mayombe, and Abakua — the Constanzo cult terrorized the college student, cut off his legs, slit open his chest and ate his heart, and placed his brains in the cauldron along with other blood, bones, animal organs, and a horseshoe. This, they thought, would make them invisible to law enforcement personnel so they could go about their drug business.

The regional police, headed by Mexican federal police commander Juan Benitez Ayala, invaded the Santa Elena Ranch on April 11, 1989, made numerous arrests, and invited the press to photograph the worship center, the cauldron, and the thirteen mutilated bodies dug up from nine graves. Mark Kilroy's body was positively identified through dental records. The Hernandez family confessed to the Kilroy killing and described the sacrificial rituals in lurid detail. Still confident in their magical power, the arrested gang snickered and laughed as the wobbly kneed police, overcome by the stench and horror of what they were seeing, rushed off one by one to vomit. At one point, the police called in a *curandero* (witch doctor) to exorcise the premises and burn everything to the ground. The bodies, the photographs, and the confessions remain as evidence.

Because of pressure from the American and European press, a manhunt of enormous proportions was established to find Constanzo. On May 6, 1989, he was tracked to an apartment in Mexico City, where he was hiding with close associates, including Sara Aldrete and his two homosexual lovers. At the last minute he tried burning suitcases full of U.S. currency so that the Mexico City police, many of whom he had previously bribed, could not get their hands on it. He was interrupted by gunfire. At this point he asked a comrade to kill him. He believed the police had come not to arrest him but to kill him in order to prevent him from reporting to the world the names of government officials he had cleansed. He wanted to deny them this satisfaction, too. Constanzo embraced one of his lovers, Martin, and then comrade Alvaro de Leon Valdez filled both of them with bullets from an AK-47.

What impact has the Matamoros case had on the dispute between the anti-anti-Satanists and the anti-Satanists? Houston psychiatrist Peter Olson is dismissive, saying, "It sounds to me like this is not a classic satanic group but a psychotic pathological group with superstitions."[25] Anti-anti-Satanist Robert Hicks complains that "because the methods of Mexican justice . . . differ significantly from those used in the United States," and because Constanzo had himself killed, "we may never know all the relevant facts." Hicks also insists that if Constanzo was a practitioner of Palo Mayombe, then on that ground alone he cannot be characterized as a Satanist. In any event, he says, "The Matamoros murders could not be sustained as proof of a satanic cult for long," because "too many people were involved, only a casual attempt was made to dispose of evidence, and the gang members seemed to disclose their crimes quite readily."[26] Thomas Green downplayed the significance of the Matamoros murders on the grounds that the newspaper reports reflected the structure of folklore, and he deliberately set aside "the precise nature of Constanzo's practices" in order to focus on the xenophobia expressed by the press label of "cult activities."[27]

Anti-Satanist Carl Raschke, in contrast, believes the Matamoros murders are significant, because now the horror of Satanic crime can no longer "be dismissed as Christian fundamentalist ravings, galloping social hysteria, or the lurid sorts of media-inspired popular imaginings" that some have labeled "urban legends."[28] As for the question of whether Constanzo can accurately be described as a believer in the Devil, Raschke says,

> Such rhetorical nitpicking tends to brush aside the fact that there is a dynamic of involvement in the occult that under the right conditions erases most of technical distinctions between "black magic" and "white magic" or between *Santeria* and *palo mayombe* or its "perverted" forms. The dynamic is, stated simply, the attainment of power for oneself and the warding off, if not the destruction, of

25. Olson, quoted by Schutze in *Cauldron of Blood*, p. 208.
26. Hicks, *In Pursuit of Satan*, pp. 72, 81-82.
27. Green, "Accusations of Satanism and Racial Tensions in the Matamoros Cult Murders," in *The Satanism Scare*, p. 238.
28. Raschke, *Painted Black* (San Francisco: Harper & Row, 1990), p. 3.

adversaries. Satanism should never be considered a religion per se; it is the carrying of magic and intrigue in its violent hues to the utmost extremes.[29]

Even those highly critical of Raschke's work admit that "the Matamoros case is Raschke's cleanest hit."[30] We would do well to take a closer look at the controversy over Raschke's interpretation.

Painting a Book Black

In 1990, University of Denver religion professor Carl Raschke dropped a bombshell: his book *Painted Black,* with the cover blurb "From Drug Killings to Heavy Metal — The Alarming True Story of How Satanism Is Terrorizing Our Communities." Raschke describes Satanism as a highly sophisticated and effective motivational system bent on tearing apart our society. United in this single dynamic force, he says, are such people and groups as the occult underground of Adolf Hitler's Third Reich, international drug cartels, child pornographers, Charles Manson, Richard "Night Stalker" Ramirez, Anton LaVey's Church of Satan, Michael Aquino's Temple of Set, the masterminds of the McMartin Preschool scandal, and the Matamoros murderers. He links public or legal Satanism with teen suicide and murder, citing Anton LaVey's *Satanic Bible,* which teaches revenge toward enemies and blood sacrifice. While LaVey himself may stay within the law, says Raschke, the teenage dabblers who read this book execute what the Scriptures say. This bothers Raschke more than a little.

In making his case, Raschke fires off a verbal mortar attack against the anti-anti-Satanism bulwark in the form of a colorful critique of FBI investigator Kenneth Lanning:

Lanning rakes the reader with volley after volley of emotional diatribe, innuendo, non sequitur, glittering and unsupported generality, and bogus appeal to his own authority as the FBI's supervisory special agent . . . to make the case that there really can be no such thing as a serious satanic crime — examines no cases, sifts through no evidence, and cites no literature. [He] merely growls, bullies, and

29. Raschke, *Painted Black,* p. 13.
30. John Strausbaugh, "Devil's Advocate," *New York Press,* 19-25 September 1990.

browbeats with all the subtlety of a charging mastodon. . . . Criminal sexual abuse has no cover under the law, even a religious one, although Lanning gives the impression that it may.[31]

Given this combative tone, one might have predicted a counterattack. It was not long in coming. The *Skeptical Inquirer* reviewed *Painted Black* along with Hicks's *In Pursuit of Satan*, repudiating Raschke and praising Hicks.[32] Blanche Barton, a spokesperson for the Church of Satan in San Francisco, agrees that the influence of Satanism is growing in America and, ironically, that people like Raschke "keep adding fuel to the flames by generating hysteria. . . . Ultimately, it just sells more *Satanic Bibles*. It makes people curious to find out for themselves what satanism is about."[33] LaVey denies any responsibility for antisocial acts committed by people who have read his *Satanic Bible*, claiming that they are taking literally what he meant metaphorically.

Kenneth Lanning has returned the fire through interviews with reviewers of *Painted Black*. He argues that Raschke and others confuse the public with indiscriminate use of such terms as *satanic, cult, occult,* and *ritualistic*. From the point of view of law enforcement, the focus should be on the crime, he says, not on the Satanic or occult context. Serial murder and child abuse are crimes regardless of any connection they might have to Satanism. Lanning points out that it is a common Mafia practice to dismember, torture, or castrate victims and then asks whether that makes the Mob part of the Satanic conspiracy. He goes on to note that numerous individuals arrested for crimes such as child abuse come out of fundamentalist Christian backgrounds and characterize the abuse as proper discipline. Should we refer to these as Christian crimes then? he asks. No. They are simply crimes. Speaking of Raschke, Lanning says, "Where he's missed the boat is that I'm not claiming that these people don't exist. I'm just saying how you should interpret, investigate and categorize these crimes."[34]

Temple of Set leader Michael Aquino also launched some verbal

31. Raschke, *Painted Black*, p. 75.

32. See Richard Noll, "Give Me That Old Time Religion: Two Books on the Modern Satanism Scare," *Skeptical Inquirer* 15 (Summer 1991): 412-15.

33. Barton, quoted by Strausbaugh in "Devil's Advocate."

34. Lanning, quoted by Michael Roberts in "Hell's Angels," *Westword*, 31 October–6 November 1990, p. 26.

missiles in Raschke's direction. He claims that Raschke lies and distorts facts in order to throw mud, and he says he's tired of it. Then he attacks Raschke's credentials. He has a Ph.D. and teaches at the University of Denver, but that institution has ties to the Methodist church, and as far as Aquino is concerned, that means he belongs in the same category as the Spiritual Counterfeits Project, "a fundamentalist hate-group." Aquino concludes by saying, "I suppose I could have more respect for modern Christianity if its proponents argued their point of view courteously and thoughtfully, showing tolerance for if not agreement with contrasting viewpoints [such as ours]. As it is, I am increasingly repelled by it."[35]

What I find curious in this explosive volley is that the target for much of the anti-anti-Satanist complaints — Christianity, especially in its fundamentalist form — is in fact missing from much of the anti-Satanist literature. Raschke's *Painted Black* is virtually devoid of theology and religious theory in general. Given the fact that Raschke is a professor of religion, one would certainly have expected some reflection on the subject matter drawn from religious resources, but there is none. Raschke shows no investment in anything other than garden-variety secular values regarding human decency. Even so, he is attacked by the anti-anti-Satanists not for the position he actually presents but rather as a front for the targeted enemy, the church.

To my observation, the amalgam of groups supporting the anti-Satanism position do not represent a single unified theology, let alone fundamentalist Christian theology. Many of the psychotherapists associated with anti-Satanist sentiment are Jewish or secular or otherwise unlikely to subordinate their psychological theories to a fundamentalist ideology. Groups rallying to expose or prevent preschool child abuse contain random mixes of individuals, including parents from a variety of religious and political backgrounds. The police departments of our states and municipalities are arms of government, not churches. There is no obvious reason for supposing that a fundamentalist conspiracy lurks behind the anti-Satanism movement, and certainly the anti-anti-Satanists have to date not provided the sort of empirical data that could prove their case. What appears to be happening here is that each side is characterizing people they happen to disagree with as a group that is conspiring to undermine our society.

35. Aquino, "Flaky Paint," *Scroll of Set* 16 (October 1990): 2.

• S I N •

Urban Legends and Subversion Ideologies

As I noted earlier, some anti-anti-Satanists account for the rise of Satanism by characterizing it as an urban legend. The strategy first appeared in Arthur Lyons's book *Satan Wants You: The Cult of Devil Worship in America*.[36] In this popular paperback, Lyons offers an informative historical survey of the concept of the Devil beginning with the Zoroastrians and Jews and then entering the Christian world-view. He distinguishes — as well he should — between witchcraft in general, which is a form of pagan nature religion, and Satanism, which is an identifiable religion based on Christian symbolism. The Satanists' use of the upside-down cross, their recitation of the Lord's Prayer backward, their rite of rebaptism in the name of the Devil, and their black mass led by an apostate priest all indicate the inverted yet dependent symbolic structure.

Satanism is a form of black magic, explains Lyons, but not all black magicians are Satanists. As with other black magic, the motive of Devil worship is to provide religious justification for self-enhancement, self-indulgence, and rebellion against the Christian church. Skeptical of any supernatural explanation for the existence of the Devil himself, Lyons sees Satanism as a social phenomenon and blames the church for its existence. Christians have been too uptight about sex and have identified self-indulgence with sin, he says, thereby pushing people with carnal desires toward nature religion and Satan. Christians have also been too hierarchical and downright oppressive, thereby encouraging a rebellious opposition. The black mass became "a way of venting hatred, of outpouring all the frustrated energy accumulated by the years of humiliation suffered at the hands of the Church."[37]

Lyons is skeptical about the contemporary hysteria over the spread of Satanic religion. He dismisses accusations of Satanic influences in heavy metal rock music, for example, as fundamentalist overreaction. He attributes the currently popular fascination with a link between Satanic groups and kidnapings, drug trafficking, child pornography,

---

36. *Satan Wants You* (New York: Warner Books, 1988) is an updated version of Lyons's book *The Second Coming: Satanism in America* (New York: Award Books, 1970).

37. Lyons, *Satan Wants You*, p. 49; cf. pp. 19, 46.

and human sacrifice largely to media hype. He cites court cases in which attempts were made to link Satanism with child molestations and murder and in which the verdict was insufficient evidence. He suggests that we think of such items as belonging to an "urban legend" (i.e., a popular story that spreads swiftly by word of mouth and is then accepted as truth).[38] There is, he argues, no proof of an organized Satanic conspiracy. Why, then, does the urban legend grow? Lyons says it is because we need scapegoats during a period of cultural *anomie:* we need someone to blame for our own excesses, and Satanists make good scapegoats because they don't exist.[39]

The Lyons accusation of scapegoatism is little better than a cheap shot. Nonexistent scapegoats are nonsense. He does not offer an analysis that could support such an accusation, leaving him vulnerable to the charge that he is himself scapegoating. When we move into the work of David Bromley, however, we find the kind of analysis that genuinely moves the discussion forward.

Bromley presents a more refined version of the urban legend theory in the form of countersubversion ideology theory. He describes anti-Satanism as an ideology that is trying to counter a subversive force — namely, Satanism. He outlines the structural conditions in our society that make Satanic subversion claims culturally plausible despite the fact that they are supposedly unfounded. He attributes both the religious cult scare of the 1970s and the Satanism scare of the 1980s to heightened social tensions caused by the ceding of previously family-held responsibilities to business or contractual agencies. Although this argument appeared reductionistic to me at first (sociologists seem to account for every upheaval on ground of social tension), I now consider Bromley's thesis well worth considering. He traces the root cause of the tension to the increase in the number of working mothers. He notes that the number of women

38. Lyons, *Satan Wants You,* p. 139.

39. Lyons, *Satan Wants You,* pp. 148, 178-79. Scapegoating does go on, but I believe we need to be more specific. Some years ago my brother telephoned me long distance to advise me to discontinue using products by Proctor & Gamble. The company's trademark, a crescent man-in-the-moon looking at thirteen stars, is a Satanic symbol, he said, indicating its corrupt nature. I wondered if this could be true. In 1991 a Kansas court ordered James and Linda Newton, distributors of Amway products, to pay Proctor & Gamble $75,000 in damages for starting the rumor and distributing literature to perpetuate it.

working outside the home increased from 39 percent in 1970 to 56 percent in 1988.[40] This has brought about a significant increase in the number of child-care providers. Whereas in the past children were raised within the family covenant, they are now raised by businesses intent on making a profit. Parents cannot help being concerned about the quality of the bond between their children and the child-care workers. Perhaps without fully being aware of it, mothers especially may experience guilt and stress for ceding their parental responsibility. In addition, they feel vulnerable to external forces. To put it simply, the growth in the child-care industry marks one more way that parents have been losing control over the socialization process to alien influences. As a purely structural concern, chaos threatens the family order. Given these emotional concerns and pressures, many parents are vulnerable to projection, self-justification, and the scapegoating of day-care workers.

The McMartin Preschool trial is a classic case in point. Seven employees of the preschool in Manhattan Beach, California, were charged with fifty-two counts of child molestation based on children's testimony describing robed adults, chanting, animal sacrifice, babies cooked and eaten, and forced participation in kiddie-porn movies. The trial began in August 1983 and concluded on January 18, 1990, and was the most expensive court case in American history. It degenerated into a circus of charges and countercharges and precedents and influences. The whole thing began when the mother of a two-year-old boy complained to Los Angeles officials that her son had been abused by McMartin employees who had worn masks and capes, taped the boy's mouth shut, stuck a tube in his rectum, made him ride naked on a horse, jabbed scissors and staples into him, stuck his finger in a goat's anus, and made him drink blood from a murdered baby. Other accusations were made that the children had been taken to a cave underneath the McMartin school for these macabre activities. Digging under the school proved that there had never been any cave there. Videotaped interviews with the children showed how the therapists had led them to construct the Satanist scheme. In the end, none of

40. What Bromley does not note is that the greatest jump in the percentage of women working outside the home took place in the 1950s, from 12 percent in 1950 to 40 percent in 1960. Perhaps the decisive factor is not the number of mothers working but the number of children in preschool day-care centers.

the fifty-two counts of child molestation was sustained, and the school's owners, Raymond Buckey and his mother, Peggy McMartin Buckey, were acquitted by a Los Angeles jury.[41]

Since the McMartin trial first hit the headlines in 1983, as many as a hundred other cases have appeared in U.S. courts accusing preschool owners or employees of child abuse with Satanic overtones. Seldom has a guilty verdict been rendered. The only result seems to be that the accused and exonerated defendants have undergone untold stress and defamation. Might we — if we dare offer a general observation without judgment pertaining to specific cases — consider the defendants in such cases scapegoats?

With this possibility in mind, I would note that Bromley offers a curious but protean suggestion — namely, that the claims regarding the existence of preschool Satanism may be metaphorically true even if empirically false. There is trouble, but the troublemaker is not an external force — a Satanic underground. Rather, the trouble is the vulnerability families feel to any and all external forces. These forces arouse anxiety, and, according to Bromley, this anxiety comes to

41. The fallout from the McMartin trial has been substantial. Bob Currie, one of the McMartin parents, seems to have been the first to offer the theory that devil worshipers were infiltrating preschools across the nation. The idea of a Satanic abuse theory did not sit well with the secular professionals involved in the prosecution, so they introduced the term "ritual abuse" in 1985 and spoke of the McMartin conspirators in terms of a "sex ring" rather than a Satanic cult. But investigative procedures continued to cast doubts on the prosecution's case, especially the role therapists played in leading the children in prescribed directions by offering positive reinforcement for allegations of abuse and negative reinforcement for denying that abuse occurred. Evidence was further contaminated through cross germination: the parents communicated constantly with one another. As a group they even consulted with Michelle Smith and Lawrence Pazder, authors of *Michelle Remembers*. The sex-ring theory, let alone the Satanic cult theory, proved unsupportable. No pornography was ever found. We know that sex ring offenders are almost always male pedophiles, whereas the McMartin defendants were mostly women. District Attorney Ira Reiner almost immediately dropped charges on five of the defendants on the grounds that the evidence against them was "incredibly weak." Eventually the jury also acquitted Peggy McMartin Buckey and Ray Buckey.

A parallel case in Jordan, Minnesota, in September 1983, produced charges against twenty-four adults for molesting preschool children during rituals that included animal sacrifice and human murder. Twenty-three of the defendants were acquitted of all charges. One man was convicted separately of pedophilia, but no evidence of any cult connection arose. The FBI and state's attorney general's office concluded that stories of torture and murder were fantasy.

245

symbolic expression in the anti-Satanism countersubversion ideology. The social construction of Satanism by the anti-Satanists reasserts family control by naming the problem, giving it a human shape, and locating its source outside. The problems within families are now thought to be the result of some malevolent outsiders, not the product of inappropriate parental conduct. If Bromley is correct, perhaps he has a helpful explanation for at least one portion of the much larger Satanic phenomenon.

Perhaps the most sober overall perspective is offered by J. Gordon Melton, director of the Institute for the Study of American Religion in Santa Barbara. He distinguishes between public Satanic groups — those that list their names in phone books — and more isolated and ephemeral cults. The former are harmless and pose no public threat. The small secret groups, however, are sometimes led by psychopaths and sociopaths. "While they pose no threat to the larger society," says Melton, "they do pose an immediate danger to those involved in them and are frequently involved in criminal activity, from dealing in drugs to rape and murder."[42] This warrants monitoring by local authorities and plans for the protection of children, but it should not be used to justify a fanatical crusade or witch-hunt.

Evangelical and Fundamentalist Literature

Even though one cannot rightly characterize anti-Satanism as solely a movement of Christian fundamentalists, it is certainly the case that conservative Christians of both fundamentalist and evangelical persuasions are deeply involved in it. Anti-Satanism was not initiated by conservative Christian ministries, but once under way the armies joined forces. If we date the beginning of the current chapter in the story of Satanism with *Michelle Remembers* in 1980, then we can note that only a half decade later evangelical bookstores began selling what is now a whole line of books, audio and video tapes, and other weapons in the spiritual warfare against the Devil.

At this point I want to register a note of concern. I am disturbed

42. Melton, "The Evidences of Satan in Contemporary America: A Survey," paper presented at a meeting of the Pacific Division of the American Philosophical Association, Los Angeles, California, 27-28 March 1986.

when I walk into a bookstore and find new releases on Satanism mixed in with books denouncing the New Age. All too frequently the New Age and Satanism are lumped together, as if the former is caused by the latter. I have been a student of the New Age for more than a decade and have found no inherent connection. There are occasional overlaps, such as the Temple of Set, but it is quite possible to engage in New Age practices and completely avoid things Satanic. While I have no intention of mounting a defense of New Age spirituality here, I would like to take a stand against the technique of guilt by association. The worst offender and perhaps the mother of the contemporary genre is Constance Cumbey's *Hidden Dangers of the Rainbow: The New Age Movement and Our Coming Age of Barbarism* (1983), which describes the New Age as not only Satanic but also Nazi-like and anti-Semitic. More recently, in *Dark Secrets of the New Age: Satan's Plan for a One-World Religion* (1987), Texe Marrs has written that "the leaders of the New Age World Religion are Satan's generals and admirals." Flatly put, those who associate the New Age with Satanism have their facts wrong.

On March 14, 1991, I was interviewed by Stacy Taylor on his WLS radio talk show in Chicago. The subject was the New Age. Numerous callers insisted that the New Age is a form of Satanism. I resisted this association. Then a man telephoned in from Urbana, Illinois. He announced that he was a practicing Satanist and that Dr. Peters was correct: Satanism and New Age are two different things. "How do you think they are different?" I asked. His answer was instructive: the New Age seeks human betterment by pursuing higher levels of spiritual reality, whereas Satanism is materialistic and pursues human fulfillment through physical pleasure. "Well, that settles that," said Stacy Taylor. I was of two minds. On the one hand, I was glad to have had my position vindicated; on the other hand, I had to wonder what my bishop would say when he discovered that the Satanists and I stood together on this issue.

What disturbs me about much of the evangelical literature is that it falls into the trap of crying wolf. If we are told to walk in the fear that Satan is hiding behind every bush, we will eventually either condemn everything the least bit unconventional as the Devil's work or begin to dismiss the idea of Satan itself as a sham. The problem is that the wolf of radical evil does exist, and we need to take it with utter seriousness. If we trivialize radical evil by identifying it with every point of view with which we disagree, we may fail to recognize the real Satan when he appears.

Anything genuinely Satanic ought to be scorned and despised. Devotees of the New Age and other innocent parties ought not to be scorned and despised, however. Remembering the subtlety of the serpent in the Garden of Eden, we need to observe a principle regarding how evil works: if we use the same Satanic brush to tar everyone we disagree with, we may only convince ourselves that scorning and despising innocent people is legitimate — making us, not them, the true disciples of Satan.

Characteristic of the current anti-Satanist genre is John Charles Cooper's book *The Black Mask: Satanism in America Today.* Cooper tries to inform and mobilize a popular Christian readership against diabolical forces that have infiltrated both our cities and our heartland. He describes Satanism with appropriate drama as "political rebellion, ethical inversion, religious heresy, and suicidal self-loathing, all mingled in one great taunting gesture of obscenity, thrown in the face of the universe."[43] Everywhere today, he adds, such Satanism is seducing our youth into antisocial and criminal activity through books, movies, drugs, and the new morality.[44] It is the occult that fosters Satanism, but we have painted a black mask over the occult so as to trivialize the threat.

The real culprit, says Cooper, is the hedonism at work in the American way of life. "The real influence of contemporary antisocial and criminal events is the spirit of the age in which we live," he writes. He refers to this spirit of the age as "the contrapuntal tradition" and includes in it such things as extremist feminism, gay liberation, the sanctioning of abortion, the destruction of the family, and the return of occultism in the New Age movement. "Popular culture, the way we see ourselves and the way we are with one another, is the source of satanic activity, not some organized conspiracy."[45]

I am bothered by a strain of doublethink in this book, by Cooper's tendency to affirm and deny the same thing. For example, he says he does not want to sensationalize Satanism, and yet the book is billed as an exposé and is filled with report after report of lurid cruelty and

43. Cooper, *The Black Mask: Satanism in American Today* (Old Tappan, N.J.: Fleming H. Revell, 1990), p. 32.
44. Cooper, *The Black Mask*, p. 59.
45. Cooper, *The Black Mask*, p. 53.

sacrilege. He denies that there is any connection between the occult or New Age and Satanism, and yet he sweeps them all up into global denunciations of the hedonism that he says is bankrupting the spiritual life of our country.[46] He describes such things as baby sacrifice in revolting detail, and then he subsequently admits that there is insufficient evidence to affirm that such practices actually take place. He describes the actions of serial killers such as Charles Manson and David Berkowitz ("Son of Sam"), and then he admits that most serial killers are loners while most Satanists are members of groups, indicating that there is only a loose tie between the two.

Cooper is a veteran writer who has treated many topics with considerable skill, and indeed he has included a good deal of accurate and pertinent information in this book. His chapter on the history of Satanism, which includes data on its rise during the reign of Louis XIV in France, is especially interesting. I like Cooper's book, and yet I cannot help but be concerned that the helpful information is so mixed with diatribes against other phenomena that Cooper opposes (e.g., the New Age, the occult, and feminism) that readers will likely lose their bearings and assume that all of these phenomena deserve the same denunciation as Satanism and on the same grounds.[47]

46. Cooper, *The Black Mask,* pp. 11, 81-82.
47. A number of books that have become popular in the conservative Christian market are flawed by an even more substantial lack of accurate information or discriminating perspective. One example is Nicky Cruz's *Devil on the Run* (Melbourne, Fla.: Dove, 1989). In this work, Cruz, famed for his dramatic conversion to Christ recounted in *The Cross and the Switchblade,* associates his own internal temptations to commit murder with everything banned by the current evangelical magisterium: astrology, reincarnation, magic, gurus, spiritualism, inner visions, mystic auras, astral travel, witchcraft, and "anything of the kind. All of it is from below, not from above — from the devil, not from God" (p. 108). Cruz even sweeps in UFOs into the net and charges that the Steven Spielberg movie *E.T.* is "manipulated by evil forces" (p. 156). Bob Larson's *Satanism: The Seduction of America's Youth* (Nashville: Thomas Nelson, 1989) is not much better. Larson properly enough warns teenagers of the dangers of drugs and heavy metal music, but then he goes on to characterize parapsychology and New Age practices as doors that open us to Satanism, offering no evidence beyond guilt by association. I give good marks to Ted Schwarz and Duane Empey's *Satanism* (Grand Rapids: Zondervan, 1988) and Jerry Johnston's *Edge of Evil: The Rise of Satanism in North America* (Waco, Tex.: Word Books, 1989) for presenting informative case-by-case descriptions of contemporary Satanism (the latter of the two is better organized than the former), and yet neither book offers a theory of evil that addresses the internal dimensions of sin, and the result is that both end up treating Satanism as a mere external social phenomenon that we need fear only if it drifts into our neighborhood.

The literature is not all bad, by any means. One beacon of sanity and discriminating insight amid the dark fog of anti-Satanist material is *The Satan Syndrome,* by British author Nigel Wright. This book presents solid theology in popular form, although unfortunately it ignores recent codes for inclusive language. Wright has carefully thought out the dynamics of evil and the theology of the Devil. He begins with a warning against adopting either of two extremes: on the one hand, following the modern post-Enlightenment inclination to dismiss the notion of the Devil as belonging solely to a now outdated myth-oriented epoch and, on the other, becoming overly fascinated with demonic forces and thereby granting them more power than they deserve. Should we believe in the Devil? Yes and no. Yes, we should believe *in the existence* of the Devil as a supra-individual or even transcendent force that presses us toward evil. No, we should not believe *in* the Devil in the sense of granting him the trust and affirmation that properly belong only to God. In the latter sense, says Wright, "The devil should be the object of disbelief."[48]

Wright's careful distinctions and insights make this book valuable. Is the Devil personal? No. Only God is personal. Satan is subpersonal, because he thrives on destroying what has been created, personality included.[49] It is regrettable that the language we use tends to personify this otherwise depersonalizing force. By referring to the Devil as "he" or "him," we impute a dignity he does not deserve. Nevertheless, says Wright, we may continue to speak this way if for no other reason than that Jesus and the New Testament use such personal pronouns when speaking of the Devil.

Wright distinguishes evil from "the shadow," a concept that Jung presents as a dark aspect of the being of God. Partly agreeing with

---

48. Wright, *The Satan Syndrome* (Grand Rapids: Zondervan, 1990), p. 24.

49. Emil Brunner would agree. He states that the power of darkness, or Satan, "destroys the personal element; for this very reason it makes it impossible to grasp its own personal character" (*The Christian Doctrine of Creation and Redemption* [Philadelphia: Westminster Press, 1952], p. 143). John Newport, on the other hand, would disagree. One of the most respected scholars in the American evangelical tradition, Newport argues that the Devil is personal: "Satan's personality cannot be characterized simply by absence, a nothingness. It is true that there is an absence of love in his personality. But his personality is also pervaded by the active presence of hate. Quite simply, Satan really exists, and he wants to destroy us" (*Life's Ultimate Questions: A Contemporary Philosophy of Religion* [Dallas: Word Publishing, 1989], p. 211; see also p. 193).

Augustine's *privatio boni* and Karl Barth's notion of evil as nothingness, Wright emphasizes that evil stands in total opposition to the holy being of God. Nothing about evil can be transmuted into something good. But the shadow is different. Although he rejects Jung's enthronement of the shadow in the being of God, Wright still likes the concept. The shadow may be dark, he says, but in itself it is not evil. It includes the sorts of experiences and sufferings that cause us difficulty but from which we emerge as better people. I note in passing that Wright accepts such things as decay and death as part of God's good creation rather than as products of the fall. In keeping with this, he views the shadow as natural and maintains that it can contribute to healthy soul-making. We can benefit from the shadow, whereas we can never benefit from outright evil. What, then, is the relationship between the two? "Evil uses the shadow as an alibi."[50] Evil hides behind the shadow, deceiving us into thinking the two are identical and, thereby, inducing toleration of evil. But Wright has no toleration for evil: "Evil is that power at work in the world about which nothing good should be said or thought. For this irrational, absurd and destructive power human beings should entertain nothing but scorn."[51]

Another of the book's strong points involves the way Wright deals with military metaphors and battle language. We are at war with the forces of evil. We seek the Devil's defeat. But such usages pose a danger for those who use them. The language, mentality, and posture of spiritual warfare may tempt us to confuse our true enemy with the people whom God enjoins us to love. We may identify evil structures in society as Satanic and then feel justified in persecuting the people involved in those structures. Wright cites witch-hunts and homophobia as examples of ways in which faithful Christians have behaved lovelessly by demonizing certain women and homosexuals and then seeking victory over them. Such moral triumphalism betrays the gospel, he says. The problem with the language of war is that in using it we risk losing our feeling for the finer qualities of justice, truth, mercy, and gentleness and fail to see that we are directed to conduct our spiritual warfare precisely through these qualities. Spiritual warfare has some analogies to battle, to be sure, but it is essentially different.

50. Wright, *The Satan Syndrome*, p. 93.
51. Wright, *The Satan Syndrome*, p. 94.

One of Wright's chief goals in this book is to get the reader to think impartially about the issues at hand. He pleads that we not focus on a host of demons and devils that are not in fact there. He promotes thoughtful discernment, rational analysis in the pursuit of truth. If the Devil be the "father of lies" (John 8:44), then it is quite important that we speak the truth in order to unmask the lies. "Enthusiasm and assertiveness are no substitute for clarity and persuasiveness of argument," he says.[52] This book helps us to think the right way.

Wright is right: we need to think. Beyond this, we need the moral resolve to act on our conclusions. And we need theological leadership that will help us to assess the significance of our current situation. Evil is a subtle thing. It involves lies, even lies to ourselves. We have not yet addressed the topic of Satanism when we treat it merely as an objective phenomenon, as one more category of crime among others that involves only those people we read about in the newspaper. We make matters worse when we characterize it as a massive social phenomenon that we, the presumably right-minded citizens, should try to wipe out with new legislation or better law enforcement or vigorous church activity. The subtlety slips away. When we speak of the Devil, there is always a subjective dimension, a hook within each of our own souls. What the bookstores have yet to put on their shelves is a volume that provides an accurate description of the breadth and seriousness of Satan-related crime in the context of an exposition of the inner workings of our own souls that does not let us easily off the hook.

Satan and Sin

The key to a proper understanding of sin is an apprehension of both its outer and inner dimensions, an awareness of it in terms of both an external force and an internal compliance. Sin is both original (it was here before we were born) and personal (we ourselves are responsible). We experience evil both as defilement or contamination and as a willful choice to pursue concupiscent ends. The symbol of Satan helps us to account for the external and original dimensions, the sense that evil precedes us and constantly threatens to take us up into its power.

Should we personify Satan? Nigel Wright says No, as we have seen,

52. Wright, *The Satan Syndrome*, p. 189.

on the grounds that Satan represents the very forces that seek to destroy all personhood. Walter Wink similarly answers No but for a somewhat different reason. He argues that those who personify Satan separate him from themselves and in so doing consign evil to something that is strictly external to themselves. It is a way of passing the buck. I can excuse my irresponsible behavior by saying "The Devil made me do it." In reality, of course, the Devil has no more power over us than what we grant him.[53] In short, the temptation to personify Satan itself leads to the possibility of human self-justification.

The idea of Satan first appears in Scripture as a sort of external conscience, an angel of God sent for the purpose of accusing us (Job 1–2). He serves as an *agent provocateur,* the left hand of God, so to speak, indirectly reminding us of our distance from God and need to rely on God's grace. The myth of the Devil's fall from heaven developed during the intertestamental period, probably as an extrapolation of the human sense of fallenness. The New Testament presupposes the image of the fallen Satan now seeking citizens for his anti-kingdom at war with the kingdom of God. Here he is called the Devil — that is, a false accuser, slanderer, or calumniator, "the evil one" (Matt. 13:19; John 17:15), "the ruler of this world" (John 12:31; 14:30), "the god of this world" (2 Cor. 4:4), "Beliar" (2 Cor. 6:15), "the ruler of the power of the air" (Eph. 2:2), "Beelzebul" (Matt. 10:25), "the destroyer" (1 Cor. 10:10), the "enemy" (Matt. 13:25), and most significantly the "murderer from the beginning" who is "a liar and the father of lies" (John 8:44).

53. Walter Wink says that the expression "The Devil made me do it" constitutes evidence that we have in fact "delivered ourselves straight into his hands. When we fail to make conscious, committed choices for God, we default on our 'dominion' over the world, and Satan becomes like a holding company that has taken over billions of mortgages in arrears through foreclosure. The satanic is actualized as evil precisely by our *failure* to choose" (*Unmasking the Powers: The Invisible Forces That Determine Human Existence* [Minneapolis: Fortress Press, 1986], p. 34). John Newport similarly contends that Satan's powers are limited: "He can tempt, deceive, accuse, and attack us, but he cannot force us to do something against our wills. We cannot truthfully say, 'The devil made me do it' " (*Life's Ultimate Questions,* p. 194). Daniel Day Williams would argue that projecting the image of the Devil in order to avoid responsibility is part of the problem. Reason dispels superstition about demonic personalized entities, he says. The assertion of demonic possession in the face of reason leads to witch-hunts and injustice. "Belief in demons as supernatural powers can itself be demonic" (*The Demonic and the Divine* [Minneapolis: Fortress Press, 1990], p. 23).

The structure of the titles betrays Satan's ultimate dependence on God — a dependence we share but that in pride we try to deny. As a false accuser, we understand Satan to have taken his task of honest accusation too far. As ruler of *this* world, it is clear that Satan does not rule the other world — namely, God's world. As the enemy or the destroyer, Satan is not engaged in creative doing but rather in undoing what has already been done by God. As a murderer and self-justifier, Satan embodies symbolically the structure of human life-stealing and scapegoating writ large. Ontologically, radical evil has to do with nonbeing, and nonbeing is but a leach off being. It is nothing in itself. Paul Tillich puts it this way: "Satan, the principle of the negative, has no independent reality."[54]

Am I asserting that Satan is merely a projection of human imagination, merely a mythical personification of our inner life? By no means. We cannot reduce Satan to a mere extension of intrapsychic processes. We actually do experience the destructive power of Satan coming to us from beyond ourselves. But we cannot permit the external visage of Satan to divorce itself from our own interior lives. Satan is a power operating within us as well as beyond us both individually and collectively.

Walter Wink may be a trifle more subjectivist than I am, but he struggles with this double dimension in a helpful manner when he describes Satan in terms of a *Zeitgeist*:

> If Satan has any reality at all, it is not as a sign or an idea or even an explanation, but as a profound *experience* of numinous, uncanny power in the psychic and historic lives of real people. *Satan is the real interiority of a society that idolatrously pursues its own enhancement as the highest good.* Satan is the spirituality of an epoch, the peculiar constellation of alienation, greed, inhumanity, oppression, and entropy that characterizes a specific period of history as a consequence of human decisions to tolerate and even further such a state of affairs.[55]

In Wink's treatment, the concept of Satan covers a multitude of sins.

54. Tillich, *Systematic Theology*, 3 vols. (Chicago: University of Chicago Press, 1951-1963), 2:171.
55. Wink, *Unmasking the Powers*, p. 25; italics in original.

Blasphemy as Symbol Stealing

Just as concupiscence is an attempt to steal mortal life from others so as to gain immortality for ourselves, blasphemy is Satan's attempt to steal eternal life from us so as to ensure our eternal death. The means by which Satan pursues blasphemy — or, more accurately, tries to evoke blasphemy from within us — is by defiling the symbols of God's grace.

Symbols provide us with access to the reality that transcends our daily world. The titles for God such as Lord, King of the universe, heavenly Father, the Almighty, and the Eternal remind us that there is a reality not limited by finitude, not subject to the destructive potential of anxiety. The titles that describe Jesus Christ at work (e.g., Savior, Redeemer) confront us with the news that God rescues us from the vicissitudes of our history fraught with greed, inhumanity, oppression, entropy, and death. References to God as Holy Spirit, Comforter, and Sanctifier communicate that we are not alone, that no matter how severely the forces of nonbeing assail us, God protects us by binding us to the power of ultimate being. In the midst of stress and distress, such symbols of a transcendent and loving God work within our psyche to give us integrity, courage, and peace of mind. To take such symbols away would leave us frightfully alone, terrorized not only by evil but also by the meaninglessness of it all.

Symbols are not mere things. They are not mere mental contrivances designating projections of psychological desire. They come to us from beyond ourselves. They speak to us of realities beyond ourselves. They draw us up and out and beyond ourselves. Like eagles' wings, they bear us above the mundane constraints of earth to the glories of heaven.

They have this power because symbols participate in the reality to which they point. Or, to view it the other way around, through the symbol the absolute can become present in the relative, the infinite in the finite, the unconditioned in the conditioned, the eternal in the temporal. Because of this, symbols come to us and open up access to new dimensions of reality, new levels of participation in being. According to Tillich, symbols unlock dimensions of our souls that correspond to the dimensions and elements of reality.[56]

56. Tillich, *Dynamics of Faith* (New York: Harper & Row, 1957), p. 42.

To put it still another way, the words we use to talk about God do not leave us unaffected. Talking about God orders our souls. Blasphemy disorders our souls. This is because the power in the words is not simply ours. The words bear a power beyond what we ourselves give them in our usage. This is especially true with regard to the Word of God. The Word of God bears an evocative and transforming power that is greater than anything we can supply: the Word of God is God at work in the world. As Karl Barth put it, "God's Word is God himself in His revelation."[57]

Hence, the seriousness of the commandment "You shall not make wrongful use of the name of the LORD your God" (Exod. 20:7). When we make wrongful use of symbols in the form of the names, titles, and stories of God, we alienate ourselves from God. We subject ourselves to the powers of destruction while denying ourselves access to the presence of divine grace. It is the Devil's delight to separate us from divine grace, because, as Barth has said, "The grace of God is the basis and norm of all being, the source and criterion of all good."[58]

Denial of access to God's grace is the goal of blasphemy in both its forms — indirectly as the use of divine symbols to justify concupiscent pride and directly as the deliberate misuse of divine symbols in ritual abuse. The indirect use is subtle; the direct misuse is overt. In both cases, blasphemy constitutes an attempt to siphon off divine power to fuel an attempt to thwart the divine design.

Perhaps the symbol most susceptible to blasphemous misuse is sacrifice. As a symbol of grace, it communicates the profundity of God's love for us. In the incarnation, God submitted to the vicissitudes of finitude, anxiety, violence, and death. God sacrificed all the protections of eternity and omnipotence in order to establish a bond with a temporal and weak human race. The preeminent sacrifice is God's sacrifice. We, in turn, love one another as a response to and extension of the divine model. Jesus put it forcefully: "Whoever wishes to be first among you must be your slave; just as the Son of Man came not to be served but to serve, and to give his life a ransom for many" (Matt. 20:27-28).

In the hands of the blasphemers, however, sacrifice becomes a means

57. Barth, *Church Dogmatics*, 4 vols., ed. Thomas F. Torrance, trans. Geoffrey W. Bromiley (Edinburgh: T. & T. Clark, 1936-1962), I/1:295.
58. Barth, *Church Dogmatics*, III/3:354.

for pressing others into one's own service. Self-justified concupiscence enslaves the working class or the underdeveloped countries or racial minorities for the aggrandizement of one's tribe. Ritual abuse physically sacrifices others, turning living beings into dead things, in the name of evil itself. The purpose in both cases is to steal life and power from others by stealing the symbols of salvation. Whether through economics or through ritual magic, our greedy desire for unlimited power leads us to sacrifice others for our own sakes in the frenzied delusion that we can take the place of God. Such blasphemy wreaks even more devastation by robbing the victims of eternal comfort in the midst of their temporal suffering. Those who twist the symbol of sacrifice to serve their own advantage may well leave their victims convinced that their loss is not divinely sanctioned but in vain.

The Call to Shed Innocent Blood

The symbols of blasphemy and the symbols of salvation are closely tied to one another. This leads me to suggest a principle to guide us: *Satan is present when we hear the call to shed innocent blood.*[59] The shedding of innocent blood is the essential structure of the symbol of sacrifice. Just as my watercooler guards wished to shed figuratively the innocent blood of Mr. Martinsen, just as the Nazis wished to shed literally the innocent blood of Jews, so also Satan wished to shed symbolically the innocent blood of the incarnate Son of God. And so Satan wishes to shed your blood and my blood, either as victims or as perpetrators and then victims of sacrifice.

An examination of demonology lies beyond the scope of this book, but I would like to to mention one item of possible relevance to the principle of shedding innocent blood in this regard. I spoke with a now-retired Anglican priest, Edison Mendis, who frequently performed exorcisms during his forty-year ministry in Sri Lanka. A composed and dignified Sinhalese gentleman, Rev. Mendis told me that demon possession is roughly the same regardless of whether the victim is Christian, Buddhist, or Hindu. Mendis said he would begin each

59. Let me stress that I am not using the word *innocent* to denote sinlessness or special virtue in this context; I am simply referring to the sort of victim who has not done anything specific to deserve being made a sacrificial victim.

exorcism with a test to see if a demon was actually present in the alleged victim of possession. He would place his hands firmly on the victim's head and then ask him or her to recite the Lord's Prayer or the Apostles' Creed. If the victim could not — Hindus and Buddhists are understandably unfamiliar with these symbols — then Mendis would himself recite the words. If a demon was present, this would throw the possessed person into convulsions or induce violent writhing or gestures. I understood Mendis to be saying that the demon was reacting against the symbols of the holy. Mendis would then ask the demon for its name, and the name given would be either a Sinhala or Tamil name, depending on the victim's native culture. Mendis would then command "in the name of Jesus Christ" that the demon depart from the person, from the room, from the village, and go to the place appointed by God to await judgment. Immediately the convulsions would stop and a previously hideous facial expression would turn serene.

"Does it matter if the victim was previously baptized?" I asked.

"No, it's the same," he said.

"Do the non-Christians suddenly get interested in Christianity?" I asked.

"Sometimes the family will try going to a Christian church," he responded, "but usually they just get what they want and go back to their normal life."

Then I asked about his actual conversations with the demons. He said that the demons tell him they enter a person who harbors revenge. Then Mendis said something most relevant to our topic at hand. Often the demons would say, "I want blood! I want blood!"

This leads me to explore another closely related topic: suicide. In his treatment of human evil, M. Scott Peck is reluctant to deal with demonic possession, but he describes two such cases nonetheless. One thing in common to both cases: something or someone told the individuals to kill themselves.[60] Something like an inner voice whispered, "Kill yourself!"

Walter Wink tells the unnerving story of a close friend who had lost a ten-year-old son to cancer. One night while sleeping with his wife in a ninth-floor hotel room, he heard a voice saying, "Why don't you

60. Peck, *People of the Lie: The Hope for Healing Human Evil* (New York: Simon & Schuster, 1983), p. 204.

go to the balcony and jump?" Though the man refused, the voice continued to tempt him by saying that if he were to die, he could go to be with his dead son. For two hours the dialogue continued until he finally woke his wife, and asked her to hold him, at which point the assault ended.[61] I can sympathize, because when depressed following the death of my parents I too felt that a similar voice was calling me to death and offering similar arguments. No doubt psychologists can identify certain dynamics of depression at work here. Yet what seems to be decisive is the voice from beyond that makes the sacrifice of the innocent — in this case the potential suicide victim is the innocent one — seem logical and desirable. Satan is present when we hear the call to shed innocent blood, even if that blood be our own.

Some Sacramental Nonconclusions

Somehow, it seems to me, these considerations have symbolic implications for our understanding of baptism and the Lord's Supper. Although these two sacraments may seem innocuous to practicing Christians because of their ritual familiarity, they may in fact mediate more power than we ordinarily observe.

I have been wondering about the power of baptism since an event in 1978. I was a super (an extra) in the opera "The Last of the Mohicans." I am no singer; I simply stood wearing a British soldier's uniform in one act and a French soldier's uniform in the next. During rehearsals, a young singer with a master's degree from a major university — we'll call him Dominic — came to me for counseling about his professional career. He was being recruited to join a New York–based coven. The Devil, he said, was offering a pact: fame in the entertainment world in exchange for his eternal soul. I could hardly believe my ears. It sounded just like the plot in *Faust, The Devil and Daniel Webster*, or even *Damn Yankees*.[62] But this was real life.

61. Wink, *Unmasking the Powers*, p. 26.

62. Ruth Nanda Anshen makes reference to historical events that may have served as a basis for the legend of Faust. In 1611 Louis Gaufridy signed a Devil's pact in which he renounced all "spiritual and temporal goods which could be conferred on me by God" to "surrender myself, body and soul, to you Lucifer." In a similar document of the same year, Urban Grandier stated, "I renounce Holy Communion and Baptism; I renounce equally all merits offered by Jesus Christ and the saints." On

I pressed him. "You have been raised in a fine Roman Catholic family," I said. "You know the difference between right and wrong. This is wrong. Just say No!"

"But Pastor Peters," he countered, "I don't know if you understand what this means. There is nothing a singer wants more, nothing else that keeps him awake nights imagining and dreaming, than to have his talent recognized, to be asked to sing by the best companies, and to become famous. This is how [he mentioned the name of the person singing the lead in the opera we were rehearsing for] made it."

"Does this apply to you?" I asked.

"Oh yes. There is nothing in this life I want more."

"Then why are you talking to me? Why haven't you already joined? What is holding you back? Something in you tells you this is not the right thing to do, right?"

He nodded affirmatively. This led to numerous conversations through the entire period the opera played. One morning he told me that the night before he had accepted an invitation to attend a sacrifice. It took place in a remote field well after our evening's performance. He explained that the group had sacrificed chickens to Satan and consumed their blood.

Among the many things I emphasized again and again over the weeks of conversation was this: "You should be able to resist such an obvious temptation. You are a baptized Christian and your disposition is kindly and loving toward other people. Just say No!"[63] It seemed so simple to me. I was assuming the truth of Augustine's contention that the Holy Spirit infuses us with the grace and power to make the right decisions and, further, that baptism is the symbol of this unfailing spiritual strength. Yet he simply sought my sympathy by repeating, "You don't know what it means for an aspiring singer such as me to envision my name up in lights. And Satan has promised to deliver it to me." What the coven was offering was full indulgence of his desire for fame.

---

his side, Lucifer granted to Grandier "irresistibility with women" and "pleasures and riches" for a twenty-year period, after which Grandier was to enter Satan's realm to "blaspheme God." The pact required the recipient of Lucifer's gifts to "trample under his foot the sacraments of the Church" (*Anatomy of Evil*, pp. 88-89).

63. This conversation took place a decade before Rev. Mendis told me that he had performed exorcisms on previously baptized persons who had later become possessed. We have need, I think, of an empirical examination of the relationship between baptism and temptation to radical evil.

The last conversation we had took place after the opera's final performance. He and I were sitting on a bench waiting for our respective rides. "You know," he said, "the church is guilty of giving the Devil a bad name. The people of Satan are really not as bad as you might think. They believe the right things. There is a strong commitment to world peace and putting a stop to war. My friends in the coven, for example, asked me to contribute some money to feed the hungry in Africa. [There was a major problem of starvation in the Sahel region of Africa at the time.] Now what church does that? And, you know, the churches are full of bigots and hypocrites. We can't get them to stop supporting apartheid in South Africa."

"Let me ask you something," I said. I believed Dominic to be a highly moral person. He had received strict religious upbringing and an advanced degree from a university that holds liberal values. "Do you believe we should work for world peace? Do you believe we should feed the starving? Do you believe it is right that we seek racial justice?"

"Absolutely."

"Then think for a minute. You're a high-minded person. You're not selfish and narrow. You have a healthy conscience. This coven cannot simply come up to you and ask you to engage in sin. You would reject them outright. So they are appealing to your better nature. Knowing your values, they appeal to those very values. But remember, Satan is a liar and the father of lies. They've given you some delectable-looking bait, but there's a hook in it."

This was our last exchange before our good-byes. My ride showed up and I left. Etched in my memory is the view through the car window of Dominic sitting on the bench pondering his eternal destiny. In the years since I have searched every opera program I could get my hands on, hoping I won't see his name.

I had not been prepared for my dealings with Dominic. There were no courses in my seminary training dealing with Devil counseling. What was I to do? What I found myself doing was trying to draw on the power of his baptism to resist temptation. I recalled how in the ancient church it was believed that the Holy Spirit actually entered the believer in baptism, that in an almost substantialist fashion God's Spirit entered and replaced our human spirit. This meant, among other things, that within each baptized person lies the very power of God to withstand if not overcome the spirit of Satan.

So I wondered: could we assume that those who are baptized are forever protected from radical evil? Later I discovered that the initiation rite into such a coven includes a renunciation of one's baptism. The initiate openly repudiates Christ and swears allegiance to Satan. The Devil's disciples know what they're doing.

Turning now to the Lord's Supper, I find it important that Satan worshipers find the Eucharist important. On the one hand, they out-literalize the fundamentalists and transubstantiationists in their use of body and blood. On the other hand, they redirect the meaning of the sacrificial symbol so that it is Satan who is honored and invoked. Real sacrifice and real death result in Satan's "real presence." Here I wish to recall my earlier enunciated principle: Satan is present when we hear the request to shed innocent blood. I suspect this was true on Golgotha.

I would like to think that the sacramental symbols within a Christian congregation could have a healing effect on victims of ritual abuse. If so, we must first surmount some complications. Recall Kathy, whom I described in Chapter 7, attending her Anglican church in Oakland. Today, when she hears the words of institution and watches the lifting up of the bread and wine symbolizing Jesus' body and blood, it strikes her with abject terror. Her former experiences with actual sacrifice and actual death come thundering into her mind. Even though the cult is in her past, the symbols of worship cannot help but keep that deathly past alive.

But this must have been the way it was for the first generation of Jesus' followers who began celebrating what eventually became our Eucharist too. The resurrection turned Jesus' last supper into a love meal, an *agape* feast, to be sure. Nevertheless, the early Christians were realistic about the suffering of Jesus. In the Eucharist they remembered the horror of innocent suffering and death. Bread and wine re-presented body and blood. Perhaps too much distance has been allowed to separate the formality of eating and drinking during communion with the original sorrow that belongs to the event it invokes. No doubt we need to find some pastoral way to ensure that the bread and wine communicate grace rather than terror to former cult members, but as things stand, perhaps we can allow their terror to have the salutary effect of reminding us of the origins of this sacrament and the divine price paid to secure our salvation.

9

Forgiveness: Grace, Love, and Unfinished Business

Thus, while His death my sin displays
In all its blackest hue,
Such is the mystery of grace,
It seals my pardon too.

John Newton, "In Evil Long I Took Delight"

It is one thing to try to understand sin. It is quite another to do something about it. If sin were at root a problem of ignorance or lack of understanding, then increased understanding would in itself improve matters. But sin is not a matter of mere ignorance; it is rooted in the human *will*. We can be warned firmly that evil is on our doorstep and still choose to go out and greet it with open arms. No amount of knowledge of the world gained through education or experience, no amount of knowledge of oneself gained through psychotherapy or mystical meditation, no amount of knowledge of any sort can in itself resist or overcome a will that desires to sow sin and reap evil.

Law

How, then, can we combat sin? More than one weapon has been used in the battle. Perhaps the most familiar weapon in the war against sin

263

is the use of law. This is the weapon most of our parents used when we were growing up. It is the one I use now that I am raising my own kids. We make rules: "Don't do this," "Don't do that." Many rules or laws are accompanied by threats of punishment. "If you suck your thumb and then put it in a wall socket, I'll slap your hand." We make such laws to teach safety and self-protection. We also make such laws to teach virtue, to provide a road map for the development of moral character. "If you steal money from my dresser drawer, I'll restrict you to the house for a month." Such a law can be quickly learned. Obeying the law is quite another matter.

Voluntary organizations such as the Boy Scouts of America also use laws in order to invite the development of moral character among our youth. Involuntary organizations such as local, state, and federal governments use laws coercively in order to prevent disorder, in order to protect the weak in our society from the ravages of the strong who lack moral character.

Religions use laws. The teachings of Confucius are known the world over as rules of wisdom that map the path toward the development of personal integrity and social harmony. The Ten Commandments brought down from Mount Sinai by Moses invoke the will of God for the purpose of ordering the human soul and ordering social arrangements so that peace and justice prevail. Religious and moral laws function *positively* to guide the growth of personal character in the direction of integrity and perhaps even holiness. They function *negatively* by providing limits to permissible human aggression, by confining sin in such a way as to limit the amount of evil that might result. Laws attempt to hold sin in check.

If we believe law to be a gift from God, and if we believe law has the power to order the very core of our personal and social being, we will find law beautiful. Certainly the Psalmist is filled with a sense of the beauty of the law:

Happy are those
    who do not follow the advice of the wicked,
  or take the path that sinners tread,
    or sit in the seat of scoffers;
but their delight is in the law of the LORD,
    and on his law they meditate day and night.
    (Psalm 1:1-2)

Probably the highest form of the law is the law of love. Jesus summed up all the law and the prophets with his two-pronged commandment to love God and love neighbor (Matt. 22:34-40).[1] Lest anyone take this to be an easy law to fulfill, Jesus presses it to the extreme by telling us, "Love your enemies and pray for those who persecute you" (Matt. 5:44). Anyone who can love God, love neighbor, and even love an enemy is not likely to engage for very long in perpetrating the evils accompanying pride or concupiscence or scapegoating. The law of love, among other things, is a road map leading us toward a beautiful life, and as such it is intended to leave sin behind.

But just how effective is the law of love? How does it work? Does it actually inspire us to live loving lives? In some cases it does, but for the most part the law of love simply reveals to us how unloving the world is. It shocks us into realizing how unloving we ourselves are. Like removing the lid of a garbage can, the law makes visible the ugliness of swarming vermin.

The law is like a measure. When we judge ourselves by it, we frequently come up short.[2] The law, like a map, points out where we ought to be and the roads we should take to get there. It also identifies wrong directions and blind alleys. If we place ourselves on the map, we can identify our location. When the map turns into a measure, we realize we have stopped short of our destination. And worse, we may even feel we do not have what it takes to press on and finish the journey. This is discouraging.

---

1. Paul follows suit by summing up the Ten Commandments and then saying that "love is the fulfilling of the law" (Rom. 13:10).

2. Theologians such as Emil Brunner follow a tradition of identifying three distinct uses of the law: (1) the political use *(usus politicus)*, which commands obedience to divine or civil laws for the purpose of maintaining justice in the social order; (2) the theological or pedagogical use *(usus elenchticus)*, which holds up as a mirror to us our sinfulness and prepares us to receive God's grace; and (3) the didactic use *(usus didacticus)*, which presents a guide for faithful living (*The Divine Imperative* [Philadelphia: Westminster Press, 1947], pp. 140-51). Most Reformed theologians embrace all three uses, whereas Lutheran theologians tend to employ only the first two. See my expanded discussion of this issue in chap. 9 of *God — The World's Future: Systematic Theology for a Postmodern Era* (Minneapolis: Fortress Press, 1992).

Forgiveness

In addition to law, there is another weapon in our arsenal aimed at combating sin: forgiveness. Rather than discouraging, however, forgiveness is encouraging. The purpose of forgiveness is to help the sinner, not to prevent the sin. Whereas law as map tries to prevent us from sinning before we get started, the combination of law as measure plus forgiveness comes to our aid once we have set out down the wrong road.

The most obvious form of forgiveness is found in the familiar response to an apology, "That's okay, forget it." Such an apology usually begins when we say, "I'm sorry." This means we are sorrowful — not about things in general but about some specific deed we regret having done. This sorrow can be motivated by one of two things: shame or guilt. It is a matter of shame when we fear exposure or, having already been exposed, we fear punishment. We are quick to apologize if it will reduce the graveness of the consequences. It is a matter of guilt when we experience a heartfelt sense of remorse. We may feel guilt even if we might appear to have gotten away with it. Whether motivated by shame or guilt, we seek forgiveness in order to reduce the evil consequences of a past sin.

It is embarrassing to ask for forgiveness. It requires confession. When we confess, we have to expose ourselves, to reveal ourselves as we are, motivated by pride or greed. When we confess, we must give up trying to justify ourselves. We have to throw off the cloak of the lie for at least a moment so that the other person can see the truth, the truth we had been trying to hide. At this moment we know how Adam and Eve felt in the Garden of Eden as they scurried to cover over their nakedness.

Perhaps this is why genuine forgiveness of sins is such a rare commodity. It may not seem to be all that rare, because a poor cousin to forgiveness is so altogether common. People are saying "Excuse me" and "I'm sorry" all day long. It is a lightweight social lubricant that we use to maintain rapport in the face of an indiscretion or accident. If we accidentally spill the coffee or show up late for an appointment or forget our spouse's birthday, we initiate the ritual of apology. We hope to hear "That's okay, forget it," as a signal that our relationship can continue as normal. In fact, a person who is known to say "I'm sorry" often is tacitly presumed to be a nice person. It's a good habit to get into if you want a good reputation.

266

But this sort of social pleasantry is something quite apart from the core experience of sin and forgiveness. To seek forgiveness for a sin — a sin, not an accident — requires that we reveal our personal character as sinner. Because of the lie of self-justification, we resist this self-revelation with every ounce of our psychic energy. When challenged to confess, we may be driven to come up with ever more subtle and creative forms of self-justification. We may even confess to something trivial in order to avoid deeper penetration into who we are. "I didn't mean to cheat on my expense account; it was an error in arithmetic." We may try to plea bargain our sin down to a misdemeanor, to get everyone involved to agree that it was an accident, elicit a "That's okay," and end any further probing. True forgiveness is quite rare because so few of us want to pay the price that true confession and self-revelation exact.

Similarly, we may shun forgiveness if we are consciously committed to a life of sin — that is, if we lack contrition. I find the testimony of Nicholas "The Crow" Caramandi, a Philadelphia hit man for Mafia figure Nicodemo Scarfo, instructive here. After he was arrested in 1987 and pled guilty to murder, racketeering, and extortion, Caramandi testified in eleven trials leading to fifty-two convictions for his former colleagues on charges of mob-related crimes. Among his own murder victims was Salvatore Testa, one of Caramandi's best friends. When asked why he would kill a friend, Caramandi answered, "If you're a gangster, you gotta be a gangster. You never know who you're gonna be told to kill in this business." He was also asked to put a hit on Pasquale Spirito. Fearing the hit, Spirito confronted Caramandi in a luncheonette the day before the scheduled murder. In this conversation, Caramandi swore his allegiance: "Buddy, my life is yours. Jesus Christ, I love you." The next night he shot Spirito twice in the back of the head. Now, we might ask, what motivated Caramandi to pursue the life of deceit and violence? He answered with unmistakable clarity: concupiscence in the form of lust for power. "When you sneeze," he said, "fifteen handkerchiefs come out. I mean, everywhere you go, people just can't do enough for you. . . . There's so much glamour and respect and money. . . . You belong to an army, something that is so powerful." When asked by *Time* magazine reporter Richard Behar whether he believed in God, Caramandi offered an answer instructive for our discussion of forgiveness:

Yeah, I believe in God. I go to church once a month, but I can't bring myself to go to confession right now. I don't have the balls yet to do that. I don't know if my sins are going to be forgiven, you know. I broke all the commandments. . . . That's the only peace I think I'll have, if I could get to God. But I don't want to use God as an excuse now, because I know in my heart that I would do it all again. I'm talking from the heart. So how could I say I'm sorry? If I say I'm sorry, who am I kidding? I did it, and I loved it.[3]

Forgiveness is rare in large part because so few genuinely ask for it.

Grace

It takes two to tango, and it takes two to accomplish true forgiveness: one party must wish to be forgiven, and the other must be willing to grant forgiveness. The character of the one granting forgiveness is decisive. He or she must be *gracious*. To be gracious toward someone offering an apology, one must be magnanimous, free to forgive without resentment or vindictiveness. To put it another way, the gracious person needs to have the ability to love even an enemy.

A gracious person is an intrinsically beautiful person. This is entailed in the very way we use the word *grace*. We think of people as graceful when they combine kindness and caringness with elegance in their manner of movement or speech. Gracious people are willing to overlook our indiscretions and faux pas. They are willing to remain our friends despite the wrongs we might have done to them. Their acts of grace in granting mercy or pardon are themselves a form of elegance that makes them inherently attractive, beautiful.

I recall a theological colleague, H. George Anderson, telling of an overnight visit in the home of some friends. The occasion included an elegant dinner party. The woman of the house, whom George described as a most gracious hostess, had brought out her finest china, crystal, silver settings, and the hand-crocheted lace tablecloth she had inherited from her mother. During the meal one of the guests overturned a dish of cranberry sauce, soiling the tablecloth. Would it leave

3. Caramandi, quoted by Behar in "A Crow Turns Stool Pigeon," *Time,* 17 June 1991, pp. 11-18.

a stain? "Oh no, it'll come right out," said the hostess, "don't worry." The embarrassed guest showed a distinct expression of relief at hearing these words. The rest of the evening proceeded as if nothing had gone wrong. In the middle of the night George awoke thirsty. He walked down the stairs and to the kitchen for a glass of water. There he found the hostess with the tablecloth in the sink, scrubbing and scrubbing the nearly indelible stain. This is grace.

Grace is perhaps the most salient character trait of God. "The fundamental meaning of grace," wrote the late Joseph Sittler, "is the goodness and loving-kindness of God and the activity of this goodness in and toward the creation."[4] Roger Haight puts it succinctly: "Grace is God's love for us."[5] Grace is not a thing or a substance but a quality that distinguishes God's loving disposition toward his creatures.[6] The God of grace is a God who loves — loves even sinners. God is magnanimous. God forgives sinners. God is beautiful.

It is this gracious and forgiving quality of God that sin conspires to cover up and hide. When we engage in unfaith, we presume that God is untrustworthy, ungracious, and therefore not deserving of our trust. When we are proud, we seek to run our lives all by ourselves without having to rely on God to give us anything. When we engage in self-justification, we may blaspheme God's name by disassociating it from grace. This is tricky. Yet we can understand the trick if we recognize that self-justification cannot work unless it relies on a false assumption about God — namely, that God is only a God of law and not of grace. It assumes that God will love us only if we are already just, that we must approach God in an already justified state. It denies that we can come to God as sinners; it denies that God will justify us by forgiving us our sin. We feel the need to justify ourselves only if we fail to accept the fact that God is willing to justify us. Finally, if we engage in cursing or Satanic rituals, we blaspheme God directly by invoking an alien power in conscious opposition to God's love. At every level, sin includes denying or hiding God's grace.

4. Sittler, "Grace in the Scriptures," in *Essays on Nature and Grace* (Philadelphia: Fortress Press, 1972), p. 24.

5. Haight, *The Experience and Language of Grace* (New York: Paulist Press, 1979), p. 8.

6. "God's love for us is gratuitous," writes Gustavo Gutiérrez; "we do not merit it. It is a gift we receive before we exist, or, to be more accurate, a gift in view of which we were created" (*We Drink from Our Own Wells* [London: SCM Press, 1984], p. 110).

Thus sin is more than simply breaking divine commandments, more than merely disobeying God's law. Sin also involves a cover-up that slanders God's character by reducing him to a God of law, by depicting him only as a God of punishment for lawbreakers, by implying that God is ugly. In this regard, it is accurate to say that Satan inspires all sin, even the most trivial. Satan is the accuser and tries to co-opt us into making indirect as well as direct accusations against God. There is little that God can do to defend the divine reputation from this coalition of human and Satanic slander. God can only be himself. God can only remain who he is, steady, standing by, offering forgiveness, and welcoming whoever comes for it.

Faith

Faith permits us to become aware of the truth about God beyond sin's slander. Recall that we earlier defined faith in terms of trust and noted how trusting God gives us the ability to gain control over the anxiety that wells up in response to the threat of nonbeing. It is divine grace that makes God trustworthy to us sinners. Regardless of who we have been or what we have done, the God of grace offers us forgiveness. We grasp this forgiveness through our faith.

Faith founded on the knowledge of forgiveness does a couple of things. First, it provides us with new insight into the nature of sin. It reveals to us what we could not see before — namely, the insult to God.

When I think of the insult to God, I think in terms of an analogy drawn from my own professional experience. I worked for a few years as a reference librarian at the Columbus (Ohio) Public Library. The librarian in charge of the reference section and my immediate supervisor was Gretchen DeWitt. I admired and liked her, and she liked me in return. We enjoyed a fine working relationship. One Friday afternoon, I was working on a particularly complicated reference problem. Knowing that the library would be closing in an hour or so, I was concentrating diligently to finish up. Miss DeWitt came to my desk and asked me to come with her to the workroom for a conference. I told her I was busy and asked if it could wait. No, it couldn't wait. I began to feel anxiety over time. I was frustrated at being interrupted. I began to remember previous occasions on which Miss DeWitt had interrupted me. Rage arose within me. Taking liberties that might strain our otherwise healthy working relationship, I insisted that I keep to my project. She insisted with equal vehemence that I drop the work and go to the workroom. Then she turned and walked, expecting me to follow. I did. All the way I nagged her by complaining. She said nothing and walked on. Seeing that my complaining was ineffective, I scolded her. Then I raised the pitch of my scolding. Soon we arrived at the workroom door. We entered and found the entire library staff standing around a table holding a cake and lit candles and singing "Happy Birthday" — to me. Miss DeWitt had planned the party in my honor. How humiliated I felt. Once the truth of Miss DeWitt's graciousness became clear to me, I became aware of how I had insulted her. However, Miss DeWitt showed not even the slightest sign of retaliation for my rudeness. She was elegantly gracious. Because of her grace, my insult didn't harm our relationship.

Our relationship to God through faith is similar. Once we understand that God forgives out of divine love, a sense of personal affront to God is added to any previous legalistic understanding of sin we might have had. Once we understand that God forgives freely, we become aware of our own ingratitude. This is not intended to be manipulative. Rather, it is intended to be revelatory of the seriousness with which God takes the task of redeeming sinners.

The point is that once we realize how God justifies us, a new dimension of the nature of sin opens up to our perception. "Only those who are justified by God are awakened from the sleep of the opinion that their acts can be justified of themselves," says Karl Barth.[7] I think he overstates the case a bit, because I think it is possible to recognize our own sin as sin apart from any willingness to receive forgiveness. The case of Nicholas Caramandi would seem to indicate as much. Yet I agree with Barth that God's justification awakens us to see what we previously could not see. It awakens us to the distinctively gracious dimension of God's character and our corresponding

---

7. Barth, *Church Dogmatics,* 4 vols., ed. Thomas F. Torrance, trans. Geoffrey W. Bromiley (Edinburgh: T. & T. Clark, 1936-1962), II/2:768. Barth goes too far, in my judgment, when he says that "it is the Gospel, and not a Law abstracted from the Gospel, that compels us to recognize our transgression" (II/2:769). The law as measure is sufficient to enable us to recognize our sin. The gospel understood as the message of forgiveness adds the ability to recognize the insult to God's grace. We can become aware of God's grace only after we have received its benefits.

ingratitude. We become aware simultaneously of the depth of our sin and the corresponding depth of God's grace.

The second thing faith does is free us and empower us from within. It frees us from being held hostage by anxiety and moral guilt. It frees us from the misleading drive to draw a line between good and evil and place ourselves on the good side.[8] We no longer feel that we have to transform ourselves into something good in order to become acceptable. Gone is the compulsion to find goodness, consume it, and then declare that we ourselves are good. Faith prompted by grace is satisfied with allowing God to be good. Furthermore, faith prompted by grace permits us to appreciate what is good in other people, eliminating any need to scapegoat them. Faith prompted by grace empowers us to live graciously.

Radical Love

The power comes from God's presence in faith. Faith is not just something we will to do, although it is at least that. Faith is a relationship in which God is vitally active, spiritually present in what we might call, for lack of a better term, a mystical bond. The Holy Spirit unites the living Christ with our entire personhood. Like the heat that turns a blacksmith's iron red hot, the love of God comes to imbue every dimension of our personal being. That heat then radiates. We love. We do not copy God's love; rather, God's love itself radiates through the life of faith.

In contrast to radical evil, radical love roots our lives in God. Like a tree rooted in the good, our fruits will be good. Augustine puts it in stark form:

A short and simple precept is given you once and for all: Love, and do what you will. Whether you keep silence, keep silence in love; whether you exclaim, exclaim in love; whether you correct, correct

---

8. The deep inner freedom that comes from faith in the God of grace is both subtle and glorious. Emil Brunner writes, "Freedom is the life founded on grace, on the gift of God. . . . Freedom means being free from the obligation to seek one's own good. Freedom is utter dependence on God, and this means the absolute renunciation to all claims of independence, of all illusory independence over against God. To be free means to be that for which God created us" (*The Divine Imperative*, p. 78).

in love; whether you forbear, forbear in love. Let love's root be within you, and from that root nothing but good can spring.[9]

It is faith that roots us in God and makes this radical love possible. Key to understanding the difference that faith makes is the recognition that people of faith do not try to be moral for the sake of making themselves good. They abandon the task of self-justification altogether, both as a genuine attempt to become virtuous and as an attempt merely to present the appearance of virtue. Personal need becomes secondary to the need of the neighbor. When we have faith, we love our neighbor — not out of our own need to be known as a person who loves but solely because the neighbor has a need. Loving becomes an activity aimed solely at edifying the life of someone else.

Martin Luther emphasized this in terms of the freedom found in faith. Once we realize that God has justified us, we are free from the obligation to justify ourselves. He says dramatically that to be a Christian is to be "a perfectly free lord of all, subject to none." Faith liberates. Then Luther turns right around and says that "a Christian is a perfectly dutiful servant of all, subject to all." By this he means that the person of faith is alert to the needs of others and quick to respond to those needs with acts of love. We should be "guided" in all our works "by this thought and contemplate this one thing alone" — namely, that we "may serve and benefit others . . . considering nothing except the need and the advantage" of our neighbor. True love is willing to serve without reward. "Through its health and comfort we may be able to work, to acquire, and lay by funds with which to aid those who are in need, that in this way the strong member may serve the weaker. . . . This is a truly Christian life. Here faith is truly active through love (Gal. 5:6)."[10]

9. Augustine, "Seventh Homily: I John 4:4-12," in *Augustine: Later Works*, Library of Christian Classics, trans. John Burnaby (Philadelphia: Westminster Press, 1965), p. 316. The Burnaby translation of Augustine's precept is potentially misleading. A more accurate rendering would be "What you will when moved by love, that do."

10. Luther, "The Freedom of a Christian," in *Three Treatises* (Philadelphia: Fortress Press, 1960), pp. 277, 302. See 1 Cor. 9:19: "For though I am free with respect to all, I have made myself a slave to all." Gutiérrez follows Aquinas and others who, following Paul, distinguish *freedom from* sin, selfishness, injustice, need, and so forth from *freedom for* love, communion, and the work of liberation. Gutiérrez adds, "Authentic love tries to start with the concrete needs of the other and act with the 'duty' of practicing love" (*We Drink from Our Own Wells*, p. 108; see also p. 92).

One of the implications of understanding love as responding to someone's needs is that loving becomes a very practical matter. The questions we ask ourselves are practical ones: What is the need? How might it be met? How might someone else's life be made richer? How can this world be made a better place? What can I do to facilitate matters? This is a rather nonromantic and nonpious and maybe even nonspiritual understanding of love. It does not increase self-esteem. It is not flamboyant. It does not seek publicity. It simply tries to get certain things done.[11]

One more thing. Forgiveness and faith do not immediately eliminate every last droplet of anxiety and fill our cup to the brim with unfailing love. We remain finite human beings. Anxiety will return to challenge us each day. Some days we will handle it better than others. In addition, we cannot extricate ourselves from the world with its heritage of sin and suffering from evil. There is nowhere we can go to avoid participation in the nexus of sin. Our hands continue inevitably to be dirty. There is no island of purity in the rough seas of this life. But forgiven sinners can accept this reality.

Existence in faith is as Luther described it: *simul justus et peccator*.

Growth in Character

This realism of the forgiven is by no means a fatalism, however. To the contrary, people with faith know best of all how life can actually be better. They know that sinners can be transformed. They know that anxiety can be transformed into peace of mind, fear into courage, pride into humility, deceit into truth, and concupiscence into charity. Forgiveness sows a seed that grows and blossoms in inner joy and strength of character. As our joy deepens and our character grows in strength, temptation loses its potency. The ugliness of sin is overcome

11. The practical approach to love is made clear by Augustine: "We should not want there to be unfortunates, so that we may exercise works of mercy. You give bread to the hungry; but it would be better that no one should hunger, and that you should not have to give. You clothe the naked; would that all were so clothed that there would be no need for it!" ("Seventh Homily," p. 321). The point is that those who love feel no need to accumulate credit for their acts of love; they are quite content to work anonymously to create a just and sustainable society, motivated solely by a desire to meet the needs of the neighbor.

by the beauty of grace. We can see the victory of virtue before our very eyes. We can feel it, appreciate it, enjoy it.

The good life is the God-centered life, and our God-centeredness comes from the power of faith rather than the power of pride. Faith prompts love, and loving forms character. What kind of character? The kind of character that produces what Paul calls the fruits of the Spirit: "love, joy, peace, patience, kindness, generosity, faithfulness, gentleness, and self-control" (Gal. 5:22). A life bearing these fruits feeds the soul — both one's own soul and those around. Once we have dined on such fruits, our hunger for the fodder of sin begins to diminish.

It would be a mistake, of course, to think that once we begin bearing these fruits all our troubles disappear. We remain in the real world, facing its daily tragedies. Yet we face them with courage and strength. It is this combination of strong character and a world of tragic evil, I think, that led Jesus to formulate the Beatitudes the way he did. They reflect both the anguish and the fulfillment that characterize the faith-filled life. Jesus said that blessings belong to those among us who may be low in spirit, who are in mourning, who are meek, who hunger and thirst for justice, who show mercy, who remain pure in heart, who strive to bring peace on earth, and who are willing to suffer persecution when standing up for what is just and right and true (Matt. 5:2-10). "There are Christian virtues," wrote theologian Georgia Harkness, and they "are the qualities of a God-centered life as one seeks, in the totality of his being, to follow the pattern of faith and love set forth by Jesus."[12]

In addition to granting us forgiveness and supplying us with the fruits of the Spirit, God gives us another even more important gift to ensure our growth in character: our vocation, our calling. I believe that God has a specific purpose for each of us and calls us to turn our lives over to that purpose. This purpose is neither elaborately detailed nor chiseled in marble. It is, rather, a direction, a beckoning, a task, a responsibility. It may be tied to our profession or to some other significant dimension of our daily life. The call to faith includes a call to open ourselves and ask for God's leading in this matter. God leads in a most gentle and unobtrusive way, yet the leading is unmistakable for those who are willing to open their eyes to see and ears to hear.

12. Harkness, *Christian Ethics* (Nashville: Abingdon Press, 1957), p. 90.

Once one makes a commitment to follow the divine call, an amazing sense of empowerment takes over. Integrity — meaning personal integration under the guidance of God — grows. Weakness and compulsion are replaced by self-control. This easily translates into strength of character and strength to deal with sin. "The most comprehensive antidotes to temptation," says Wayne Oates, "are a clear sense of personal integrity and a strong sense of mission."[13]

In sum, we need not accept our world as fatally enchained by the forces of sin and evil. Nor need we accept a destiny wherein our inner self is locked into itself by fear and compulsion. Freedom and transformation are possible. God's grace is the key. By forgiving our sins, God liberates us from guilt and the need for self-aggrandizement. By promising resurrection to everlasting life, God liberates us from the sting of death produced by anxiety. By the presence of the Holy Spirit in our faith, God transforms our lives from within. Character grows toward greater personal integrity, and this empowers us for victory over sin.

The Dynamics of Sin

It has been my task in this book to throw some light on the experiential dynamics of sin so that we might better understand both sin and ourselves. I admitted at the outset that a complete understanding would be too much to hope for — in part because of the limited scope of this study but even more because of the intrinsically mysterious character of the sinful side of human nature. Because sin involves lies and cover-ups, it almost by definition protects large patches of darkness from the revealing light of truth.

I have worked with the assumption that the experience of sin is universal, that it involves all human beings in every society and at every age and station in life. Sin belongs to the human condition. Sin ought not to be trivialized by identifying it strictly with sexual indiscretion and overlooking such horrors as injustice, war, and environmental destruction. Nor ought sin to be trivialized by limiting it to so-called unjust social structures or systemic evil under the illusion that the human soul is unaffected and that a mere improvement in the edu-

13. Oates, *Temptation* (Louisville: Westminster/John Knox Press, 1991), p. 80.

cational system or a change in political leadership could rid us of the problem. Nor ought sin to be trivialized ideologically, by attributing the source of evil to one's enemies and exonerating one's own political party, tribe, gender, race, or nation. Nor ought sin to be trivialized through an outright denial of its existence, by suggesting that the idea of sin is merely the invention of a power-hungry priesthood for the purpose of inculcating a sense of guilt so that people will come to them for absolution. Sin does in fact exist. It is serious. Sin may derive from nonbeing, but as such it is the principle of destruction at work in the realm of being. It reaps an untold harvest of evil and suffering in every field of the world's activity. The attempt to trivialize sin, I have argued, itself belongs to sin, belongs to the lie.

I have also worked from the assumption that sin is simultaneously harmful to ourselves and harmful to God. Sin wounds both the creation and its Creator; sin is both *conversio ad creaturam* and *aversio a Deo.* To break this down further, sin is a cancer ever threatening death to our own inner life, to our intimate relationships, to larger social structures, to the interdependence of the human race with nature, and all of the above in relation to God. There is no zone of health that is not infected by the disease. But healing is possible through grace in both its human and divine forms.

Theodicy

Having limited our agenda here to the experiential dynamics of sin, I have necessarily left many related and fascinating topics unaddressed. Even so, a number of them have been hovering on the borders of our discussion all along. In some cases I have had to invoke certain commitments as presuppositions to sustain the description of sin with which we have been working. Perhaps some of these adjacent topics should be identified and considered as possible items on a future agenda of inquiry.

The first such topic is *theodicy*. Since the Second World War, whenever theologians have discussed evil, they have focused on the problem of theodicy. It has been a pastoral concern all along, because at the moment of tragedy such as disease or death people ask deep questions about the meaning of suffering. It recently became a topic of popular discussion when it made the cover of *Time* magazine with the word in giant capital letters: EVIL. Calling it a "theologian's problem," *Time* essayist Lance Morrow defined the theodicy problem in terms of three irreconcilable propositions.

> God is all powerful.
> God is all good.
> Terrible things happen.[14]

This is a problem of logic. It is difficult to see how all three statements could be true. If God is all powerful and terrible things happen, then God must not be all good — that is, God must be the author of evil. If God is all good and terrible things happen, then God must not be all powerful — that is, God must be unable to control evil forces. If God is both all powerful and all good, then it must be that terrible things do not happen — that is, what we call evil does not in fact exist. So what's the answer? As some are given to put it, how can we justify God in an evil world?

The question of theodicy comes to us with great existential force as we ponder the overwhelming weight of human sin and the havoc it has wreaked in our own century: the attempted genocide of the Armenians and the Jews, the self-destruction of European civilization in two world wars, the massive systems of imprisonment and execution by communists in Stalinist Russia and Maoist China, the advent of nuclear weaponry and push-button destruction of cities, international drug trafficking and arms sales profiteering, dictators and death squads supported by stable economies, and at this writing the starvation of tens of millions in Africa unable to grow food while civil wars rage to determine who will have the power over the devastated remains. Evil seems to roar down upon us like water over Niagara Falls, inundating and drowning the human race in an uncontrollable flood of hatred, mayhem, bloodshed, agony, and death.

It is in this context that the theodicy question has arisen with such urgency. Yet it seems odd to me that in asking it we tacitly dump the problem at God's feet. Why do we demand that God justify Godself? Most of the greatest evils of the twentieth century have been the

---

14. Morrow, "Evil," *Time,* 10 June 1991, p. 48. The use of the theodicy problem in an attempt to disprove the existence of God as Christians conceive it goes back at least to Celsus in the Roman period.

products of human sin. Should we not follow Ernest Becker and define the problem in terms of an *anthropodicy* rather than a theodicy?

Some philosophers of religion and philosophical theologians count the fact that such terrible things have happened as evidence that God does not exist. Or they lay the gauntlet down by saying either that the sort of God who would allow such terrible things to happen would not be worthy of our faith. They demand that God show just cause for such behavior; that God provide some sort of divine self-justification in the face of evil. It has been my assumption throughout this discussion of the experiential dynamics of sin that such theologians are themselves providing a prime example of sin. When they argue in this way, they are engaging in self-justification and scapegoating. In demanding divine self-justification, they are making God a scapegoat, however hidden it might be under the cover of theological logic. By setting up the problem in such a way that God is put on the defensive, the theologians give the appearance of being engaged in an honest inquiry. But that is a lie. They conveniently leave out of the formulation of the problem the key fact that many of the terrible things they ask God to account for are things that human beings do to each other. The philosophical theologians factor in the evil but factor out the sin. With a logical sleight of hand, these scholars justify humanity by scapegoating humanity's Creator and Redeemer.

This is the assumption with which I have been working. But it demands further examination to see if it will stand critical review. I would like in the near future to see a reassessment of the theodicy problem that takes into account the actual history of evil as well as the history of redemption.

One more thing before we depart from the problem of theodicy: we should take care not to reduce the issue to a mere assignment of blame, either to God or to ourselves. At a deeper level, the theodicy problem arises from the human sense of helplessness in the face of the impenetrable mystery surrounding suffering. It arises especially out of anxiety as we anticipate potential suffering. In such circumstances, we naturally ask about God. But we need to resist the temptation to rush in and define God in ways that are most convenient for ourselves; we need to recognize the freedom of God to define himself as God. Karl Rahner reminds us that God remains mysterious, beyond the reach of our definitions. Our experience of suffering may enhance the mystery, but it does not deny the reality of God.

The acceptance of suffering without an answer other than the in-comprehensibility of God and his freedom is the concrete form in which we accept God himself and allow him to be God. If there is not directly or indirectly this absolute acceptance of the incompre-hensibility of suffering, all that can really happen is the affirmation of our own idea of God and not the affirmation of God himself.[15]

Timothy Lull puts it this way: "One thing we know about God, or ought to know about God, is that God is God and we are not."[16] Regardless of how we answer the theodicy question, a great deal of mystery surrounding both suffering and God will remain.

Natural Evil

A second connected topic worthy of further discussion is *natural evil,* by which I mean suffering caused by forces of nature that apparently lie beyond human control — what insurance companies call "acts of God": earthquakes, storms, floods, drought, and such. Also included are diseases such as cancer and AIDS that, despite our most valiant medical efforts, kill mercilessly. Here we have evil without sin.

Or at least apparently. The horrendous damage inflicted on Ban-gladesh by the spring cyclone and flood of 1991 would seem to be a case of natural evil. The ten million vulnerable delta dwellers were inundated by wind, rain, and tidal waves that made water and land indistinguishable, washing away entire islands with all their inhabitants. As the storm waned, the corpses of countless cattle and perhaps 125,000 people washed up on what was left of the shoreline. Survivors then faced weeks and months of contaminated water, food shortages, malnutrition, disease, and more death. The loss of the year's crop meant more poverty and death yet to come. Natural evil? Yes, of course. But more. The geographically impoverished and overpopulated Bangladesh is a nation the world forgot. Unwanted by its grandmother India because its population is largely Muslim, and unwanted by its wealthier mother [West] Pakistan because of the economic burden it represents, Bangladesh has been a wandering orphan of poverty since

15. Rahner, "Why Does God Allow Us to Suffer?" in *Theological Investigations,* vol. 19 (New York: Crossroad, 1983), p. 207.
16. Lull, "God and Suffering: A Fragment," *Dialog* 25 (Spring 1986): 94.

1947. The cyclone and flood that struck in 1970, when it was called East Pakistan, killed 200,000 people. The Pakistani government did not react at that time to bring aid to the suffering nor to do what reason guided by love would dictate — namely, construct a protective dike system, control population growth, and seek a better standard of living for the people. The East Pakistanis revolted and gained independence in 1971, but since then population growth and continuing poverty have prevented preparations for the next natural disaster. It was only a matter of time, and the time came in 1991. A combination of human concern and foresight would not have prevented the cyclone, but it could have prevented the disaster. And the vulnerability remains. It takes no prophet to predict that the next cyclone and the one after that will continue to take massive tolls in human misery.

Much of the misery attributed to natural disasters derives from the human factor. Be that as it may, I do not dispute that natural evil exists in its own right. A fruitful direction for future inquiry, I think, would be to explore in greater detail the connection between natural evil and human sin. This would include, among other things, the tie between finitude and sin. What I have identified as anxiety due to the threat of nonbeing begins as a problem of finitude. It begins with finitude in relation to the human imagination that can envision infinity. Death makes us finite. Yet we can imagine the alternative. We have need of a more thorough examination of the relationship between finitude and anxiety than I have been able to perform here.

Another line of inquiry into natural evil that has only recently appeared on the horizon is the possible significance of entropy. According to the second law of thermodynamics, closed systems tend to move from states of high energy and high order to states of low energy and low order. Unless energy is pumped in from outside, systems dissipate. Unless energy is pumped into the universe from beyond, it too will dissipate. Many physical cosmologists believe that the cosmos is winding down, moving toward a future in which all things will dissipate into homogenous frozen disorder. At least at the metaphorical or comparative level, this looks like evil.[17] Is it? Is it only another

---

17. See Robert John Russell's pioneering essay, "Entropy and Evil," *Zygon* 19 (December 1984): 440-68. Juan Luis Segundo uses the terms *entropy* and *negentropy* as analogies for the tension in human existence; see *Evolution and Guilt*, trans. John Drury (Maryknoll, N.Y.: Orbis Books, 1974).

characteristic of temporal finitude? Should such questions be explored further?

Still another line of inquiry here would turn our attention to natural evil as a factor within human biology. The rise of the field of sociobiology in the 1970s and startling new discoveries expected from the Human Genome Project have raised again the question of how much human behavior is determined by our genes. Is anxiety genetic? Is aggression genetic? Are some individuals genetically determined to be more anxious or more aggressive? If so, should this enter into an accounting of their relative innocence or guilt? Might we eventually find a gene for sin? If we pursue this line of inquiry, we may find that the line between natural evil and human sin will blur if not fade away altogether.

The Ecological Myth of Holism

A third and closely related topic also involves our relationship with the natural world. It begins with the question of holism and then proceeds to guilt consciousness. The holism question is being raised today by environmentalists and New Age spokespersons who are trying to explain the sense of estrangement we feel toward the natural world of which we are a part. The explanation takes the form of an ecological myth that is a sort of parallel of the story of the fall of Adam and Eve from paradise. According to the ecological myth, there was once a time when the human race lived in perfect harmony with nature. Everything was in balance. We humans enjoyed a naive symbiosis with the plants and animals. Then we fell. What we fell into was objectivist thinking, the kind of thinking that gives rise to science and technology. We began to see nature as an object over against ourselves as subjects. Our present state of fallenness is referred to derisively as subject-object "dualism." Redemption, according to this developing ecological myth, would consist of a new form of thinking that affirms human oneness with nature — that is, holistic thinking.

Whom do we blame for our fall from natural wholeness? The philosopher G. W. F. Hegel thought he located the fall in two stages. The first was the ancient Hebrew experience with a transcendent God. Prior to Moses, humanity allegedly lived in harmony with the world. Nature was sacred. It embodied a spiritual order. But this spiritual presence was lost when God revealed the Godself at Sinai. If God transcends nature, then nature stands as an object over against God. It loses its sacredness. The second stage of the fall, according to Hegel, was the rise of the modern world and the objectification of nature by science and technology. If nature is not sacred, then we can treat it like a thing. This is what we do when we employ technology.

Twentieth-century versions of the ecologist's myth echo the Hegelian scheme and add variants in an effort to retrieve some of the pre-Hebrew paganism. Neopagan feminism, for example, asserts that the original harmony occurred during a primal matriarchal epoch. The human race then fell when society became patriarchal. This is buttressed by assertions that women are more in tune with nature, that nature can be thought of as a goddess, and that the male gender is responsible for the dualistic thinking that founded both ancient Hebrew and modern technological dualism. If we could return to feminine sensibilities, feminist ecologists argue, we could solve our environmental problems.

The immediate and obvious difficulty with this ecological myth is its gnostic structure. It locates the problem in human knowing — the problem of our ignorance regarding the oneness we humans share with all of nature — rather than in willing. It locates the problem in terms of right thinking. Dualistic thinking is said to be inferior to holistic thinking. If we think correctly, we will regain our lost harmony. The ecological myth fails to recognize that it is entirely possible for us to think correctly and yet still choose to do evil. I have already argued that the environmental crisis is due fundamentally to concupiscence and its accompanying willful short-sightedness, not to subject-object or technological thinking. There may very well be problems associated with dualistic thinking, but the root of the crisis is our sin.

Now, I happen to be a strong advocate of holistic thinking. I am also committed to a concerted effort on the part of the human race to preserve the habitability and the ecological integrity of our planet. Yet I worry that a combination of naiveté and ideological opportunism may be retarding an honest analysis and the development of a practical set of proposals for taking the kind of action that would have a positive effect. A worthwhile future agenda, I think, would be to take greater care than we have thus far in examining the relationship between concupiscence or other forms of sin and the identifiable trajectories of environmental deterioration.

The Unhappy Consciousness

A closely related fourth topic is guilt in the form of the unhappy consciousness, what Hegel called *das unglückliche Bewußtsein*. The unhappy consciousness arises from the primal human awareness of being tied to and yet estranged from nature. We are aware of our separation. We are also aware that, despite our best efforts, we cannot return to primitive wholeness. Hegel located his answer in the concept of the *absolute spirit*.[18] That answer may be interesting to some, but it is not what I wish to address here. I want to take a closer look at a point that he touches on only in passing in his treatment of the issue — namely, the way guilt works in a downward spiral.

Hegel charged medieval Christian spirituality with having repudiated human pleasure. Human pleasure, especially bodily pleasure, is the way we humans enjoy the natural world around and in us. According to Hegel, the medievals taught that a person of faith should renounce all worldly pleasure and press all energy into the pursuit of virtue — that is, the pursuit of love for God. And, since they believed that God transcends the world of nature, they believed that our true pleasure must consist in transcending the natural world. This led to a spirituality of asceticism, of renouncing the world and mortifying the flesh. It led, according to Jean Delumeau, to outright contempt for the world *(contemptus mundi)*.[19] Some advocates of the ecological myth would add that this contempt for the world underlies the modern Western reluctance to take the steps necessary to preserve the planet. Instead of contempt, we should love — or, according to some ecologists, *worship* — the world of nature.

What interests me here is the twisted logic that might account for the torturous misery of so many souls. The argument is that, having stipulated that there exist two competing pleasures, one this-worldly and the other otherworldly, the medievals pressed on to assert that they were mutually exclusive. One could not enjoy natural pleasure and at the same time enjoy the presence of God. One had to choose:

18. See Hegel, *The Phenomenology of Mind*, trans. J. B. Baillie (New York: Harper & Row, 1967), pp. 251-52, 752ff.; and Charles Taylor, *Hegel* (Cambridge: Cambridge University Press, 1975), pp. 57ff., 63, 159-60.

19. See Delumeau, *Sin and Fear: The Emergence of a Western Guilt Culture, Thirteenth-Eighteenth Centuries,* trans. Eric Nicholson (New York: St. Martin's Press, 1990), chap. 1.

either God or the world, not both. In fact, one could ascertain an increase in divine pleasure by observing a relative decrease in worldly pleasure. Conversely, the more one enjoyed natural life, the more one had reason to worry that he or she was denying God. The argument is that if I deny myself such things as food, money, sex, and close friendships — things that fulfill my nature and thereby make me happy — then I will become happier in my relationship to God. The net objective, it turns out, was to make oneself totally miserable in order to find total happiness.[20] This is the core of the unhappy consciousness.

The Protestant Reformation did nothing to improve matters in this regard. Despite the Reformers' earnest desire to spread a sense of comfort by pronouncing believers justified by God rather than by what they achieved by their own spiritual accomplishments, the message backfired. In order to be comforted, we need to receive God's forgiveness. In order to receive God's forgiveness, the logic goes, we need to acknowledge our guilt. The greater the sense of guilt, it seems to follow, the greater the sense of God's grace. Soon Protestants found themselves focusing not on God's grace but rather on their own guilt. The creation of a guilt consciousness became common fare in Protestant pulpits and devotional literature. Nineteenth-century revivalist orators stressed radical conversion, encouraging exaggerated accounts of personal sins and miseries prior to joyous conversion. Liberal Protestants have borne the mantle of the unhappy consciousness into the twentieth century by identifying social criticism with prophecy and castigating themselves mercilessly for complicity in all the world's problems. The unspoken maxim has become: the guiltier I feel, the closer to God I am.

It gets still nastier. The nature we oppose in the unhappy consciousness is our own God-given nature. We fight against our own natural tendencies. Sometimes we win, sometimes we lose. When we lose, we may get angry at ourselves. We may get angry enough that we punish ourselves. God does not need to punish us. We do it

---

20. A contemporary rendering of the unhappy consciousness can be found in Christopher Lasch's protest against the chauvinism of modernity that repudiates the truths found in religion — specifically, that obligation to live with limits. Once we willingly commit ourselves to living within our limits, says Lasch, we will be able to recognize "the central paradox of religious faith: that the secret of happiness lies in renouncing the right to be happy" ("The Illusion of Disillusionment," *Harper's,* July 1991, p. 22.

ourselves. Philosophers such as Nietzsche and psychologists such as Freud have rightly criticized the sort of theology that supports such self-destruction.[21]

Guilt seems to feed on itself. It grows all by itself. Why? How does it distort our attempts to understand ourselves realistically as sinners, as forgiven? How can we extricate ourselves from a spirituality that confuses nature with sin and then repudiates both?

Free Will

Fifth, although I have steadfastly taken the position throughout this book that sin is rooted in the human will, I still believe the matter needs further investigation. I am reasonably confident that the role of will is more fundamental than that of ignorance, and that the will to sin actually leads to blindness rather than the other way around. Nevertheless, I am less confident about another dimension of the human will — namely, its freedom. When we speak of the human will, we typically do so in Pelagian terms, assuming that it is simply free to decide on each occasion whether to sin or not to sin. We assume that freedom is an essential prerequisite for sin. Modern jurisprudence has secularized this inherited theological assumption and established that only a free person can be held responsible for a crime. If we are compelled by reason of external force or if we lack the knowledge of right and wrong, a modern court will judge us innocent. The tacit assumption in all this is that there exists some sort of primordial freedom.

Yet, I have my doubts. As I reflect on some of the earlier discussion of original sin, especially tribalism in the form of racial prejudice, I wonder just how the concept of freedom applies. As a young boy growing up in Dearborn, I wonder if I was free in any meaningful sense to make choices that would not have reinforced white racism. Even when I made moral choices in keeping with what I believed then to be the good, I was unwittingly giving expression to systemic prejudice. The option to do otherwise was not available in any real sense. The evil was systemic, but I was no less culpable for that reason. My

---

21. See Pannenberg, *Anthropology in Theological Perspective* (Philadelphia: Westminster Press, 1985), p. 151.

situation may very well be similar now that I find myself in pluralistic and liberal Berkeley: I may very well be reinforcing prejudices that are invisible to me. Who knows what time or the shock of a new set of circumstances might reveal to me?

Roger Haight has wrestled with this problem. On the one hand, he wants to assert without qualification that human sin arises out of freedom. Yet he recognizes that this does not quite square with our experience. So he admits that "the freedom that is human existence is not unmixed; there is no pure freedom."[22] Our social situation conscripts us into social sin frequently whether we know it or not, whether we will it or not. "The social determinisms of the institutions that make up the second nature of human existence amount to a concupiscence and temptation that are often stronger than the impulses of one's individual nature."[23]

Thus, another area that might be fruitful for inquiry is the relation between freedom, knowledge, and will along with our inescapable tie to tribal traditions and social institutions.

A Theological View of Satan

A sixth topic that has been hovering on the edge of our discussion all along is the reality and role of Satan. We have dealt directly with the practice of Satanism, but not much with Satan himself. We need to ask how we should think about Satan theologically. A couple of questions come immediately to mind. Is Satan merely the projected personification of human sin, or is Satan an independent reality enticing us from beyond?[24] Would a doctrine of Satan aid us in making a realistic assessment of human responsibility, or would it merely provide a supernatural scapegoat whom we could blame for our own frailties?

With regard to the first question, Martin Luther answers categorically: "It is undeniable that the devil lives, yes, rules, in all the

22. Haight, "Sin and Grace," in *Systematic Theology: Roman Catholic Perspectives*, vol. 2, ed. Francis Schüssler Fiorenza and John P. Galvin (Minneapolis: Fortress Press, 1991), p. 96.

23. Haight, "Sin and Grace," p. 104.

24. "It is by no means certain that the Devil exists," writes Ruth Nanda Anshen. "Such uncertainty, however, cannot comfort the pious; for it is uncertainty that makes hell of our life" (*Anatomy of Evil* [Mt. Kisco, N.Y.: Moyer Bell, 1972], p. 17).

world."[25] A bit more circumspect, Karl Rahner establishes some of the parameters within which an inquiry into the Devil's reality should take place. He begins by asserting that Satan "is not to be regarded as a mere mythological personification of evil in the world; the existence of the Devil cannot be denied." He then adds a prohibition against dualism, against setting Satan up as an independent counterpart to God. Following Augustine, Rahner emphasizes that Satan is a finite creature whose "evil remains comprised within the scope of the power, freedom and goodness of the holy God."[26] The negativity of the Devil is a leach off God's created goodness. Evil, even in this radical form, is a perversion of the good. "The devil is a creature who must retain a created essence which is good."[27] Or, as Tillich

25. Luther, *Lectures on Galatians I*, vol. 26 of *Luther's Works*, ed. Jaroslav Pelikan (St. Louis: Concordia, 1962), p. 190. Heiko A. Oberman makes two interpretive points worth noting. First, it would be a distortion to dismiss Luther's concept of the Devil as merely a holdover from medieval belief: "Christ and the Devil were equally real to him" (*Luther: Man between God and the Devil* [New Haven: Yale University Press, 1982], p. 104). Second, Luther deviates from the medieval concept of the Devil, "according to which the evil one is drawn by the smell of sin, the sin of worldly concern. In Luther's view, it is not a life dedicated to secular tasks and worldly business that attracts the Devil. On the contrary, where Christ is present, the adversary is never far away" (p. 106). The Devil comes to harass us just when we are closest to God's grace. Luther gives the devil four titles: (1) *doctor consolatorius*, Dr. Comforter; (2) *magister conscientiae*, master of the conscience; (3) *princeps mundi*, prince of this world; and (4) *ein saur Geist*, a sour spirit. See Oberman, "Luther and the Devil," *The [Lutheran Theological Seminary at Gettysburg] Bulletin* 69 (Winter 1989): 8-10.

26. Rahner, "The Devil," in the *Encyclopedia of Theology: The Concise Sacramentum Mundi* (New York: Seabury, 1975), p. 341. Emil Brunner would agree emphatically, arguing that to set Satan up as a rival god would be to make the mistake of dualism as in Zoroastrianism or Manicheanism. Says Brunner, "Satanic sin, conceived as a possibility, as a phenomenon is quite different from human sin, by the very fact that it is not due to temptation, but is purely spontaneous sin, that is, self-generated. It would not be the sin of the tempted but of the Tempter. . . . The Christian faith is bound to admit the existence of a sinful supernatural power, and indeed of a purely spiritual sinful being, to which we can ascribe what we may call 'Satanic' sin, in contrast to human sin" (*The Christian Doctrine of Creation and Redemption* [Philadelphia: Westminster Press, 1952], pp. 139-40). A problem with Brunner's argument is that his "purely spiritual sinful being" is set over against physical or sense-bound beings such as us humans. Brunner thus inadvertently falls into the trap he otherwise repudiates of making physical finitude a decisive factor in human sin, in this case a positive factor. In my judgment, the physical-spiritual dichotomy is irrelevant. What is relevant is that Satan deliberately opposes God through the shedding of innocent blood.

27. Rahner, "The Devil," p. 343.

puts it, "Satan, the principle of the negative, has no independent reality."[28]

Rahner also adds some further advice that might be worth taking. When looking for evidence of the Devil, do not look at cases of demon possession. Rahner's shyness here has to do with the low credibility that practices such as exorcism have among the secular and scientific minded people of today. Whether this is a sufficient reason to ignore demonic activity is beside the present point. What I find significant is Rahner's suggestion that we turn instead to "the sinister suprahuman power of evil in history."[29] We should turn to the crushing avalanches of political and economic and cultural events that have swept down upon us, wiping away freedom, tradition, prosperity, wholesome values, health, and even life itself. The principalities and powers are threatening. Like an invading army that conscripts conquered people to fight on its side, the helter-skelter of a violent movement engulfs us and makes us accomplices in its downward rush. This is the place to look for the Devil's work, says Rahner.

Turning to the next question, I believe we must be wary that talk of the Devil might trivialize evil rather than contribute to a better understanding of it. The Devil as an image and figure of speech has become common in the final quarter of the twentieth century, filling political rhetoric. Muslim leaders, especially in Iran and Iraq, have developed a tradition of identifying the president of the United States with Satan and the American people with demons. The American counter has been to invoke the name of Hitler to describe its enemy. Although Satan is supernatural and Hitler is natural, they both function to connote the epitome of evil. Perhaps the secularization of the American psyche leads to the preference for a natural version of the Devil. Be that as it may, we can easily see that such rhetoric is serving as propaganda to whip up enthusiasm for war. The symbols of sin are being transformed into tools of sin. We must ask at this point whether such language about Satan increases our perception of the depth of evil or numbs us to it.

28. Tillich, *Systematic Theology*, 3 vols. (Chicago: University of Chicago Press, 1951-1963), 2:171. Wayne Oates is similarly convinced: "Satan's being is counterfeit. Satan is not a being in the sense that God is a being. Satan's being is borrowed or stolen; it participates in unreality and deception" (*Temptation*, p. 20).
29. Rahner, "The Devil," p. 343.

Gustaf Aulén reminds us that engaging in Devil talk is no guarantee that we will achieve a more profound understanding of sin and evil than we would achieve had we avoided it. Aulén is more dualistic than Rahner, using the notion of dualism to emphasize the severity of evil's opposition to the divine will:

> The use of the conception of the devil is not in and by itself the least guarantee of a profound insight into the nature and terrific power of evil. Many examples can be cited to show that the idea of the devil has been used in such a way that the conception of evil has been weakened. It is of greatest importance for Christian faith that the "dualistic" element contained in this conception not be obscured, or, in other words, that the element in creation which is hostile to God be allowed to appear with all the realism and intensity it possesses for faith. It is not a demonic mythology which is important, but an insight into the nature of evil, its power and extent.[30]

In sum, once the parameters and cautions are duly noted, a more extensive exploration into the theology of Satan seems to be called for.

Hope and the Double Tie to Eternity

Finally, I would like to return briefly to our point of departure, the point where faith provides what we need to redirect our anxiety. Faith is one of the three theological virtues identified in the closing verse of 1 Corinthians 13; the other two are hope and love. I have spoken briefly about the freedom to love that is afforded by faith founded on forgiveness. I would like now to offer a closing word about hope.

We have defined faith in terms of trust. When we mix in hope, faith becomes trust in God *for the future*. I am concerned here about two closely tied futures — our own personal future and the future of world history.

The presence of God in faith constitutes our personal tie to eternity, our transcendence of the time and place in which we find ourselves. Our present situation is not our only reality. Whether we find ourselves the initiators of sin, whether we find ourselves unwilling accomplices

---

30. Aulén, *The Faith of the Christian Church,* trans. Eric H. Wahlstrom (Philadelphia: Fortress Press, 1960), p. 244.

in original sin or coerced into cooperation with forces of evil stronger than we, or whether we are merely the innocent victims of inflicted suffering, the eternal God is present while our time passes. God is present in the midst of time, granting eternal forgiveness, justification, comfort, and redemption. No matter how grave the crisis of the moment, it will pass, but our tie to God's eternity will endure.

In addition to faith, we have hope. The symbol of hope is resurrection. Believing that God raised Jesus from the dead on the first Easter, we hope that God will raise us as well. Sin, evil, suffering, and death will not have the last word. They may have the next to the last word, but God will utter the final call, "Rise!" Confidence in God's promise of resurrection affords us incalculable courage and endurance and patience for the present time. We come to a point where we can accept our own limits, even our own death. This in turn eliminates the sting of death, the anxiety that tempts us to defiant self-sufficiency. Anticipating the fulfillment God has in store for me in my personal future, I find inner fulfillment in my personal present even if my immediate surroundings are threatening, bleak, or meaningless.[31]

Our personal tie to God's eternity gives us a certain freedom or independence from the time-bound course of historical events. Yet, we cannot extricate ourselves fully from the ongoing story of our world.[32] Reinhold Niebuhr helps make us aware of this metaxy, this

---

31. Reinhold Niebuhr puts it this way: "The hope of the resurrection affirms that ultimately finiteness will be emancipated from anxiety and the self will know itself as it is known" (*The Nature and Destiny of Man,* 2 vols. [New York: Scribner's, 1941-1943], 2:312).

32. Here I embrace for the most part the work of the theology-of-hope school, principally that of Jürgen Moltmann, Wolfhart Pannenberg, and Carl Braaten. These theologians interpret the biblical promise in terms of a future event of new creation, a transformation of the world that will eradicate sin and evil for the everlasting future. They contend that this prospect should inspire us to work for transformation in the present. Daniel Day Williams appeals similarly to hope, although he rejects the idea of a consummate fulfillment in favor of an ongoing openness to creativity and the everlasting possibility of evil. The value of hope is for the present, says Williams, not the future. "Christian hope . . . lends support to every effort to meet human needs," he writes. "We are obligated as Christians to work within the orders of human life for new good. There have been strong protests in theology against identifying the Kingdom of God with any human program. With this protest we must agree. But if God is as we know the divine in Christ, then it is an equally fatal error to treat creative effort to solve human problems as irrelevant to our salvation" (*The Demonic and the Divine* [Minneapolis: Fortress Press, 1990], p. 50). In sum, future hope inspires us to combat present evil.

state of existing in-between. As individuals standing before God, we face the eternal in every moment and every action. We confront the end of history when we confront our own death. In this way we transcend our social situation. Our own personal spirits cannot attain fulfillment in even the highest achievements of the human history that surround us. Whether our nation wins or loses in war, whether our family becomes wealthy or remains poor, whether we are caught up in scandal or maintain an exemplary reputation, our tie to eternity bears a fulfillment that carries us beyond all these things. Yet, on the other hand, our individual lives are meaningful only in their organic relation to our historical communities. We cannot understand ourselves for who we are without reference to our nation, ethnicity, or social image. These communal and time-bound dimensions so influence our psyche that they largely determine the very criteria by which we understand what counts as fulfillment for us.

We are bound in a sense to the world's future. But it is a future embraced by hope. The Easter resurrection, when combined with the biblical symbol of the new creation, gives us grounds for hope on behalf of the world. Despite its past and present history, the world is slated for a future fulfillment. Its glorious fulfillment will be God-given, the result of a transformation on a cosmic scale comparable to the new life granted Jesus at the resurrection.

Enter the symbol of the Antichrist. As long as history endures under the aegis of what we call the present order, every good is liable to be countered by a reactive evil. In the New Testament, this principle of history is represented by the Antichrist. The future is not to be considered on its own terms as a safe haven. There is no such thing as inevitable moral progress. The open future, says Niebuhr, is "never presented as a realm of greater security than the present or as the guarantor of a higher virtue. The Antichrist stands at the end of history to indicate that history culminates, rather than solves, the essential problems of human existence."[33] No matter how bad things are now, they could get worse. Furthermore, at the very moment of God's maximum grace, the opportunity appears for maximum evil. Only a decisive end to the present order and resurrection to a new creation — only decisive action by the divine power — will free us forever from the scourge. This is entailed in a hope that relies on the promised

33. Niebuhr, *The Nature and Destiny of Man*, 2:318.

defeat of the Antichrist. "The Antichrist who appears at the end of history can be defeated only by the Christ who ends history."[34]

Our personal future and the world's future constitute our double tie to eternity. Eternity comes to us now, in the midst of time, in the form of forgiveness and the promise of resurrection. Forgiveness, when we receive it in faith, cools the fires of anxiety, soothes the sting of death, and fills us with life-giving hope.

34. Niebuhr, *The Nature and Destiny of Man*, 2:319.

10

Genes and Sin: More Unfinished Business

Genetic information does not dictate everything about us.

Walter Gilbert[1]

Perhaps one of the topics of potential relevance in connection with our understanding of sin can be developed a bit more fully, even if briefly. In the discussion of natural evil in Chapter 9, I made reference to the possible significance of sociobiology and new discoveries in genetic research. The specter of biological determinism seems to be looming on our horizon. More and more voices seem willing to say, "It's all in the genes!" Many seem to be saying that it's not just the color of our eyes that's determined by our genetic inheritance; patterns of behavior are genetically coded as well — including such things as aggression and altruism, vice and virtue.[2] "In the long debate over

1. Gilbert, "A Vision of the Grail," in *The Code of Codes: Scientific and Social Issues in the Human Genome Project,* ed. Daniel J. Kevles and Leroy Hood (Cambridge: Harvard University Press, 1992), p. 96.
2. The following discussion reflects issues raised at the frontier of research in human genetics plus related but as yet inconclusive discussions regarding biological determinism. At this writing, I and some of my colleagues at the Center for Theology and the Natural Sciences — a research center at the Graduate Theological Union in Berkeley, California — are engaged in a study entitled "Theological and Ethical Questions

the relative influences of 'nature and nurture,'" Dorothy Nelkin and Laurence Tancredi have suggested, "the balance seems to have shifted to the biological extreme."[3]

In the face of this continuing ascendancy of nature over nurture, we need to pose a few questions. First, is it scientifically justifiable to take biological determinism seriously? If so, just how seriously? Second, if it is scientifically justifiable to ascribe large portions of human behavior to genetic determinants, then might this confirm what traditional Christians have understood by the concept of original sin? Augustine and his heirs have argued that original sin is hereditary. Do we now have a scientific version of original sin? Third, what does biological determinism do to moral responsibility? Does it increase our moral responsibility or does it pass the buck to a genetic inheritance over which we have no control? Should genetics become the new excuse? Can we legitimately scapegoat our genetic makeup?

Is It All in the Selfish Gene?

At the outset we need to distinguish between science and pop science — that is, between what the laboratory scientists are thinking and the images of the gene found in the popular media. Over the last two decades a culturally constructed image of the gene has been developed that is reductionistic: "It's all in the genes!" Genes have become the all-determining reality. Molecular biologists and other scientists who perform the actual experiments do not see it this way, however. They tend to see the gene as one factor among many determining human behavior and even determining our biological inheritance. To be sure, experiments frequently begin with a deterministic hypothesis — the scientist sets out to find the gene that governs a certain trait — but philosophically experimenters believe the jury is out regarding genetic determinism. Perhaps the researchers can best be described as holding a wait-and-see attitude, looking for genetic determinants but tem-

---

Raised by the Human Genome Initiative," funded by National Institutes of Health grant HG00487. What is reflected here in a preliminary way are the initial items on the team's agenda regarding our biological human nature and their possible implications for understanding human sin.

3. Nelkin and Tancredi, *Dangerous Diagnostics: The Social Power of Biological Information* (New York: Basic Books, 1989), p. 12.

porarily suspending judgment as to whether or not we will finally be able to reduce all human behavior to our DNA. Theologians, of course, must attend to both the cultural image of the gene and the more tentative thinking of the actual research scientists.

One of the formative forces in developing the current deterministic image is the popularity of the works of Richard Dawkins. The purpose of Dawkins's theory of "the selfish gene" is to give a biological account of selfishness and altruism.[4] His audacious yet tantalizing theory is that genes are by nature selfish — ruthlessly selfish! — and that genes are ultimately driving natural and human history. The organism is but DNA's way of making more DNA, he says. Human beings as individuals and as a species serve their genes as vehicles for their replicating process and the achievement of their ultimate objective, survival long enough to reproduce. We humans are but pawns in a genetic chess game wherein each gene seeks to checkmate all competitors. Every aspect of our social lives — our loving and hating, our fighting and cooperating, our giving and stealing, our greed and generosity — are but subplots within the broader evolutionary drama. What we experience in our daily life as human selfishness has an underlying biological explanation. We are selfish because the genes are selfish.

In addition, curiously enough, even when we are altruistic to the point of self-sacrifice, our behavior is still explicable in terms of the selfishness of the gene. Dawkins argues that the selfish gene uses altruism to perpetuate its own survival through the hereditary process. He notes that altruism is tied to kinship. We as individuals are willing to sacrifice ourselves for a brother or sister or someone to whom we feel loyal. We are willing to ensure the survival of someone belonging to our own group, our own family, our own race, our own nation in the interest of the greater good — which is, precisely, preserving the gene pool. This explains territorialism, xenophobia, and war as expressions of altruism. This explains why we accord hero status to soldiers who die bravely in battle: they have sacrificed themselves for others — the others being those belonging to our own nation or group and not our enemies. In short, says Dawkins, what we take to be the highest human virtue — namely, self-sacrificial love in behalf of another — is in fact blind sacrifice in service to the perpetuation of

4. See Dawkins, *The Selfish Gene,* 2d ed. (New York: Oxford University Press, 1989).

privileged genes.[5] Altruism as we know it can be reduced to biological determinants.[6]

In explicating the Dawkins theory, we need to clarify the source of selfishness. He is not arguing that there is a specific gene located on a specific chromosome that codes for selfishness. The concept of the selfish gene here is based on a general principle — namely, that the purpose of DNA is self-replication. The blind ongoing process of DNA replication is the source of what Dawkins calls genetic selfishness.

Edward O. Wilson has also lent scientific credibility to genetic determinism through his work in the area of "sociobiology." According to Wilson, what we think of as sin is in fact genetic.

> Human beings are strongly predisposed to respond with unreasoning hatred to external threats and to escalate their hostility sufficiently to overwhelm the source of the threat by a respectably wide margin of safety. Our brains do appear to be programmed to the following extent: we are inclined to partition other people into friends and aliens. . . . We tend to fear deeply the actions of strangers and to solve conflict by aggression. These learning rules are most likely to have evolved during the past hundreds of thousands of years of human evolution and, thus, to have conferred a biological advantage on those who conformed to them with the greatest fidelity.[7]

5. Dawkins is one of the soldiers in an army of scientists marching against the forces of religion in society. In an acceptance speech after receiving the 1992 "In Praise of Reason" award from the Committee for the Scientific Investigation of Claims of the Paranormal, he said, "Don't let us allow religion to walk away with the awe factor. Science has orders of magnitude more to offer in this field. . . . And, to become a bit mercenary about it, there's that 54 percent of the charitable donations!" He is referring to the fact that 54 percent of American charitable donations go to religious work. "We should be able to at least shave off a bit of that 54 percent by putting the right amount of emphasis on the romance and the inspiring aspect of science" ("The Awe Factor," *Skeptical Inquirer* 17 [Spring 1993]: 243).

6. The claim here is that our values — such as altruism — are the result of biological evolution. One could easily take a step further and found an ethical system on our evolutionary history, establishing an ethic of biological naturalism. But this would commit the naturalistic fallacy — that is, it would falsely assume that what is natural is good. It would base the *ought* on the *is*. "It is important to emphasize this point," writes William Irons, who is an advocate of Human Behavior Ecology, "because people frequently assume that any attempt to address morality in evolutionary terms must include some argument to the effect that it is somehow morally good to do the things that we evolved to do. This is emphatically not what I argue" ("How Did Morality Evolve?" *Zygon* 26 [March 1991]: 51).

7. Wilson, *On Human Nature* (New York: Bantam Books, 1978), pp. 122-23.

Thus he accounts for certain forms of human sin in Darwinian and Spencerian terms as products of evolutionary development that secure a "biological advantage" for those who sin most skillfully.[8]

Does the human race have any hope of rising above its biological base through cultural efforts? Does the future hold any hope of our escaping the determinism of our evolutionary past? Not according to Wilson.

> Can the cultural evolution of higher ethical values gain a direction and momentum of its own and completely replace genetic evolution? I think not. The genes hold culture on a leash. The leash is very long, but inevitably values will be constrained in accordance with their effects on the human gene pool.[9]

The image developed by science writers such as Dawkins and Wilson suggests that biological determinants render the human race inescapably selfish and that we must cultivate this very selfishness if we are to achieve a greater degree of social harmony. They view love as biologically constrained reciprocity between individuals who share a genetic identity. What we celebrate as love they characterize as just one more selfish expression of genes seeking their own survival through maximizing their replication generation after generation. The particular genes that lie at the basis of contemporary society have been selected by evolution because the traits they govern result in higher reproductive fitness of the persons who carry them. This is biological determinism to the extreme.[10]

8. Wilson says this descriptively, of course, not prescriptively. The mere fact that we can describe a pattern of human behavior developed through our evolution does not mean that we should prescribe this behavior or make it a moral standard. Arthur Caplan reminds us not to confuse conclusions drawn from "the evolution of human ethics" with commitment to "the ethics of evolution" ("Ethics, Evolution, and the Milk of Human Kindness," in *The Sociobiology Debate,* ed. Arthur L. Caplan [New York: Harper & Row, 1978], p. 313).

9. Wilson, *On Human Nature,* p. 175. Responding to critics, Wilson goes on to say, "Human nature can adapt to more encompassing forms of altruism and social justice. Genetic biases can be trespassed, passions averted or redirected, and ethics altered; and the human genius for making contracts can continue to be applied to achieve healthier and freer societies. Yet the mind is not infinitely malleable" ("For Sociobiology," in *The Sociobiology Debate,* p. 267).

10. Wilson maintains that this biological determinism does not necessarily translate into academic reductionism. He respects the creative adversarial relations between the

As mentioned above, molecular biologists and other genetic researchers generally do not operate with this overly deterministic perspective. In fact, they repudiate such determinist claims, denying that genes have such omnipotence. Walter Gilbert, for example, states that "genetic information does not dictate everything about us."[11] He bases this assertion on the grounds that the genotype does not by itself determine the phenotype of an individual. The phenotype — that is, the actual physical form of a particular individual — does not fully mirror the individual's genetic code. In the replication process wherein DNA is transcripted into a nucleotide sequence by RNA, the passing of genetic information is contingent. Some genes are expressed and others are not. Mutations take place at a rate of about one in each ten thousand replications. Our experiences with the environment may precipitate adaptations that are passed on through the future history of the cell. This leads Berkeley molecular biologist R. David Cole to say that DNA has a nuanced role in authoring our nature. "As the author of our biological destiny, DNA has been reduced to the role of co-author, even if it might be the senior author."[12]

Responding to these sorts of observations from the geneticists, sociobiologists have refined their claim to read that the genes determine the possible range of behavior and culture, not the specific behaviors of individuals. What the genes are responsible for, say sociobiologists, is the range of biological possibility. It takes human history to actualize this possibility. This more modest claim borders on the vacuous, however, because it merely asserts that whatever has actually happened must have been within the range of biological possibility.

The deterministic claims made by proponents of the selfish gene theory are precipitating a rebellion. It may appear that in the nature-nurture war the nature armies have temporarily gained the upper hand, but the nurture forces are now regrouping to launch a counterattack. Ruth Hubbard, emerita professor of biology at Harvard and board

---

natural sciences and the social sciences in the context of their studies of the human phenomenon. Each discipline can serve as the antidiscipline for another, with biology serving as the antidiscipline for all of the social sciences. See Wilson, "Biology and the Social Sciences," *Daedalus* 106 (Autumn 1977): 127-40.

11. Gilbert, "A Vision of the Grail," in *The Code of Codes: Scientific and Social Issues in the Human Genome Project,* ed. Daniel J. Kevles and Leroy Hood (Cambridge: Harvard University Press, 1992), p. 96.

12. Cole, "Genetic Predestination?" *Dialog* 33 (Winter 1994).

member of the Council for Responsible Genetics, believes that assertions that it's all in the genes are leading us astray. "The myth of the all-powerful gene is based on flawed science that discounts the environmental context in which we and our genes exist," she has written with co-author Elijah Wald.[13] Hubbard is objecting to the reductionist effort to explain living organisms simply in terms of the workings of important molecules. Who we are, she argues to the contrary, is a matter of the interaction of genes and environment — nature plus nurture.

The sociobiology of E. O. Wilson has come under attack on two fronts: the methodological and the ethical.[14] On the methodological front, Wilson's critics charge him with skewing data, making hasty generalizations based on inappropriate observations, and ultimately with being internally incoherent. Solomon Katz, for example, criticizes Wilson for overgeneralizing: "None of the current concepts of altruism satisfactorily explains the kind of self sacrifice that takes place in more complex societies in which the individuals are so distantly related that the genetic advantages of the altruism are essentially zero."[15]

On the ethical front, critics have charged Wilson with using science to baptize conservative social theory. "The reason for the survival of

13. Hubbard and Wald, *Exploding the Gene Myth* (Boston: Beacon Press, 1993), p. 5. It seems to me that in the end Hubbard and Wald are less troubled by "flawed science" than by what they view as ungrounded expectations that human beings should be able to provide simple laboratory solutions to complex problems.

14. Viggo Mortensen has actually identified four categories of criticism leveled against Wilson: (1) a political argument, which I here call the ideological or ethical argument; (2) the argument from the world of culture, which I think overgeneralizes the biological evidence; and (3) a methodological argument and (4) a reduction argument, both of which I view as extensions of the argument from overgeneralizing the biological evidence. Mortensen says that "a deterministic, biological theory is inadquate for explaining human culture, because, among other things, it cannot take into account the independence of mental phenomena and the intentionality and direction of human actions" ("Free Will, Determinism and Responsibility," in *Free Will and Determinism,* ed. Viggo Mortensen and Robert C. Sorensen [Aarhus, Denmark: Aarhus University Press, 1987], p. 204).

15. Katz, "Free Will: Does it have a Bio-Cultural Evolutionary Basis?" in *Free Will and Determinism,* p. 37. Katz holds that culture takes us beyond our biological starting point. Hans Fink disagrees, arguing that varieties of human freedom do "not even rest upon a bio-cultural basis. They are Nature in one of its manifest operations" ("Mountain Peaks Do Not Float Unsupported," in *Free Will and Determinism,* p. 51).

these determinist theories," writes Elizabeth Allen, "is that they consistently tend to provide a genetic justification of the status quo and of existing privileges for certain groups according to class, race or sex."[16] I don't know how much weight we should give to ad hominem arguments of this sort. They are directed more at presumptions about the scientists' ideological prejudices than at the actual facts of the case.

Nevertheless, the critics march on. R. C. Lewontin and colleagues Steven Rose and Leon J. Kamin, for example, argue that Wilson's sociobiology serves as a scientific justification for bourgeois politics. Just as the church gave ideological comfort to medieval feudalism, they argue, so today science provides ideological justification for the privileged classes within a democratic society. The doctrine of genetic determinism, these critics believe, is nothing more than a misuse of science for the purposes of keeping African Americans, women, and other oppressed minorities in their place. The Lewontin position is based on a neo-Marxist reading of the situation that makes class interests determinative of scientific claims to truth. Because nurture is not the pawn of nature, they say, their school of thought can provide hope for the future by affirming that "it is possible to create a better society than the one we live in at present; that inequalities of wealth, power, and status are not 'natural' but socially imposed obstructions to the building of a society in which the creative potential of all its citizens is employed for the benefit of all."[17]

Lewontin's team also raises the already mentioned scientific objection that sociobiologists underestimate the importance of the variance between genotype and phenotype. The manifest or expressed traits of an organism (its phenotype) are not determined strictly by the genes (the genotype). Some genes are expressed. Others are not. The pheno-

---

16. Allen et al., "Against Sociobiology," in *The Sociobiology Debate*, p. 260. See also R. C. Lewontin, Steven Rose, and Leon J. Kamin, *Not in Our Genes* (New York: Pantheon Books, 1984), p. 236. "Given the explicit claims of sociobiology to be the extension of Darwinist and Mendelian mechanism, its contradictory devotion, in practice, to the adaptive mode of argument can only be understood as flowing from an independent ideological basis. By arguing that each aspect of the human behavioral repertoire is specifically adaptive, or at least was so in the past, sociobiology sets the stage for legitimation of things as they are" (*Not in Our Genes*, p. 264).

17. Lewontin, Rose, and Kamin, *Not in Our Genes*, p. 9. Lewontin and colleagues argue that sociobiology is reductionistic, whereas their own alternative is nonreductionistic, relying as it does on a nature-nurture dialectic in which the properties of parts and wholes codetermine each other (p. 11).

301

type of each actual organism is a consequence of the interaction of genes with environment.[18] Variability of environment — that is, nurture — must be factored in here.

Even though they are emphasizing nurture over nature, Lewontin and colleagues do not ignore the significance of what is in the genes. They call for a dialectical balance between organism and environment. A full understanding of human nature requires "an integration of the biological and the social in which neither is given primacy or ontological priority over the other but in which they are seen as being related in a dialectical manner."[19] Over against sociobiology, they end up saying, "It is our biology that makes us free."[20]

What Is Freedom?

Is it really our biology that makes us free? At this point I feel constrained to interject at least a brief comment regarding the almost forgotten understanding of human freedom developed over the centuries by Christian thinkers relying on the grace of God.[21] According to the Christian tradition, freedom is not merely a product of our biology but an achievement of divine grace working in the human will that takes us beyond our biology. Perhaps it would be better to say that freedom in the fullest sense stretches us beyond our given human nature.

To make this point, let's take a closer look at the ideal of altruism. The Christian category here is love. The grace of God operative in the human will enables me to love another being for itself rather than for what it can do for me. This includes God. Our love for God may develop in stages. We may first love God in response to the news of salvation, as a gesture of gratitude for benefits gained from God's love toward us. Yet it is possible for us to go further and love God for who

18. Lewontin, Rose, and Kamin, *Not in Our Genes,* p. 252.

19. Lewontin, Rose, and Kamin, *Not in Our Genes,* p. 75.

20. Lewontin, Rose, and Kamin, *Not in Our Genes,* p. 290.

21. In the context of arguing against Cicero on fate, Augustine makes the point that human free will does not stand in contrast to divine determinism. "It does not follow that, though there is for God a certain order of causes, there must therefore be nothing depending on the free exercise of our own wills, for our wills themselves are included in that order of causes which is certain to God and is embraced by his foreknowledge, for human wills are also causes of human action" (*The City of God,* 5.9).

God is apart from reciprocity, apart from any benefit we might receive from God's love for us. God can be the sole object of our love.

This understanding of freedom also includes love for our neighbor. We are capable of loving our neighbor as ourselves — that is, of treating our neighbors as equal in value to ourselves. And, taking the matter beyond kin selection, Jesus commands us to love even our enemy. Love of enemy in the fullest sense would be impossible if our behavior were determined solely by the selfish gene.

Further, this experience of loving elicits within us a grand vision of all humanity and even all of creation participating in a single inclusive network of mutual love. The love of God becomes simultaneously the love of all, and this inspires the desire that all be loved.[22]

Now, why do we refer to this as freedom? Because it liberates us from our given natures. Or perhaps it would be more accurate to say that it places the human will in a position to harness the resources and energies of our given natures in the service of the broadest conceivable altruism. Rather than being driven solely by the agenda of a human nature designed by selfish genes, we transcend our genetic code. Whatever human nature is, it is more than merely what we find in our genes. Rather than being mere puppets in the genetic drama, we become actors and even playwrights developing a plot that includes making this a better world. Even if we grant that in the past we have been biologically programmed to be selfish (programmed to be what many would call sinful), the future can be different. The future can transcend the past. As individuals we can live today with a self-transcending freedom that envisions a future of total altruism, the

22. Roman Catholic ethicist and theologian Thomas A. Shannon has developed this notion of love in the context of a critique of sociobiology and explication of the concept of *affectio justitiae* in the work of Duns Scotus, in "The Matter of Genetics and Freedom," an unpublished paper written for the Center for Theology and the Natural Sciences, Graduate Theological Union, January 1993. In affirming this vision, I do not want to fall into unrealistic idealism. Reinhold Niebuhr wrestled with the knotty problem of human selfishness and the Christian vision of altruistic love for the whole human race that extends beyond family, clan, race, and nation. The problem is that, while "the law of love is indeed the basis of all moral life, . . . it can not be obeyed by a simple act of the will because the power of self-concern is too great." Divine grace is required and available (*Man's Nature and His Communities* [New York: Scribner's, 1965], p. 125). Paradoxically, even when endowed with divine grace and empowered to love all as God loves, the human self remains self-concerned. Perpetual awareness of this fact is at the heart of Christian realism.

vision of total cooperation centered in love for a single divine good. The key to such self-transcending freedom is the operative power of God's grace, a power we invite into our lives through prayer, praise, and thanksgiving. It is God's grace that makes us free.

Having said this, the question remains open regarding just how God's grace effects this freedom. Can divine grace be mediated through our biology? If our genes can dispose us to sin, can they also dispose us to freedom from sin? Lindon Eaves, Distinguished Professor of Human Genetics at the Medical College of Virginia, says that our genes are not only a force determining our behavior but also a source of God's grace in our lives.[23]

God, Genes, and Freedom

At least three theologians have sought to integrate the new genetics and to some extent the sociobiological vision of human development into an understanding of God's ongoing creative work. Arthur R. Peacocke has stated, "Theologians would do well to recognize, more explicitly than they have done in the past, the complexity of human nature and the fact that its basic foundational level is biological and genetic, however overlaid by nurture and culture." Peacocke's view is distinguished by the bold manner in which he asserts that God works within the bio-evolutionary process. Yet, biology is not enough. Human freedom and cultural creativity go beyond biology, says Peacocke. "God has made human beings thus with their genetically constrained behaviour — but, through the freedom God has allowed to evolve in such creatures, he has also opened up new possibilities of self-fulfillment, creativity, and openness to the future that requires a language other than that of genetics to elaborate and express."[24]

23. Eaves made a statement to this effect during the third consultation of the Center for Theology and the Natural Sciences' human genome research project, 17 January 1993.

24. Peacocke, *God and the New Biology* (San Francisco: Harper & Row, 1986), pp. 110-11; see also pp. 65-72 and his *Creation and the World of Science* (Oxford: Clarendon Press, 1979), pp. 161-64. The sociobiology debate reflects at least in part a continuation of the debate over the theological implications of Darwin's theory of evolution, which in the minds of many replaced purpose with chance in nature and reduced the human race to one more animal species among others. "The problem was that a description

In a manner similar to that of Peacocke, Philip Hefner affirms that "coevolution of genetic and cultural information, mediated by the brain and selected by the system of forces that selects all things, can be said to be the means that God has chosen to unfold the divine intention and to bring nature/matter to a new stage of fulfillment."[25] Hefner takes the long view, the coevolutionary view, according to which today's cultural freedom is the result of yesterday's biological determinism. He grants that yesterday's determinism persists today in the form of our genetic heritage and our environmental limits but insists that this by no means restricts freedom. To the contrary, says Hefner, freedom is inescapable: evolution has determined that we would be free. "We are deterministically defined as free."[26] He defines freedom in terms of four human dispositions: exploration of the environment, conscious deliberation and decision making, a sense of responsibility, and a sense of liberty and autonomy.[27] He believes that biological evolution is the means by which God has brought culturally free human beings into existence, and now with this freedom we seek a destiny that actualizes the will of God for the future. "The activity that we fashion to meet the requirements of our destiny should conform to the sacrifice of Christ for the whole world," he says, "and in such self-giving we find our deepest harmony with our destiny."[28]

-----

of man had become a statement concerning the nature of man," writes John Dillenberger about the nineteenth-century debate. "Hence, both biologists and theologians fought over man as if man's descent determined his nature. . . . For the Darwinians, man was not unique in nature. . . . For the most conservative theologians, man was considered to be essentially distinct and unique" (*Protestant Thought and Natural Science* [Garden City, N.Y.: Doubleday, 1960], p. 221). Today's debate centers on whether our genetic descent determines — exhaustively determines — our nature.

25. Hefner, "Sociobiology, Ethics, and Theology," *Zygon* 19 (June 1984): 200.

26. Hefner, *The Human Factor* (Minneapolis: Fortress Press, 1993), p. 121; see also his essay "Freedom in Evolutionary Perspective," in *Free Will and Determinism*, p. 138. Hefner offers a very subtle and nuanced understanding of the relation between freedom and determinism. "Determinism is often defined as the attribute appropriate to actions that are fully caused by antecedent factors," he writes, "whereas freedom is defined as an attribute of actions that are not caused by antecedents, but rather by autonomous choice. Such definitions are unhelpful, largely because they isolate freedom and determinism from the relevant context. Humans really have no interest in either freedom or determinism except as they are relevant, either positively or negatively, to our becoming what we ought to be" (*The Human Factor*, p. 112).

27. Hefner, *The Human Factor*, p. 112.

28. Hefner, "Freedom in Evolutionary Perspective," p. 139.

This wider evolutionary vision provides the backdrop for what Hefner wants to say about sin. He is convinced that "biology enriches our understanding of the inherent character of sin,"[29] and he identifies areas in which this is the case: "(1) Sin is an inherent factor in human awareness. (2) We participate in sin as a condition pertaining to our very origin as persons. (3) Sin seems to be inherited in some fashion. (4) Sin is associated with our freedom. (5) Sin is marked by a sense of guilt and estrangement, thus requiring the gift of grace."[30]

The tie between genetic inheritance and original sin is a point of special interest in this regard. Hefner maintains that we inherit both determinism and freedom both genetically and culturally from our evolutionary past and that this inheritance is the condition that makes human sinning possible. In this sense, sin belongs to our origin and therefore can rightly be called "original sin." Thus Hefner links "original sin" not with actual sins committed by our ancestors such as Adam and Eve but rather with the human condition of finitude and fallibility, which naturally opens the door to human sin.

> What we have called sin is inherent in human being because it is a constituent of the process that makes life possible in the first place and that contributes to life's development. Thus, even though we are aware of sin and feel its pain (guilt), sin is not present because of some prior evil action or evil nature. The guilt is better understood as a response to our inherent inability to satisfy all of the messages that are delivered to our central nervous system, rather than as a response to an evil act committed in the primordial past of the race.[31]

What is the relationship between past dispositions, present sins, and future possibilities? With his sense of divine involvement in our bio-evolutionary destiny, Hefner tackles the problem raised by Dawkins and Wilson — namely, how to produce an altruism that goes beyond immediate kin selection to encompass all of humanity. Because of the desparately dangerous situation in which the contemporary world finds itself, he says, "society demands altruism beyond the kin group for its survival." In this regard, the theologian has something specific to say:

29. Hefner, *The Human Factor,* p. 141.
30. Hefner, *The Human Factor,* p. 129.
31. Hefner, *The Human Factor,* p. 139.

"The fact that Christianity elevates the sacrificial action of Jesus on the cross to a central position, in symbol, in faith, and in ethics is of striking significance against the sociobiological background."[32] The symbol of the cross — the symbol of God's sacrifice and the call for the human race to emulate God — makes altruism a cultural value and generates religious schemes of meaning to uphold that value. Hefner is offering here a "coadaptation theory," according to which "religion plays a significant role, since it is one of the chief value-generating institutions and since it also provides an overarching system of meaning to support its values."[33]

A third theologian who takes the new genetics with utmost seriousness is Ronald Cole-Turner. Cole-Turner accepts the premise that genes influence behavior, even sinful behavior, but he maintains that genes are not the sole determinants. "As research clarifies the role of genes in behavior," he writes, "theology will be pressed to clarify the role, if any, of personal responsibility and of divine grace. If genetics research succeeded in convincing people that their beliefs and behaviors are *nothing but the effect of their genes,* theology would be seriously threatened. Theologians, drawing upon genetics research itself, need to argue against this possible confusion."[34] Cole-Turner works through the implications of genetic engineering in terms of both creation and redemption, in terms of both what is presently the case and how it can be transformed into something better. Genetic technology can improve the human lot. The Christian doctrine of redemption calls us to enter our own evolutionary development and engage in human transformation. Although sinful human beings can press biotechnology into the service of disorder and even evil, we human beings are creative creatures and responsible for transcending and improving what nature has bequeathed to us thus far. "Science and technology serve God's ongoing creative work. Together they offer God a new way to create and a new modality of divine agency in the physical world."[35]

32. Hefner, "Sociobiology, Ethics, and Theology," pp. 197-98.
33. Hefner, "Sociobiology, Ethics, and Theology," p. 201.
34. Cole-Turner, *The New Genesis: Theology and the Genetic Revolution* (Louisville: Westminster/John Knox Press, 1993), p. 87; italics in original.
35. Cole-Turner, *The New Genesis,* p. 101.

Genes and Crime

Returning to the topic at hand — the question of biological determinants for human sinning — I would note a resurgence of interest in identifying individual biological factors in criminal behavior. This marks a shift from what has been the dominant perspective, however. The dominant approach to crime with which we in the modern world are most familiar is the social scientific approach that deals not with individuals but with broad cultural, economic, racial, and class factors. The sociological approach grew out of the philosophy of Jean-Jacques Rousseau, which presumes human nature to be innately good and blames social structures for corrupting this essential goodness. Social scientific efforts to locate the cause of crime look to family practices, poor education, racial prejudice, and economic disadvantage. The sociological approach has simply assumed that criminal behavior can be explained — and even altered — by nurture, not nature. The empirical weakness in this approach is that it fails to explain why in cases of shared social circumstance some individuals become criminals and others do not. So, we ask, might we look again to nature?[36]

Two Harvard professors, James Q. Wilson in government and Richard J. Herrnstein in experimental psychology, are looking again to nature, to our biological or "constitutional" nature. They begin by noting that some features of crime are universal. For example, all societies and all classes have historically agreed that murder, theft, robbery, and rape are crimes. This consensus diminishes with regard to some activities — abortion and homosexual behavior, for instance — but the overwhelming majority of people of all locations and all classes agree that certain acts are unqualifiedly wrong and subject to social sanction. Armed with this list as criterion, Wilson and Herrnstein further note that criminal activity is greatest among young urban males everywhere in the world, regardless of race or class. Furthermore, within this group the largest percentage exhibit behavior consistent with criminality already at a very early age. Although crime is not

36. Drawing on family studies that include a comparison of the behavior of twins with that of adopted siblings, Patricia A. Brennan, Sarnoff A. Mednick, and William F. Gabrielli Jr. have concluded that "genetic factors can and do influence certain types of criminal behavior" ("Genetic Influences and Criminal Behavior," in *Genetic Issues in Psychology and Epidemiology,* ed. Ming T. Tsuang, Kenneth S. Kendler, and Michael J. Lyons [New Brunswick, N.J.: Rutgers University Press, 1991], p. 243).

wholly absent in rural areas or among women, crime is dramatically more prevalent among young urban males. It is reasonable to ask, then, whether there may be some constitutional factors that account for this relative prevalence.

Wilson and Herrnstein think they have found certain physical features that can be associated with criminality. Criminals are more likely than noncriminals to have mesomorphic body types, to have biological fathers who were criminals (and this applies even to cases of adoptive sons who never knew their birth fathers), to be of somewhat lower intelligence, to be impulsive or extroverted, and to have autonomic nervous systems that respond more slowly and less vigorously to stimuli.[37] They contend that these constitutional factors predispose some individuals toward socially unacceptable behavior. They are not saying that these factors by themselves determine whether a given individual will engage in criminal activity. They maintain that individuals choose whether to commit a crime on the basis of of their own unique and personal assessment of the rewards and punishments that might be involved. They are simply arguing that social factors are not the sole influence on our perceptions regarding reward and punishment, that physical factors also play a role in the calculations.

Wilson and Herrnstein would not likely seek residence in the camp of strict biological determinists. Like Lewontin and his colleagues, they affirm a dialectical or interactive relationship between nature and nurture, between an individual's physical constitution and environment. They assert that "there *is* a human nature that develops in intimate settings out of a complex interaction of constitutional and social factors, and that this nature affects how people choose between the consequences of crime and its alternatives."[38] They reject the notion of a "crime gene" without rejecting the possibility of a genetic predispostion to commit crimes: "There is no such thing as a 'born criminal,' but some traits that are to a degree heritable, such as intelligence and temperament, affect to some extent the likelihood that individuals will engage in criminal activities."[39] Despite these disclaimers, however, Wilson and Herrnstein clearly do assert that

37. Wilson and Herrnstein, *Crime and Human Nature* (New York: Simon & Schuster, 1985), p. 66.

38. Wilson and Herrnstein, *Crime and Human Nature,* p. 508.

39. Wilson and Herrnstein, *Crime and Human Nature,* p. 69.

some of us inherit biological temperaments conducive to criminality — especially the sons of criminal fathers.

This thesis about the genetics of young urban males has led University of California sociologist Troy Duster to sound a skeptical alarm. He is not so much dubious of the findings of molecular biologists concerning the power of the genes to influence us as he is worried that we might jump prematurely to conclusions regarding the social import of such findings.

> In the last few decades, gradually, almost imperceptibly, our thinking about human social life has shifted to accept a greater role for genetics. . . . The last decade has seen a geometric increase in publications pronouncing the genetic basis of such disparate phenomena as shyness, rape, mental illness, alcoholism, crime, even social and economic position. How did we get here? . . . I will argue that the social concerns of an age, not the scientific status of the new knowledge-structure of genetics, offer the most compelling answer to this question.[40]

Because he believes that the social forces governing the interpretation of scientific findings are more influential than the findings themselves, Duster is worried about the role that an apparently scientifically derived image of criminality might play in our society. He notes that between 1981 and 1991, the U.S. prison population grew from 330,000 to 804,000. He further notes that the vast majority of the new inmates are black. In 1991 African Americans were being incarcerated at a rate seven times higher than that of whites. Fifteen per cent of black males between the ages of sixteen and nineteen are arrested in any given year. In the light of such statistics, Duster wonders whether researchers taking samples from inmates might not someday draw the conclusion that one race is more genetically disposed to crime than another race. Duster sees a grave problem in looking for the source of crime in prison cells. Some people overlook the obvious fact that there is a difference between committing a crime and being convicted of a crime. Only a small percentage of those who commit crimes are arrested, a smaller number are prosecuted, and a still smaller number are incarcerated. Duster, a social scientist, is well aware that incarceration rates are a function of social, economic, and political forces. He is concerned

---

40. Duster, *Backdoor to Eugenics* (New York: Routledge, 1990), p. vii.

310

that a methodologically biased science might lead our society to think that African Americans are genetically predisposed to commit more crimes than others. Such a conclusion, he says, would simply constitute one more expression of an as yet unexpurgated racism.

So, what Duster fears from theories such as that proposed by Wilson and Herrnstein is the possible public acceptance of a genetic explanation for crime not just in individuals but in social groups. Such a genetic explanation could constitute an illegitimate scientific whitewash that would obscure or even hide our massive social justice problem regarding race relations.[41] Science would tell the lie that hides scapegoatism.

Intellectual honesty requires that we push on with laboratory research to determine the extent to which our genes do in fact contribute to making us who we are, yet we dare not permit ourselves to be lulled into a scientific pangloss that diverts our attention away from moral responsibility for seeking social justice.

A major controversy broke out over this issue in the fall of 1992. David Wasserman at the University of Maryland had secured a grant from the special program of the National Institutes of Health (NIH) dealing with Ethical, Legal, and Social Implications of the Human Genome Project to fund a conference entitled "Genetic Factors in Crime: Findings, Uses and Implications." Wasserman had planned an open academic discussion of the scientific findings — findings that would most likely have shown that to date no serious biological evidence exists directly linking genes to crime. That conference never took place.[42] A brochure advertising the conference was misleadingly

41. Duster, "Human Genetics, Evolutionary Theory, and Social Stratification," unpublished paper delivered to the third consultation of the Center for Theology and Natural Sciences genome research project, 18 January 1993. See also Duster, "Genetics, Race, and Crime: Recurring Seduction to a False Precision," in *DNA On Trial*, ed. Paul R. Billings (Plainview, N.Y.: Cold Springs Harbor Press, 1992), pp. 129-40.

42. An important part of the context that led to the cancellation of the conference is often overlooked in discussions of the incident. In 1992, Louis W. Sullivan, a black physician who at the time was serving as secretary of Department of Health and Human Services, conceived of a federal funding plan to help African Americans. He noted the prevalence of violent crimes in black communities and the fact that the homicide rate for blacks is five times that for whites. He proposed a "psycho-social" program that would examine a wide array of phenomena such as child abuse, drug addiction, and other potential factors in crime. He included a small biological research component (it was to take only 5 percent of the proposed budget). The assumption here was clearly that crime is socially linked to poverty and drug traffic. There was certainly no attempt to try to explain crime in terms of genes. Yet the public atmosphere was poisoned by

inflammatory, and a public protest arose.[43] A black interest magazine ran a story under the headline "U.S. Government Wants to Sedate Black Youth" charging that the conference would endorse the use of drug therapy to counteract the genetic predisposition of blacks to commit crime. Howard University political scientist Ronald W. Walters publicly opposed all research into the biological causes of crime. Washington was bombarded with complaints. The Black Caucus in Congress responded. The government capitulated. Bernadine Healy, then director of the NIH, demanded that funding be revoked. NIH Deputy Director John Diggs canceled the conference.

Opinions are divided as to whether Dr. Healy did the right thing. Among those who approve of Healy's action are Ruth Hubbard and Elijah Wald, who accused Wasserman of drawing "attention away from the societal reasons for why poor people, especially African-Americans, make up a disproportionate share of America's prison population." They added that "the very definition of criminal behavior is flawed, and that it is meaningless to talk about genetic predispositions for behaviors that are socially constructed." They concluded by saying that "there is no scientific merit to looking for genetic factors in crime."[44] Taking the opposing view was medical geneticist Paul Billings, widely known for his defense of rights to privacy in genetic matters. He joined Hubbard and Wald in doubting that scientists will find a direct link between genes and crime, but he disagreed with the decision to cancel the conference. "The NIH did a disservice to academic freedom," he said, "and allowed the fantasy that there is a science behind the discussion of the genetics of criminality to con-

---

Frederick K. Goodwin, who was then directing the Alcohol, Drug Abuse and Mental Health Administration and now heads the National Institute of Mental Health. Citing research on monkey violence and sexuality, Goodwin offhandedly commented, "Maybe it isn't just the careless use of the word when people call certain areas of certain cities 'jungles.'" This statement had civil rights leaders fuming on the eve of the ill-fated University of Maryland conference. See John Horgan, "Genes and Crime," *Scientific American,* February 1993, pp. 24-29.

43. The brochure inviting participants included the following statement: "Genetic research holds out the prospect of identifying individuals who may be predisposed to certain kinds of criminal conduct, of isolating environmental features which trigger those predispositions, and of treating some predispositions with drugs or unobtrusive therapies." Some readers interpreted it as racist propaganda.

44. Hubbard and Wald, "Responsible Science," *GeneWatch* 8 (November 1992): 3.

tinue."[45] In sum, the scientific consensus seems to be that genes and crime have at best an indirect connection, and some scholars are anxious that drawing premature conclusions regarding genetic causes of crime might have deleterious repercussions for race relations.

Is Alcoholism in the Genes?

Now let's narrow the field and look at a specific example — alcoholism. The statistical association between alcohol use and crime is overwhelming. Fourteen studies have shown that alcohol plays an influential role in 60 per cent of all murders and 40 per cent of all rapes.[46] Does this mean that alcohol causes crime? Not according to Wilson and Herrnstein. They cautiously suggest that alcoholism is a statistically significant factor only among specifically neurotic criminals. Extroverted aggressive criminals, in contrast, may not be alcoholics even if they drink frequently. In their assessment, the most notorious threat to the public safety — the drunk who causes traffic accidents — seems not to be accorded criminal status. So the two Harvard researchers conclude, "Alcoholics tend to be neurotic personalities; overtly aggressive men tend to be impulsive ones. Both alcoholism and aggressiveness may have some genetic component, but, if it is a different component, there would be no reason to assume that a predisposition to alcoholism and a predisposition to criminality would appear in the same person more frequently than by chance."[47]

But is susceptibility to alcoholism itself genetically inherited? Quite possibly yes, answers psychiatrist C. Robert Cloninger. He distinguishes two types of alcoholism. Type I alcoholism is the more common and less severe form. It has a clearly environmental cause — that is, it results from the consumption of strong drink over a long period of time. A smaller group of alcoholics — perhaps one fourth of the total — seem predetermined to alcohol addiction. These Type II al-

45. Paul Billings, "Academic Freedom," *GeneWatch* 8 (November 1992): 2. On 3 September 1993, the NIH Grant Appeals Board ruled that the decision to cancel the University of Maryland grant was based on spurious reasoning, and it reapproved funding for the program. See "NIH Told to Reconsider Crime Meeting," *Science,* 1 October 1993, p. 23.

46. Wilson and Herrnstein, *Crime and Human Nature,* p. 356.

47. Wilson and Herrnstein, *Crime and Human Nature,* p. 361.

coholics typically begin drinking to drunkenness already as teenagers, find it difficult to keep jobs, and create difficulties within their families. Type II men seem to outnumber Type II women by a ratio of four or five to one. And, as in the case of crime statistics, boys often inherit this propensity from their fathers.[48]

Cloninger has identified three personality traits associated with Type II alcoholism, personality traits that appear to have a physiological basis. The first trait is novelty-seeking, "a heritable tendency toward frequent exploratory activity and intense exhilaration in response to novel or appetitive stimuli."[49] This natural exhilaration in response to stimuli is related to the release of chemical dopamine in the nervous system. Dopamine production is stimulated by alcohol. The presumed mechanism at work here, then, is that the Type II alcoholic receives a sense of exhilaration as a reward for consuming alcohol. Experiments have shown that sons of alcoholics tend to experience a much stronger response to dopamine than those of nonalcoholics. Second, alcohol tends to block the serotonin system, which is associated with feelings including fear, inhibition, shyness, and the like. Type II alcoholics are born with a rather sluggish serotonin system and hence tend to be comparatively less inhibited and more carefree. Third, Type II alcoholics are born with a low sensitivity to norepinephrine, the neurotransmitter for signals announcing possible rewards and punishments; as a result, they tend to be less daunted than average individuals by concerns about social approval for their actions. In sum, Type II alcoholics seem to be genetically predisposed to seek novelty, to be relatively less inhibited, and to be less subject to control by traditional social rewards and punishments.

Is Type II alcoholism then genetic? Some think that the gene responsible for the dopamine receptor on nerve cells can be found on chromosome 11. Is this enough evidence? No. More than likely it would take more than a single gene to predispose a person to a given

48. Do genes play a role in alcoholism in women too? Lindon Eaves and colleagues conclude a study saying, "In women, genetic factors play a major etiologic role in alcoholism" (Kenneth S. Kendler, Andrew C. Heath, Michael C. Neale, Ronald C. Kessler, and Lindon J. Eaves, "A Population-Based Twin Study of Alcoholism in Women," *Journal of the American Medical Association,* 14 October 1992, p. 1881.

49. Cloninger, "Neurogenetic Adaptive Mechanisms in Alcoholism," *Science* 236 (1987): 413. See also Jerry E. Bishop and Michael Waldholz, *Genome* (New York: Simon & Schuster, 1990), p. 261.

pattern of behavior — perhaps a configuration of a dozen or more contributing genes. To date, the Cloninger research has been suggestive but not independently confirmed. The scientific jury is still out.[50]

While the scientific jury is still deciding how much credibility we should grant to these theories regarding the genetic disposition to criminal and alcoholic behavior, I believe theologians should begin asking about possible ramifications for understanding sin and moral responsibility. In the event that scientific research is eventually able to demonstrate that genes or other biological processes are more influential on human behavior than previously thought, theologians will be challenged to explicate the symbol of sin in light of the new knowledge. Let me suggest what direction we might take using the example of alcoholism.

Is alcoholism sinful? That depends. Many would argue that if alcoholism is either caused or cured by willpower, then it belongs in the moral category of sin. Prior to the 1950s, the dominant view in Western society was that alcoholic behavior *was* a matter of will and hence that the alcoholic was morally responsible. At the end of the eighteenth century in Britain and the United States, alcoholics were widely despised for wasting their families' money and mistreating their spouses and children. The most effective remedy was considered to be repentance. The Christian revivalist movements such as that of John and Charles Wesley prayed for the indwelling of the Holy Spirit, for a conversion of the heart, and for the strength of will to stop drinking. Those who repented and received the Spirit received the power to cease and desist from drinking alcohol and immediately became loving spouses and responsible parents. The method worked, and by employing it the Methodist churches made a dramatic impact on society. The Woman's Christian Temperance Union and Alcoholics Anonymous simply began with the view that alcoholism is a matter of personal will and sought divine power to choose to overcome the inner compulsion to drink.

During the 1950s, the view began to change in English-speaking societies, however. People began to argue that alcoholism is not a

50. The popular turn-of-the-century novelist Jack London postulated that there are two types of alcoholism, the inherited type and the learned type. In his autobiographical book of 1913, *John Barleycorn,* he placed himself in the latter category. The eugenics movement already growing in London's day placed "drunkards" along with prostitutes, criminals, and the feebleminded on their list of people who should not pass on their defective genes.

matter of sin but of sickness. They urged alcoholics to go to their doctors rather than to church. People abandoned moral language in discussions of alcoholism and turned instead to medical metaphors. Alcoholism was no longer characterized as a compulsion arising from within that should be overcome by an act of will but rather as an invader from without, like a virus, that called for medical treatment. Today television commercials advertise the services of clinics that promise a cure for the disease. Anyone speaking of alcoholism as a sin these days would be viewed as religiously parochial if not atavistic.

Other factors may be in the process of shifting our perception of alcoholism once again, however. Recent years have brought a heightened sense of the problem of abuse in our society — spousal abuse, child abuse, substance abuse. And, given the fact that alcoholic men are disproportionately guilty of abusing their wives and children, a backlash may be building against them. Abuse is widely viewed as a moral failing. Perhaps alcoholism is on its way to being viewed as a moral matter once again.

The point of this brief side trip was to show the shifting nature of social perceptions regarding one identifiable form of human behavior. Whether a specific behavior is judged to be sinful depends in large part on its social context.

With this in mind, let's look to the future regarding possible social appropriations of genetic research. If it can be demonstrated conclusively that a propensity to alcoholism or even to crime is genetically determined, will this count against or in favor of one's moral responsibility? Will genes become a scapegoat, permitting us to sidestep guilt by saying, "The genes — not the Devil — made me do it"? Or might it work the other way around — might we conclude that our genes make us guilty? It could go either way.

We have already had at least one skirmish, and it appears that the scapegoating strategy won the day. In 1990 the California Supreme Court heard the case of *Baker v. State Bar* in which Mr. Baker was accused of embezzlement. The accusation of embezzlement went uncontested. His defense consisted of asking the court for leniency on the grounds that he "had a genetic predisposition to alcoholism" and had committed the crime under the influence of alcohol. The court seemed persuaded by this argument and mitigated his sentence. Evidently in this case genetic predisposition toward alcoholism relieved the perpetrator of the crime from at least some portion of his responsibility for it.

This precedent alarms Dorothy Nelkin, a scholar who has tried to assess the impact of genetic research on society. She dubs the position taken by the California Supreme Court genetic "essentialism." She contends that if the essentialist position spreads, it could mean that all those proven to be biologically wired for alcoholism or criminality or both could use their genetic inheritance as a defense. To be biologically determined is to be innocent. If essentialism is set loose on the court system, and if Wilson and Herrnstein are correct, then the vast majority of predatory criminals will have a good shot at avoiding incarceration, and our society will face unparalleled anarchy.

The alternative possibility — assigning guilt to persons due to genetic inheritance — also has pitfalls. If genetic predisposition is used to support enhancing rather than mitigating punishment, and if society determines that persons so genetically predisposed should not be set free to create anarchy, then we might find ourselves in a situation similar to that created by the insanity defense. Under current law, when defendants are found to be legally insane, the courts may have the option of institutionalizing them for periods longer than those of the maximum criminal sentences they might have received had they been found guilty of the offenses in question. In the future, courts may decide to base sentences on predictions of dangerousness, and such predictions could be based on a genetic calculus. Genetic predisposition would constitute a sort of status offense, and this might very well be susceptible to racial or ethnic prejudice. "If it is accepted that genetic endowment determines the propensity to commit bad acts, then hereditary traits, which often reduce to ethnic group membership, may one day be considered evidence of the commission of a crime."[51] Troy Duster's fears would be confirmed.

Is Homosexuality in the Genes?

A parallel controversy is heating up regarding homosexuality, following the possible discovery of a "gay gene." In April 1993 a team of researchers headed by Dean H. Hamer at the National Cancer Institute discovered "a statistically significant correlation between inheritance of genetic markers on chromosomal region Xq28 and sexual

51. Dorothy Nelkin, "The Jurisprudence of Genetics," *Vanderbilt Law Review* 45 (March 1992): 331.

orientation in a selected group of homosexual males."[52] The study examined forty pairs of homosexual brothers and found that thirty-three pairs shared a set of five genetic markers located near the end of the long arm of the X chromosome. Males have a combination of X and Y sex-determining chromosomes. They receive the Y chromosome from their fathers and the X chromosome from their mothers. Thus, Hamer's team contends that its research has "produced evidence that one form of male homosexuality is preferentially transmitted through the maternal side."[53] Follow-up studies will try to replicate and confirm these findings regarding the X chromosome and will also look for other causes of homosexuality that might apply to the seven pairs of gay brothers in the study who did not evidence this genetic marker. Hamer reports that he believes homosexuality arises from a variety of causes, genetic and perhaps environmental as well.[54]

What will this mean for the ethical and political debate over homosexuality? *Time* magazine immediately solicited a reaction to the study from gay rights advocates. They interpreted the results as an endorsement of the assertion that homosexual persons "are acting as God or nature — in other words, their genes — intended." Note the identification of genes with God and nature. The logic is clear: if nature or God has gifted certain individuals with a genetic predisposition toward homosexual behavior, then those persons have a moral license and a legal right to adopt a gay lifestyle. As they see it, science is providing ethical muscle to the gay rights movement. "If gays can establish a genetic basis for sexual preference, like skin color or gender, they may persuade judges that discrimination is unconstitutional."[55]

The assertion of a genetic basis for homosexuality raises countless issues. If homosexuality is genetically inherited, is homosexual behavior sinful? Is social discrimination against homosexuals or homosexual behavior warranted? Should homosexuals be granted legal protections

52. Dean H. Hamer, Stella Hu, Victoria L. Magnuson, Nan Hu, and Angela M. L. Pattatucci, "A Linkage between DNA Markers on the X Chromosome and Male Sexual Orientation," *Science,* 16 July 1993, p. 321.

53. Hamer et al., "A Linkage between DNA Markers on the X Chromosome and Male Sexual Orientation," p. 325.

54. Hamer's remarks are cited by Robert Pool in "Evidence for Homosexuality Gene," *Science,* 16 July 1993, p. 291.

55. William Henry III, Ellen Germain, and Alice Park, "Born Gay?" *Time,* 26 July 1993, p. 38.

on the basis of their sexual orientation? At the heart of all such issues is a pair of related questions: Are we exempt from moral responsibility for what we inherit, and is what we inherit determinative of who we are and what we do? Many people seem quick to assume that we should not be assigned guilt for what is found in our genes. As a society, we seem to believe that if our behavior is biologically determined, then the genes we inherit — not we ourselves — can be held responsible for what we do. Confronted by moments of moral crisis, we are often quick to scapegoat our genes.

If these early investigations into possible genetic links to alcoholism and homosexuality are any indication, the next decade will find our entire society wrestling with a dramatic array of questions regarding the cultural, philosophical, and legal implications of genetic research and proposals for biological determinism. This should prompt theologians to open up discussion on a number of doctrinal fronts, especially the doctrine of sin. One obvious point of contact is the concept of inheritance. Christian and Jewish thinking about sin and its consequences is steeped in the idea of inheritance. Given this point, I would like to take a closer look at the idea that the propensity for sin originated with Adam and Eve and has been passed down congenitally from generation to generation since.

As we turn to this component in our understanding of original sin, let me interject a brief comment regarding the relationship between theology and natural science. Of the various ways to conceive of the interface between these two giant fields of human intellectual endeavor, the way I prefer is that of *hypothetical consonance*. Guided by the desire to find consonance if and where it is to be found, I look for those areas in which there might be a correspondence between what can be said scientifically about the natural world and what can be said theologically about God's creation.[56] The proposals offered by biological determinists regarding genetically inherited predispositions to alcoholism and criminality look at first glance to be quite similar to traditional depictions of original sin. This initial sense of similarity, it seems to me, provides sufficient warrant for theologians to ask about existing correspondences. Then, further, we might ask if what we learn from science should inform what theologians think; and, conversely, we might ask if

56. See *Cosmos as Creation: Theology and Science in Consonance,* ed. Ted Peters (Nashville: Abingdon Press, 1989), p. 13.

what theologians think should inform what we learn through science. Might the interaction between theology and science expand or deepen our understanding of the human condition?

Is Original Sin Hereditary Sin?

Long before the appearance of modern genetic science, Christian theologians used the metaphor of inheritance to explicate the symbol of human sinfulness. John Calvin speaks for much of Western Christianity when he says, "Original sin . . . seems to be a hereditary depravity and corruption of our nature, diffused into all parts of the soul, which makes us first liable to God's wrath, then also brings forth in us those works which scripture calls 'works of the flesh.' "[57] Although he affirms that the predisposition to sin is inherited, it is clear that he is not asserting that this predisposition belongs to our nature. To the contrary, he characterizes it as a *corruption* of our nature. If there be consonance between what Dawkins means by the selfishness of our genes and what Calvin means by original sin, a difference would nonetheless remain — namely, the issue of whether sin is natural. Original sin may be inherited, but it is a superaddition to an originally good nature. This distinction is significant: Christians affirm the goodness of creation as the gift of a good Creator. No matter how pervasive human sin may be in our world today, it is is an alien virus infecting an otherwise healthy creation.[58] Original sin, then, is something like a disease that is passed on congenitally.

57. Calvin, *Institutes of the Christian Religion*, 2.1.8. For the assembly of materials connecting inherited sin with inherited genes I am indebted to the work of Ronald Cole-Turner in "The Biology of Original Sin," a paper delivered to third consultation of the Center for Theology and the Natural Sciences' genome research project, 17 January 1993.

58. What about nature in the form of nonhuman creation? Gustaf Wingren holds that "the things of creation are always purer than man is. Sin does not lie in the things that are created, but in man's use of them" (*Creation and Law*, trans. Ross Mackenzie [London: Oliver & Boyd, 1961], p. 44). The matter cannot be as simple as Wingren suggests, especially when we note that we human beings share a large portion of our DNA with plants and as much as 98 percent of our DNA with higher primates. Genetically speaking, there is no sharp line between the human and the nonhuman. Theologically speaking, the categories of sin and grace should apply to the whole scope of creation, not merely the human.

With this observation in mind, we can foresee an entanglement coming. Let's speculate. Suppose it could be shown that sin is in the genes either as a disposition toward anxiety or as a disposition toward specifiable forms of aggressive and violent behavior. The assumption from a scientific point of view would have to be that sin is natural. All genes belong to nature, regardless of whether we view them as helpful or harmful. This would apply equally to disease-related genes such as those for Huntington's disease on chromosome 4 and cystic fibrosis on chromosome 21. Any genetic disease is equaprimordial with our genetic nature. All genes belong to nature. Clearly the Christian habit of referring to original sin as a disease that infects a previously healthy human nature would not be consonant with this view; scientifically speaking, human sin would be just as natural as everything else human. Perhaps we need to reexamine the hereditary disease metaphor to see just what is at stake in the Christian concept of original sin.

The hereditary-disease metaphor began to make its mark on Western Christendom when Augustine wrestled with biblical texts such as the following:

> Sin came into the world through one man, and death came through sin, and so death spread to all because all have sinned. . . . For if the many died through the one man's trespass, much more surely have the grace of God and the free gift in the grace of the one man, Jesus Christ, abounded for the many. And the free gift is not like the effect of the one man's sin. For the judgment following one trespass brought condemnation, but the free gift following many trespasses brings justification (Rom. 5:12, 15b-16)

> For since death came through a human being, the resurrection of the dead has also come through a human being; for as all die in Adam, so all will be made alive in Christ (1 Cor. 15:21-22)

What Augustine felt obligated to say regarding the meaning of these texts proved decisive for the tradition that followed for a millennium and a half. Augustine believed it was not enough to say that those of us who sin today merely imitate the sin that Adam committed many years ago. It is not enough to say that each of us behaves *like* Adam. Somehow Adam's act and our acts are tied together. Somehow we participate in Adam, and Adam participates in us. The prepositional phrase, *"in* Adam," is key here. Why does Augustine stress this? Because of what the text says about Christ and the work of salvation. The saving power of the gospel is that Christ enters into us and we into him. Christians do not merely imitate Christ. By the power of the Holy Spirit, the resurrected Christ himself enters the inner life of the person of faith, and "his grace works within us our illumination and justification."[59] Apparently using reverse logic in an effort to remain true to the Pauline juxtaposition, Augustine asserts that our relation to Adam must parallel our relation to Christ.

If that is so, the question becomes how Adam's sin of yesterday is *in* our sin today? Can we describe it in terms of propagation through biological inheritance? The idea of a congenital disease begins to bear the conceptual burden of explaining the unity of the human race as sinful. Sin passes to all of us by natural descent, not merely by imitation. Augustine distinguished our actual sins from original sin, to be sure, but he also affirmed that by being born into an already fallen human race, we inherit the originating sin of our primeval parents. In asserting this he did not intend to argue for some sort of biological determinism that erases our moral responsibility. Rather, his intent was to affirm a wholeness principle that would underscore the fact that all members of the human race are bound together in sin just as all members of the human race are destined to enjoy the benefits of Christ's saving work: "We have derived from Adam, in whom all have sinned, not all our actual sins, but only original sin; whereas from Christ, in whom we are all justified, we obtain the remission not merely of that original sin, but of the rest of our sins also, which we have added."[60] So we see that the weight of Augustine's explication of the symbol of sin

59. Augustine, "On the Merits and Remission of Sins," 1.10. Jaroslav Pelikan believes Augustine may have made an error in exegesis here, being misled by the Latin translation he was using. The key clause in Romans 5:12 is properly interpreted "because all have sinned," but the text on which Augustine was relying reads "in whom all have sinned" (*The Christian Tradition: A History of the Development of Doctrine*, 5 vols. [Chicago: University of Chicago Press, 1971-1989], 1:299). I believe it is Pelikan, not Augustine, who makes the error. The problem with Pelikan's reading here is twofold. First, "in Adam" also appears in 1 Cor. 15:22, so Augustine is not dependent on only one ambiguous text. Second, and more importantly, Augustine's interpretation depends on more than merely the prepositional phrase; it depends on Paul's juxtaposition of Adam with Christ.

60. Augustine, "On the Merits and Remissions of Sins," 1:16. See "Original Sin," p. 31.

rests not on the biological mechanism of transmission but on the need to affirm unity in Christ and a corresponding unity in sin.

This image of the inherited disease itself was passed down from theological generation to theological generation. A thousand years after Augustine, article 2 of the Augsburg Confession of 1530 was formulated as follows:

> Since the fall of Adam all men who are born according to the course of nature are conceived and born in sin. That is, all men are full of evil lust and inclinations from their mother's wombs and are unable by nature to have true fear of God and true faith in God. Moreover, this inborn sickness and hereditary sin *(Erbsünde)* is truly sin and condemns to the eternal wrath of God all those who are not born again through Baptism and the Holy Spirit.

Here the emphasis is less on the bond we share with Adam and more on the bad genes we have inherited, on our inborn dispositions toward "evil lust and inclinations." We might also note the bald identification of original sin with nature. This statement lacks the subtle distinction between an originally good creation and a contaminated or diseased natural process.[61]

How can this congenital disease infecting the human race be cured? Gerhard Forde, interpreting Martin Luther, says, "There is no cure; the patient must die."[62] Jesus Christ, the Son of God and savior of the human race, dies. It is the Easter resurrection that sounds the trumpet of victory, a healing of both sin and death. The Reformation theology of the cross, says Forde, makes this point: "If you wish to be raised with him you must die with him. This is to say that there is no way to

---

61. The matter of the relationship between nature and sin is clarified in the Formula of Concord: "There is a distinction between man's nature and original sin, not only in the beginning when God created man pure and holy and without sin, but also as we now have our nature after the Fall" (*The Book of Concord,* ed. Theodore G. Tappert [Philadelphia: Fortress Press, 1959], p. 466). Hefner comments, "The mainstream of the tradition wishes to avoid two extremes in thinking about this sin: on the one hand, a cool view of sin as defect, overlooking the ferocity of sinful intention; on the other hand, a view of sin as total depravity that demolishes the God-given original goodness that pertains to humans. I cite the Lutheran versions of the doctrine because they seem, when taken as a whole, to represent the main tradition without the extremes — the *Augsburg Confession* articulating the inherent ferocity of the sin, the *Formula of Concord* insisting upon human created goodness" (*The Human Factor,* p. 127).

62. Forde, *Where God Meets Man* (Minneapolis: Augsburg, 1972), p. 32.

appropriate the cross other than to go through it. . . . Then something absolutely new begins: the life of *faith*, the life of trusting God."[63]

With the advent of modern Christianity in its liberal and neo-orthodox forms, the tie between original sin and biological transmission begins to loosen. The Augustinian notion of inherited disease presupposed the existence of a literal Adam and a literal Eve, the first parents of the human race, in conjunction with a linear history from the beginning down to the present. With the rise of rationalism, critical consciousness, and historical relativism in the modern period, such historical literalism was replaced by general sociological or psychological or existential principles. Friedrich Schleiermacher, for example, affirmed the doctrine of original sin in the form of "universal sinfulness" but argued that our consciousness of universal sinfulness is something inward and immediate, that it does not depend on the story of the fall and associated biological history. He dismissed the notion that our sin today is an inherited derivation of Adam's sin as an unnecessary extra. According to Schleiermacher, the idea of inherited sin is not in itself an element of our faith. He followed Augustine's interpretation of Romans 5:12: "The apostle refers to the origin of sin only with a view to elucidating the doctrine of the restoration of life through Christ, and the point of comparison is simply that each originates in and emanates from one."[64] Alluding more to cultural inheritance rather than biological inheritance, Schleiermacher declared that "sin in general, and original sin in particular, are seen to be the corporate action and the corporate guilt of the whole human race."[65]

Turn-of-the-century Social Gospel theologian Walter Rauschenbusch further explicated the notion of socially inherited sin. Older boys in the neighborhood, he observed, pass on to the younger ones evil habits of boyhood such as lying, stealing, cigarette smoking, profane and obscene talk, and self-pollution. Then he turned to the adults, whose "vices and crimes are not transmitted by heredity, but by being socialized," listing such things as alcoholism, drug evils, cruel sports, sex perversity, blood feuds, and lynching.[66] These sins are lodged in

63. Forde, *Where God Meets Man,* p. 39; italics in original.
64. Schleiermacher, *The Christian Faith* (Edinburgh: T. & T. Clark, 1960), pp. 299-300.
65. Schleiermacher, *The Christian Faith,* p. 304.
66. Rauschenbusch, *A Theology for the Social Gospel* (1917; reprint, Nashville: Abingdon Press, 1945), p. 60.

social customs and institutions and then absorbed by the individual, he said. The preexisting group infects the individual. Hence, the disease metaphor perdures, but now we have a social disease.

Yet, despite this clear preference for a social or cultural understanding of inherited sinfulness, Rauschenbusch was so impressed with the developing insights of the evolutionary vision that he said, "Science, to some extent, corroborates the doctrine of original sin. Evil does flow down the generations through the channels of biological coherence." Perhaps, he pondered, stubbornness and antisocial impulses in children "have had their adequate biological causes somewhere back on the line, even if we lack the records."[67] Concerning this remark, I would note two things: (1) Rauschenbusch combined biological with social inheritance, and (2) he traced the possible biological source of original sin back not to Adam and Eve but rather to "causes somewhere back on the line" for which we lack records.[68]

With the development of neo-orthodoxy, Christian theologians began to demonstrate an antipathy toward the idea of a biologically inherited original sin. Karl Barth defended the doctrine of original sin but opposed the metaphor of biological inheritance saying, "'Hereditary sin' has a hopelessly naturalistic, deterministic and even fatalistic ring."[69] Barth went back to the biblical account of Adam and Eve to suggest that the actual sin which they committed was quite trivial. We today are capable of much worse. And we are free.

> This does not mean that he [Adam] has bequeathed it to us as his heirs so that we have to be as he was. He has not poisoned us or passed on a disease. What we do after him is not done according to

67. Rauschenbusch, *A Theology for the Social Gospel*, p. 58.

68. Contemporary feminist theologian Rosemary Radford Ruether may have something in common with Rauschenbusch at this point. "Feminism continues, in a new form," she writes, "the basic Christian perception that sin, as perversion of the good potential into evil, is not simply individual but refers to a fallen state of humanity, historically" (*Sexism and God-Talk* [Boston: Beacon Press, 1983], p. 161). Note the word *historically* here. She is not referring to Adam and Eve, but could she be referring to an ancient historical event "somewhere back on the line" when she speaks of a fall into alienation between the sexes? She rejects the interpretations of the fall that scapegoat women, to be sure, yet she affirms the notion of a fall from harmony. "Not sex, but sexism . . . is central to the origin and transmission of this alienated, fallen condition," she says (p. 37).

69. Barth, *Church Dogmatics*, 4 vols., ed. Thomas F. Torrance, trans. Geoffrey W. Bromiley (Edinburgh: T. & T. Clark, 1936-62), IV/1:501.

an example which irresistibly overthrows us, or in an imitation of his act which is ordained for all his successors. No one has to be Adam. We are so freely and on our own responsibility.[70]

Although Barth avoided the metaphor of inherited disease, he certainly recognized the universal scope of human sin. All of us find ourselves "in Adam," and hence in sin. The story of Adam is the truth about us.

Reinhold Niebuhr similarly argued against using the metaphor of inheritance, referring to it as a "literalistic error." What Augustine had wanted to affirm was the idea of mystical identity, said Niebuhr, the sense of human solidarity in sin.[71] This insight stands. Niebuhr proceeded to argue for the viability of the Christian insight, yet he recognized that it is both realistic and absurd at the same time. Why? Because human sin is universal but not necessary. "Here is the absurdity in a nutshell," he wrote. "Original sin, which is by definition an inherited corruption, or at least an inevitable one, is nevertheless not to be regarded as belonging to [man's] essential nature and therefore is not outside the realm of his responsibility. Sin is natural for man in the sense that it is universal but not in the sense that it is necessary."[72] That is, sin is not built into nature, and yet it is inevitable. It is predictable, not in any given instance but as an overall prediction regarding the human future. Sin is a universal contingent, and the truth of the matter can be confirmed by simply observing what human beings do over a period of time.[73] Niebuhr was fond of quoting the assertion of the *London Times Literary Supplement:* "The doctrine of original sin is the only empirically verifiable doctrine of the Christian faith."[74]

Extending this type of argument in our own day, we find Gerhard Forde alerting us to an apparent danger of thinking of sin as hereditary.

70. Barth, *Church Dogmatics,* IV/1:509.
71. Niebuhr, *Nature and Destiny of Man,* 2 vols. (New York: Scribner's, 1941), 1:260-61.
72. Niebuhr, *Nature and Destiny of Man,* 1:242.
73. The term "universal contingent" is employed by Robert John Russell to draw out the implications of Niebuhr's notion of "inevitable but not necessary." See Russell, "The Thermodynamics of Natural Evil," *CTNS Bulletin* 10 (Spring 1990): 20-25.
74. Niebuhr, *Man's Nature and His Communities,* p. 24. Karl Barth's observation was similar: "Is the doctrine of original sin merely one doctrine among many? Is it not rather . . . the doctrine which emerges from all honest study of history?" (*The Epistle to the Romans* [New York: Oxford University Press, 1968], pp. 85-86.

That original sin exists is obvious, of course, he says, but the idea of hereditary sin is "best avoided in an age that thinks of heredity in terms of genes and DNA. Such talk might lead us to think that genetic engineering could discover and remove original sin. In any case it makes the mistake of offering a biological answer to a theological question."[75]

So at the close of the twentieth century we find ourselves in the curious situation in which Christian theologians affirm the notion of original sin but are reluctant to affirm its biological transmissibility, whereas natural scientists are debating the possibility that human predispositions toward what hitherto has been known as sinful behavior is genetically inherited. Rather than writing these two off as ships that pass in the night, I recommend that scientific and theological crews be encouraged to board one another's vessels to examine their respective intellectual cargoes.

75. Forde, *Theology Is for Proclamation* (Minneapolis: Fortress Press, 1990), p. 53.

Index of Subjects and Names

Neo-orthodoxy, 6, 23, 112, 324, 325
Neopaganism, 112, 232, 283
New Age, 3, 54n.18, 247-49, 282
New creation, 121, 292
Niebuhr, Reinhold, 6, 63-64, 65, 101, 191, 291, 292-93, 303n.22, 326
Nietzsche, Friedrich, 286
Noddings, Nel, 111n.22, 155n.50, 167n.5
Non posse non peccare, 118
Nuclear threat, 7, 18, 116-18, 278

Occult, 239, 240, 249
Original sin, 24-31, 115, 116, 119, 139, 158, 252, 286, 291; and genetic research, 295, 306, 319, 320-27; and grace, 79-82; and racial prejudice, 169, 172. *See also* Augustine; Determinism

Pagels, Elaine, 148-51
Paglia, Camille, 146
Pannenberg, Wolfhart, 6n.1
Paradise, 31-33, 282
Patriarchy, 105-7, 113, 114, 147
Patriotism, 175. *See also* Nationalism
Peacocke, Arthur, 304
Peccatum, 7
Peck, M. Scott, 20, 96, 169, 181, 258
Pelagius, 148, 286
Phenotype, 299, 301
Pleasure, 124-25, 140n.26, 165, 194, 210-11, 284-85
Power over, 98-99, 106, 109, 114, 135
Prejudice, 24, 168-72, 176, 179, 182, 192, 234, 286, 308, 317. *See also* Racism
Presbyterian Church USA: and sexuality, 145-47
Pride, 66-67, 112, 254, 265, 274; and ancient Israel, 91-94; definition of, 12-13; and male aggression, 99, 114; and prejudice, 170; universality of, 91, 94

Principalities and powers, 289
Protestant Reformation, 285
Psychopathology, 70, 74, 78, 207-9, 246. *See also* Antisocial Personality Disorder
Purity codes and the New Testament, 141-44

Quietism, 192

Racism, 7, 104, 234, 286; and crime 310-13
Radical evil: definition of, 9, 16. *See also* Evil
Rage, 11, 35, 43, 59, 66, 80, 85, 100, 167-68; and psychopathology, 72, 74-79; and violence, 39-40, 183
Rahner, Karl, 279, 288-89
Raschke, Carl, 224, 238-41
Rauschenbusch, Walter, 324-25
Real presence, 262
Reconciliation, 189
Redemption, 16, 279, 282, 291, 307
Repression, 158
Resurrection: general, 6, 17, 81, 181, 190, 191, 276, 291, 293; of Jesus, 121, 190, 262, 291, 292, 323
Ricoeur, Paul, 25
Ritual abuse, 2, 215, 219, 226, 228, 231, 232, 245n.41, 256, 262; and cruelty, 16; and death, 187; and sacrifice, 53, 237; and torture, 221; and violence, 186
Romero, Oscar, 202
Rousseau, Jean-Jacques, 47, 50, 308
Ruether, Rosemary Radford, 325n.68
Russell, Jeffrey Burton, 18-19, 211
Russell, Letty, 155

Sacraments, 259-62
Sacrifice, 119, 183-89, 296; of Christ, 16; human, 16; symbols of, 256, 257, 307
Sade, Marquis de, 210, 212

Terrorism, 18
Tertullian, 88, 113, 148, 153n.49
Theft, 139
Theodicy, 46, 212, 277-80
Theology and natural science, 319
Theology of the cross, 323
Third World, 128-29
Tillich, Paul, 6, 57, 60-61, 66-69,
  87, 89-90, 123n.1, 255; and the
  definition of sin, 23; and grace,
  83-84; and Satan, 254, 288-89
Torture, 15, 174, 194, 199-205,
  210, 235, 240; psychological,
  200, 203
Transcendence, 6, 59
Transcendental Meditation, 54n.18
Tribalism, 101-5, 175, 177, 178,
  286
Triviality, 109-11
Troeltsch, Ernst, 140n.26
Trust, 8, 39, 63, 66, 67, 69-70, 81,
  90, 159, 269, 270

Ultimate concern, 90
Unfaith. See Faith

Vietnam, 103, 105, 169
Violence, 12, 13, 15, 20, 29, 59,
  66, 102, 118; and the social
  order, 116, 182-89, 202

Virtue, 109, 210, 264, 273, 275,
  294
Vitiatum in radice, 219
Vocation, 275
Voodoo, 235. *See also* Black magic;
  Santeria

War, 41, 53, 55, 119, 127, 135,
  251, 276, 296; and *power over,*
  98, 135; and prejudice, 13-14,
  182, 289
Wesley, John and Charles, 315
White supremacists, 191
Wicca, 232
Will, 114, 159, 263, 303. *See also*
  Determinism; Free will
Williams, Daniel Day, 61n.26,
  253n.53, 291n.32
Wilson, Edward O., 297-300
Wink, Walter, 187n.27, 188n.30,
  253, 254, 258-59
Witchcraft, 232, 242, 249n.47
Wolf, 13, 197-99
Word of God, 256
World War II, 175, 277
Wright, Nigel, 250-52

Xenophobia, 234, 296

Yom Kippur, 181

Index of Scripture References